Fix-It and Forget-It Vegetarian Cookbook is for you if —

✓ You're looking for tasty, easy-to-prepare vegetarian recipes, with easy-to-find ingredients.

✓ You want to include more meatless meals in your cooking.

✓ You have vegetarian friends and family members, and you want to cook confidently for them.

✓ You would like a little help in putting complete meals together without meat at their center. Here are 50 menus for completely vegetarian meals!

✓ You want slow-cooker recipes, roasting and stir-frying recipes, stove-top, oven, and salad recipes.

✓ You are looking for proven recipes from home cooks that you know will work!

✓ You wish for one go-to vegetarian cookbook that offers breakfasts and desserts, along with appetizers and snacks, pizzas and sandwiches—as well as main dishes.

Fix-It and Forget Vegetarian Cookbook is your trusted companion, whether you are a committed vegetarian or wanting to add more meatless meals to your cooking and eating!

National Bestsellers! More than 12 million copies already sold!

Fix-It and Forget-It Cookbook *(Revised and Updated)*

Fix-It and Forget-It Vegetarian Cookbook

Fix-It and Forget-It 5-Ingredient Favorites

Fix-It and Forget-It Cooking Light for Slow Cookers

Fix-It and Forget-It Slow Cooker Diabetic Cookbook

Fix-It and Forget-It Big Cookbook

Fix-It and Forget-It Christmas Cookbook

Fix-It and Forget-It Cooking with Kids

Fix-It and Forget-It Slow Cooker Magic

Fix-It and Forget-It Pink Cookbook

Fix-It and Forget-It Box Set

Fix-It and Forget-It New Cookbook

Fix-It and Forget-It Baking with Your Slow Cooker

Fix-It and Forget-It Slow Cooker Champion Recipes

Fix-It and Forget-It®
Vegetarian Cookbook

565 Delicious Slow-Cooker, Stove-Top,
Oven, and Salad Recipes, plus
50 Suggested Menus

Phyllis
Good

New York, New York

Good Books books may be purchased in bulk at special discounts for sales promotion, corporate gifts, fund-raising, or educational purposes. Special editions can also be created to specifications. For details, contact the Special Sales Department, Good Books, 307 West 36th Street, 11th Floor, New York, NY 10018 or info@skyhorsepublishing.com.

Good Books is an imprint of Skyhorse Publishing, Inc.®, a Delaware corporation.

Visit our website at www.goodbooks.com.

10 9 8 7 6 5 4 3 2

Library of Congress Cataloging-in-Publication Data is available on file.

Cover design by Cliff Snyder
Cover illustration and illustrations throughout the book by Cheryl Benner

Comb edition ISBN: 978-1-68099-196-3
Paperback edition ISBN: 978-1-68099-193-2
Ebook ISBN: 978-1-68099-195-6

The information in this book has been developed with care and accuracy and is presented in good faith. However, no warranty is given nor are results guaranteed. Neither the author nor the publisher has control over the materials or procedures used, and neither has any liability for any loss or damage related to the use of information contained in the book.

Printed in China

Table of Contents

Welcome to Fix-It and Forget-It Vegetarian Cookbook

First, the Truth About Me

Folks, I am actively working at making and eating more meatless meals. This takes practice. This requires a new way of thinking about how to put a meal together.

I'm not giving up meat. But I am asking it to move aside. I'm upping the vegetables and grains that I eat—and cook—day-to-day.

You see, I wanted to do this *Vegetarian Cookbook* because I need a little help here. My life's pretty full, so during the week when I don't have a lot of time to think, I tend to drop back to the familiar. Often our evening meals are built around chicken that I can cook quickly or some beef that provides a flavorful center to our dinner.

Phyllis Good

But I want to form some new habits that have me thinking "Vegetable Variety" and "Whole Foods."

I've told my helpers on our staff this. I told our home-cook recipe-contributors about my fresh resolve. I think of this *Cookbook* as representing a gentle uprising.

Tasty, Easy-to-Prepare, Non-Meat Recipes—Plus Companionship!

If you're looking for some tasty, whole-food recipes without meat, they're here.

If you're also looking for some companionship as you move toward more meatless dishes in your cooking, you'll find it here. (We've included some "bridge" recipes that point in the direction you want to go.)

If you want to cook confidently for your vegetarian friends or family, *Fix-It and Forget-It Vegetarian Cookbook* is full of tasty ideas.

Our First Hybrid

Ever since *Fix-It and Forget-It Cookbook* (our first in the series) appeared, people have been asking for a *Fix-It and Forget-It Vegetarian Cookbook*. "My kids are vegetarians," they tell me. Or "I want to eat more vegetables, but I need the convenience of my slow cooker to help me."

Yes, beans and potatoes and carrots and lentils love a slow cooker's low, moist heat. But not all vegetables do.

Plus, other cooking methods can highlight vegetables' star qualities, making them irresistible to behold—and to eat. I couldn't bear not to include recipes for roasting and stir-frying and steaming vegetables, as well as eating them raw in salads, in this *Cookbook*.

So you're looking at our first hybrid cookbook—a collection of slow-cooker, stove-top, oven, and salad recipes. But true to our *Fix-It and Forget-It* style, all are easy to prepare and all are made with easy-to-find ingredients.

Fix-It and Forget-It Vegetarian Cookbook can meet all your meatless cooking needs, from appetizers to desserts. The whole meal is here.

A Different Way to Think

Think of a vegetarian meal as several dishes of equal importance, rather than a main dish with side dishes built around it.

Not sure how all the parts of a vegetarian meal come together? Flip to the 50 menus in the *Cookbook* (see pages 6-15) to find well-balanced meals and tasty food combinations. Now you can confidently serve a nutritionally complete vegetarian meal for a weekday family supper, or a feast for a special day. These menus will get you started, or give you fresh inspiration.

No Apologies for Vegetables Here!

When my mother's generation first discovered canned cream soups, they couldn't believe the ease they brought to cooking. Then someone mixed the creamed soup into vegetables and felt almost French! With the appearance of processed cheese, vegetables receded further into the background flavor-wise.

Some of our kids think they want to eat only well-masked vegetables. But we've steered almost completely clear of this approach to vegetables here. We're making vegetables and whole foods the leads, in as natural a state as possible.

Yes, your husband and your kids can get full when they eat a meatless meal. Yes, you might have to search a new aisle in the grocery store to find an ingredient you haven't used before. Yes, you might need to think of yourself as an explorer.

Just remember that these recipes come from home cooks who've made them successfully and served them to happy friends and family. You're joining great company when you try these recipes, whether you start with one meatless meal a week or eat only vegetarian dishes!

Phyllis Good

How To Put Together a Vegetarian Meal:
50 Menus

A traditional menu often has a main dish—frequently a meat—at the center, with side dishes to complement its flavor. However, **vegetarian menus usually have several equal dishes whose flavors complement each other.** So in this cookbook, we have dropped references to main dishes and side dishes, and focus instead on balanced meals.

For each menu, we have aimed to include protein, fruits and/or vegetables and carbohydrates. Carbohydrates are root vegetables, pasta, rice, bread and other grains. Protein for vegetarians comes from dairy products, beans and legumes. (Meat proteins contain all essential amino acids and are called "complete proteins.")

Other foods can make complete proteins when eaten together. Milk makes a complete protein when combined with wheat. Beans make a complete protein when combined with rice or corn. Eggs, soybeans, buckwheat, amaranth and quinoa are complete proteins in themselves, just as meat is.

Dessert is not included with all the menus. When it is included, it is providing some part of the nutritional or celebratory make-up of the meal.

Those recipes on the menus which appear in *Fix-It and Forget-It Vegetarian Cookbook* are capitalized and include their page numbers. Recipe names in lower case letters are not in this cookbook but are simple foods to make or buy.

Breakfast and Brunch

1. Quick Breakfast

- Blueberry Banana Smoothie (page 29)
- *toasted* Peanut Butter Bread (page 50)

2. Spring Breakfast

- Cream-of-Brown-Rice Cereal (page 45)
- Banana Split Salad (page 194)

3. Summer Breakfast

- Strawberries and Cream Mini Muffins (page 58)
- Cold Strawberry Soup (page 46)
- Granola (page 42)

4. Holiday Breakfast

- Gift of the Magi Bread (page 55)
- Overnight Danish Braids (page 36)
- Fruit Salad (page 193)
- Caramel Frappés (page 28)

5. Festive Brunch

- Baked Apple Cranberry Pancake (page 31)
- Pumpkin Custard (page 46)
- *orange wedges*

6. Another Festive Brunch

- Cheesy Bread Pudding (page 39)
- Mango Salsa (page 26)
- Apple Streusel Muffins (page 56)

Plan a variety of colors in a menu to create an appetizing appearance on the plate.

Betty K. Drescher, Quakertown, PA

Lunch

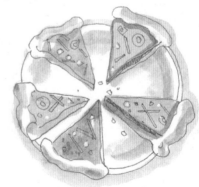

Spring

Summer

Autumn

To decrease the amount of meat in your diet, adopt the idea of "Meatless Monday" where you swap out meat for vegetarian dishes for one day each week. You'll save money, have a positive impact on the environment, and improve your family's health.

Janelle Glick, Lancaster, PA

Winter

Family Suppers

38. Comfort Food Supper
by Ruth Miller

- Cheese Potatoes (page 165)
- *applesauce*
- *peas*
- Chocolate Date Cake (page 240)

39. Family Supper
by Ellie Oberholtzer

- Cornbread Salad (page 225)
- *steamed kale*
- Maple Peach Crumble Pie (page 243) *with vanilla ice cream*

40. Family Supper *by Lois Hess*

- Spicy Mexican Bean Burgers (page 69)
- Carrot and Raisin Salad (page 219)
- *applesauce*
- Cranberry Oatmeal Cookies (page 257)

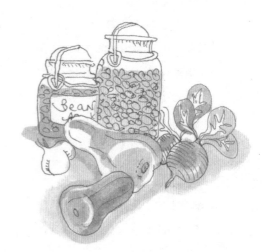

Our household includes both vegetarians and non-vegetarians who all take turns cooking. Early on, when the vegetarian members first converted to not eating or cooking with meat and were experimenting with new recipes, we found that we began to have a lot of tension at mealtime over what was served. In order to keep mealtimes as peaceful as possible, we all agreed that if someone didn't care for what was served, it was both their responsibility and their right to prepare themselves something else. We also agreed that the cook was not allowed to take offense. Slowly, over time, our taste preferences have merged, and the tension has decreased, as the vegetarian cooks have become more practiced and the meat-eaters have expanded their palates.

Leanne Yoder, Tucson, AZ

Holidays and Celebrations

41. Celebration Meal

by Crystal Trost

- Swiss Chard Scramble (page 195)
- Black Beans and Rice (page 130)
- *tortillas*
- *sliced avocado*
- *fried plantains with sour cream*

42. Celebration Meal

- Nepal Vegetable Curry (page 186)
- Baked Rice (page 146)
- Rasam (page 84)
- Indian Naan Bread (page 49)
- Fruit Salad with Yogurt and Nuts (page 194)

43. Festive Vegan Dinner

- Simple French Onion Soup (page 90)
- Wheat Bread (page 48)
- California Salad (page 209)
- Mushrooms in Red Wine (page 188)
- Farfalle with Tomatoes, Garlic and Basil (page 122)
- Chocolate Mousse (page 252)

44. Elegant Dinner *by Bob Coffey*

- Spring Greens with Roasted Rhubarb and Parmesan Crisps (page 213)
- White Beans with Sun-Dried Tomatoes (page 129)
- Rigatoni with Grilled Vegetables (page 122)
- *flan with blackberries*

45. Winter Holiday Meal

- Holiday Punch (page 30)
- Sweet Onion Dip (page 23) *with crudités*
- Spinach Balls (page 19)
- Twice-Baked Sweet Potatoes (page 160)
- Coleslaw (page 226)
- 100% Whole Wheat Refrigerator Rolls (page 52)
- Coconut Buttermilk Pound Cake (page 241)
- Hot Fruit Casserole (page 192)

46. Thanksgiving Dinner

- Sweet Potato Soufflé (page 160)
- Artichoke Stuffing (page 157)
- Mustard Green Beans (page 173)
- Cranberry Apple Salad (page 212)
- Herb Rolls (page 53)
- Pecan Pumpkin Pie (page 245)

Write out menus for the week before you go shopping.

Colleen Heatwole, Burton, MI

Appetizers, Snacks, and Beverages

Swiss Cheese Puffs

Becky S. Frey
Lebanon, PA

Makes 12 servings

Prep. Time: 20-30 minutes
Baking Time: 1-3 minutes

½ cup salad dressing, *or*
   mayonnaise
¼ cup chopped onions
2 Tbsp. chopped fresh
   parsley
2 cups grated Swiss, cheddar,
   or pepper jack cheese
⅛ tsp. pepper
24 party-loaf bread slices
24-36 slices of green, black
   or Kalamata olives

1. Mix salad dressing, onions,
parsley, cheese and pepper.
2. Place bread on baking
sheet. Spread a thin layer of
cheese mixture on each slice
of bread.
3. Garnish each with 2-3
olive slices.

4. Put bread under broiler
until cheese melts, 1-3
minutes. Watch carefully!
5. Serve immediately.

Feta Bruschetta

Rosie Glick
Perry, NY

Makes 10 toasts

Prep. Time: 10 minutes
Baking Time: 16-20 minutes

half stick (¼ cup) butter,
   melted
¼ cup olive oil
10 slices French bread, 1"
   thick
4 oz. crumbled feta cheese
2-3 garlic cloves, minced
1 Tbsp. minced fresh basil
   or 1 tsp. dried basil
1 large tomato, seeded and
   chopped

1. In a bowl, combine
butter and oil.
2. Brush onto both sides of
bread slices.
3. Place on baking sheet.
4. Bake at 350° for 8-10
minutes or until lightly
browned on top. Remove
from oven.
5. In a small bowl, combine
feta, garlic, and basil. Sprinkle
evenly over toast.
6. Top with tomatoes.
7. Return to oven and bake
8-10 minutes longer or until
heated through.
8. Serve warm.

Go-Along:
• Serve as a party food, or
alongside a pasta dish.

Vegan

Bruschetta with Avocado and Basil

Janelle Glick
Lancaster, PA

Makes 6 servings

Prep. Time: 20 minutes
Baking Time: 5 minutes

1½ ripe fresh Hass avocados, pitted and peeled
3 medium Roma tomatoes, sliced lengthwise and diced
3 Tbsp. diced red onions
1½ Tbsp. olive oil
3 tsp. chopped fresh basil leaves, plus additional whole leaves for garnish
1 medium clove garlic, minced
freshly ground pepper and salt, to taste
12 ½"-thick baguette slices

1. Thinly slice an avocado half. Set aside.
2. Dice the remaining avocado.
3. In medium bowl, gently combine the diced avocado, tomatoes, onions, olive oil, chopped basil leaves, garlic, pepper and salt.
4. Toast the baguette slices in a toaster oven or under the broiler until warmed and lightly tan.
5. Top each slice of toasted bread with two or three of the reserved avocado slices. Then top with 1 heaping tablespoon of tomato/avocado mixture.

6. Garnish each with a small whole leaf of basil, if you wish.
7. Serve within an hour of making.

Go-Alongs:
• Vegetarian Pasta Salad
• Fresh Fruit Salad with Mint

Blue Cheese Tarts

JB Miller
Indianapolis, IN

Makes 18 tarts

Prep. Time: 15 minutes
Baking Time: 10-12 minutes

1 10"×12" sheet frozen puff pastry
4 oz. blue cheese, room temperature
8 oz. cream cheese, room temperature
2 oz. sun-dried tomatoes
½ cup pesto
½-1 oz. shredded Parmesan cheese
¼ cup chopped walnuts

1. Partially defrost puff pastry and cut sheet into 9 equal squares, and then cut each square diagonally to create 18 triangles.
2. Lay the triangles on a baking sheet. Bake in 450° oven 10 to 12 minutes until golden brown.
3. Combine blue cheese and cream cheese with sun-dried tomatoes. Blend and mash with a fork.

4. Equally divide cheese mixture over 18 triangles.
5. Spread pesto over cheese.
6. Sprinkle with Parmesan cheese.
7. Sprinkle walnuts on top.
8. Place under broiler and broil briefly until bubbly. Watch carefully so they don't darken too much! Serve warm.

Tip:
Tarts may be made several hours in advance except for the last step of finishing under the broiler.

Sweet and Sour Neatballs

Charlotte Burkholder
East Petersburg, PA
Esther Nafziger
La Junta, CO

Makes 15 servings

Prep. Time: 1 hour
Cooking/Baking Time: 25 minutes

4 eggs
1 small onion, minced
3 Tbsp. minced, fresh parsley
2 garlic cloves, minced
1¼ cups finely crushed saltine crackers *or* bread crumbs
1 cup minced walnuts *or* pecans
½ cup cottage cheese
1 cup shredded cheddar cheese
½ tsp. salt, *or* to taste
1 tsp. Italian Mrs. Dash, *optional*
¼ tsp. dried sage
½ tsp. dried thyme
2 Tbsp. vegetable *or* canola oil
¼ cup lemon juice *or* white vinegar
¾ cup apricot jam
1 cup ketchup
¼ cup minced onion
½ tsp. dried oregano
dash hot sauce, *optional*

1. Mix eggs, minced small onion, parsley, garlic, crushed crackers, ground nuts, cottage cheese, and cheddar cheese together.
2. Add salt, Mrs. Dash, sage and thyme. Mix well.
3. Form the mixture into 2" balls.
4. Place them in a 9 × 13 baking dish.
5. In another bowl, whisk together the vegetable oil, vinegar, apricot jam, ketchup, ¼ cup minced onions, oregano and optional hot sauce.
6. Pour evenly over meatballs.
7. Bake at 350° for 35-40 minutes, until meatballs are firm and the sauce is thick and bubbly.

Tips:
1. You can also boil sauce separately on stovetop. Bake uncovered balls for 25 minutes. Stick each ball with a toothpick. Put sauce on side for dip.
2. These balls freeze well, and can be made in advance. Add cilantro leaves to sauce for Mexican flavor.
3. Replace 2 eggs and cottage cheese with 3 egg whites, beaten until stiff.

Charlotte Burkholder

Spinach Balls

Miriam Detweiler
Hickory, NC

Makes 6-8 servings

Prep. Time: 20-30 minutes
Cooking/Baking Time: 30 minutes
Standing Time: 20 minutes

20 oz. frozen chopped spinach, thawed
6 eggs
1 medium onion, minced
1 stick (½ cup) butter, melted
½ cup grated Parmesan cheese
1 Tbsp. garlic salt
⅔ tsp. dried thyme
2 cups bread crumbs

1. Cook spinach as directed on package. Drain well. When cool enough to handle, squeeze dry.
2. Beat eggs in a large mixing bowl. Mix in cooked spinach, minced onions, butter, cheese, garlic salt and thyme.
3. Add bread crumbs to mixture.
4. Form mixture into small balls, approximately 48 of them. Place on greased baking sheet.
5. Bake at 350° for 20 minutes.

Tip:
These balls are also great additions to the main course of a meal.

I like to buy nut pieces. They cost less than whole nuts and save chopping time.
Sherri McCauley, Lakeway, TX

Stuffed Mushrooms

Barbara Hoover
Landisville, PA

Makes 12 mushrooms

Prep. Time: 15-20 minutes
Cooking/Baking Time: 20 minutes

12 large, fresh mushrooms
1 stick (½ cup) butter,
   divided
¼ cup grated Parmesan
   cheese
2 Tbsp. seasoned bread
   crumbs
2 Tbsp. minced fresh parsley
2 Tbsp. white wine *or*
   apple juice

1. Wipe the mushrooms clean with a damp paper towel. Remove stems and reserve.
2. Finely chop the stems.
3. Melt 2 Tbsp. butter in small skillet over medium heat. Add chopped mushroom stems and cook until softened, 5 minutes.
4. Remove skillet from heat. Add the Parmesan, bread crumbs, parsley and wine. Toss lightly.
5. Place remaining 6 Tbsp. butter in small microwave-safe shallow bowl. Melt it in the microwave.
6. Carefully spoon the mushroom mixture into the mushroom caps.
7. Dip the mushroom caps in the butter. Place cap-side down in 8 × 12 baking dish.
8. Bake at 350° until heated through, 10-15 minutes.

Wild Mushroom Dip

Monica Wagner
Quarryville, PA

Makes 6 cups

Prep. Time: 20 minutes
Cooking Time: 3-4 hours
Ideal slow-cooker size: 4-qt.

2 cups dry white wine,
   such as Chardonnay
2½-oz. container dried
   wild mushrooms, mixed
   variety
2 8-oz. pkgs. cream cheese,
   cut into 1" cubes
2 10¾-oz. cans condensed
   cream of mushroom soup
2 cups shredded mozzarella
   cheese
1 tsp. dried tarragon
1 tsp. salt
½ tsp. ground black pepper

1. In a microwave-safe bowl, heat white wine on high until steaming hot.
2. Place dried mushrooms in hot wine and let sit for 10 minutes to rehydrate.
3. With a slotted spoon, transfer mushrooms to a food processor, reserving liquid. Cover and process mushrooms until they form a coarse paste.
4. In a large bowl combine mushroom paste, ⅔ cup reserved mushroom liquid and remaining ingredients.

Mix thoroughly and pour into a 4-quart slow cooker.
5. Cover. Cook on low for 2-3 hours, stirring once halfway through.

Tip:
   Find dried wild mushrooms in grocery-store produce departments or at Asian grocery stores.

To make your own cream of mushroom soup, please turn to pages 260-261.

Hot Mexican Spinach Dip

Laura Peachey
Goshen, IN

Makes 6 cups

Prep. Time: 15 minutes
Cooking Time: 15 minutes
Ideal slow-cooker size: 4-qt.

10 oz. frozen spinach,
    thawed and squeezed dry
16-oz. jar salsa
2 cups shredded
    Pepper Jack cheese
8 oz. cream cheese, at room
    temperature
1 cup evaporated milk *or*
    light cream
2-oz. can black olives,
    chopped
1 Tbsp. red wine vinegar
salt and pepper, to taste
chips *or* bread cubes

1. Chop spinach.
2. Mix together spinach, salsa, cheese, cream cheese, evaporated milk, olives, vinegar, salt and pepper.
3. Place in slow cooker. Heat on low for 2-3 hours. Stir occasionally.
4. Serve as a dip for chips or bread cubes.

Variation:
    You can bake this at 400° for 12-15 minutes if you wish.

Go-Along:
• Mexican meal.

Game-Day Blue-Cheese Dip

Sharon Timpe
Jackson, WI

Makes 2 cups

Prep. Time: 5 minutes
Cooking Time: 1 hour
Ideal slow-cooker size: 3-qt.

8 oz. cream cheese, softened
½ cup ranch salad dressing
½ cup crumbled blue cheese
hot sauce, to taste
¼-½ cup re-fried beans,
    optional

1. Mix cream cheese, salad dressing, blue cheese, hot sauce and beans if you wish.
2. Place in small slow cooker.
3. Cook on low 1 hour or until bubbly.

Variation:
    Add cooked, crumbled veggie burgers, or crisp-fried vegetarian bacon to the dip.

Go-Along:
• Serve at room temperature with crackers, bagel chips, toast or raw vegetables.

Bean Cheese Dip

Wafi Brandt
Manheim, PA
Diana Kampnich
Croghan, NY

Makes 3 cups

Prep. Time: 5-10 minutes
Cooking Time: 1-2 hours
Ideal slow-cooker size: 3-qt.

2 cups kidney beans,
    drained and mashed
1 cup salsa
1 cup shredded cheddar
    cheese
¼ tsp. garlic powder
½ tsp. chili powder
¼ tsp. ground coriander
½ tsp. ground cumin
tortilla chips

1. Mix all ingredients except chips in slow cooker.
2. Cook on low 1-2 hours until hot through.
3. Serve with tortilla chips.

Tip:
    Mash the beans with the bottom of a cup or in a food processor.

Variation:
    Omit spices. Use whole pinto beans instead of mashed kidney beans. Add 8 oz. softened cream cheese.

Diana Kampnich

Hot Artichoke & Parmesan Dip

Melissa Cramer
Lancaster, PA

Makes 4 cups

Prep. Time: 15 minutes
Cooking Time: 1-2 hours
Ideal slow-cooker size: 3-qt.

2 8-oz. pkgs. cream cheese, softened
1 cup mayonnaise *or* cottage cheese
1 cup shredded Parmesan cheese, packed
7 cloves garlic, minced
12-oz. jar marinated artichoke hearts, drained and chopped
crusty bread *or* pita chips

1. In a large mixing bowl, mix softened cream cheese, mayonnaise and shredded Parmesan cheese.
2. Add minced garlic and chopped artichoke hearts.
3. Place mixture in slow cooker for 1-2 hours until bubbly and hot.
4. Serve hot as a dip for crusty bread or pita chips.

Tip:
This recipe can also be frozen and then cooked at a later time.

Variation:
Low-fat cream cheese may be substituted for regular cream cheese.

Go-Along:
• Also good on baked potatoes for a meal.

Jalapeño Popper Dip

Jackie Finstad
New Ulm, MN

Makes 3 cups

Prep. Time: 10 minutes
Cooking Time: 1 hour
Ideal slow-cooker size: 3-qt.

2-oz. can jalapeño peppers, *or* 4-6 fresh jalapeños
2 8-oz. pkgs. cream cheese, softened
1 cup mayonnaise
4-oz. can green chilies, drained and chopped
1 cup grated Parmesan cheese
chips, crackers *or* baguette slices

1. If using canned jalapeños, drain and chop them. If using fresh, remove seeds and chop.
2. Mix together cream cheese, mayonnaise, green chilies, peppers and cheese. Stir until smooth.
3. Place in slow cooker on low until hot and bubbly, about 1 hour.
4. Serve with dippers of your choice.

Tips:
1. This can be served without cooking it first, just as a cold dip.
2. If you like extra kick, stir in a few more jalapeños or use some Pepper Jack cheese.

Slow-Cooked Salsa

Andy Wagner
Quarryville, PA

Makes 2 cups

Prep. Time: 15 minutes
Cooking Time: 2½-3 hours
Standing Time: 2 hours
Ideal slow-cooker size: 3-qt.

10 plum tomatoes
2 garlic cloves
1 small onion, cut into wedges
1-2 jalapeño peppers
¼ cup chopped fresh cilantro
½ tsp. salt, *optional*

1. Core tomatoes. Cut a small slit in two tomatoes. Insert a garlic clove into each slit.
2. Place all tomatoes and onions in a 3-qt. slow cooker.
3. Cut stems off jalapeños. (Remove seeds if you want a milder salsa.) Place jalapeños in the slow cooker.
4. Cover and cook on high for 2½ to 3 hours or until vegetables are softened. Some may brown slightly. Cool at least 2 hours with the lid off.
5. In a blender, combine the tomato mixture, cilantro and salt if you wish. Cover and process until blended.
6. Refrigerate leftovers.

Tip:
Wear disposable gloves when cutting hot peppers; the oils can burn your skin. Avoid touching your face when you've been working with hot peppers.

Sun-Dried Tomato and Olive Spread

JB Miller
Indianapolis, IN

Makes 3 cups
Prep. Time: 15 minutes

1 cup sun-dried tomatoes, oil-packed, drained, but oil reserved
1 cup pitted Kalamata olives
1 cup coarsely chopped fresh parsley
4-5 cloves garlic, peeled
½ cup pine nuts, toasted
ground black pepper

1. Combine tomatoes, olives, parsley, garlic and pine nuts in bowl of food processor. Pulse to blend. Add enough reserved oil and blend until contents are chunky but can be easily spread. Do not blend into a paste.
2. Remove mixture to a bowl. Season with pepper. Stir gently.
3. Serve with crackers or toast points.

Go-Along:
• Serve with mild crackers to enjoy the flavors of the spread.

Sweet Onion Dip

Mary Fisher
Leola, PA

Makes 1½ cups
Prep. Time: 10 minutes
Cooking Time: 15 minutes

1 Tbsp. butter
1 medium onion, sliced
2 Tbsp. cider vinegar
2 Tbsp. honey
1 Tbsp. prepared mustard
1 cup mayonnaise
salt and pepper, to taste

1. Melt butter in a skillet.
2. Add onions. Cook 15 minutes, stirring occasionally, until onions are soft and caramelized. Add vinegar.
3. Place onions and vinegar in food processor.
4. Add honey and mustard. Process until smooth. Place in bowl.
5. Stir in mayonnaise, salt and pepper.

Go-Along:
• Baked zucchini sticks, or any dipper you like.

Vegetable Dip from Scratch

Trudy Guenter
Vanderhoof, BC

Makes 1½ cups
Prep. Time: 10 minutes
Chilling Time: 1 hour

¾ cup mayonnaise
¾ cup sour cream
1 tsp. seasoned salt
1 tsp. onion flakes
1 tsp. dried parsley
1½ tsp. dried dill weed

1. Mix all ingredients. Cover.
2. Refrigerate at least 1 hour before serving.
3. Serve with fresh, raw vegetables.

When you have an abundance of parsley in your garden, wash and chop it fine. Freeze it for use in the winter. Its flavor and color is much better than dried parsley.
Becky S. Frey, Lebanon, PA

Garlic Hummus

Donna Suter
Pandora, OH

Samantha Seifried
Lancaster, PA

Lindsay Spencer
Morrow, OH

Makes 2 cups

Prep. Time: 10 minutes

15-oz. can garbanzo beans
¼ cup tahini (nut butter made from sesame seeds)
1-4 garlic cloves, depending on your taste preference
½ cup olive oil
3 Tbsp. lemon juice
½ tsp. salt
dash pepper, *optional*
½ tsp. roasted garlic powder, *optional*
1 tsp. ground cumin, *optional*

1. Drain the garbanzos, but reserve ½ cup liquid.
2. Combine beans, tahini, garlic, oil, lemon juice, salt, optional pepper, optional garlic powder and optional cumin in a food processor or blender.
3. Blend until smooth. Add a little bean liquid if needed to reach desired spreading or dipping consistency.

4. Store in the refrigerator. Serve with pita bread or homemade pita chips.

Tips:
1. To make homemade pita chips, cut pita bread into 8 triangles. Drizzle with olive oil, sprinkle with Mrs. Dash seasoning or seasoned salt, and bake in a 350° oven for 20 minutes.
Donna Suter

2. Add 1 cup chopped red bell peppers. Omit olive oil. Puree as directed.
Lindsay Spencer

3. To make Tex-Mex Hummus, replace garbanzos with black beans. Add 6 oz. plain Greek yogurt and ½ packet taco seasoning. Reduce tahini to 1 Tbsp. Omit cumin, salt, pepper and olive oil.
Samantha Seifried

Garbanzo Olive Dip

Lois Mae E. Kuh
Penfield, NY

Makes 2 cups

Prep. Time: 10 minutes

1½ cups cooked garbanzo beans, drained
2 cloves garlic
3 Tbsp. chopped scallions
juice of 1½ lemons, including pulp
6 Italian black olives, chopped
1-2 Tbsp. olive oil

1. Combine beans, garlic, scallions, lemon juice, olives and oil.
2. Put in a food processor and process until smooth.

Tip:
Serve with pita bread or pita chips.

The flavor of fresh garlic is more intense than powdered. Purchase a good garlic press for ease in using these healthful bulbs.

Becky S. Frey, Lebanon, PA

Greek Layer Dip

Jessica Stoner
West Liberty, OH

Makes 10 servings

Prep. Time: 20-25 minutes

16 oz. plain Greek yogurt
½ cup unpeeled cucumber, finely chopped, *divided*
1 Tbsp. finely chopped red onions
2 tsp. snipped fresh mint
10 oz. plain hummus
½ cup chopped, seeded tomatoes
½ cup crumbled feta cheese
3 large white *or* wheat pita rounds

1. In a small bowl, stir together yogurt, ¼ cup cucumber, onions and mint.
2. Spread hummus in bottom of 10" quiche dish or pie plate.
3. Spread yogurt mixture evenly over hummus.
4. Sprinkle with tomatoes, remaining cucumber and feta cheese.
5. Split each pita round horizontally and cut into 8 wedges.
6. Serve with dip.

Tip:
Make just before serving. If the dip stands in the refrigerator, it tends to get a little watery around the edges.

Pimento Cheese

Lucille Amos
Greensboro, NC

Makes 1½-2 cups

Prep. Time: 20 minutes
Chilling Time: 1 hour

½ lb. sharp cheddar cheese
2 oz. pimentos, chopped
1 Tbsp. sweet relish
½ cup mayonnaise
1 Tbsp. chopped jalapeño pepper
salt and pepper, to taste

1. Grate cheese into bowl.
2. Add pimentos, relish, mayonnaise, jalapeño pepper, salt and pepper. Mix gently.
3. Chill at least 1 hour before serving. Stir again.

Tip:
Do not use pre-grated cheese.

Go-Along:
• Soup with Pimento Cheese and tomato sandwiches on crusty bread.

Vegan

Pico de Gallo

MaryAnn Beachy
Dover, OH

Makes 4 cups

Prep. Time: 15 minutes

1 large onion, chopped
1½ cups tomatoes, chopped
1-1½ cups chopped fresh cilantro
½ tsp. salt
juice of one lime
1-2 jalapeños, minced, *optional*, if you like the heat

1. Combine onions, tomatoes, cilantro, salt, lime juice and optional jalapeños. Stir together.
2. Taste and add salt as needed. Serve with tortilla chips.

The ratio of fresh herbs to dry herbs is 3:1; 3 fresh to 1 dry.
Colleen Heatwole, Burton, MI

Mango Salsa

Heidi Wood
Vacaville, CA
Cathy Scholz
Beavercreek, OH

Makes 2 cups

Prep. Time: 20 minutes
Chilling Time: 30-60 minutes

1 fresh mango, peeled,
  pitted and chopped
¼ cup finely chopped red
  bell pepper
1 Tbsp. diced red onion
2 Tbsp. chopped fresh
  cilantro
1 jalapeño pepper, seeded
  and minced
2 Tbsp. lime juice
1 Tbsp. olive *or* grapeseed
  oil
salt, to taste

1. Combine mango, red
pepper, onion, cilantro and
jalapeño in a bowl.
2. Sprinkle lime juice on
top of mango mixture and
stir to coat fruit to prevent
discoloration.
3. Gently stir in oil and
salt.
4. Cover and refrigerate
30 minutes to 1 hour before
serving.

Tip:
  Add ½ cup diced avocado,
1 cup diced tomatoes, 2
minced garlic cloves. Omit
red bell pepper. Increase
cilantro to ¼ cup.
                 Cathy Scholz

Go-Along:
• This rainbow-hued salsa
is a surefire way to spice up
a salad. Simply nestle it on
top of a bed of greens. It is
also fabulous in burritos with
black beans.

Zucchini and Tomato Salsa

Andrew Schrock
Catlett, VA

Makes 4-5 cups

Prep. Time: 5 minutes

1 large onion, diced
2 medium zucchini, diced
1 jalapeño, diced
2 tomatoes, diced
juice of 2 limes
½ cup minced fresh
  cilantro
1 tsp. salt
1 tsp. pepper
2 tsp. red wine vinegar
2 Tbsp. oil
2 tsp. sugar

1. Combine all ingredients
and mix together.
2. Allow to marinate at
room temperature for 2-3
hours.

Go-Along:
• Serve with chips or as a
topping to vegetarian burgers
or eggs.

*Wear throw-away vinyl gloves when chopping
jalapeño or other hotter peppers! The oils can sting
your skin. I learned this the hard way...*

Elaine Sue Good, Tiskilwa, IL

Christmas Popcorn

Barbara Grannemann
Gerald, MO

Makes 15 cups

Prep. Time: 15 minutes
Cooking Time: 2-3 minutes
Standing Time: 1 hour

2 3.3-oz. bags microwave-
   popcorn, popped, about
   8 cups popcorn
3 cups crispy rice cereal
2 cups peanuts *or* any nut
   you like
24 oz. vanilla almond bark
½ cup peanut butter

1. Cover a large flat surface, like a tray or kitchen counter, with waxed paper.
2. Discard any unpopped kernels from popcorn.
3. In a big bowl, mix together popped popcorn, cereal and nuts.
4. Place almond bark and peanut butter in glass bowl. Microwave in 45-second increments, checking and stirring after each time, until melted.
5. Pour over the popcorn mixture and mix well.
6. Pour onto waxed-paper-covered surface. Allow to cool at least 1 hour.
7. Store in airtight container.

Parmesan Garlic Popcorn

Abby Diller
Delphos, OH

Makes 20 cups

Prep. Time: 10 minutes
Cooking Time: 10 minutes

3 Tbsp. butter
2 cloves garlic, minced
2 Tbsp. oil
1 cup unpopped popcorn
   kernels
½ cup grated Parmesan
   cheese
½ tsp. cayenne pepper, *or*
   to taste
salt

1. In microwave-safe bowl, place butter and garlic. Microwave for 30 seconds or until butter is melted. Set aside.
2. In large, deep pot, heat oil over high heat. When hot, add popcorn kernels. Cover. Cook and shake pot back and forth until popping stops.
3. Pour popcorn into large bowl.
4. Pour butter-garlic mixture over popcorn. Sprinkle with Parmesan and cayenne. Toss to coat.
5. Salt as needed and serve.

Sour-Cream Candied Walnuts

Sharon Easter
Yuba City, CA

Makes 4 cups

Prep. Time: 15 minutes
Cooking Time: 10-15 minutes
Standing Time: 1 hour

1 cup brown sugar
½ cup white sugar
½ cup sour cream
1 tsp. vanilla
pinch salt
4 cups walnuts

1. Combine sugars and sour cream in 3-quart saucepan with candy thermometer.
2. Bring to boil. Cook for approximately 10 minutes or until soft-ball stage is reached, 236°.
3. Remove from heat. Add vanilla and salt.
4. Beat 5-10 minutes, or until mixture is thick and has lost its gloss.
5. Add nuts and stir to coat.
6. Spread out quickly on waxed or parchment paper to dry and cool.

Energy Balls

Jean Turner
Williams Lake, BC

Makes 20 balls

Prep. Time: 15 minutes

1 cup sunflower seeds,
  toasted
1 cup sesame seeds, toasted
1 cup uncooked rolled oats
1 cup chocolate chips
1 cup raisins
1 cup dried cranberries
½ cup unsweetened cocoa
  powder
2 cups peanut butter
½-¾ cup honey
1 cup shredded coconut,
  toasted

1. Combine sunflower
seeds, sesame seeds, rolled
oats, chocolate chips, raisins,
cranberries, cocoa powder,
peanut butter and ½ cup
honey in bowl.
2. Mix well, using your
hands. You may need a
bit more honey to hold it
together.
3. Roll ¼ cup scoops of
dough into balls. Roll balls in
the toasted coconut.
4. Store Energy Balls in an
airtight container in the refrigerator for up to one week, or
in the freezer for two months.

Variation:
  You can easily substitute
other dried fruits in this
recipe by using your favorite
combinations.

High-Energy Trail Bars

Tamera Baker
Lafayette, IN

Makes 12 servings

Prep. Time: 15 minutes
Cooking Time: 25-30 minutes

1 cup brown suger
⅔ cup peanut butter
1 stick (½ cup) butter,
  melted
½ cup light corn syrup
2 tsp. vanilla
1½ cups dry quick oats
1½ cups crispy rice cereal
1 cup chocolate chips *or*
  cocoa nibs
1 cup raisins
½ cup shredded coconut
½ cup sunflower seeds
⅓ cup wheat germ
2 Tbsp. sesame seeds

1. Mix brown sugar, peanut
butter, butter, corn syrup and
vanilla together in a good-
sized bowl.
2. Mix in oats, cereal,
chocolate chips, raisins, coconut, sunflower seeds, wheat
germ and sesame seeds.
3. Spread into a greased
9 × 13 pan.
4. Bake at 350° for 25-30
minutes.
5. Cool. Cut into squares.

Tip:
  Wrap squares individu-
ally. Place in freezer to enjoy
a healthy energizing snack
anytime!

Caramel Frappés

Anita Troyer
Fairview, MI

Makes 2 servings

Prep. Time: 15 minutes

3 cups ice cubes
2 cups milk
½ cup caramel syrup
  (coffee flavoring), plus
  extra for garnish
1½ Tbsp. instant coffee
¼ cup sugar
whipped cream, for garnish

1. Place all ingredients
except cream into blender.
2. Blend until smooth.
Top each glass with a little
whipped cream and drizzle
with additional caramel
syrup.

Green Tea Smoothie

Teresa Martin
Strasburg, PA

Makes 2 servings

Prep. Time: 10 minutes
Chilling Time: 8 hours or overnight

¾ cup water
2 green tea bags
2 cups frozen blueberries
3 ice cubes
12 oz. fat-free vanilla yogurt
12-15 whole dry-roasted, unsalted almonds
2 Tbsp. ground flaxseed

1. Bring water to steaming hot, not boiling, and pour over tea bags.
2. Allow to steep 1-2 minutes. Squeeze and remove tea bags and discard.
3. Chill tea 8 hours or overnight.
4. Place tea, blueberries, ice, yogurt, almonds, and flaxseed in blender. Process until smooth.

Tip:
This is a very satisfying drink, although it will not be completely smooth because of the almonds and flaxseed. Brewing the tea the night before saves time in the morning because the tea is already chilled.

Orange-Pineapple Shake

Anita Troyer
Fairview, MI

Makes 4 servings

Prep. Time: 5 minutes

2 cups orange juice
20-oz. can crushed pineapple in pineapple juice
1½ cups vanilla ice cream

1. In a blender, combine orange juice, pineapple and ice cream.
2. Blend until smooth and frothy.
3. Pour into glasses and serve.

Blueberry Banana Smoothie

Charlotte Shaffer
East Earl, PA

Makes 4 cups

Prep. Time: 5 minutes

1 banana, peeled and cut into 2" chunks
1 cup blueberries, fresh *or* frozen
½ cup soft tofu
¾ cup soy milk
1 Tbsp. ground flaxseeds
1 tsp. honey

1. Place banana, blueberries, tofu, milk, seeds and honey in blender and purée until smooth.
2. Pour into glasses and serve.

Holiday Punch

Cathy Kruba
Baltimore, MD

Makes 30 cups

Prep. Time: 15 minutes
Cooking Time: 10 minutes

3 cups sugar
3 cups water
4 cups cranberry juice
  cocktail
3 cups lemon juice
2 cups orange juice
2 cups unsweetened
  pineapple juice
2 quarts ginger ale

1. Combine sugar and water in saucepan and stir over medium heat until sugar dissolves.
2. Bring to a boil and boil, without stirring, for 7 minutes.
3. Cool at least 45 minutes.
4. Combine with fruit juices.
5. When ready to serve, stir in ginger ale.
6. Pour over ice in individual glasses and serve.

Variation:
  Float scoops of sherbet or ice cream on top of each glass if you wish.

Orange-Lemon Drink

Rhonda Freed
Croghan, NY

Makes 16 cups

Prep. Time: 5 minutes

1½ cups sugar
12-oz. can frozen orange
  juice concentrate
½ cup lemon juice
about 3 qts. water, *divided*

1. Put sugar, orange juice and lemon juice in a gallon pitcher.
2. Add 2 quarts cold water and mix well until sugar is dissolved.
3. Add ice cubes and cold water to make 1 gallon. Mix before serving.

Go-Along:
• Great for summer picnics.

30

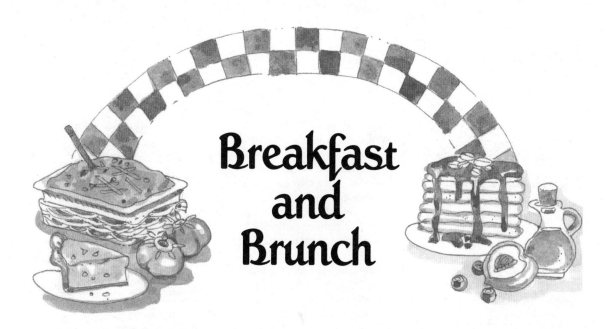

Breakfast and Brunch

Baked Apple Cranberry Pancake

Annabelle Unternahrer
Shipshewana, IN

Makes 8 servings

Prep. Time: 20 minutes
Cooking/Baking Time: 15 minutes

2 Tbsp. butter
¼ cup dried cranberries
1 small apple, cored and
    diced
¼ cup brown sugar
¼ cup orange juice
¾ cup all-purpose flour
4 tsp. granulated sugar
½ tsp. baking powder
½ tsp. baking soda
⅛ tsp. salt
1 egg, beaten
½ cup buttermilk
4 tsp. canola oil
1 tsp. finely shredded
    orange peel

1. Place butter in 10" pie plate. Place in 350° oven to melt butter.

2. Remove from oven. Stir in cranberries and apples. Set aside.

3. In small saucepan, combine brown sugar and orange juice. Bring to boil. Reduce heat to medium and boil, uncovered, 5 minutes.

4. Pour mixture over fruit in pie pan.

5. Mix together flour, sugar, baking powder, baking soda and salt. Set aside.

6. In small bowl, combine egg, buttermilk, oil and orange peel.

7. Add to flour mixture and stir gently.

8. Pour batter evenly over fruit and syrup in pie plate.

9. Bake, uncovered, at 350° for 15 minutes, or until top springs back when lightly touched.

10. Cool in pie plate on wire rack for 5 minutes.

11. Invert pancake onto serving platter.

12. Cut into 8 wedges and serve warm.

Tip:
    This recipe does not need additional syrup. It is sweet.

If you like all the ingredients in a recipe, you'll probably like the dish.
    Orpha Herr, Andover, NY

Pumpkin Pancakes

Susan Henne
Fleetwood, PA
Denise Nolt
Fleetwood, PA

Makes 24 pancakes

Prep. Time: 20 minutes
Cooking Time: 4-5 minutes per pancake

4 cups flour
2 Tbsp. baking powder
1 tsp. salt
4 Tbsp. brown sugar
1 Tbsp., plus 1 tsp., ground cinnamon
2 tsp. pumpkin pie spice
½ tsp. ground nutmeg
4 eggs
2 12-oz. cans evaporated milk
1 cup canned pumpkin
4 Tbsp. canola oil
2 tsp. vanilla extract
½ cup chopped pecans, *optional*
pure maple syrup, for serving
butter, for serving

1. In a medium mixing bowl, sift together the flour, baking powder, salt, brown sugar, cinnamon, pumpkin pie spice and nutmeg.
2. Stir to combine. Make a well in the center of the bowl and set aside.
3. In another medium mixing bowl, beat the eggs with a whisk. Add the evaporated milk, pumpkin, oil and vanilla and whisk until smooth.
4. Pour the wet-ingredient mixture into the prepared well in the dry ingredients. Whisk until just combined.
5. Add the pecans and stir them into the batter.
6. Use a ⅓-cup measure to pour batter onto a hot, greased griddle or frying pan.
7. Fry pancakes until bubbles appear in the middle and the edges are set. Flip and fry briefly on the other side.
8. Put cooked pancakes on a plate and place in a 250° oven to keep warm until serving time.
9. Serve with maple syrup and butter, if you wish.

Tip:
Left-over batter can be refrigerated and used the next day, if you don't want to make it all in one day.
Susan Henne

Variation:
To save time, if you are in a hurry, you can use 4 cups of biscuit or baking mix, in place of the flour, baking powder, and salt.

Susan Henne

Apple Oatmeal Pancakes

Laraine Good
Bernville, PA

Makes 14 servings

Prep. Time: 20 minutes
Cooking Time: 15 minutes

¾ cup flour
1 Tbsp. sugar
1 tsp. salt
1 tsp. baking soda
1 tsp. baking powder
1 tsp. cinnamon
1½ cups quick oats
2 medium apples, grated
2 eggs, beaten
1¾ cups sour cream
¼ cup oil

1. Sift flour, sugar, salt, baking soda, baking powder and cinnamon into a bowl. Mix in oats.
2. Add apples, eggs, sour cream and oil. Stir just until moistened.
3. To make 1 pancake, pour ½ cup batter into hot greased frying pan. When bubbles appear in middle and edges look set, flip and cook the other side briefly.

Melt-in-Your-Mouth Pancakes

Jessalyn Wantland
Arlington, WA

Makes 4 servings

Prep. Time: 5 minutes
Cooking Time: 15 minutes

2 cups buttermilk baking
  mix
1 cup milk
1 Tbsp. sugar
2 Tbsp. lemon juice
2 tsp. baking powder
2 eggs

1. Mix baking mix, milk,
sugar, lemon juice, baking
powder and eggs together. Do
not overmix. Batter will be a
little lumpy.
2. Fry on a hot, lightly
greased griddle. Flip when
pancakes start to appear dry
along the edges.

PB&J French Toast

Denise Nolt
Fleetwood, PA

Makes 6 servings

Prep. Time: 15 minutes
Cooking Time: 15 minutes

12 slices white bread
¾ cup peanut butter
¾ cup jam, any flavor
3 eggs
¾ cup milk
¼ tsp. salt
2 Tbsp. butter *or* margarine
confectioners sugar

1. Spread 6 slices of bread
with peanut butter and 6
slices with jam. Put the slices
together to make sandwiches.
Set aside.
2. In a shallow bowl, beat
eggs, milk and salt.
3. Melt butter in a large
skillet or griddle over
medium-high heat.
4. Dip sandwiches in egg
mixture.
5. Lay in skillet. Brown in
butter on both sides.
6. Dust with confectioners
sugar and serve immediately.

Cinnamon Toast Sticks

Janet L. Roggie
Lowville, NY

Makes 6-8 servings

Prep. Time: 20 minutes
Baking Time: 10 minutes

6-8 white *or* whole wheat
  bread slices
half stick (¼ cup) butter, at
  room temperature
½ cup sugar
1 tsp. cinnamon
⅓ cup chopped walnuts

1. Cut bread in 1½" strips.
2. In a mixing bowl, cream
butter.
3. Add sugar and cinnamon
to create a paste.
4. Spread paste on bread
strips and sprinkle with nuts.
5. Bake at 350° until paste
melts, about 10 minutes.

Go-Along:
• Applesauce or other fruit.

Refrigerate or freeze nuts, seeds, whole wheat flour, and grains.
Janice Sams, Lancaster, PA

Baked Apple French Toast

Ruth Nolt
Leola, PA

Makes 8 servings

Prep. Time: 30 minutes
Cooking/Baking Time: 45 minutes
Chilling Time: 8 hours or overnight
Standing Time: 30 minutes

1 cup brown sugar
one stick (½ cup) butter
2 Tbsp. honey *or* light corn syrup
4 tart apples, peeled and sliced
3 Tbsp. sugar
1 tsp. cinnamon
1 loaf French *or* Italian bread, sliced
6 eggs
1½ cups milk
1 tsp. vanilla

1. Cook brown sugar, butter and honey in a saucepan, stirring continually until sugar is melted.
2. Pour mixture evenly into buttered 9 × 13 baking pan.
3. Place sliced apples on top.
4. In a small bowl, mix sugar and cinnamon together. Sprinkle over apples.
5. Arrange 2 layers of bread on top of apples.
6. Whisk eggs, milk and vanilla together. Pour egg mixture over bread.
7. Cover and refrigerate overnight.
8. Remove from refrigerator 30 minutes before baking.
9. Bake, uncovered, at 350° for 45 minutes.

Go-Along:
• Pancake syrup.

Delicious Coffee Cake

Andrea Bjorlie
Grand Rapids, MI

Makes 6-8 servings

Prep. Time: 20 minutes
Baking Time: 45-50 minutes

1 egg
half stick (¼ cup) butter, at room temperature
¾ cup sugar
¾ cup milk
2½ tsp. baking powder
¾ tsp. salt
2 cups flour
2 cups frozen fruit, thawed and drained, *optional*

Topping:
½ cup sugar
⅓ cup flour
½ tsp. cinnamon
half stick (¼ cup) butter, softened

Glaze:
½ cup confectioners sugar
¼ tsp. vanilla
1½-2 tsp. hot water

1. To make the cake, cream together eggs, butter and sugar in a mixing bowl.
2. Add milk, baking powder, salt and flour. Beat for 30 seconds. If you wish, stir in fruit with a spoon.
3. Spread batter in greased 9 × 9 baking pan.
4. For the topping, combine sugar, flour, cinnamon and butter. Mix until crumbly.
5. Crumble topping evenly over batter.
6. Bake at 375° for 45-50 minutes, or until tester inserted in middle comes out clean.
7. While cake is baking, combine confectioners sugar, vanilla and water.
8. Drizzle glaze over cake top just after it is removed from the oven.

Variation:
You can add 2 Tbsp. ground flaxseed to the batter for extra nutrition.

Never-Fail Waffles

Rae Ann Henry
Conestoga, PA

Makes 10 servings

Prep. Time: 15 minutes
Cooking Time: depends on
waffle iron

2 eggs
1 cup milk
1 cup flour
1 tsp. sugar
¼ tsp. salt
2 tsp. baking powder
¼ cup vegetable oil

1. Separate eggs. In a small bowl, whip whites until soft peaks form.
2. In a another bowl, blend yolks, milk, flour, sugar, salt and baking powder.
3. Add vegetable oil, and mix just until combined. Do not overmix.
4. Fold in beaten egg whites with a rubber spatula.
5. Lightly oil the waffle iron. Pour batter into waffle iron by measured amounts according to appliance's instructions. Repeat with remaining batter.

Slow-Cooker Baked Oatmeal

Karen Burkholder
Narvon, PA
Susan Heil
Strasburg, PA
Tamera Baker
Lafayette, IN
Loretta Brubaker
Mount Joy, PA
Beverly Hummel
Fleetwood, PA
Rhonda Freed
Croghan, NY
Marlene Weaver
Lititz, PA

Makes 4-6 servings

Prep. Time: 10 minutes
Cooking Time: 2-3 hours
Ideal slow-cooker size: 3-qt.

3 cups quick oats
½-1 cup brown sugar
2 tsp. baking powder
1 tsp. cinnamon
1 tsp. salt
1 cup milk
1 stick (½ cup) butter,
    melted, *or* oil
2 eggs

1. Combine oats, sugar, baking powder, cinnamon, salt, milk, butter and eggs.
2. Spoon into a 3-quart slow cooker.
3. Cover. Cook on low 2-3 hours, or until set.

Tips:
    This can be cut into squares, put into baggies, and frozen. Defrost and microwave for a quick breakfast, lunch, or snack.
Susan Heil

Variations:
    1. To make it festive, add ¾ cup dried cranberries and 1⅔ cups chopped apples.
Marlene Weaver

    2. Add 1 tsp. vanilla.
Tamera Baker

    3. You can bake this in the oven instead. Put it in a greased 8 × 8 baking dish. Bake at 350° for 30 minutes.
Loretta Brubaker

    4. Use applesauce for half the butter.
Rhonda Freed
Beverly Hummel

Go-Alongs:
• Serve with vanilla ice cream for a dessert.
Susan Heil

• Delicious served with milk.
Karen Burkholder

• Fresh or frozen blueberries are a great topping!
Loretta Brubaker

Keep a plastic knife in flour and sugar canisters to level off a cup for accurate measurements.
Bonnie Whaling, Clearfield, PA

Blueberry Kuchen

Edna Good
Richland Center, WI

Makes 10-12 servings

Prep. Time: 15 minutes
Baking Time: 40 minutes

1½ cups all-purpose flour
2 tsp. baking powder
½ tsp. nutmeg
¾ cup sugar
1½ tsp. grated lemon peel
¼ tsp. salt
⅔ cup milk
1 egg, beaten
half stick (¼ cup) butter,
    melted
1 tsp. vanilla
2 cups blueberries, fresh *or*
    frozen

Topping:
    ½ cup flour
    ¾ cup sugar
    half stick (¼ cup) butter,
        melted

1. To make the cake, in mixing bowl, combine flour, baking powder, nutmeg, sugar, lemon peel and salt.
2. Add milk, egg, butter and vanilla. Beat for 2 minutes or until well blended.
3. Pour into greased 9 × 13 baking dish. Sprinkle blueberries evenly over batter.
4. In a small bowl, combine topping ingredients and toss with a fork until crumbly. Sprinkle over blueberries.
5. Bake at 350° for 40 minutes, or until lightly browned.

Overnight
Danish Braids

Joanna Bear
Salisbury, MD

Makes 8-10 servings

Prep. Time: 30 minutes
Baking Time: 35-40 minutes
Chilling Time: 12 hours or
overnight

5 cups all-purpose flour
½ cup sugar
½ tsp. salt
2 sticks (1 cup) butter, at
    room temperature
1 Tbsp. yeast
1 cup warm water
3 eggs, beaten

Filling:
    1½ sticks (¾ cup)
        softened butter
    1 cup brown sugar
    1 Tbsp. cinnamon
    1 cup nuts, *optional*

1. Put flour, sugar and salt in large bowl. Using two knives or a pastry cutter, cut 1 cup butter into dry ingredients.
2. In a separate bowl, dissolve yeast in warm water. Add eggs.
3. Add wet ingredients to dry and mix with your hands until soft dough forms.
4. Cover tightly and refrigerate overnight.
5. Remove from fridge. Allow dough to stand at room temperature for 1 hour.
6. Meanwhile, mix filling ingredients together in a small bowl.
7. Divide dough into 4 equal parts. Roll each part into a ¼"-thick rectangle.
8. Divide filling evenly among the 4 rectangles, placing it in the center and down the length of each dough rectangle.
9. Cut slits in the long sides of each rectangle. Pull the dough pieces up over the filling in the center, crossing the pieces to look like a braid.
10. Carefully place each braid on greased baking sheets. Bake at 350° for 35-40 minutes.

Variation:
    Drizzle baked braid with frosting if you wish.

Save the wrappers from sticks of margarine or butter. Fold them in half (sticky sides together) and store in the refrigerator. When you need to grease a pan, unfold, use, and throw away. Saves messing up your hands!

Debra Kilheffer, Millersville, PA

Pumpkin Ginger Scones

Arianne Hochstetler
Goshen, IN

Makes 12 servings

Prep. Time: 15-20 minutes
Baking Time: 12 minutes

½ **cup sugar,** *divided*
2 **cups all-purpose flour**
2 **tsp. baking powder**
½ **tsp. baking soda**
½ **tsp. salt**
1 **tsp. cinnamon**
5 **Tbsp. butter,** *divided*
1 **egg, beaten**
½ **cup cooked pumpkin**
¼ **cup sour cream**
½ **tsp. peeled, grated fresh ginger**

1. Reserve 1 Tbsp. sugar and set aside.
2. In a mixing bowl, combine remaining sugar, flour, baking powder, baking soda, salt, and cinnamon.
3. Cut in 4 Tbsp. butter with pastry blender until mixture resembles coarse crumbs.
4. In small bowl, combine egg, pumpkin, sour cream and ginger. Add to flour mixture.
5. Stir until mixture forms soft dough that pulls away from side of bowl.
6. Turn onto well-floured surface. Knead 10 times.
7. Roll out dough into six 3"-squares. Cut squares diagonally.
8. Place on ungreased baking sheet.
9. Brush with remaining butter and sprinkle with reserved sugar.
10. Bake at 425° for 10-12 minutes.

Tip:
These are best served warm from the oven.

Variation:
You may replace up to one cup of the all-purpose flour with whole wheat flour.

Apricot and White Chocolate Scones

Ruth Nolt
Leola, PA

Makes 12 servings

Prep. Time: 20 minutes
Baking Time: 15-18 minutes

1¾ **cups flour**
¼ **cup sugar**
2 **tsp. baking powder**
¼ **tsp. salt**
⅓ **cup (5⅓ Tbsp.) chilled butter, cut in ¼" pieces**
⅓ **cup, plus 2 Tbsp., chopped, dried apricots,** *divided*
1 **cup white chocolate baking chips,** *divided*
1 **egg, beaten**
⅓ **cup half-and-half**

1. Sift together flour, sugar, baking powder, and salt in a mixing bowl.
2. Using a pastry blender, cut butter into flour mixture until butter is the size of peas.
3. Stir in ⅓ cup apricots and ⅔ cup white chocolate chips.
4. Add egg and half-and-half.
5. Mix with fork until just mixed. Do not overmix.
6. Knead lightly a few times. Place dough on greased baking sheet.
7. Form dough into 8" circle.
8. Score with sharp knife into 8 wedges.
9. Bake at 400° for 15-18 minutes.
10. Melt remaining ⅓ cup white chocolate chips.
11. Remove baked scones immediately from baking sheet, carefully separating wedges.
12. Sprinkle with remaining apricots and drizzle with melted white chocolate.

Italian Frittata Cups

Rebekah Zehr
Lowville, NY

Makes 6 servings

Prep. Time: 25 minutes
Cooking/Baking Time: 15 minutes
Standing Time: 5 minutes

4 garlic cloves, minced
2 Tbsp. extra-virgin olive
    oil
1 cup diced whole wheat
    baguette bread
1 cup shredded yellow
    summer squash
1 cup shredded zucchini
2 Tbsp. butter
½ tsp. salt
¼ tsp. pepper
½ cup white whole wheat
    flour *or* all-purpose flour
4 eggs, beaten
2 Tbsp. grated Parmesan
    cheese
1 tsp. dried basil
½ tsp. garlic salt
5 Tbsp. chopped green
    olives
1 small onion, thinly sliced
1-2 tomatoes, diced
½ cup shredded Monterey
    Jack cheese

1. In a rimmed baking
sheet, toss together minced
garlic, olive oil and diced
bread. Bake in oven at 450°,
stirring once, for 8-10 minutes. Set aside.
2. In a large skillet, sauté
squash, zucchini and butter
until softened. Add salt and
pepper.
3. In a separate bowl,
whisk the flour and eggs,
Parmesan cheese, basil and
garlic salt.
4. Stir in sautéed vegetables
and olives.
5. Grease 12 muffin cups.
Fill each half-full with egg
mixture.
6. Carefully place onion
slices on top of egg mixture,
dividing them evenly.
7. Bake at 450° for 8
minutes.
8. Take out of oven and
place diced tomatoes and
reserved croutons over eggs.
Sprinkle with shredded
Monterey Jack cheese.
9. Bake 5 more minutes.
Allow to stand 5 minutes
before serving.

Tip:
    This is great for brunch
as it is very easy to serve.
It is also great for reheating
and eating on the go. You
can make the garlic croutons
ahead of time if you want.

Baked Cheese Grits

Janie Steele
Moore, OK

Makes 6 servings

Prep. Time: 20 minutes
Cooking Time: 2 hours
Ideal slow-cooker size: 3- or 4-qt.

4 cups water
1 tsp. salt
1 cup grits, uncooked
2 eggs
1 stick (½ cup) butter, cut
    into chunks
1¼ cups grated cheese
additional cheese, *optional*

1. In a medium saucepan,
bring water and salt to a boil.
2. Slowly pour in dry grits,
stirring constantly. Keep stirring
for 1 minute to avoid lumps.
3. Cover. Cook until grits
are thick and creamy, 5-10
minutes.
4. Beat eggs in a small
bowl. Add about ½ cup
cooked grits to eggs stirring
continuously. This tempers
the eggs.
5. Pour the grits/egg
mixture back into the hot
grits, stirring.
6. Add butter and cheese. Stir.
7. Pour into slow cooker.
Cover.
8. Cook on high 2 hours or
until set.
9. Top with additional
cheese if you wish.

Tip:
    You can use any combination of cheddar, Monterey
Jack, or pepper jack cheese.

*When zucchini is in season, shred it into 2-cup
amounts for future recipes. Freeze until needed.*

Betty Moore, Avon Park, FL

Cheese Vegetable Strata

June S. Groff
Denver, PA

Mary Fisher
Leola, PA

Makes 8-10 servings

Prep. Time: 20 minutes
Cooking/Baking Time: 45 minutes
Standing Time: 10 minutes

8 slices bread
3 Tbsp. vegetable oil
1 medium bunch broccoli, cut in bite-size pieces
1 medium onion, diced
½ lb. fresh mushrooms, sliced
1½ tsp. salt, *divided*
8-oz pkg. Muenster cheese slices
6 eggs
4 cups milk
½ tsp. dry mustard

1. With 3" round cookie cutter, cut 6 rounds from bread slices and set aside.
2. Tear remaining bread into small pieces and place in bottom of greased 9 × 13 baking pan.
3. Heat oil in skillet over medium heat.
4. Add broccoli, onion, mushrooms and ½ tsp. salt. Cook until vegetables are tender. Stir frequently.
5. Place vegetables on top of bread pieces in pan.
6. Place cheese slices over vegetable mixture.
7. In a bowl, whisk eggs, milk, mustard and remaining 1 tsp. salt until blended.
8. Dip bread rounds in egg mixture and place on top of cheese.
9. Pour remaining egg mixture over cheese.
10. Bake at 350° for 45 minutes. Allow to stand for 10 minutes before slicing and serving.

Tip:
If bread browns too quickly, cover with foil during last 10 minutes.

Cheesy Bread Pudding

Sara Harter Fredette
Williamsburg, MA

Makes 6-8 servings

Prep. Time: 15 minutes
Cooking/Baking Time: 30-35 minutes

1 onion, chopped
1 Tbsp. olive oil
1 Tbsp. butter
4 cups cubed bread
2 cups milk
1 egg
½ tsp. salt
pepper, to taste
dash of hot pepper sauce
¼ cup sunflower seeds, *optional*
¼ cup wheat germ
1 cup grated sharp cheese

1. In a frying pan, sauté onion in oil until soft.
2. Melt butter in the microwave or a small pan. Pour in 8 × 8 baking dish.
3. In large bowl, mix sautéed onion, bread, milk, egg, salt, pepper, hot pepper sauce, sunflower seeds, wheat germ and cheese.
4. Pour into buttered baking dish.
5. Bake at 350° for 30-35 minutes.

Tip:
This is good hot or cold. Use an assortment of breads. I freeze odds and ends of breads until I have enough for this recipe.

Go-Along:
• Fruit salad.

Impossible Brunch Pie

Joanne E. Martin
Stevens, PA

Makes 6-8 servings

Prep. Time: 10 minutes
Cooking Time: 2-3 hours
Ideal slow-cooker size: 3- or 4-qt.

10-oz. pkg. frozen broccoli, thawed and chopped
1 cup sour cream
1 cup creamed cottage cheese
½ cup buttermilk baking mix
half stick (¼ cup) butter, melted
2 eggs
1 tomato, sliced
¼ cup grated Parmesan cheese

1. Spread broccoli in greased 3-quart slow cooker.
2. Beat sour cream, cottage cheese, baking mix, butter and eggs for 15 seconds in a blender.
3. Pour over broccoli in slow cooker.
4. Top with tomato and Parmesan cheese.
5. Cook covered on high 2-3 hours, or until set.

Variation:
Add a tablespoon or two of chopped onion if you like to step 2.

Mexican Egg Casserole

Margaret Wenger Johnson
Keezletown, VA

Makes 8 servings

Prep. Time: 15 minutes
Baking Time: 45 minutes
Standing Time: 5 minutes

½ cup all-purpose flour
1 tsp. baking powder
12 eggs, lightly beaten
4 cups shredded Monterey Jack cheese, *divided*
2 cups small-curd cottage cheese
2 plum tomatoes, seeded and diced
4-oz. can green chilies, drained and chopped
4 green onions, sliced
½ tsp. hot pepper sauce
1 tsp. dried oregano
2 Tbsp. minced fresh cilantro *or* parsley
½ tsp. salt
½ tsp. pepper
salsa, *optional*

1. In a large bowl, combine the flour and baking powder.
2. Add the eggs, 3½ cups Monterey Jack cheese, cottage cheese, tomatoes, chilies, onions, hot pepper sauce, oregano, cilantro, salt and pepper.
3. Pour into a greased 9 × 13 baking dish. Sprinkle with the remaining Monterey Jack cheese.
4. Bake at 400° for 15 minutes. Reduce heat to 350° and bake 30 minutes longer, or until a knife inserted near the center comes out clean.
5. Let stand 5 minutes before cutting. Serve with salsa if you wish.

When adding eggs to a dish that you're preparing, crack the eggs over a separate bowl so shells do not get into the recipe.

Lynn Higgins, Marion, OH

Quiche Mediterranean

June S. Groff
Denver, PA

Makes 6-8 servings

Prep. Time: 20 minutes
Cooking/Baking Time: 30 minutes

¼ cup vegetable oil
¼ cup chopped onion
½ small eggplant, cubed into ½" pieces (about 2 cups)
2 medium tomatoes, diced
2 Tbsp. chopped fresh parsley
¼ tsp. dried basil
9" *or* 10" unbaked pie crust
¾ cup cream
3 eggs
3 Tbsp. grated Parmesan cheese
¼ tsp. minced garlic
¾ tsp. salt

1. Heat oil in skillet over medium heat.
2. Add onion and eggplant and cook until fork-tender.
3. Add tomatoes, parsley and basil.
4. Cook 5 minutes longer.
5. Spoon mixture into pie shell.
6. In medium bowl, whisk cream, eggs, cheese, garlic and salt until well blended.
7. Pour over vegetable mixture.
8. Bake at 400° for 20-30 minutes, until set in the middle.

Potato-Crust Quiche

Vonda Ebersole
Mt. Pleasant Mills, PA
Marlene Zimmerman
Bradford, PA
Colleen Heatwole
Burton, MI
Donna Conto
Saylorsburg, PA
Jean Turner
Williams Lake, BC

Makes 6-8 servings

Prep. Time: 30 minutes
Cooking/Baking Time: 55 minutes

4 raw potatoes, grated
half stick (¼ cup) butter, melted
3 cups broccoli
5 eggs
⅔ cup milk
½ tsp. salt
¼ tsp. pepper
1 cup shredded cheddar cheese

1. Press potatoes into bottom and sides of greased 10" pie plate.
2. Melt butter in skillet. Drizzle butter over potatoes.
3. Bake at 425° for 20-25 minutes, until browned.
4. Meanwhile, sauté broccoli in skillet used to melt butter. Broccoli should be softened, but not mushy.
5. In small bowl, beat eggs, milk, salt and pepper.
6. Spoon broccoli evenly over hot crust.
7. Top with cheese.
8. Pour egg mixture over top.
9. Bake at 350° for 25-30 minutes, until set in the middle.

Variations:
1. Use 10-oz. package of frozen spinach, thawed and squeezed dry, instead of sautéed broccoli. Add ⅓ cup sautéed, chopped onion. Add 1 tsp. oregano and ¼ tsp. nutmeg.
Jean Turner

2. Make a different crust with 3 cups cooked, shredded potatoes. You can buy these as frozen hash brown potatoes.
Marlene Zimmerman
Colleen Heatwole
Jean Turner

3. Omit broccoli and use 1 cup diced mushrooms, ½ cup diced peppers, and ¼ cup pimento. No need to sauté the vegetables first.
Marlene Zimmerman

4. Make a crust from 1⅓ cups leftover mashed potatoes. No need to bake before filling with egg mixture.
Donna Conto

Go-Along:
• Zucchini Tomato Salsa is good served on top.

Overnight Veggie Omelet

Doug Garrett
Palmyra, PA

Makes 6 servings

Prep. Time: 30 minutes
Cooking/Baking Time: 60 minutes
Chilling Time: 4 hours to overnight

½ cup diced onion
1 medium carrot, pared
　and sliced thinly
2 Tbsp. butter
6 slices whole-grain bread,
　torn into pieces
2 cups fresh broccoli
　florets, cut small
¾ cup grape tomatoes,
　sliced lengthwise
4 oz. cream cheese
1 cup grated colby cheese
6 eggs
1½ cups milk
½ tsp. dry mustard
½ tsp. salt
dash cayenne pepper

1. Sauté diced onion and carrots in butter in skillet, until onion is light brown and softened.

2. Distribute torn bread in bottom of greased 9 × 9 baking dish.

3. Add onion/carrot mixture. Evenly sprinkle broccoli and grape tomatoes on top.

4. Cut cream cheese into small pieces. Sprinkle it and grated cheese evenly over top.

5. Mix eggs, milk, mustard, salt and cayenne. Pour over top.

6. Cover with aluminum foil. Refrigerate for 4 hours or overnight.

7. Bake, still covered, at 325° for 50 minutes. Uncover. Bake 10 minutes more.

Go-Along:
• This complements breakfast pastries such as sticky buns or muffins.

Granola

Julia Burkholder
Robesonia, PA

Makes 12 cups

Prep. Time: 15 minutes
Baking Time: 1 hour

5 cups dry quick *or* rolled
　oats
3 cups whole wheat flour
1¼ cups brown sugar
1 cup sunflower seeds
1 cup wheat germ
½ cup nuts of your choice
1 cup oil
½ cup water

1. Mix oats, flour, sugar, sunflower seeds, wheat germ and nuts.

2. Add oil and water and mix well.

3. Divide mixture into two 9 × 13 baking pans.

4. Bake at 300° for 1 hour, stirring every 15 minutes.

5. Cool. Store in airtight containers.

Go-Along:
• Serve with fruit and milk, soy milk, or vanilla yogurt. Or eat as a crunchy snack.

If you only need half an onion, save the root half because it will last longer.

Orpha Herr, Andover, NY

Soy-Flax Granola

Doug Garrett
Palmyra, PA

Makes 10 cups

Prep. Time: 20 minutes
Baking Time: 45 minutes
Standing Time: 2 hours

12 oz. soybeans, roasted
    with no salt
4 cups rolled oats
¾ cup soy flour
¾ cup ground flaxseed
1¼ cups brown sugar
1 tsp. salt
2 tsp. cinnamon
⅔ cup walnuts, coarsely
    chopped
⅔ cup whole pecans
½ cup canola oil
¾ cup applesauce
2 tsp. vanilla extract
dried cranberries, dried
    cherries, chopped dried
    apricots, chopped dried
    figs, or raisins, *optional*

1. Put roasted soybeans in a blender and blend briefly until coarsely chopped. Place in large mixing bowl.

2. Add oats, flour, flaxseed, brown sugar, salt, cinnamon, walnuts and pecans. Mix thoroughly with spoon, breaking up any brown sugar lumps.

3. In a 2-cup measuring cup, combine oil, applesauce and vanilla extract. Mix.

4. Thoroughly mix dry and wet ingredients together until mixture is uniformly moist.

5. Turn into a roasting pan. Clean off mixing spoon with spatula into the roasting pan.

6. Bake at 325° for 15 minutes, and then stir. Repeat two more times for a total baking time of 45 minutes.

7. After baking, add dried fruit if you wish.

8. Let cool at least 2 hours. When cool, store in airtight containers.

Tip:

You can be very flexible with this granola's dry ingredients. Just keep the dry/wet proportions similar.

Go-Along:

• Top granola with some yogurt and fresh fruit - it's like dessert for breakfast!

Muesli

Loretta Lapp
Kinzer, PA

Makes 2 servings

Prep. Time: 10 minutes

¼ cup almonds
¼ cup sunflower *or*
    pumpkin seeds
¼ cup walnuts
1 fresh pitted date
1 dried apricot
¼ tsp. cinnamon
½ cup uncooked oatmeal
milk
maple syrup *or* agave
    nectar, to taste

1. Place almonds, sunflower seeds, walnuts, date, apricot, cinnamon and oatmeal in small food processor or chopper.

2. Pulse briefly to desired chunkiness.

3. Serve with milk. Drizzle with maple syrup or agave nectar.

Tips:

1. Do not cook this recipe.

2. This is a delicious breakfast food that gives lots of energy. It is a good start for the day.

Grain and Fruit Cereal

Cynthia Haller
New Holland, PA

Makes 4-5 servings

Prep. Time: 5 minutes
Cooking Time: 3 hours
Ideal slow-cooker size: 4-qt.

⅓ cup uncooked quinoa
⅓ cup uncooked millet
⅓ cup uncooked brown rice
4 cups water
¼ tsp. salt
½ cup raisins *or* dried cranberries
¼ cup chopped nuts, *optional*
1 tsp. vanilla extract, *optional*
½ tsp. ground cinnamon, *optional*
1 Tbsp. maple syrup, *optional*

1. Wash the quinoa, millet and brown rice and rinse well.
2. Place the grains, water and salt in a slow cooker. Cook on low until most of the water has been absorbed, about 3 hours.
3. Add dried fruit, milk and any optional ingredients, and cook for 30 minutes more. If the mixture is too thick, add a little more water or milk.
4. Serve hot or cold.

Breakfast Quinoa with Cranberries

Mary Ann Lefever
Lancaster, PA

Kate Good
Intercourse, PA

Makes 4 servings

Prep. Time: 10 minutes
Cooking Time: 20 minutes

1 cup water
1½ cups vanilla soy milk, plus more for serving
1 cup uncooked quinoa, rinsed, drained
½ cup dried cranberries
2 Tbsp. maple sugar *or* maple syrup *or* brown sugar
1 tsp. ground cinnamon
½ tsp. ground ginger
¼ tsp. ground allspice
¼ tsp. ground nutmeg
½ cup chopped pecans, toasted

1. In medium saucepan, bring water and soy milk to a boil.
2. Stir in quinoa and cranberries.
3. Reduce heat to medium low. Cover. Simmer 15-20 minutes, or until liquid is absorbed and grains are tender. Stir occasionally.
4. Remove from heat and stir in maple sugar, cinnamon, ginger, allspice and nutmeg.
5. Serve warm.

6. Top with more soy milk and pecans.

Tip:
Quinoa is a whole grain complex carbohydrate and very high in protein. This is great to try when you are tired of oatmeal for breakfast.

Mary Ann Lefever

Variations:
1. Any dried fruit may be used in place of cranberries: prunes, dates, raisins, dried cherries, and apricots. If fresh fruit is used, add after cooking.

Mary Ann Lefever

2. Reduce cinnamon to ⅛ tsp. and omit other spices. Add ½ tsp. vanilla extract. You can use regular milk instead of soymilk and water.

Kate Good

Use a small mesh strainer to rinse quinoa.

Colleen Heatwole, Burton, MI

Steel-Cut Oats with Bananas

April Green
Aurora, CO

Makes 4 servings

Prep. Time: 5 minutes
Cooking Time: 25 minutes

2 cups water
2 cups vanilla soy milk
1 cup uncooked steel-cut oats
¼ tsp. salt
2 bananas, mashed
2 Tbsp. ground flaxseed
2 tsp. cinnamon
2 Tbsp. pure maple syrup
1½ tsp. vanilla extract

1. Bring water and soy milk to a boil in a medium pan.
2. Stir in oats and salt. Reduce heat to low. Stir in bananas and flax.
3. Simmer uncovered on low for 20 minutes, or until oats are tender, stirring every 5 minutes.
4. Remove from heat. Stir in cinnamon, syrup and vanilla.

Go-Along:
• Serve with your favorite hot-cereal toppings such as raisins, walnuts, granola or brown sugar.

Cream-of-Brown-Rice Cereal

June Hackenberger
Thompsontown, PA

Makes 3-4 servings

Prep. Time: 5 minutes
Cooking Time: 10 minutes

¾ cup brown rice, uncooked
4 cups water, *divided*
scant teaspoon salt

1. Grind rice in blender until fine and powdery.
2. Bring 3 cups of water to a boil in a covered saucepan.
3. Add ground rice and salt to the remaining 1 cup of water in a bowl. Stir well. Slowly stir into the boiling water.
4. Cook on low for 10 minutes or until cereal is thick and creamy.

Go-Along:
• Serve with butter, milk and brown sugar.

Be adventurous with recipes! Try something that is different from anything you've made before. You'll learn something new and build on your prior experience in the kitchen. Janelle Glick, Lancaster, PA

Pumpkin Custard

Audrey Hess
Gettysburg, PA

Makes 4-6 servings

Prep. Time: 10 minutes
Cooking Time: 1-1½ hours
Ideal slow-cooker size: 2½-qt.

2 cups cooked pumpkin, *or*
   any winter squash
3 Tbsp. molasses
3 eggs
1 tsp. cinnamon
½ tsp. ground ginger
½ tsp. ground cloves
dash salt

1. Place ingredients in blender and purée until smooth.
2. Pour into 2½ quart greased slow cooker.
3. Cook, covered, on high for 1-1½ hours, until set.
4. Serve warm or chilled over hot cereal. Keep leftovers in fridge.

Tip:
The custard will separate and weep a little in the fridge, but it's still fine to use.

Go-Along:
• Delicious topped with walnuts.

Cold Strawberry Soup

Polly Winters
Lancaster, PA

Makes 8 cups

Prep. Time: 15 minutes

1 quart strawberries
2 cups plain yogurt
½ cup orange juice
¼-½ cup sugar, to taste
strawberries for garnish,
   optional

1. Wash and stem berries.
2. Combine strawberries, yogurt, juice and sugar in blender.
3. Process in blender until smooth. Serve in bowls. Top with whole berries if you wish.

Variation:
Refreshing any time of year! Use frozen strawberries when you can't get fresh.

Breads, Sandwiches, and Pizzas

Vermont Honey Wheat Bread

Rachel Yoder
Dundee, OH

Makes 3 loaves

Prep. Time: 30 minutes
Rising Time: 3 hours
Baking Time: 30-35 minutes

2 ¼-oz. pkgs. (2 Tbsp.) yeast
¾ cup warm water
1¼ cups rolled oats, *divided*
1 cup buttermilk, room temperature
⅓ cup (5⅓ Tbsp.) butter, softened
1½ cups whole wheat flour
½ cup maple syrup
½ cup honey
⅓ cup wheat germ
2 eggs, beaten
1 tsp. salt
3¾-4½ cups all-purpose flour
1 egg white
1 Tbsp. water

1. In small bowl, dissolve yeast in warm water.
2. In large mixing bowl, combine 1 cup oats, buttermilk and butter. Add yeast mixture.
3. Add whole wheat flour, syrup, honey, wheat germ, eggs and salt. Beat for 30 seconds.
4. Stir in flour until dough is firm.
5. Knead 6-8 minutes. Grease bowl. Add dough to bowl, turning once to grease top.
6. Cover. Let rise for 1 hour in a warm place.
7. Punch down. Allow to rise a second time.
8. Grease three loaf pans. Divide dough into three parts and shape into loaves. Place in loaf pans.
9. Cover. Let loaves rise again in a warm place until double.
10. In a small bowl, beat egg white and water. Brush tops of loaves. Sprinkle with remaining ¼ cup oats.
11. Bake at 350° for 30-35 minutes. Turn out of pans to cool on wire rack.

Go-Along:
• Cinnamon butter.

When shaping bread, I roll it out into a rectangle, then roll it up and flop it onto the counter a few times before placing in pans. This prevents the bread from having large holes inside. Also, pricking the newly-shaped loaves with a fork will prevent bubbles.
Natalie Butikofer, Richland Center, WI

French Bread

Renae Hege
Midville, GA

Makes 2 loaves servings

Prep. Time: 30 minutes
Rising Time: 2 hours
Baking Time: 25 minutes

2 Tbsp. instant yeast
2½ cups warm water
1 Tbsp. salt
1 Tbsp. butter, softened
2 cups whole wheat flour
⅓ cup wheat bran
4½-5 cups all-purpose *or*
   unbleached flour, *divided*
1 Tbsp. oil

1. In large bowl, combine yeast, water, salt, butter, whole wheat flour, bran and 2 cups all-purpose flour. Mix well with wooden spoon.

2. Add remaining flour to form dough that is slightly sticky.

3. Knead 2 minutes. Form into a big ball.

4. Pour oil into mixing bowl. Place ball of dough in oil and rub oil over bowl and dough so ball of dough is completely oiled.

5. Cover bowl with kitchen towel. Let rise in a warm place for 1 hour, or until double.

6. Punch dough down and divide in half.

7. Roll each half into 12 × 15" rectangle.

8. Starting at long side, roll up rectangles tightly, creating two long loaves. Pinch seam hard to seal. Taper ends.

9. Place loaves, seam-side down, on a greased baking sheet.

10. Cover again with kitchen towel. Let rise 1 hour, or until double.

11. Bake at 450° for 20-25 minutes, or until loaves are golden brown and hollow-sounding when tapped.

Go-Along:
• Soup.

Potato water is liquid drained from cooking potatoes. It enhances yeast bread.

Ruth Mast, Crossville, TN

Vegan

Wheat Bread

Edna Good
Richland Center, WI

Makes 24 servings

Prep. Time: 25 minutes
Rising Time: 2-4 hours
Baking Time: 35 minutes

2 Tbsp. yeast
2 cups warm water
¼ cup brown sugar
¼ cup oil
¼ cup sorghum
2 tsp. salt
3 cups whole wheat flour
3 cups all-purpose flour

1. In a large mixing bowl, dissolve yeast in warm water. Add brown sugar, oil, sorghum and salt.

2. Mix in whole wheat flour and stir until smooth.

3. Add remaining flour. Knead for 5-10 minutes or until dough is smooth and elastic.

4. Shape dough into a smooth ball and place in a greased bowl.

5. Cover and put in warm place. Let rise until doubled in size, 1-2 hours.

6. Punch down and shape into 2 loaves. Place into 2 greased 9 × 5 bread pans.

7. Cover. Let rise until doubled again.

8. Bake at 325° for 10 minutes. Then at 300° for 25 minutes. Remove from pans and cool on wire rack.

9. Brush olive oil over tops of loaves while hot, if you wish.

Indian Naan Bread

Wilma Stoltzfus
Honey Brook, PA

Makes 15 servings

Prep. Time: 20 minutes
Rising Time: 1½ hours
Cooking Time: 40 minutes

1 Tbsp. yeast
1 cup lukewarm water
¼ cup sugar
3 Tbsp. milk
1 egg, beaten
2 tsp. salt
4½ cups bread flour
half stick (¼ cup) butter, melted
2 cloves minced garlic

1. In a mixing bowl, dissolve yeast in warm water.
2. Add sugar, milk, egg and salt.
3. Stir in flour to make a soft dough. Knead briefly.
4. Put dough in well-oiled bowl. Turn to grease top. Cover with kitchen towel.
5. Allow to rise for one hour or until double.
6. Pinch off golf-ball-sized balls of dough. Allow dough balls to rise for 30 minutes on the counter.
7. Roll each dough ball into a thin disc.
8. Lightly oil a griddle and heat to medium high. Meanwhile, mix melted butter with garlic and set aside.
9. Fry each dough disc 2-3 minutes, until puffy or light brown.
10. Brush uncooked side with melted butter mixed with garlic.
11. Turn over to brown.
12. Brush with garlic butter after each side is browned.

Tip:
Use several pans to fry to decrease preparation time.

Go-Along:
• Nepal vegetable curry with rice.

Tomato Dill Bread

Anna King
Andover, NY

Makes 2 loaves

Prep. Time: 30 minutes
Rising Time: 2 hours
Baking Time: 40 minutes

¼-oz. package (1 Tbsp.) active dry yeast
2 Tbsp. sugar
½ cup warm (110-115° F) water
1 cup chopped peeled tomatoes
2 Tbsp. vegetable oil
1 Tbsp. minced fresh parsley, *or* 1 tsp. dried
1 Tbsp. fresh dill, *or* 1 tsp. dried
1 Tbsp. fresh oregano, *or* 1 tsp. dried
2 tsp. salt
3½-4½ cups all-purpose flour
3 Tbsp. butter, melted

1. Dissolve yeast and sugar in warm water in a mixing bowl.
2. In a blender or food processor, purée tomatoes with oil, parsley, dill, oregano and salt. Add to yeast mixture.
3. Add enough flour to make a smooth dough.
4. Turn onto a floured surface. Knead until smooth and elastic, about 6-8 minutes.
5. Place in a greased bowl, turning once to grease top.
6. Cover and let rise in a warm place about 1 hour.
7. Punch down and divide dough in half. Shape into loaves. Place into two greased 8 × 4 loaf pans.
8. Cover. Let rise until doubled, about 1 hour.
9. Bake at 400° for 15 minutes. Reduce heat to 350° for 25 minutes.
10. Brush loaves with melted butter as soon as they come out of the oven. Remove from pans and cool on wire rack.

Tip:
To help bread rise in a cool house, set bread bowl directly in slow cooker base with no crock or lid. The bowl should not touch the sides. Turn cooker on low. Cover the rising dough with waxed paper or a kitchen towel.

49

Cinnamon Raisin Bread

Beverly Hummel
Fleetwood, PA

Makes 3 loaves

Prep. Time: 30 minutes
Rising Time: 1½-2½ hours
Cooking/Baking Time: 40 minutes

1½ cups milk
1 cup warm water
2 Tbsp. *or* 2 pkgs. yeast
3 eggs
½ cup sugar
1 stick (½ cup), plus 2
   Tbsp., butter, softened,
   divided
1 tsp. salt
1 cup raisins
8 cups all-purpose flour
1 cup sugar
3 Tbsp. cinnamon

1. In a saucepan, heat the milk until it begins to boil. Remove from heat. Let cool until lukewarm.

2. In a large mixing bowl, dissolve yeast in warm water. Mix in eggs, ½ cup sugar, ½ cup butter, salt, raisins and cooled milk.

3. Stir in flour gradually to make a stiff dough. Knead until smooth, 4-6 minutes.

4. Form dough into a ball. Grease mixing bowl. Add

dough back to bowl and turn to grease top. Cover bowl with kitchen towel.

5. Let rise until double, about 1-2 hours.

6. Roll dough out into a large rectangle ½" thick.

7. Mix together 1 cup sugar and cinnamon, and sprinkle evenly over the dough.

8. Roll tightly, starting with the long side. Pinch seam to seal.

9. Cut long roll into three equal pieces. Place each into a greased 9 × 5 loaf pan.

10. Rub tops of bread with remaining 2 Tbsp. softened butter.

11. Bake at 350° for 35-40 minutes, until golden brown and hollow-sounding when tapped.

Tip:
   Eat one loaf, and freeze the other two, or give as gifts.

Variation:
   Replace 2 cups of the all-purpose flour with whole wheat flour.

Go-Along:
• Lemon curd.

Peanut Butter Bread

Marla Folkerts
Geneva, IL

Makes 1 loaf

Prep. Time: 20 minutes
Rising Time: 2-3 hours
Cooking/Baking Time: 45 minutes

1 cup milk
½ cup creamy peanut
   butter, not reduced-fat
   or natural
2 Tbsp. sugar
1 tsp. salt
2 tsp. yeast
¼ cup warm water
1 large egg
⅔ cup whole wheat flour
2⅓ cups bread flour,
   divided

1. In a saucepan, heat milk to almost boiling. Pour into a large mixing bowl.

2. Add peanut butter, sugar and salt. Beat well and set aside until lukewarm.

3. In a small bowl, dissolve yeast in ¼ cup warm water.

4. Add yeast mixture to peanut-butter mixture. Add egg and beat.

5. Add whole wheat flour and 1 cup bread flour. Beat well.

6. Stir in enough additional flour to form a stiff dough.

7. Knead dough on floured surface. Grease bowl. Put dough in greased bowl, turning once to grease top.

8. Cover with kitchen towel. Let rise in warm place

To test if bread is done, insert a toothpick into the center of the loaf. If it comes out clean the bread is done. If not, bake an additional 5 minutes.

Annabelle Unternahrer, Shipshewana, IN

50

until double in size, 1-2 hours.

9. Knead briefly. Shape into a loaf. Place into greased 9 × 5 loaf pan.

10. Cover. Allow to rise again in a warm place until double, or about 1 hour.

11. Bake at 350° for 35-40 minutes.

Tip:

To make in a bread machine:
Mix milk, adding 2 Tbsp. extra milk, and peanut butter.

Add egg, salt, bread flour, whole wheat flour, sugar and yeast according to bread machine's suggested instructions.

Pumpkin Knot Rolls

Leah Hersberger
Dundee, OH

Makes 24 rolls

Prep. Time: 45 minutes
Rising Time: 2 hours
Baking Time: 15-17 minutes

2 ¼-oz. pkgs. (2 Tbsp.) dry yeast
1 cup warm milk
⅓ cup (5⅓ Tbsp.) butter, softened
½ cup sugar
1 cup cooked pumpkin
2 eggs
1½ tsp. salt
5½-6 cups bread flour, *divided*
1 Tbsp. water
1 egg
sesame *or* poppy seed, *optional*

1. In large mixing bowl, dissolve yeast in warm milk.

2. Add butter, sugar, pumpkin, 2 eggs, salt and 3 cups flour. Beat until smooth.

3. With a spoon, stir in remaining flour to form a soft dough.

4. Turn onto lightly floured surface and knead 6-8 minutes, or until smooth and elastic.

5. Place in greased bowl, turning once to grease top.

6. Cover. Let rise in warm place for 1 hour, or until doubled.

7. Punch dough down. Turn onto lightly floured surface and divide in half.

8. Shape each portion into 12 equal balls. Roll each ball into a 10" rope.

9. Tie into knot and tuck ends under.

10. Place knots 2" apart on greased cookie sheet.

11. Cover. Let rise until doubled, approximately 1 hour.

12. Mix water and egg in small bowl. Brush over rolls.

13. Sprinkle with sesame or poppy seeds, if you wish.

14. Bake at 350° for 15-17 minutes.

15. Remove from pans to wire rack. Serve hot or warm.

Tip:

These complement a holiday meal.

Go-Along:
• Serve with Harvest Pumpkin Butter.

Easy Rolls

Gloria Julien
Gladstone, MI

Makes 24 rolls

Prep. Time: 20 minutes
Rising Time: 2 hours
Baking Time: 15 minutes

2 cups warm water
2 Tbsp. dry yeast
⅓ cup vegetable oil
2 tsp. salt
1 egg, beaten
½ cup sugar
6½-7½ cups all-purpose
   flour, *divided*
melted butter

1. In a large bowl, use electric beater and mix water, yeast, oil, salt, egg, sugar and 4½ cups flour.
2. Stir in 2 or 3 more cups of flour until dough comes away from sides of bowl. Push dough into a ball.
3. Remove dough ball from bowl. Pour a little oil in bowl. Place dough ball back in the oil in bowl, turning to grease all sides.
4. Cover bowl with a kitchen towel. Let rise until double in size, approximately 1 hour.
5. Punch down. Roll dough on floured surface with rolling pin.
6. Cut into 24 pieces using a biscuit cutter or knife.
7. Place rolls on 11×17 cookie sheet. Cover with towel. Let rise again until doubled, approximately 45-60 minutes.

8. Bake at 350° for 15 minutes.
9. Brush hot rolls with melted butter. Remove to cooling rack to finish cooling.

Go-Along:
• Stews, casseroles, salad, or vegetable soup.

100% Whole Wheat Refrigerator Rolls

Lois Hess
Lancaster, PA

Makes 36 rolls

Prep. Time: 15 minutes
Chilling Time: 12-36 hours
Baking Time: 10-12 minutes

2 cups warm (110-115°)
   water
2 Tbsp. yeast
½ cup sugar
2 tsp. salt
¼ cup oil
1 egg
6-6½ cups whole wheat
   flour

1. In large mixing bowl, dissolve yeast in water.
2. Add sugar, salt, oil and egg.
3. Knead in flour, but keep dough slightly sticky.
4. Place in greased bowl. Cover with kitchen towel.
5. Set in refrigerator and let rise to top of bowl.
6. Form into 24-36 dinner rolls. Place on baking sheet. Allow to rest 15-20 minutes.

7. Bake at 400° for 10-12 minutes.

Tips:
1. Dough can be kept in refrigerator up to 3 days, ready for fresh dinner rolls each day.
2. You can mix the dough, allow it to rise, and shape it into rolls immediately without refrigerating it.

Herb Rolls

Rebecca Beery
Mt. Crawford, VA

Makes 15-20 servings

Prep. Time: 15 minutes
Rising Time: 1-2 hours
Baking Time: 15-20 minutes

1 cup warm water
⅓ cup sugar
2 Tbsp. yeast
¾ stick (6 Tbsp.) butter, softened, *divided*
1 egg
1 tsp. salt
3½ cups all-purpose flour
1 Tbsp. dried parsley
½ tsp. dried basil
½ tsp. dried dill
½ tsp. dried rosemary
2 Tbsp. grated Parmesan cheese

1. In a good-sized mixing bowl, dissolve yeast and sugar in warm water.
2. Add 4 Tbsp. butter, egg, salt, flour and herbs. Stir until dough forms.
3. Press into a 9 × 13 baking pan. With a sharp knife, score dough diagonally to form diamonds.
4. Cover with a towel. Let rise until doubled, 1-2 hours.
5. Bake at 375° for 15-18 minutes.
6. Brush rolls with remaining 2 Tbsp. melted butter and sprinkle with Parmesan cheese. Break into diamonds to serve.

Variation:
Replace some or all of the all-purpose flour with white whole wheat flour.

Sour Cream Cornbread

Dorothy Vandeest
Memphis, TN

Makes 8 servings

Prep. Time: 10 minutes
Baking Time: 22-24 minutes

1½ cups self-rising white cornmeal mix
½ cup all-purpose flour
14¾-oz. can low-sodium cream-style corn
8 oz. light sour cream
3 large eggs, lightly beaten
2 Tbsp. chopped fresh cilantro
½ cup shredded cheddar cheese

1. Heat lightly greased, 10" cast-iron skillet in 450° oven for 5 minutes.
2. Meanwhile, in large bowl, stir together cornmeal and flour.
3. Add corn, sour cream, eggs and cilantro.
4. Pour corn batter into hot skillet.
5. Top with cheese.
6. Bake at 450° for 22-24 minutes or until golden brown and cornbread pulls away from sides of skillet.

Variation:
If you don't have self-rising white cornmeal, use instead: ¾ cup cornmeal, 3 Tbsp. all-purpose flour, 1 Tbsp. baking powder, ½ tsp. salt.

Go-Along:
• Any cabbage dish!

Broccoli Cornbread

Darla Sathre
Baxter, MN

Makes 12 servings

Prep. Time: 10 minutes
Baking Time: 25-30 minutes

1 stick (½ cup) butter
16-oz. pkg. frozen chopped broccoli, thawed
4 eggs
1 onion, finely chopped
8½-oz. box cornbread mix
2 cups shredded Mexican cheese

1. Turn oven on to 400°. Place butter in 9 × 13 baking pan and place in oven to melt.
2. Meanwhile, in a bowl, mix broccoli, eggs, onion, cornbread mix and cheese.
3. Pour onto melted butter in baking pan.
4. Bake at 400° for 25-30 minutes or until tester inserted in middle comes out clean.

Tip:
Thaw broccoli in bag in refrigerator.

To make your own cornbread mix, please turn to page 261.

Pineapple Cheddar Cornbread

Moreen and **Christina Weaver**
Bath, NY

Makes 10-12 servings

Prep. Time: 15-20 minutes
Baking Time: 35 minutes

1 cup all-purpose flour
1 cup cornmeal
½ cup sugar
2 tsp. baking powder
1 tsp. salt
1 stick (½ cup) butter, softened
4 eggs, lightly beaten
14¾-oz. can cream-style corn
8-oz. can crushed pineapple, drained
1 cup shredded cheddar cheese, *or* Monterey Jack cheese

1. In medium bowl, combine flour, cornmeal, sugar, baking powder and salt. Set aside.
2. In large mixing bowl, beat butter with electric mixer on medium speed for 30 seconds.
3. Add eggs, one at a time. Beat well after each addition.
4. On low speed, beat in flour mixture until combined.
5. Stir in corn, pineapple and cheese.
6. Pour into greased, 2-quart, rectangular baking dish.
7. Bake at 375° for 35 minutes or until toothpick comes out clean.
8. Cut in squares and serve warm.

Go-Along:
• Spicy chili.

Banana Cookie Bread Deluxe

Willard Swartley
Elkhart, IN

Makes 1 loaf

Prep. Time: 30 minutes
Baking Time: 55-60 minutes

¾ cup sugar
3 Tbsp. margarine *or* butter, melted
4 oz. yogurt, almost any flavor works
2 eggs
2 Tbsp. orange juice
3 bananas, mashed
pinch of salt, *optional*
1 tsp. baking soda
½ tsp. baking powder
1¾ cups all-purpose flour
¼ cup raisins *or* dried cranberries, or some of both
½ cup chopped walnuts, *optional*
9 dried apricots *or* dried kiwi, chopped fine
1 cup quick oats
1 cup raisin bran
1 cup crisp rice cereal
1 cup low-fat granola

1. Mix together sugar, butter, yogurt and eggs.
2. Add in orange juice and bananas. Mix.
3. Add in salt, baking soda, baking powder and flour. Mix again.
4. Add in apricots or kiwi, oats, raisin bran, crisp rice cereal and granola.
5. Pour into a greased 9 × 5 bread pan.
6. Bake at 325° for 55-60 minutes, or until top is brown and split a bit and tester inserted in middle comes out clean.

Tip:
Excellent for any meal, even dessert.

Go-Along:
• Fruit, tea, or coffee.

When baking, always follow directions and measure ingredients.
Lynn Higgins, Marion, OH

Gift of the Magi Bread

Arianne Hochstetler
Goshen, IN

Makes 2 loaves

Prep. Time: 15-20 minutes
Baking Time: 55 minutes

1 stick (½ cup) butter *or*
   margarine, softened
1 cup sugar
2 eggs
1 tsp. vanilla extract
2 cups flour
1 tsp. baking soda
½ tsp. salt
1 cup mashed ripe bananas
11-oz. can mandarin
   oranges, drained
½ cup chopped dates
1 cup flaked coconut,
   optional
1 cup semi-sweet chocolate
   chips
⅔ cup sliced almonds,
   divided
½ cup chopped maraschino
   cherries

1. In mixing bowl, cream butter and sugar.
2. Beat in eggs and vanilla. Set aside.
3. Combine flour, baking soda and salt in a separate bowl.
4. Add flour mixture to creamed mixture alternately with bananas.
5. Stir in oranges, dates, coconut, chocolate chips, ½ cup almonds, and cherries.
6. Pour into two greased 8 ×5 loaf pans.

7. Sprinkle with remaining almonds.
8. Bake at 350° for 50-55 minutes, or until toothpick comes out clean.
9. Cool for 10 minutes before removing from pans. Continue cooling on wire racks.

Go-Along:
• Fresh fruit slices, tea or coffee.

Wheat Germ Zucchini Bread with Chocolate Chips

Steven Lantz
Denver, CO

Makes 2 loaves

Prep. Time: 15 minutes
Baking Time: 1 hour
Standing Time: 10 minutes

3 eggs, beaten
½ cup white sugar
1 cup brown sugar, not
   packed
1 cup vegetable oil
dash maple flavoring
2 cups shredded zucchini
2 tsp. baking soda
½ tsp. baking powder
2 tsp. salt
1½ cups wheat germ
2½ cups all-purpose flour
1 cup chocolate chips

1. In a large bowl, beat together eggs, both sugars, oil and maple flavoring until foamy and thick.
2. Stir in zucchini.
3. In a separate bowl, mix baking soda, baking powder, salt, wheat germ and flour. Add to zucchini mixture and mix well.
4. Stir in chocolate chips.
5. Pour batter into two greased 9 ×5 loaf pans.
6. Bake in 350° oven for 1 hour or until toothpick inserted in center comes out clean.
7. Cool bread in pans for 10 minutes before removing to rack to cool completely.

Orange-Coconut Zucchini Bread

Moreen and **Christina Weaver**
Bath, NY

Marla Alger
Timberville, VA

Makes 2 loaves

Prep. Time: 20 minutes
Baking Time: 50-55 minutes

1 cup canola oil
1¾-2¼ cups sugar
3 eggs
2 tsp. almond extract,
    optional
¾ cup orange juice
1 Tbsp. finely grated
    orange rind
1½ cups shredded coconut
2 cups grated zucchini
3 cups flour
1 tsp. baking soda
1 tsp. baking powder
½-1 tsp. salt

1. Mix oil, sugar, eggs, almond extract, orange juice, orange rind, coconut and zucchini together. Mix well.

2. Stir in flour, baking soda, baking powder and salt.

3. Divide batter into two greased 9×5 bread pans.

4. Bake at 350° for 50-55 minutes or until tester inserted in middle comes out clean.

Apple Streusel Muffins

Ruth Nolt
Leola, PA

Makes 12 muffins

Prep. Time: 25 minutes
Baking Time: 15-20 minutes
Standing Time: 65 minutes or more

2 cups all-purpose flour
¾ cup sugar
1 tsp. baking powder
½ tsp. baking soda
½ tsp. salt
2 eggs
1 stick (½ cup) butter,
    melted
1¼ tsp. vanilla
1½ cups chopped, peeled
    tart apples

Topping:
    ⅓ cup brown sugar
    1 Tbsp. flour
    ⅛ tsp. cinnamon
    1 Tbsp. cold butter

Glaze:
    1½ cups confectioners
        sugar
    1-2 Tbsp. milk
    1 tsp. butter, melted
    ¼ tsp. vanilla
    ⅛ tsp. salt

1. In bowl, combine flour, sugar, baking powder, baking soda and salt.

2. In separate bowl, whisk eggs, butter and vanilla together.

3. Stir into flour mixture.

4. Fold in apples. Divide among 12 greased muffin cups.

5. For topping, combine brown sugar, flour and cinnamon.

6. Cut in butter with a pastry cutter until crumbly.

7. Sprinkle over batter.

8. Bake at 375° for 15-20 minutes, or until toothpick comes out clean.

9. Cool 5 minutes. Remove from pan and cool completely, at least an hour.

10. To make glaze, combine confectioners sugar, milk, melted butter, vanilla and salt.

11. Drizzle over muffins.

Spelt Applesauce Muffins

Linda Tyson
Brownstown, PA

Makes 24 muffins

Prep. Time: 10-15 minutes
Baking Time: 20 minutes

1 cup oil
½ cup sugar
2 cups applesauce
2⅔ cups spelt flour
⅓ cup sweet white rice flour
2 tsp. baking soda
2 tsp. cinnamon
1 cup raisins

1. In small bowl, combine oil, sugar and applesauce.
2. In a larger mixing bowl, stir together spelt flour, rice flour, baking soda, cinnamon and raisins. Mix well.
3. Add the wet ingredients to the dry and mix until just moistened.
4. Spoon batter into muffin tins lined with baking cups. Fill baking cups ⅔ to ¾ full.
5. Bake at 375° for 20 minutes or until toothpick inserted in center comes out clean.
6. Cool muffins in pan before removing.

Tip:
These freeze well. And they're quick to make!

Ready Bake Muffins

Dottie Geraci
Burtonsville, MD

Makes 24-36 muffins

Prep. Time: 15 minutes
Standing Time: 20 minutes
Baking Time: 20 minutes

3 cups bran cereal
1 cup boiling water
2 eggs, slightly beaten
2 cups buttermilk
½ cup oil
1 cup grated carrots
1 cup raisins *or* chopped dates *or* chopped prunes
2½ tsp. baking soda
½ tsp. salt
1 cup sugar
2½ cups all-purpose flour

1. In a heat-proof mixing bowl, mix cereal with boiling water. Stir to moisten evenly. Set aside until cool, about 20 minutes.
2. When cooled, add eggs, buttermilk, oil, carrots, and raisins. Blend well.
3. In a separate small bowl, combine baking soda, salt, sugar, and flour.
4. Add to cereal mixture and stir batter to distribute fruit.

5. Spoon batter into buttered 2½" muffin cups until ¾ full.
6. Bake at 425° for 20 minutes, or until top springs back when touched.
7. Serve hot.

Tip:
This batter may be refrigerated in a tightly-covered container for as long as two weeks. Muffins can ready in about 25 minutes!

Enjoy your work, share your discoveries, and give thanks for all the gifts.

Rose Stewart, Lancaster, PA

Whole Wheat Zucchini Muffins

Sharon Yoder
Doylestown, PA

Makes 12 muffins

Prep. Time: 15 minutes
Baking Time: 18-22 minutes

2 cups whole wheat flour
½ cup brown sugar, packed
3 tsp. baking powder
1 tsp. cinnamon
¼ tsp. salt
2 eggs
¾ cup milk
⅓ cup vegetable oil
1 cup grated zucchini
½ cup mini chocolate chips
  or raisins

1. Combine the dry ingredients.
2. Beat the eggs, milk, and oil in a large separate bowl.
3. Fold the zucchini and chocolate chips into the wet ingredients.
4. Add the dry ingredients, stirring only until combined.
5. Spoon into greased muffin tins.
6. Bake at 375° for 18-22 minutes.

Strawberries and Cream Mini Muffins

Jenny Unternahrer
Wayland, IA

Makes 6-8 servings

Prep. Time: 20 minutes
Baking Time: 10 minutes
Standing Time: 5 minutes

1 cup diced strawberries
2 tsp. lemon juice
1 cup flour
½ cup sugar
1 tsp. baking powder
¼ cup vegetable oil
4 oz. low-fat cream cheese, at room temperature and cut into small chunks
¼ cup orange juice
1 tsp. vanilla
1 egg
confectioners sugar

1. Line mini muffin tins with baking cups and set aside.
2. Put strawberries in small bowl. Toss with lemon juice.
3. In medium bowl stir together flour, sugar and baking powder.
4. In another small bowl stir together oil, cream cheese, orange juice, vanilla and egg.
5. Pour over dry ingredients, stirring just until combined with a spoon.
6. Fold in strawberries and lemon juice.
7. Spoon into mini muffin tins (a small cookie scoop is handy).
8. Bake at 400° for about 9-10 minutes or until toothpick inserted comes out clean.
9. Remove from oven and cool in the tins on a cooling rack for 5 minutes. Take out the muffins and continue to cool.
10. If serving right away, let them stand for 5 minutes before dusting with confectioners sugar. If serving later, dust just before serving.

Banana Millet Muffins

Christie Detamore-Hunsberger
Harrisonburg, VA

Makes 12 muffins

Prep. Time: 20 minutes
Baking Time: 18-22 minutes

2 cups whole wheat flour *or* whole wheat pastry flour
¼ cup uncooked quick oats
2 tsp. baking soda
½ tsp. salt
⅓ cup uncooked millet
½ cup applesauce
2 Tbsp. ground flax
3 Tbsp. water
2 cups mashed over-ripe bananas, about 4-5 large bananas
¼ cup raisins

1. In a large bowl, mix together flour, oats, baking soda, salt and millet. Set aside.
2. In blender, purée on high speed the applesauce, ground flax, water, bananas and raisins.
3. Add wet ingredients to dry, stirring just until moist.
4. Fill 12 greased muffin tins. Bake at 350° for 18-20 minutes.

Tips:
1. These muffins have only fruit sugars and no added fat.
2. They also freeze well.

Variation:
You can use 1 egg instead of ground flax and water.

Raspberry Chocolate Chip Muffins

Roanna Martin
Morgantown, WV

Makes 12-15 muffins

Prep. Time: 15 minutes
Baking Time: 25 minutes

1⅔ cups all-purpose flour
¾ cup rolled oats
⅔ cup sugar
2 tsp. baking powder
1 tsp. baking soda
½ tsp. ground cinnamon
1 egg, lightly beaten
¾ cup skim milk
⅓ cup canola oil
2 Tbsp. orange juice
1 tsp. vanilla extract
¾ cup fresh *or* frozen unsweetened raspberries
½ cup miniature semi-sweet chocolate chips

1. In a large bowl, combine flour, oats, sugar, baking powder, baking soda and cinnamon.
2. In a separate bowl, combine egg, milk, oil, orange juice and vanilla.
3. Stir wet ingredients into dry ingredients until just moistened.
4. Gently fold in raspberries and chocolate chips.
5. Fill paper-lined muffin cups coated with nonstick cooking spray ⅔ full.
6. Bake at 375° for 20-25 minutes or until toothpick inserted in center of a muffin or two comes out clean.
7. Cool for 5 minutes before removing from pan to wire rack to cool.

Tip:
If using frozen raspberries, do not thaw before adding to batter.

Go-Along:
• My family enjoys crumbling fresh muffins into a bowl and serving with milk.

Pumpkin Chip Muffins

Ruth Miller
Wooster, OH

Makes 24 muffins

Prep. Time: 15 minutes
Baking Time: 16-20 minutes
Standing Time: 10 minutes

4 eggs
2 cups sugar
16-oz. can pumpkin
1½ cups vegetable oil
3 cups all-purpose flour
2 tsp. baking soda
2 tsp. baking powder
1 tsp. ground cinnamon
1 tsp. salt
¼ tsp. ground nutmeg
⅛ tsp. ground ginger
⅛ tsp. ground cloves
2 cups chocolate chips

1. In large mixing bowl, beat eggs, sugar, pumpkin and oil until smooth.
2. In separate bowl, combine flour, baking soda, baking powder, cinnamon and salt.
3. Add dry ingredients to pumpkin mixture and mix well.
4. Fold in chocolate chips.
5. Pour into paper liners or greased muffin pan, making each ¾ full.
6. Bake at 400° for 16-20 minutes or until tester inserted in middle of a muffin comes out clean.
7. Cool in pan 10 minutes before removing to wire rack.

Go-Along:
• Casseroles or soups.

Orange Bran Flax Muffins

Mary Emma Zook
Hutchinson, KS

Makes 24 muffins

Prep. Time: 20 minutes
Baking Time: 18-20 minutes

2 oranges, peeled, seeded, and chopped
½-1 tsp. finely grated orange rind
1 cup brown sugar
1 cup buttermilk *or* sour milk
½ cup canola *or* olive oil
2 eggs
1 tsp. baking soda
1½ cups raisins
1½ cups oat bran
1 cup all-purpose flour
1 cup ground flaxseed
1 cup wheat bran *or* wheat germ
1 Tbsp. baking powder
½ tsp. salt

1. Blend oranges, orange rind, sugar, buttermilk, oil, eggs, baking soda and raisins in a blender.
2. In a large bowl, mix oat bran, flour, flaxseed, wheat bran, baking powder and salt.
3. Pour orange mixture into dry ingredients. Mix well.
4. Divide batter evenly into greased or paper-lined muffin tins.
5. Bake at 375° for 18-20 minutes.

Variation:
Raisins may be stirred in separately at the end rather than blended.

Cheddar Garlic Biscuits

Amy Bauer
New Ulm, MN

Barbara Grannemann
Gerald, MO

Makes 9 biscuits

Prep. Time: 10 minutes
Baking Time: 8-10 minutes

2 cups buttermilk baking mix
⅔ cup milk
½ cup shredded sharp cheddar cheese
2 Tbsp. butter, melted
⅛ tsp. garlic powder

1. Mix together buttermilk baking mix, milk and cheese to form a soft dough.
2. Drop 9 spoonfuls onto ungreased baking sheet.
3. Bake at 450° for 8-10 minutes.
4. Mix butter and garlic powder and brush over warm biscuits.

Sweet Potato Biscuits

Elva Evers
Wayland, IA

Makes 18 biscuits

Prep. Time: 20 minutes
Baking Time: 12-15 minutes

2½ cups unbleached all-purpose flour
2 Tbsp. brown sugar
2 tsp. baking powder
1 tsp. baking soda
½ tsp. ground nutmeg
½ tsp. salt
¼ cup canola oil
¾ cup, plus 2 Tbsp., cultured nonfat buttermilk
¾ cup cooked, mashed sweet potato

1. Lightly spray a baking sheet with cooking spray.
2. In a large bowl, combine flour, brown sugar, baking powder, baking soda, nutmeg and salt and set aside.
3. In a small bowl, combine oil, buttermilk and sweet potato. Add to dry ingredients and mix until just combined. If dough is sticky, add a little more flour.
4. Transfer dough to a floured work surface. Knead a few times and pat an 8 × 5 rectangle that's 1" thick.
5. Dip a sharp knife in flour and cut dough into thirds lengthwise. Dip knife into flour again and cut each long strip into 6 equal pieces, making 18 squares in all.
6. Transfer biscuits to baking sheet.
7. Bake at 425° for 12-15 minutes, or until tops are golden and firm to the touch. Serve warm.

Tip:

Sometimes I cut these with a floured round biscuit cutter.

Go-Along:
• They're good served with butter, honey or apple butter.

Vegan

All-Day Apple Butter

Andy Wagner
Quarryville, PA

Makes 4 pints

Prep. Time: 30 minutes
Cooking Time: 11-13 hours
Ideal slow-cooker size: 4-qt.

5½ lbs. apples, peeled, cored and finely chopped
4 cups sugar
2 tsp. cinnamon, ground
¼ tsp. cloves, ground
¼ tsp. salt

1. Place the apples in a slow cooker.
2. In a medium bowl, mix the sugar, cinnamon, cloves and salt. Pour the mixture over the apples and mix well.
3. Cover. Cook on high 1 hour.
4. Reduce heat to low and cook 9-11 hours, stirring occasionally, until the mixture is thickened and dark brown.
5. Uncover and continue cooking on low 1 hour. Stir with a whisk, if desired, to increase smoothness.
6. Spoon the mixture into sterile containers, cover and refrigerate or freeze.

Take advantage of classes provided by local extension service if offered in your area. The food safety course is especially helpful.

Carolyn Leaman, Strasburg, PA

Fay Etta's Apple Butter

Leanne Yoder
Tucson, AZ

Makes 13 cups

Prep. Time: 30 minutes
Cooking Time: 5 hours

10-12 apples, a mix of McIntosh, Yellow Delicious, Jonathan, and Ida Red
½ cup water
5-6 cups sugar depending on how sweet you like your apple butter
1 Tbsp. cinnamon
¼ tsp. ground cloves
1 cup orange juice
¼ cup lemon juice

1. Peel and chop apples. Place apples and water in cast-iron Dutch oven over low heat. Cover.

2. Cook until apples are totally soft, 30-45 minutes. Stir often.

3. Puree in food processor, blender, or food mill. There should be 2 quarts apple purée.

4. Return purée to Dutch oven. Add sugar, cinnamon, cloves, orange juice and lemon juice.

5. Cook uncovered, stirring occasionally with a straight-edged utensil so nothing sticks to the bottom and burns.

6. After cooking at least 4 hours, drop a little onto a plate and test its spreadability with a knife. It will thicken slightly as it cools.

7. Turn hot apple butter into pint jars, leaving ¼" head space. Process according to your canner's instructions. Alternatively, store in the fridge or freeze.

Tips:

1. McIntosh, Yellow Delicious, Jonathans and Ida Reds are good choices of apples to use. Use a variety in the same batch for the best flavor.

2. Store-bought apple butter doesn't come close to matching the pleasing flavor of homemade. It is worth every minute of the time it takes to make.

3. Tie a ribbon around a jar of apple butter for a lovely teacher's gift that is guaranteed to please!

Variation:

Cook 4 hours on low in slow cooker, leaving lid off for last hour.

Go-Along:
• Serve on homemade bread, muffins, or crackers as you would jam, or alongside cottage cheese.

Practice safety with heat. Watch hair and loose clothing. Turn handles away from edges. Turn burners on only with pots or pans on them. Use mitts and hot pads. Presume metal is hot. Respect boiling water, and respect hot oil even more.

Rose Stewart, Lancaster, PA

Harvest Pumpkin Butter

Leah Hersberger
Dundee, OH

Makes 1½ cups

Prep. Time: 10 minutes
Cooking Time: 15 minutes
Chilling Time: 1 hour

1 cup cooked pumpkin
½ cup applesauce
⅓ cup honey
¼ cup sorghum, *or* molasses
¾ tsp. cinnamon
½ Tbsp. lemon juice

1. In saucepan, combine pumpkin, applesauce, honey, sorghum, cinnamon and lemon juice.
2. Bring to boil, stirring frequently.
3. Reduce heat. Simmer, uncovered, for 10-15 minutes, or until thickened.
4. Refrigerate for 1 hour before serving.

Go-Along:
• Eat with toast or crackers. Or serve with pancakes.

Microwave Lemon Curd

Sharon Easter
Yuba City, CA

Makes 1½-2 cups

Prep. Time: 5 minutes
Cooking Time: 6-10 minutes

2½ cups sugar
3 lemons, juiced, yielding about 1 cup juice
1 stick (½ cup) butter, cut in chunks
3 eggs, well beaten

1. In microwave, cook sugar and lemon juice 3 minutes on high. Stir after each minute with wire whisk.
2. Add butter and cook 1 minute. Stir.
3. Add beaten eggs.
4. Heat on high 2-5 minutes, or until thickened.
5. Whisk after every 1-2 minutes.

Go-Along:
• Serve on toast or pound cake.

Jalapeño Pepper Jelly

Jenna Yoder
Floyd, VA

Makes 3-4 pints

Prep. Time: 30 minutes
Cooking Time: 10 minutes

10 jalapeño peppers, chopped (remove seeds for a milder jelly)
1 green bell pepper, finely chopped
1 red bell pepper, finely chopped
3¼ cups sugar
¾ cup vinegar
2 3-oz. packets Certo *or* fruit pectin

1. In a large saucepan simmer together peppers, sugar and vinegar for 5 minutes.
2. Add Certo or pectin. Boil 1 minute.
3. Remove from heat and allow to cool.
4. Put in pretty glass jelly jars. Cover. Keeps in the refrigerator for several weeks.

Tip:
This jelly may be canned for even longer storage. Follow directions from your favorite canning resource.

Go-Alongs:
• Stir and pour a few spoonfuls over a block of cream cheese. Spread on snack crackers.
• Also very good on eggs at breakfast.

Breads, Sandwiches, and Pizzas

Carrot Egg Sandwich Filling

Patricia Howard
Green Valley, AZ

Makes 1½ cups

Prep. Time: 10 minutes
Chilling Time: 2 hours

4 eggs, hard-boiled and
  finely chopped
½ cup grated carrots
¼ tsp. curry powder
¼ tsp. salt
dash of pepper
¼ cup mayonnaise

1. Combine ingredients in a small bowl. Mix well.
2. Chill at least 2 hours before serving.

Egg Salad Sandwiches

Nadine Martinitz
Salina, KS

Irene Miller
Seymour, MO

Makes 3 cups

Prep. Time: 15 minutes

½ cup mayonnaise
2 tsp. vinegar
½ tsp. salt
¼ tsp. celery salt
¼ tsp. onion salt
1 Tbsp. prepared mustard
1 Tbsp. sugar
1 dozen hard-boiled eggs,
  peeled and chopped
12-16 slices bread

1. Mix mayonnaise, vinegar, salt, celery salt, onion salt, mustard and sugar together in a big bowl.
2. Add chopped eggs and mix well.
3. Spread egg filling on bread slices and assemble sandwiches.

Variations:
1. You may add 1-2 ribs chopped celery if you like a crunchy texture in egg salad.
2. Instead of vinegar, celery salt, onion salt, and mustard, add ¼ cup pickle relish and 2 Tbsp. minced fresh onion. Put a sliced tomato in the sandwich too.

Irene Miller

Chickpea of the Sea Spread

Mabel Shirk
Mt. Crawford, VA

Makes 2 cups

Prep. Time: 15 minutes

15-oz. can garbanzo beans,
  rinsed and drained
½ cup finely chopped
  celery
¼ cup finely chopped
  onions
1 Tbsp. lemon juice
¼ cup mayonnaise *or* salad
  dressing
2 Tbsp. pickle relish
crackers *or* bread

1. Place beans in food processor and process until coarsely chopped, or mash with potato masher.
2. Place in bowl. Add celery, onions, lemon juice, mayonnaise and pickle relish.
3. Mix well. Chill for 1 hour before serving. Serve on crackers or as a sandwich spread.

Go-Along:
• Soup, relish tray, apple-sauce, and cookies.

Grilled Cheese & Mushroom Sandwiches

Mary Anne Cressman Musser
Lancaster, PA

Makes 4 sandwiches

Prep. Time: 15 minutes
Cooking Time: 10-15 minutes

⅓ cup mayonnaise
2 tsp. vegetarian
   Worcestershire sauce
1 tsp. prepared mustard
2 cups shredded cheese
2 cups finely chopped
   mushrooms
2 Tbsp. minced onion
8 slices whole wheat bread
butter

1. Mix together mayonnaise, Worcestershire sauce, mustard, cheese, mushrooms and onion.
2. Spread butter on slices of bread.
3. Place mushroom mixture between two slices of bread with buttered sides out.
4. Place sandwiches on hot griddle or skillet.
5. Cook on both sides for 4-6 minutes per side until cheese is melted and bread is golden.

Gourmet Oven Grilled-Cheese Sandwiches

Jennifer Kauffman
Ames, IA

Makes 2 sandwiches

Prep. Time: 10 minutes
Baking Time: 16 minutes

4 slices of bread
butter *or* olive oil
1 Tbsp. pesto
½ cup minced black olives,
   or kalamata olives
4 slices cheddar cheese,
   divided
1 tomato, thinly sliced

1. Butter or brush with olive oil one side of each of the 4 slices of bread.
2. Place 2 of the slices butter-side down on a baking sheet.
3. Spread a thin layer of pesto on those two pieces of bread.
4. Divide olives among bread slices spread with pesto. Add one slice of cheese on top of each one.
5. Top each with a slice of tomato. Add the remaining pieces of cheese on top of tomatoes.
6. Cover each with the last slice of bread, butter-side up.
7. Bake at 450° for 6-8 minutes until golden brown on the bottom, the side touching the baking sheet. Flip and bake an additional 6-8 minutes, or until golden brown on the other side and cheese is melted.

Tip:
   This recipe can easily be multiplied to serve hot grilled cheese sandwiches to a group of people. It's much easier and more efficient than standing over the stove-top!

Go-Along:
• Tomato Basil Bisque.

Three-Cheese Quesadillas

Judi Robb
Manhattan, KS

Makes 4 servings

Prep. Time: 20 minutes
Cooking Time: 4 minutes per quesadilla

1 Tbsp. butter
4 8" flour tortillas
2 oz. (¼ of 8-oz. pkg.) cream cheese, softened
¼ cup shredded sharp cheddar cheese
¼ cup shredded Monterey Jack cheese
2 Tbsp. chopped onion
2 Tbsp. minced fresh cilantro
2 tsp. chopped ripe olives
¼ cup salsa
sour cream, *optional*

1. Spread butter lightly on one side of each tortilla.
2. Spread cream cheese on half of the side without butter.
3. Sprinkle cheeses, onion, cilantro and olives over cream cheese.
4. Fold other half of each tortilla over cheeses, buttered side up, making each tortilla a half-moon shape.
5. Cook on griddle over medium heat, 1-2 minutes on each side.
6. Cut into wedges.
7. Serve with salsa and sour cream if you wish.

Soy Sloppy Joes

Andrew Schrock
Catlett, VA

Vegan

Makes 6-8 servings

Prep. Time: 5 minutes
Cooking Time: 15 minutes

1 Tbsp. oil
1 onion, diced
1 bell pepper, diced
1 celery rib, diced
1 jalapeño, seeds removed, diced
1 tomato, diced
1 Tbsp. minced garlic
½ tsp. salt
1 tsp. black pepper
2 tsp. cumin
½ tsp. cayenne
2 cups ketchup
2 cups tomato juice
2 lbs. soy crumbles, *or* broken soy rolls
burger buns, *or* bread

1. In a nonstick skillet, heat oil. Sauté onion, bell pepper, celery, jalapeño, tomato and garlic until soft, about 5 minutes.
2. Add salt, pepper, cumin, cayenne, ketchup, tomato juice and soy crumbles.
3. Bring to a boil and simmer until desired consistency is reached, 5-10 minutes.
4. Serve on burger buns or your favorite bread.

Tip:
This is a little bit spicier than traditional sloppy joes. If you prefer it less spicy, do not use the jalapeños and/or the cayenne.

Go-Along:
• Home fries and salad.

Veggie Sandwiches

Esther S. Martin
Ephrata, PA

Makes 2 servings

Prep. Time: 15 minutes
Cooking Time: 3-5 minutes

4 slices crusty French bread
butter *or* cooking spray
6 button mushrooms, sliced
½ cup shredded carrots
2 Tbsp. hot pepper jam, *or* to taste
4 slices mozzarella cheese
1 avocado, sliced
1 cup baby spinach
4 slices tomato

1. Butter each piece of bread on both sides, or spray with cooking oil.
2. Grill over medium heat until golden brown, flipping once.
3. In a skillet, lightly sauté mushrooms and carrots.
4. To make sandwiches, spread pepper jam on two pieces of grilled bread.
5. Divide cheese, avocado, mushrooms and carrots, spinach and tomato evenly between the two pieces of bread spread with jam.
6. Place second piece of bread on top.

Go-Along:
• Dill pickle and salad.

Broiled Vegetable Sandwiches

Pat Bechtel
Carlisle, PA

Makes 2-3 servings

Prep. Time: 20 minutes
Baking Time: 10-14 minutes

6 slices peeled eggplant, ¼"
  thick
½ cup sliced yellow squash
⅓ cup sliced zucchini, ¼"
  thick
2 slices red onion, ¼" thick
cooking spray *or* olive oil
1 tsp. Italian herb
  seasoning
dash cayenne pepper
2-3 hard rolls, split and
  toasted
5 tsp. mayonnaise
2 fresh basil leaves
2-4 spinach leaves
1 cup julienned roasted red
  sweet pepper
2 slices tomato
2 tsp. minced seeded
  jalapeño pepper

1. In large bowl, combine eggplant, squash, zucchini, and onion.

2. Spray lightly with cooking spray or toss with olive oil.

3. Add Italian seasoning and cayenne and toss to coat vegetables.

4. Arrange in single layer in 10 × 15 baking pan coated with cooking spray.

5. Broil 4-6" from heat for 5-7 minutes on each side or until tender and browned.

6. Spread rolls with mayonnaise. Layer with basil, spinach, red peppers, tomato and jalapeño on bottom half of rolls.

7. Top with broiled vegetables. Cover with top half of roll.

Variation:
The vegetables may be grilled in a basket for 5-7 minutes on each side.

Go-Along:
• Macaroni or potato salad.

Mushroom Sliders

Donna Treloar
Muncie, IN

Makes 4 servings

Prep. Time: 15 minutes
Standing Time: 1 hour
Cooking Time: 10 minutes

2 large portabello
  mushrooms, stems
  removed
¼ cup balsamic vinaigrette
¼ tsp. salt
¼ tsp. freshly ground
  pepper
½ cup garlic herb spread
8 small rolls, slider-size
8 tomato slices
8 red onion slices

1. Place mushrooms and vinaigrette in large resealable bag.

2. Toss to coat, and then marinate for 1 hour.

3. Remove mushrooms. Season both sides with salt and pepper.

4. Spray a grill pan with cooking spray.

5. Place mushrooms on grill and cook over medium heat, 8-10 minutes, turning once.

6. Meanwhile, split the rolls. Toast in toaster oven or place on grill with mushrooms. Allow rolls to warm up and get crispy on edges.

7. Remove mushrooms from grill to drain on paper towels.

8. Cut each mushroom in 4 pieces.

9. Spread garlic spread on both sides of toasted rolls.

10. Top with mushrooms, tomato, and onion. Serve hot.

Tip:
If you wish, melt a slice of cheese on top of the mushrooms on each sandwich.

Go-Along:
• Raw vegetables and chips.

Mushroom Burgers

Melva Baumer
Mifflintown, PA

Makes 4 servings

Prep. Time: 15 minutes
Cooking Time: 6 minutes

2 eggs, beaten
2 cups (about 8 oz. whole) finely chopped fresh mushrooms
½ cup dry bread crumbs
½ cup shredded cheddar cheese
½ cup finely chopped onion
¼ cup all-purpose flour
½ tsp. salt
¼ tsp. dried thyme
¼ tsp. pepper
1 Tbsp. oil

1. In large bowl, combine eggs, mushrooms, bread crumbs, cheese, onion, flour, salt, thyme and pepper.
2. Shape into 4 patties.
3. In large skillet, cook patties in oil over medium heat, for 3 minutes on each side or until crisp and lightly browned.
4. Serve on rolls.

BBQ Tofu Baguette

Meg Suter
Goshen, IN

Makes 2 servings

Prep. Time: 15 minutes
Standing Time: 2-12 hours
Cooking Time: 8 minutes

1 Tbsp. honey *or* sweet chili sauce
1 Tbsp. tomato ketchup
1 Tbsp. soy sauce
¼ tsp. smoked paprika, *optional*
4½ oz. firm tofu, patted dry and cut into 4 long slices
olive oil, for brushing
1 small baguette
1 lettuce leaf, shredded
1 tomato, seeded and thinly sliced

1. In a shallow dish, mix together honey, ketchup, soy sauce and paprika for the marinade.
2. Place the tofu slices in the dish with the marinade. Spoon the marinade over the tofu so it is well coated. Let set for at least 2 hours or overnight.
3. Generously brush a griddle pan with olive oil, then heat until hot.
4. Carefully put the tofu slices in the pan. Cook 4 minutes on each side until golden, occasionally spooning marinade over top.
5. Slice the baguette lengthwise. Cut each half in half.
6. Place two of the tofu slices in the baguette and top with half the lettuce and tomato. Close up the baguette and press down lightly.
7. Repeat with the remaining two halves of the baguette and vegetables.

Spicy Mexican Bean Burgers

Lois Hess
Lancaster, PA

Makes 6 servings

Prep. Time: 20 minutes
Baking Time: 15-20 minutes

16-oz. can red kidney beans
½ onion, chopped
½ green bell pepper, chopped
1 carrot, steamed and mashed
2 Tbsp. salsa, plus more for serving
1 cup whole wheat bread crumbs
½ cup whole wheat flour
½ tsp. black pepper, *optional*
dash of chili powder
6 whole wheat buns
lettuce
6 tomato slices

1. Rinse and drain the kidney beans. Pour the beans into a medium mixing bowl. Mash.
2. Add onion, pepper, carrot, salsa, bread crumbs, flour, black pepper if you wish, and chili powder. Mix well.
3. Add more flour to create a firmer mixture or more salsa if mixture is too stiff.
4. Divide and form into 6 balls. Flatten into patties.

5. Place on a baking sheet, lightly oiled. Bake at 400° for 15-20 minutes, or until firm and brown.
6. Serve on a whole wheat bun with lettuce, tomato and salsa.

Go-Along:
• Carrot salad.

Soybean Burgers

Teresa Martin
Strasburg, PA

Makes 4 servings

Prep. Time: 30 minutes
Cooking Time: 8-12 minutes

1 cup cooked soybeans, drained
1 cup cooked brown rice
1 onion, coarsely chopped
1 cup whole wheat bread cubes
2 Tbsp. chopped fresh parsley
2 eggs, beaten
1 tsp. salt
½ tsp. celery salt
½ tsp. garlic salt
2 tsp. vegetarian Worcestershire sauce
½ cup dry bread crumbs *or* wheat germ
oil

1. Combine soybeans, rice, onion and bread in a food processor. Blend until mostly smooth.
2. Add parsley, eggs, salt, celery salt, garlic salt and Worcestershire sauce. Pulse briefly until mixed.
3. Form into 4 patties. Coat each patty with dry bread crumbs or wheat germ.
4. Fry in hot skillet with a small amount of oil for 4-6 minutes on each side, until browned.

Tip:
After step 3, the patties can be stacked between waxed paper and frozen. Thaw and cook later. They can also be grilled instead of fried.

Go-Along:
• Warm buns, lettuce, tomato, and homemade relish.

When you need bread crumbs, grate slices of frozen bread on a grater to make crumbs.

Bonnie Whaling, Clearfield, PA

Bean Burgers
Gloria Yurkiewicz
Washington Boro, PA

Makes 8 servings

Prep. Time: 20 minutes
Baking Time: 18-20 minutes

2 cups cooked beans of
  your choice, drained
⅔ cup sunflower seeds,
  ground
¼ cup chopped onion
½ tsp. chili powder
1 tsp. salt
2 Tbsp. olive oil
4 Tbsp. ketchup
½ cup wheat germ
8 slices cheese, American
  or cheddar
8 whole-grain buns

1. Put beans in a mixing
bowl. Mash.
2. Add seeds, onion, chili
powder, salt, oil, ketchup and
wheat germ.
3. Form into 8 patties.
4. Cover each patty with a
cheese slice.
5. Place on a lightly oiled
baking sheet.
6. Bake at 350° for 12-15
minutes, until hot through.
7. Add a cheese slice to each
burger and bake 3-5 minutes
longer, until cheese is melted.
8. Serve on a whole-grain
bun.

Variation:
  You can use dried beans,
soaked overnight and cooked
until soft. You can also experiment with raw or toasted sunflower seeds and wheat germ.

Go-Along:
• Chips, pickles, salad.

Lemon Dill Garbanzo Patties
Kim Patrick
Norwood, PA

Makes 4 servings

Prep. Time: 20 minutes
Cooking Time: 20 minutes

2 garlic cloves
½ red onion, cut into 3 cubes
1 chopped celery rib
1 cup cremini mushrooms
¼ cup flat-leaf parsley,
  packed
¼ cup chopped fresh dill
15-oz. can garbanzo beans,
  rinsed and drained
juice of 1 lemon
zest of 1 lemon
½ cup rolled oats
1 egg white
1 tsp. salt
1 Tbsp. olive oil
2 whole wheat pitas,
  halved and warmed
2 cups shredded romaine
  lettuce

1. Place
garlic, onion,
celery, mushrooms,
parsley and dill
in food processor.
Pulse until finely
chopped.
2. Add garbanzo
beans, lemon juice,
lemon zest, oats,
egg whites and salt.

3. Pulse 3-4 times until a
chunky mixture forms.
4. Form into 4 patties.
5. Heat oil in large skillet
over medium heat.
6. Add patties and cook 4-5
minutes per side, until lightly
browned and heated through.
7. Place each patty into half
a pita and top with lettuce.

Go-Along:
• Cucumber salad.

70

Judy's Bean Burgers

Judy Houser
Hershey, PA

Makes 4-6 servings

Prep. Time: 10 minutes
Cooking Time: 10-15 minutes

2 cups cooked lentils,
  drained
1 cup cooked garbanzo
  beans, drained
1 Tbsp. soy sauce
1 Tbsp. chopped fresh
  parsley
¼ cup ketchup
¼ cup finely chopped onion
¼ cup quick oats
1 egg
salt and pepper, to taste

1. In a medium bowl, mash
lentils and garbanzos with
potato masher.
2. Add soy sauce, parsley,
ketchup, onion, oats, egg, salt
and pepper. Mix well.
3. Shape into 4-6 patties.
4. Fry in lightly oiled skillet
over medium heat for 5-6
minutes on each side.

Go-Along:
• These burgers are delicious
in a roll with sliced tomato,
onion and lettuce.

Garbanzo Vegetable Burgers

Elaine Hostetler
Goshen, IN

Makes 6 servings

Prep. Time: 15 minutes
Cooking Time: 10-14 minutes

2 cups cooked, mashed
  garbanzo beans
1 rib celery, finely chopped
1 carrot, finely chopped
3 Tbsp. minced onion
¼ cup whole wheat flour
salt and pepper, to taste
2 tsp. oil
sandwich buns
lettuce
tomato

1. Mix beans, celery, carrot,
onion, flour, salt and pepper
in a bowl.
2. Form 6 flat patties.
3. Heat oil in frying pan
over medium heat. Fry
burgers in oiled pan until
golden brown on each side,
5-7 minutes per side.
4. Serve in a bun with
lettuce and tomato.

Golden Garbanzo Patties

Mabel Shirk
Mt. Crawford, VA

Makes 8 servings

Prep. Time: 15 minutes
Cooking Time: 20 minutes

2 15-oz. cans garbanzo
  beans
1½ cups quick oats
¼ tsp. garlic powder
1 tsp. salt
dash of pepper
2-4 Tbsp. olive oil

1. Drain garbanzo beans,
reserving ½ cup liquid.
2. Process beans and ½ cup
liquid in food processor or
blender to achieve a smooth
thick paste.
3. Place garbanzo purée in
mixing bowl. Add oats, garlic
powder, salt, and pepper. Mix.
4. Shape into 8 patties.
5. In heavy skillet, heat oil
and fry patties until golden
brown on each side.

Tip:
  Garnish the serving platter
of patties with fresh parsley.

Go-Along:
• Baked potatoes, cranberry
sauce, green beans.

71

Sunburgers

Christie Detamore-Hunsberger
Harrisonburg, VA

Makes 12 servings

Prep. Time: 30 minutes
Standing Time: 30 minutes
Cooking/Baking Time: 25-30
*   minutes*

3¼ cups water
¼ cup soy sauce
1 tsp. onion powder
¼ tsp. garlic powder
⅛-¼ tsp. cayenne pepper to
    taste, *optional*
1 tsp. dried thyme
1 tsp. dried sage
1 tsp. dried marjoram
¼ cup raw sunflower seeds
2 Tbsp. nutritional yeast
    flakes, *optional*
3 cups rolled oats

1. Combine water, soy
sauce, onion powder, garlic
powder, cayenne, thyme, sage,
marjoram, sunflower seeds
and nutritional yeast flakes.
Bring to a boil.
2. Add rolled oats to boiling
mixture. Remove from heat
and stir, mixing well.
3. Cover with lid. Let sit for
20 minutes.
4. When cool enough to
handle, drop by 12 spoonfuls
onto greased baking sheet.
Press down into patties.
5. Bake at 350° for 15 minutes. Turn patties over and
bake for another 15 minutes.

Tips:
1. You can double this
recipe and pat into a greased

rimmed baking sheet. Bake
25-30 minutes. Cut into
squares to serve.
2. Cool completely after
baking, wrap, and freeze.
These freeze well and pack
well in a lunch. When
reheating, thaw and heat on
a non-stick skillet or in the
microwave.

Go-Along:
• We like to eat them
plain or with ketchup/Dijon
mustard mixed.

Crazy-Crust Pizza

Amy Bauer
New Ulm, MN

Makes 4 servings

Prep. Time: 15 minutes
Baking Time: 40 minutes
Standing Time: 10 minutes

½ cup all-purpose flour
dash of salt and pepper, to
    taste
¼ tsp. Italian herb
    seasoning
1 egg
⅓ cup milk
¼ cup black *or* green olives
¼ cup chopped red and
    green bell peppers
2 Tbsp. chopped onion
any other veggie pizza
    toppings you like
1 cup pizza sauce
1 cup shredded mozzarella
    cheese

1. Mix flour, salt, pepper,
Italian seasonings, egg and
milk in a bowl.
2. Pour into a 9" greased
pie pan. Spread with olives,
peppers, onions, and other
veggie pizza toppings you like.
3. Bake at 350° for 25
minutes.
4. Remove from oven and
top with sauce and cheese.
Return to oven.
5. Bake another 10-15
minutes at 350°. Allow to sit
10 minutes before cutting in
wedges.

Go-Along:
• A lettuce salad.

Vegetable Rice Pizza

Karen L. Gingrich
Bernville, PA

Diane Myers
Brunswick, ME

Makes 8-10 servings

Prep. Time: 30 minutes
Baking Time: 15 minutes

3 cups cooked rice
1 egg, beaten
⅔-1 cup tomato sauce
2 tsp. Italian herb seasoning
¼ tsp. garlic powder
1 tsp. pepper
1 Tbsp. grated Parmesan
   cheese
1 cup sliced mushrooms
¾ cup sliced zucchini
¼ cup diced red bell
   peppers
1 Tbsp. dried parsley
2-3 cups shredded
   mozzarella cheese

1. Combine rice and egg in mixing bowl.
2. Spread on pizza pan or 9 × 13 baking dish.
3. Bake at 400° for 5 minutes.
4. Combine sauce, Italian seasoning, garlic powder and pepper.
5. Spread on rice.
6. Sprinkle with Parmesan cheese.
7. Layer with mushrooms, zucchini, peppers and parsley.
8. Top with mozzarella cheese.
9. Bake at 400° for 8-10 minutes.

Variations:
1. You may bake the rice and spread with re-fried beans and top with cheese. Bake and serve.

Karen L. Gingrich

2. Use your choice of pizza toppings.

Diane Myers

Go-Along:
• Salad goes well with any pizza!

Zucchini Pizza

Anna King
Andover, NY

Orpha Herr
Andover, NY

Makes 6-8 servings

Prep. Time: 30 minutes
Baking Time: 25-30 minutes

3 cups shredded zucchini
3 eggs, beaten
⅓ cup all-purpose flour
1 tsp. dried oregano,
   divided
1 tsp. dried basil, *divided*
¼ teaspoon salt
1 cup sliced ripe olives
⅔ cup sliced green onions
½ cup chopped green
   pepper
2 cups shredded mozzarella
   cheese
2-3 medium
   tomatoes,
   peeled and
   thinly sliced

1. Press excess liquid from zucchini by putting it in a mesh strainer or kitchen towel. Place drained zucchini in a bowl.
2. Add eggs, flour, ½ teaspoon oregano, ½ teaspoon basil and salt. Mix well.
3. Spread evenly over the bottom of a greased 9 × 13 baking pan.
4. Bake at 450° for 8-10 minutes. Remove from oven and set on a wire rack.
5. Reduce heat to 350°. Sprinkle zucchini crust with olives, onion slices, green peppers, cheese, and remaining oregano and basil.
6. Cover with tomato slices.
7. Return pan to oven and bake at 350° for 10-15 minutes.

Hoagie Pizza

Jolene Good
Lebanon, PA

Makes 4 servings

Prep. Time: 15 minutes
Baking Time: 15 minutes
Standing Time: 30-60 minutes

¾ cup mayonnaise
¼ cup Dijon mustard
4 Tbsp. dill pickle juice
12" baked pizza crust
8 oz. shredded mozzarella
  cheese
½ head lettuce, torn into
  bite-sized pieces
2 tomatoes, sliced
sweet peppers, black olives,
  onions, or any vegetable
  you like
Italian dressing

1. Mix mayonnaise, mustard and pickle juice. Spread over pizza crust.
2. Sprinkle cheese on top.
3. Bake at 400° for 15 minutes. Let pizza cool 30-60 minutes.
4. Top with lettuce, tomatoes, and other veggies.
5. Drizzle with Italian dressing.

New Mexican Pizza

Doreen Miller
Albuquerque, NM

Makes 4 servings

Prep. Time: 45 minutes
Baking Time: 28-32 minutes

1½ cups all-purpose flour
½ cup cornmeal
3 tsp. baking powder
½ tsp. salt
⅓ cup shortening
⅓ cup grated cheese
¾ cup milk
½ cup chopped onion
½ cup chopped bell pepper
1 clove garlic, minced
2 Tbsp. olive oil
15-oz. can re-fried beans
15-oz. can garbanzo beans,
  drained
4½-oz. can green chilies
4-oz. can sliced
  mushrooms, drained
1 cup salsa
¾ cup grated cheese

1. In a large bowl, mix flour, cornmeal, baking powder, salt, shortening, cheese and milk for the crust. Knead until smooth.
2. Roll out or pat into a 12" pizza pan.
3. Bake at 375° for 8 minutes. Remove from oven.

4. Meanwhile, sauté onion, peppers and garlic in olive oil in skillet. Drain.
5. Spread the re-fried beans over the partially baked crust.
6. Sprinkle the drained garbanzo beans evenly over the pizza.
7. Add the green chilies, mushrooms,and sautéed onion, peppers and garlic. Spoon salsa over all.
8. Top with grated cheese.
9. Bake at 375° for 20-25 minutes.

Go-Along:
• Salsa and sour cream as dipping sauces. Crisp green salad with light dressing.

When reheating pizza, use the defrost setting in the microwave for 1-2 minutes. Then, heat on high for 15-30 seconds. The pizza will not become hard or dry.
Edwina Stoltzfus, Narvon, PA

Caprese Pizza

Leanne Yoder
Tucson, AZ
Abigail Thompson
Millersville, PA

Makes 4 servings

Prep. Time: 20 minutes
Baking Time: 20 minutes

2 cups fresh basil leaves, packed
¼ cup pine nuts *or* walnuts
¼ cup olive oil
½ cup grated Parmesan cheese
3 cloves garlic, minced
1 whole wheat pizza dough of your choice
1-2 large tomatoes, thinly sliced
2 cups ricotta cheese

1. Make the pesto. Put the basil, pine nuts or walnuts, olive oil, Parmesan cheese and garlic in a food processor.
2. Blend until the basil is finely chopped. Turn off processor and scrape down the sides. Add a little extra oil as needed to make the pesto blend better.
3. Press out dough on a greased pizza pan or cookie sheet. Spread pesto evenly over the dough.
4. Top generously with tomato slices and dollops of ricotta cheese.
5. Bake in a 400° oven for 20 minutes or until crust is turning brown.

Tip:
This pesto sauce is also delicious over pasta. This recipe makes ½ pint, and it freezes well. Freezing it in ice-cube trays, then storing the cubes in a freezer bag, makes it easy to take out just the amount needed, usually about one cube per serving.

Variation:
Use ½ cup Buitoni Pesto instead of making it. Use 1½ cups grated mozzarella instead of the ricotta. Layer tomato slices between layers of mozzarella.

Abigail Thompson

Tuscan Pizza with Garlic Cream Sauce

Jenny Unternahrer
Wayland, IA

Makes 8-10 servings

Prep. Time: 25 minutes
Cooking/Baking Time: 50 minutes

1 Tbsp. olive oil
½ tsp. minced garlic
1 Tbsp. flour
2 cups half-and-half
½ cup white wine
⅓ cup chopped cooked spinach (frozen or fresh is fine)
1-1½ cups shredded Parmesan cheese
your favorite pizza crust, homemade *or* store-bought
1-2 cups spinach leaves
4-6 Roma tomatoes, thinly sliced
2 cups shredded mozzarella

1. Make the garlic cream sauce. Drizzle olive oil in saucepan.
2. Add garlic and sauté briefly so as not to burn the garlic.
3. Add flour. Whisk and cook until bubbly.
4. Add half-and-half, wine and spinach. Cook over low heat, stirring, until just barely boiling.
5. Turn off heat. Add Parmesan and stir until blended. Set aside.
6. To make the pizza, press pizza crust into 11 × 15 rimmed jelly-roll pan.
7. Spread garlic cream sauce onto pizza crust.
8. Top with spinach leaves using as much or as little as you like.
9. Layer over sliced tomatoes and cheese.
10. Bake according to your pizza crust directions, or until lightly brown.

White Veggie Pizza

Marjorie Nolt
Denver, PA

Makes 6-8 servings

Prep. Time: 45 minutes
Baking Time: 20-25 minutes

pizza dough of your choice, enough to make 1 crust
3 Tbsp. ranch dressing
1 tsp. garlic salt
2 cups shredded mozzarella cheese
1 cup shredded Monterey Jack cheese
½ cup shredded provolone cheese
3 medium tomatoes, thinly sliced
1 medium green bell pepper, thinly sliced into rings
1 small onion, thinly sliced
½ tsp. dried basil
½ tsp. dried oregano
¼ tsp. pepper
½ cup shredded Parmesan cheese

1. Lay pizza crust on pizza pan. Build up edges slightly. Cover and let rise for 30 minutes.
2. Spread with thin layer of ranch dressing. Sprinkle with garlic salt.
3. Combine mozzarella, Monterey Jack and provolone cheese in small bowl.
4. Sprinkle cheese over ranch dressing and garlic salt.
5. Layer the tomatoes, peppers and onion over top.

Sprinkle with basil, oregano, pepper and Parmesan cheese.
6. Bake at 425° for 20-25 minutes or until crust is golden brown and cheese is melted.

Personal Portabello Pizzas

Barb Yoder
Angola, IN

Makes 4 servings

Prep. Time: 10-15 minutes
Baking Time: 15-20 minutes

4 large portabello mushrooms
1 cup spaghetti sauce, *divided*
¼ cup diced onions, *divided*
¼ cup sliced green olives, *divided*
½ cup shredded mozzarella cheese, *divided*

1. Clean and remove stems from mushrooms.
2. Place portabello caps on sprayed cookie sheet with stem-side up.
3. Pour ¼ cup sauce on each mushroom.
4. Sprinkle with onions, olives, and cheese.
5. Bake at 375° for 15-20 minutes.

Tip:
Cut into quarters for a tasty, attractive appetizer.

Variation:
If you have time, bake the caps alone for 15 minutes. Then pile on toppings and bake 15-20 more minutes. This makes the pizzas less watery.

Go-Along:
• Fresh lettuce salad.

Soups, Stews, and Chilis

Vegan

Jamaican Red Bean Stew

Andy Wagner
Quarryville, PA

Makes 6 servings

Prep. Time: 30 minutes
Cooking Time: 6-8 hours
Ideal slow-cooker size: 4-qt.

1 Tbsp. extra-virgin olive oil
2 cloves garlic, minced
2 cups sliced carrots
3 scallions, chopped
1 sweet potato, diced
15-oz. can tomatoes, drained and diced
2 tsp. curry powder
½ tsp. dried thyme
¼ tsp. red pepper flakes
¼ tsp. ground allspice
salt and freshly ground black pepper, to taste
2 16-oz. cans dark red kidney beans, rinsed and drained

1 cup unsweetened coconut milk
1-2 cups unsalted vegetable broth *or* water

1. Pour the oil into a 4-qt. slow cooker and set the cooker on high. Add the garlic and put the lid on the cooker while you prepare the rest of the ingredients.
2. Add carrots, scallions, sweet potato and tomatoes to the cooker.
3. Stir in the curry powder, thyme, red pepper flakes, allspice, and salt and pepper to taste.
4. Add the beans, coconut milk and broth.

5. Reduce heat to low, cover, and cook on low for 6-8 hours.

Variations:
1. Use light coconut milk or reduce the amount to ½ cup for less saturated fat and calories.
2. Reduce sodium in this recipe by eliminating added salt, by thoroughly rinsing the canned beans and by using unsalted canned tomatoes.

Cut back on the amount of meat in your family's meals by using a can of drained, rinsed beans or 2 cups of cooked starchy beans for half of the meat in your casseroles, chili, etc. You'll save money, while increasing fiber, vitamins, and minerals.

Janelle Glick, Lancaster, PA

Chipotle Navy Bean Soup

Rebecca Weybright
Manheim, PA

Makes 6 servings

Prep. Time: 10 minutes
Cooking Time: 8 hours
Standing Time: 12 hours
Ideal slow-cooker size: 5-qt.

1½ cups dried navy beans, soaked overnight
1 onion, chopped
1 dried chipotle chili, soaked 10-15 minutes in cold water
4 cups water
1-2 tsp. salt
2 cups canned tomatoes with juice

1. Drain soaked beans.
2. Add to slow cooker with onion, chili and water.
3. Cover and cook on low for 8 hours until beans are creamy.
4. Add salt and tomatoes.
5. Puree soup, using an immersion blender.

Tips:
1. You can serve this soup without puréeing it.
2. Dried chipotles can be found in Hispanic grocery stores and most large grocery stores. A few canned chipotles may be puréed with the beans if dried are not available.

Go-Along:
• Serve with warmed corn tortillas or cheese quesadillas and a salad of crunchy greens, such as Romaine lettuce with a creamy dressing.

Butter Bean Veggie Soup

Irene Zimmerman
Lititz, PA
Kay Magruder
Seminole, OK
Renae Hege
Midville, GA

Makes 8-10 servings

Prep. Time: 20 minutes
Cooking Time: 2-3 hours
Ideal slow-cooker size: 4-qt.

3 ribs celery, chopped
3 medium carrots, chopped
1 small onion, chopped
2 Tbsp. olive oil
3 Tbsp. flour, *or potato flakes*
2 14-oz. cans vegetable broth
2 15-oz. cans butter beans, rinsed and drained
15-oz. can stewed tomatoes, diced
1 tsp. dried basil
½ tsp. salt
½ tsp. dried parsley flakes
¼ tsp. pepper

1. In a saucepan, sauté and stir celery, carrots and onions in olive oil until tender.
2. Stir in flour until blended. Turn off heat. Stir in vegetable broth.
3. Pour mixture into slow cooker, swishing to get all the vegetables out of the saucepan.
4. Add beans, tomatoes, basil, salt, parsley and pepper.
5. Cook on low for 2-3 hours.

Variation:
Add 1½ cups cooked brown rice at the end. Omit basil and add ¼ tsp. ginger. Use seasoned salt instead of regular salt.

Renae Hege

Southwestern Soup

Elena Yoder
Albuquerque, NM

Makes 6-8 servings

Prep. Time: 20 minutes
Cooking Time: 4 hours 10 minutes
Ideal slow-cooker size: 5-qt.

1 Tbsp. olive oil
1 cup chopped onions
1 cup chopped celery
6 cups vegetable broth
10-oz. pkg. frozen corn
15-oz. can black beans, rinsed and drained
15-oz. can diced tomatoes
4-oz. can chopped green chilies
1 tsp. ground cumin
2 tsp. chili powder
salt to taste
chopped fresh cilantro, for garnish

1. In a skillet, heat oil. Add onions and celery. Stir and fry until tender, 5-10 minutes.

2. Place onions, celery, broth, corn, beans, tomatoes, chilies, cumin, chili powder and salt in slow cooker.

3. Cook, covered, on low 4 hours.

4. Sprinkle fresh cilantro into soup before serving.

Go-Along:
• Tortilla chips and potato salad.

Large Quantity Pasta Bean Soup

Betty Moore
Avon Park, FL

Makes 8-10 (45-55) servings

Prep. Time: 10 minutes
Cooking Time: 30 minutes

(large quantity amounts are in parentheses)
2 (6) large onions, diced
2 Tbsp. (⅔) cup oil
4 (18) garlic cloves, minced
3 (12) 16-oz. cans kidney beans, rinsed, drained
1 (4) 28-oz. cans Italian crushed tomatoes
1 (3) 32-oz. cans vegetable broth
1 (4) Tbsp. salt
1 Tbsp. (¼ cup) dried oregano
½ (1-2) tsp. pepper
1 (3) 1-lb. pkgs. spaghetti, pasta strands broken into 4 pieces
Parmesan cheese, *optional*

1. In large soup kettle, sauté onions in oil.
2. Add garlic. Cook and stir 2 minutes.
3. Add beans, tomatoes, broth, salt, oregano and pepper.
4. Separately, cook spaghetti according to package directions. Drain.
5. Just before serving, stir in spaghetti.
6. Serve sprinkled with Parmesan cheese if you wish.

Tip:
The large quantity is great for soup suppers at church.

Keep chopped and measured onions in the freezer for including in recipes.
Ruth Miller, Wooster, OH

Beans 'n' Greens

Teri Sparks
Glen Burnie, MD

Makes 10 servings

Prep. Time: 30 minutes
Cooking Time: 6-8 hours
Ideal slow-cooker size: 4- or 5-qt.

1 lb. dried 13-bean mix
5 cups vegetable broth
¼ cup green onions, chopped
½ tsp. black pepper
2 Tbsp. dried parsley
1 yellow onion, coarsely chopped
3 cloves garlic, chopped
1 Tbsp. olive oil
6 cups fresh kale, torn in 2" pieces
Greek yogurt *or* sour cream, *optional*

1. Rinse and place beans in 4-quart slow cooker.
2. Add broth, green onions, pepper and parsley.
3. In skillet, sauté yellow onion and garlic in oil. Add to beans in slow cooker.
4. Pile kale on top of bean mixture and cover with lid (crock will be very full).
5. Cook on high for 1 hour. Greens will have wilted some, so stir to combine all ingredients. Replace lid.
6. Cook on low for 6-8 hours.
7. Top individual servings with dollops of Greek yogurt if you wish.

Go-Along:
• Good crusty brown bread.

Veggie Pea Soup

Diana Kampnich
Croghan, NY

Makes 6-8 servings

Prep. Time: 10 minutes
Cooking Time: 6 hours
Ideal slow-cooker size: 5-qt.

1 lb. package (2 cups) dry
   split green peas
1 large onion, diced
2 ribs celery, diced
4 carrots, diced
2 medium potatoes,
   unpeeled, diced
8 cups water
2 tsp. garlic
1 tsp. seasoned salt
⅛ tsp. pepper
2 Tbsp. cider vinegar,
   optional

1. Mix peas, onion, celery,
carrots, potatoes, water, garlic,
seasoned salt and pepper in
slow cooker.
2. Cover. Cook on low
6 hours. If you wish, add
vinegar just before serving.

Go-Along:
• Cornbread.

Pea and Rice Soup

Diana Kampnich
Croghan, NY
Ruth Nolt
Leola, PA

Makes 8-10 servings

Prep. Time: 15 minutes
Cooking Time: 6-7 hours
Ideal slow-cooker size: 5-qt.

1 cup dried green peas
1 cup dried yellow peas
3 carrots, diced
2 ribs celery, diced
1 onion, diced
1 cup raw brown rice
1½ tsp. salt
¼ tsp. pepper
½ tsp. dried marjoram
4 cups water
4 cups tomato juice

1. Mix ingredients in slow
cooker.
2. Cook on high 1 hour.
Reduce heat to low for 5-6
hours.

Spicy Pea Soup

Janice Sams
Lancaster, PA

Makes 4 servings

Prep. Time: 15 minutes
Cooking Time: 70 minutes

¾ cup dried green split
   peas
2 Tbsp. canola oil
2 cups chopped plum
   tomatoes
4 scallions, sliced
1 cup chopped carrots
1½ Tbsp. curry powder
5 cups water *or* vegetable
   stock
1 Tbsp. tamari *or* soy sauce
salt, to taste
freshly ground pepper, to
   taste
minced fresh parsley, for
   garnish
sour cream, for garnish

1. Rinse the split peas,
drain and set aside.
2. Heat the oil in a soup
pot. Stir in the tomatoes and
cook over medium-high heat
for 2 to 3 minutes, stirring
frequently.
3. Toss in the split peas,
sliced scallions and carrots.
Continue to cook for 5
minutes.
4. Stir in the curry powder
and cook for 1 minute, stirring continually.
5. Add water and lower the
heat to simmer. Cover the pot
and cook for 1 hour.
6. Stir in the tamari and
season to taste with salt and
freshly ground pepper.

7. Garnish soup bowls with chopped parsley and a dollop of sour cream.

Tip:

Omit sour cream for a vegan dish.

Baby Beans Soup

Rebekah Zehr
Lowville, NY

Makes 6-8 servings

Prep. Time: 10 minutes
Cooking Time: 3 hours
Ideal slow-cooker size: 6-qt.

2 cups chopped onions
6 garlic cloves, minced
2 Tbsp. olive oil
½ tsp. salt
1 cup diced celery
2 cups chopped red and green bell peppers
1 small fresh chili, seeds removed, minced
1 tsp. dried oregano
½ tsp. dried thyme
2 tsp. ground cumin
½ tsp. black pepper
2 cups water
1½ cups canned diced tomatoes, undrained
15-oz. can black-eyed peas, rinsed and drained
15-oz. can black beans, rinsed and drained
15-oz. can other small bean of your choice, rinsed and drained
¼ cup smoke-flavored barbecue sauce
tortilla chips, crushed, for garnish

jalapeño Jack cheese, shredded, for garnish
Greek yogurt, for garnish

1. Combine everything in slow cooker except garnishes.
2. Cook on low until vegetables are tender, 3-4 hours.
3. Taste for salt. Add more if needed.
4. Ladle into soup bowls and top each with tortilla chips, shredded cheese, and a dollop of Greek yogurt.

Variation:

Fresh or frozen corn can be added to the soup near the end of the cooking time.

Ribollita

Orpha Herr
Andover, NY

Makes 6-8 servings

Prep. Time: 20 minutes
Standing Time: 8 hours or overnight
Cooking Time: 6-7 hours
Ideal slow-cooker size: 5-qt.

1 cup dried white beans
4 cups water, *divided*
3 Tbsp. olive oil
¾ cup chopped onion
2 tsp. minced garlic
1 cup finely chopped celery
1 cup finely chopped carrots
3 cups water
4 cups thinly sliced green cabbage
2 cups chopped tomatoes, fresh or canned

1 Tbsp. dried parsley leaves
1 tsp. dried rosemary
1 tsp. dried oregano
½ tsp. dried thyme leaves
⅛ tsp. black pepper
1 cup water, *optional*
2 tsp. salt
grated Parmesan cheese, for garnish

1. In slow cooker, cover beans with 2" water. Allow to soak overnight or 8 hours.
2. Drain.
3. Heat oil in a saucepan. Sauté onion, garlic, celery and carrots.
4. Transfer sautéed vegetables to slow cooker with beans.
5. Add 3 cups water.
6. Cook on low 4-6 hours until beans are almost soft.
7. Add cabbage and tomatoes and parsley, rosemary, oregano, thyme and pepper. Add another cup of water if needed. Cook on low another hour.
8. Add salt. Ladle into bowls.
9. Garnish with grated Parmesan cheese and serve.

Tuscan Bean Soup

Jean Turner
Williams Lake, BC

Makes 4-6 servings

Prep. Time: 15 minutes
Cooking Time: 2 hours
Ideal slow-cooker size: 4-qt.

2 14-oz. cans chopped
  crushed tomatoes with
  herbs
1⅔ cups warm water
salt and pepper to taste
2 cups Tuscan *or* curly
  kale, roughly shredded
  or chopped
14-oz. can cannellini beans
  or white beans, rinsed
  and drained
4 Tbsp. extra-virgin olive
  oil

1. Combine tomatoes,
warm water, salt, pepper and
kale in slow cooker.
2. Cook on high for 1 hour.
3. Add beans. Cook on high
another hour.
4. Place soup into bowls
and drizzle each bowl with
a little olive oil. Serve with
warm crusty bread for dipping.

Hungarian Soup

Leanne Yoder
Tucson, AZ

Makes 4 servings

Prep. Time: 30 minutes
Cooking Time: 30 minutes

3-4 Tbsp. olive oil
2 cups chopped onions
2 cloves garlic, crushed
½ cup chopped celery
2 cups sweet potatoes *or*
  winter squash, peeled
  and chopped
2 tsp. paprika
1 tsp. turmeric
1 tsp. dried basil
1 tsp. salt
dash of cinnamon
dash of cayenne
1 bay leaf
3 cups stock *or* water
1 cup chopped fresh
  tomatoes
¾ cup chopped bell
  peppers
1½ cups garbanzo beans,
  cooked
1 Tbsp. tamari *or* soy sauce

1. In a soup kettle sauté
onions, garlic, celery and
sweet potatoes in olive oil for
about five minutes.
2. Add paprika, turmeric,
basil, salt, cinnamon, cayenne, bay leaf and the stock
or water. Simmer, covered, 15
minutes.
3. Add tomatoes, peppers
and garbanzo beans. Simmer
another 10 minutes or so,
until all the vegetables are as
tender as you like them.
4. Stir in tamari. Serve.

Variations:
1. You can use raw chick-
peas instead of canned. Soak
¾ cup garbanzos at least 4
hours. Allow 1½ hours for
them to cook alone before
starting this soup.
2. Any orange vegetable
can be replaced with another
orange vegetable (carrots for
squash, for example) and
any green vegetable can be
replaced with green (green
beans for the peppers).

Go-Along:
• Crusty bread with salad, or
a fresh fruit platter.

Red Lentil Soup

Barbara Landis
Lititz, PA

Makes 4 servings

Prep. Time: 10 minutes
Cooking Time: 4-8 hours
Ideal slow-cooker size: 5-qt.

6 cups vegetable broth
1 cup dry red lentils
3 carrots, sliced
1 medium onion, chopped
3 celery ribs, chopped
3 Tbsp. uncooked brown
  rice
2 Tbsp. minced garlic
1½ tsp. herbes de Provence
½ tsp. salt
¼ tsp. pepper

1. Mix all ingredients in
slow cooker.
2. Cover. Cook on low 7-8
hours, or high 4-5 hours.

Lentil Spinach Soup

Marilyn Widrick
Adams, NY

Makes 4-6 servings

Prep. Time: 10 minutes
Cooking Time: 2½ hours
Ideal slow-cooker size: 5-qt.

1 Tbsp. olive oil
4 medium carrots, chopped
1 small onion, diced
1 tsp. ground cumin
14½-oz. can diced tomatoes
14½-oz. can vegetable
  broth
1 cup dry lentils
2 cups water
¼ tsp. salt
⅛ tsp. pepper
5 oz. bag fresh spinach,
  chopped

1. Heat 1 Tbsp. olive oil in cooking pot. Add carrots and onion. Cook 8-10 minutes over medium heat.

2. Place in slow cooker. Add cumin, diced tomatoes, vegetable broth, dry lentils, water, salt and pepper.

3. Cover and cook on low 2 hours.

4. Add spinach. Cook on low an additional 15-25 minutes.

Variation:
You may sprinkle Parmesan cheese on each bowl prior to serving for extra flavor.

Go-Alongs:
• Crackers, crusty bread, pickled beets or cucumber pickles.
• Green salad with apple or orange chunks.

Lentil Soup with Lemon

Heidi Wood
Vacaville, CA

Makes 6 servings

Prep. Time: 30 minutes
Cooking Time: 20-30 minutes

⅓ cup olive oil
2 large sweet onions,
  chopped
4 cloves garlic, minced
2 tsp. ground cumin
½ tsp. salt
½ tsp. freshly ground black
  pepper
¼ tsp. chili powder
8 cups water *or* vegetable
  broth
2 cups dry red lentils
2 large carrots, diced
2 Tbsp. tomato paste
4 Tbsp. lemon juice
1 cup chopped fresh
  cilantro
plain yogurt, *optional*

1. Heat olive oil in a large pot over medium-high heat. Stir in the onion and garlic, and cook until the onion is golden brown, about 5 minutes.

2. Stir in the cumin, salt, black pepper and chili powder. Cook and stir until fragrant, about 2 minutes.

3. Add water or broth, lentils and carrots to the spiced onions. Bring to a boil over high heat, then reduce the heat to medium-low.

4. Cover and simmer until the lentils are soft, stirring frequently so lentils don't stick to the bottom of the pan. This can take anywhere from 20 to 30 minutes.

5. Add tomato paste to soup pot and stir to combine thoroughly.

6. Just before serving, stir lemon juice into the pot of soup.

7. Ladle soup into bowls. Serve cilantro on the side to be added as a garnish. It is also good with a dollop of plain yogurt for a slightly different taste.

Go-Along:
• This is delightful served with a crusty loaf of whole grain bread and a green salad.

Lentils have a mild flavor and are a good source of protein, iron and fiber, so they are a healthy and tasty ingredient.
Linda Yoder, Fresno, OH

Curried Lentil Soup

Deanne Gingrich
Lancaster, PA

Makes 4-6 servings

Prep. Time: 15 minutes
Cooking Time: 8 hours
Ideal slow-cooker size: 5-qt.

4 cups hot water
8-oz. can crushed tomatoes
3 medium potatoes, diced
3 medium carrots, sliced
1 large onion, chopped
1 celery rib, chopped
1 cup dry lentils
2 cloves garlic, minced
2 bay leaves
1 Tbsp. curry powder
1½ tsp. salt

1. Combine everything in slow cooker.
2. Cover. Cook on low for 8 hours. Remove bay leaves before serving.

Go-Along:
• Excellent with a piece of crusty bread and a salad with sweet dressing.

Rasam

Anita Carlson
Jacksonville, FL

Makes 4-6 servings

Prep. Time: 10 minutes
Cooking Time: 30 minutes

1 cup split peas (mung *or* masoor dal)
3 cups water
2 Tbsp. olive oil
1 tsp. mustard seeds
¼ tsp. whole cumin seeds
14½-oz. can diced tomatoes
1¼ tsp. black pepper
1 tsp. ground cumin
2 cloves garlic, minced
1 tsp. salt
2 Tbsp. lemon juice
fresh cilantro, chopped, *optional*

1. In a soup pot, cook split peas in water until soft, about 20-30 minutes. As they cook, check and add water if they are getting dry.
2. Meanwhile, heat oil in heavy 2-quart pan with lid. Add mustard and cumin seeds. Cook on medium-high until the seeds begin to pop.
3. Cover immediately. Turn heat to low.
4. Quickly add tomatoes, pepper, ground cumin, garlic and salt so the seeds don't burn.
5. Stir in split peas and add another cup of water.
6. Simmer uncovered 10 to 20 minutes.

7. Blend briefly with an immersion blender, or remove 1 cup of the soup and purée it in a blender. Return purée to soup pot.
8. Add lemon juice. Serve each bowl with a sprinkle of chopped cilantro leaves if you wish.

Tip:
Yellow split peas will work but take longer to cook than the mung or masoor dal which I usually buy at an Indian grocery store.

Go-Along:
• Eat with pitas or chapattis or any flat bread.

Fully-Loaded Baked Potato Soup

Beverly Hummel
Fleetwood, PA
Penny Blosser
Beavercreek, OH

Makes 8 servings

Prep. Time: 20 minutes
Cooking Time: 3 hours
Ideal slow-cooker size: 4-qt.

4 large potatoes, baked
1 Tbsp. butter
1 small onion, chopped, *or*
   4 scallions, sliced
1 clove garlic, minced
4 Tbsp. all-purpose flour
1 tsp. salt
1 tsp. dried basil
½ tsp. pepper
4 cups vegetable broth
2 cups milk
shredded cheese, for garnish
chopped fresh parsley, for
   garnish
sour cream, for garnish

1. Peel the baked potatoes if you wish. Cube the baked potatoes. Place in slow cooker.
2. In a skillet, melt butter and sauté onion and garlic.
3. Stir in flour, salt, basil and pepper. Add broth, whisking continuously. Heat and stir until hot.
4. Pour over potatoes in slow cooker.
5. Cook on low for 2 hours.
6. Add milk. Cook an additional 30-40 minutes on low.
7. Garnish with cheese, parsley and sour cream.

Tip:
   Great way to use leftover baked potatoes!

Variation:
   Omit basil. Cook only the white part of the scallions with the soup and reserve the chopped green ends to garnish the bowls of soup. Stir 1 cup sharp cheddar cheese directly into the soup just before serving.
   Penny Blosser

Potato Chowder

Marlene Weaver
Lititz, PA
Elaine Rineer
Lancaster, PA
Marlene Graber
Sparta, WI
Polly Winters
Lancaster, PA
Jana Beyer
Harrisonburg, VA

Makes 6-8 servings

Prep. Time: 30 minutes
Cooking Time: 2½ hours
Ideal slow-cooker size: 6-qt.

4 cups peeled, diced potatoes
½ cup finely chopped onions
1 cup grated carrots
1 tsp. salt
¼ tsp. pepper
1 Tbsp. dried parsley flakes
4 vegetable bouillon cubes
water
6 cups milk, *divided*
half stick (4 Tbsp.) butter
½ cup flour

1. In slow cooker, combine potatoes, onions, carrots, salt, pepper, parsley and bouillon.
2. Add water to cover vegetables.
3. Cook on high 2 hours, or until vegetables are tender.
4. Do not drain.
5. Heat milk in microwave until steaming. Add 4 cups to slow cooker.
6. Melt butter in saucepan. Add flour and whisk in over medium heat. Cook for a minute or 2 to prevent a raw flour taste.
7. Pour remaining 2 cups hot milk into saucepan slowly, stirring continuously with wire whisk. Stir and cook until thickened.
8. Stir thickened milk mixture into slow cooker until blended.
9. Replace lid. Cook on high an additional 30 minutes.

Variations:
1. Add 2 hard-boiled, chopped eggs and 2 cups grated cheddar cheese at end.
   Polly Winters

2. Substitute chopped celery for the grated carrots.
   Marlene Graber

Asparagus Potato Soup

Wilma Haberkamp
Fairbank, IA

Makes 4-6 servings

Prep. Time: 30 minutes
Cooking Time: 30 minutes

3 potatoes, peeled or
　unpeeled, and cubed
2 cups asparagus, cut into
　½" pieces
⅓ cup chopped onion
1 tsp. salt
1¾ cups vegetable broth
1½ cups milk
2 Tbsp. flour
1 cup good melting cheese
　of your choice, grated
additional grated cheese,
　optional

1. In a large saucepan,
combine potatoes, asparagus,
onion, salt and vegetable
broth.
2. Cook 30 minutes, or
until vegetables are tender.
3. In a small bowl, whisk
together milk and flour.
Slowly add to soup, stirring
continually over medium
heat.
4. Turn heat to low. Add 1
cup cheese. Stir until melted.
5. Pour into warmed soup
bowls. Garnish with grated
cheese if you wish.

Homemade Vegetable Soup

Audrey Romonosky
Austin, TX

Makes 10-12 servings

Prep. Time: 20 minutes
Cooking Time: 4-5 hours
Ideal slow-cooker size: 5-qt.

1 bay leaf
1 onion, diced
3 carrots, diced
2 celery ribs, diced
2-3 potatoes, diced
14½-oz. can stewed
　tomatoes
8-oz. can tomato sauce
4-5 cups water
½ cup frozen corn
½ cup frozen green beans
½ cup frozen peas
2-3 cups chopped cabbage
salt, to taste
pepper, to taste

1. Put bay leaf, onions,
carrots, celery, potatoes,
stewed tomatoes and tomato
sauce in slow cooker. Add
water to cover. Cook on low
for 3 hours.
2. Add rest of vegetables.
Cover and cook an additional
1-2 hours until vegetables are
as tender as you like them.
3. Add salt and pepper.
Taste and adjust if needed.

Variation:
When you add the second
batch of vegetables, add dried
herbs that your family likes.

Vegetable Soup

Diana Kampnich
Croghan, NY

Makes 10-12 servings

Prep. Time: 10 minutes
Cooking Time: 4-6 hours
Ideal slow-cooker size: 6-qt.

2 26-oz. jars spaghetti
　sauce of your choice
3 cups diced carrots
3 cups chopped zucchini
3 cups chopped summer
　squash
3 cups frozen peas
3 cups cut green beans
1 onion, diced
1 green bell pepper, diced,
　optional
1 tsp. minced garlic
1 tsp. dried basil
1 tsp. dried rosemary
3 cups water

1. Combine all ingredients
in a slow cooker. Mix well.
2. Cook on high for 4-6
hours. Taste and add salt if
needed.

Variation:
You can add cooked maca-
roni at the end, if you wish.

Go-Along:
• Challah bread.

Vegetable Chowder

Charmaine Caesar
Lancaster, PA

Makes 8-10 servings

Prep. Time: 15 minutes
Cooking Time: 4½-5 hours
Ideal slow-cooker size: 6-qt.

5-6 medium potatoes, cubed small
3 16-oz. cans vegetable broth
4 carrots, diced
2-3 onions, diced
half stick (¼ cup) butter, cut into pieces
1 tsp. dried thyme
salt to taste
¼ tsp. dried marjoram
¼ tsp. garlic powder
20-oz. bag frozen mixed vegetables
¼ cup all-purpose flour
1¼ cups milk

1. Place potatoes, broth, carrots, onions, butter, thyme, salt, marjoram, garlic powder and vegetables in slow cooker.
2. Cover. Cook on high 4½-5 hours.
3. Combine flour and milk in bowl. Mix until there are no lumps.
4. Add to slow cooker, stirring. Replace lid and cook on high for an additional 15 minutes, or until chowder is slightly thickened.

Vegetable Bean Chowder

Elaine Hostetler
Goshen, IN

Makes 6 servings

Prep. Time: 15 minutes
Cooking Time: 25 minutes

1 Tbsp. olive oil
½ cup chopped onion
½ cup sliced celery
2 cups water
½ tsp. salt
2 cups cubed, peeled potatoes
1 cup chopped carrots
15-oz. can cream-style corn
15-oz. can cannellini beans, rinsed and drained
¼ tsp. dried tarragon leaves
¼ tsp. black pepper
2 cups milk
2 Tbsp. cornstarch

1. Saute onion and celery in oil for 3 minutes or until crisp tender.
2. Add water and salt. Bring to a boil.
3. Add potatoes and carrots. Reduce heat to medium-low. Simmer, covered, 10 minutes or until potatoes and carrots are tender.
4. Stir in corn, beans, tarragon and pepper.
5. Simmer, covered, for 10 minutes or until heated through.
6. Stir milk into cornstarch in a small bowl until smooth. Stir into vegetable mixture.
7. Simmer, uncovered, until thickened.

Cabbage Soup

Ruth C. Hancock
Earlsboro, OK

Makes 6 servings

Prep. Time: 15 minutes
Cooking Time: 3-4 hours
Ideal slow-cooker size: 5-qt.

1 quart tomato juice
1 medium head cabbage, chopped
1 bell pepper, chopped
1 cup finely chopped celery
15-oz. can French-style green beans
3 vegetarian bouillon cubes
1 Tbsp. soy sauce
2 Tbsp. onion flakes
1 Tbsp. dried parsley
1 tsp. garlic

1. Mix all together in 5-quart slow cooker. Cover.
2. Cook on low 3-4 hours, until vegetables are as tender as you like them.

Country Fresh Soup

Susan Guarneri
Three Lakes, WI

Makes 4-6 servings

Prep. Time: 30 minutes
Cooking Time: 45 minutes

½ cup chopped onions
2 cloves garlic, minced
2 Tbsp. butter
2 Tbsp. all-purpose flour
10½ oz. can condensed
   vegetable broth
2 cups cubed zucchini
2 cups cubed yellow
   squash
2 cups shredded cabbage
16-oz. can whole tomatoes,
   chopped, undrained
15¼-oz. can dark kidney
   beans, rinsed and
   drained
¼ tsp. salt
¼ tsp. sugar
½ tsp. dried thyme
½ tsp. dried oregano
dash of pepper

1. In 6-quart Dutch oven,
over medium-high heat, sauté
onion and garlic in butter
until golden brown.
2. Add flour and cook and
stir until bubbly, 1-2 minutes.
You've just made the roux.
3. Gradually add broth,
stirring continuously. Add
zucchini, squash, cabbage,
tomatoes, kidney beans, salt,
sugar, thyme, oregano and
pepper.
4. Bring to boil. Reduce
heat to low.
5. Cover. Simmer for 30
minutes.

Variation:
Add 2 Tbsp. chopped fresh
parsley and 1 cup cooked
pasta at the end.

Go-Along:
• Toasted cheese sandwiches.

Latin Stew

Diann Dunham
State College, PA

Makes 8-10 servings

Prep. Time: 30 minutes
Cooking Time: 3 hours
Ideal slow-cooker size: 4-qt.

4-oz. can green chilies,
   diced
½ lb. string beans, sliced
   into 2"-long pieces
1 tsp. chili powder
dash hot sauce
1 cup cooked brown rice
¾ cup raw bulgur
1 cup water
⅔ cup cooked soybeans
16-oz. can stewed tomatoes
12-oz. can corn
dash of salt
dash of pepper

1. Combine everything in
4-quart slow cooker.
2. Stir well. Cook on low 3
hours.

Tip:
Prepare rice and beans the
day before to save time, or
use leftovers.

Go-Along:
• Serve with cornbread and
green salad.

Do not let garlic burn or it will taste bitter.
Carol Sherwood, Batavia, NY

Tortellini Soup

Esther Porter
Minneapolis, MN

Makes 6 servings

Prep. Time: 5-10 minutes
Cooking Time: 4-6 hours
Ideal slow-cooker size: 5-qt.

1 cup chopped onions
2 garlic cloves, sliced
olive oil
5 cups vegetable-cocktail juice
2 cups chopped tomatoes
1 zucchini, sliced
1 large carrot, sliced
1 cup green beans
1 Tbsp. Italian herb seasoning
10 oz. fresh cheese tortellini

1. In a large heavy saucepan, sauté onions and garlic in oil.
2. Transfer to slow cooker. Add vegetable-cocktail juice, tomatoes, zucchini, carrots, green beans and Italian seasoning.
3. Cook on low 3-4 hours until vegetables are tender.
4. Add tortellini and cook 10-15 minutes, until tortellini are done to your liking.

Go-Along:
• French bread and salad.

5-Minute Heat-and-Go Soup

Esther J. Yoder
Hartville, OH

Makes 2-4 servings

Prep. Time: 5 minutes
Cooking Time: 10 minutes

16-oz. can navy beans, rinsed and drained
14½-oz. can diced tomatoes
1 cup water
1½ tsp. dried basil, *or* 2-4 tsp. freshly snipped basil
½ tsp. sugar
1 vegetable bouillon cube
¼ cup finely cut onions
½ cup chopped zucchini, *optional*
2 tsp. extra-virgin olive oil

1. Place beans, tomatoes, water, basil, sugar, bouillon, onion, and zucchini if you wish, in saucepan.
2. Bring to boil.
3. Reduce heat. Simmer 5 minutes.
4. Remove from heat and stir in oil.

Variation:
Replace the water, tomatoes, and bouillon cube with 2 cups vegetable- cocktail juice.

Corn Chowder

Jana Beyer
Harrisonburg, VA

Makes 8-10 servings

Prep. Time: 15 minutes
Cooking Time: 4-8 hours
Ideal slow-cooker size: 5-qt.

10-oz. bag frozen corn
1 small onion, chopped
½ cup chopped celery
6 medium to large potatoes, diced
parsley, to taste
salt and pepper, to taste
milk to cover

1. Combine corn, onions, celery, potatoes, parsley, salt and pepper in slow cooker.
2. Pour milk over mixture, enough to cover.
3. Cook on high 4-6 hours or low 8 hours.

Tip:
This is a very mild soup. Feel free to add spices and herbs if you like.

I dry celery leaves instead of throwing them away. I sprinkle them over soups and stews.

Norma Musser, Womelsdorf, PA

Spicy Corn on the Cob Soup

Monica Wagner
Quarryville, PA

Makes 6-8 servings

Prep. Time: 20 minutes
Cooking Time: 40 minutes

6 medium ears of corn,
  husked, cobs reserved
1½ Tbsp. olive oil
3 garlic cloves, minced
2 medium jalapeño
  peppers, minced
1 cup chopped onions
½ cup chopped celery
1½ tsp. ground cumin
1 tsp. turmeric
4 cups vegetable stock
2 cups water
1½ tsp. salt
1 tsp. freshly ground pepper
½ cup chopped red bell
  pepper, for garnish
¼ cup chopped cilantro,
  for garnish
¼ cup chopped scallions,
  for garnish

1. Slice corn from the cob with knife. Reserve the cobs. Set aside 1 cup of kernels.

2. Heat oil in a large stockpot over medium heat. Add garlic and sauté about 1 minute.

3. Add jalapeño and onions. Sauté about 5 minutes.

4. Add celery, cumin and turmeric. Cook for 1-2 more minutes.

5. Add stock, water and cobs. Bring to a boil. Reduce heat to low and simmer for 15 minutes. Remove and discard cobs.

6. Add corn except for 1 reserved cup. Add salt and pepper. Simmer 15 more minutes.

7. Purée soup until smooth with immersion blender or stand blender.

8. Garnish with red pepper, cilantro, scallions and reserved corn. Serve hot or at room temperature.

Simple French Onion Soup

Christen Chew
Lancaster, PA

Makes 6 servings

Prep. Time: 15 minutes
Cooking Time: 9-11 hours
Ideal slow-cooker size: 4- or 6-qt.

¼ cup olive oil
4 medium sweet onions,
  thinly sliced
8 cups vegetable stock
⅓ cup burgundy wine
salt and pepper, to taste

1. Spread the oil in the bottom of a 4-to 6-quart slow cooker. Add onions and cover.

2. Cook on low 8-10 hours, until onion are soft and well caramelized.

3. Add the stock and wine and season with salt and pepper. Cover.

4. Cook on high for 30-60 minutes.

Go-Along:
• Grilled cheese sandwiches.

French Onion Soup

Rosemarie Fitzgerald
Gibsonia, PA

Makes 4 servings

Prep. Time: 25 minutes
Cooking/Baking Time: 5-6 hours
Ideal slow-cooker size: 5-qt.

3 Tbsp. butter
2 Tbsp. olive oil
4 large yellow onions,
  thinly sliced
1 tsp. sugar
1 tsp. salt
½ tsp. freshly ground
  pepper
2 Tbsp. all-purpose flour
1 cup white wine
4 cups vegetable stock,
  canned *or* homemade
1"-thick slices French
  bread, toasted
shredded Swiss cheese

1. In large sauté pan, heat butter and oil on medium high heat until butter is melted.

2. Add onions, sugar, salt and pepper.

3. Reduce heat to medium for 15 minutes, stirring frequently.

4. Add flour and stir for 2 minutes.

5. Transfer to slow cooker. Add wine and stock.

6. Cover and cook on low 5-6 hours.

7. Serve soup in oven-proof bowls. Place one slice toasted French bread onto each bowl of soup. Sprinkle with cheese. Put under broiler for a few minutes until browned.

Barley and Mushroom Soup

Jean Turner
Williams Lake, BC

Makes 8 servings

Prep. Time: 30 minutes
Cooking Time: 3 hours
Ideal slow-cooker size: 5-qt.

⅔ cup uncooked pearl
 barley
7 cups vegetable stock
3 onions, chopped
4 carrots, chopped
2 ribs celery, chopped
2 cups chopped fresh
 mushrooms
2 Tbsp. butter
1 tsp. salt
1 tsp. pepper
1-1½ cups sour cream
chopped fresh parsley

1. Combine barley, stock, onions, carrots, celery, mushrooms, butter, salt and pepper in slow cooker.
2. Cover. Cook on low 3 hours or until barley is soft. Remove from heat.
3. Stir in sour cream and parsley.

Tip:
 You can serve this soup hot or cold.

Go-Along:
• Irish soda bread.

Zucchini Soup Base

Jana Beyer
Harrisonburg, VA

Makes 4 servings

Prep. Time: 15 minutes
Cooking Time: 2-3 hours
Ideal slow-cooker size: 4-qt.

Soup Base:
 3 cups unpeeled diced
  zucchini
 ½ cup chopped onions
 1 tsp. seasoned salt
 ½ cup water
 1 tsp. powdered
  vegetarian bouillon

White Sauce:
 2 Tbsp. butter
 2 Tbsp. all-purpose flour
 2 cups whole milk

1. To make soup base, combine zucchini, onions, seasoned salt, water, and powdered bouillon in slow cooker. Cook on low 2-3 hours until tender.
2. Put into blender and whiz until very smooth.
3. Store in the freezer until needed.
4. To serve, thaw soup base.
5. Make white sauce. Melt butter in saucepan. Add flour and whisk until smooth and bubbly.
6. Slowly, stirring continuously, pour milk into butter-flour mixture. Cook and stir over low heat until thickened, approximately 10 minutes. Do not allow white sauce to boil.
7. Add soup base to white sauce. Stir well. Heat and serve.

Tip:
 This base can be increased as many times as you like and then frozen for a quick soup.

Use a whisk when stirring sauce to do away with the lumps.
Susan Kasting, Jenks, OK

Zucchini Garden Chowder

Dawn Alderfer
Oley, PA

Makes 8-10 servings

Prep. Time: 5 minutes
Cooking Time: 3-4 hours
Ideal slow-cooker size: 5-qt.

2 medium zucchini,
  chopped
3 Tbsp. minced fresh
  parsley
1 tsp. dried basil
1 tsp. salt
¼ tsp. pepper
pinch sugar
14½-oz. can diced
  tomatoes, undrained
10-oz. pkg. frozen corn
3 cups water, *divided*
3 tsp. vegetarian bouillon
1 tsp. lemon juice
⅓ cup all-purpose flour
12-oz. can evaporated milk
¼ cup grated Parmesan
  cheese
2 cups shredded cheddar
  cheese

1. Combine zucchini,
parsley, basil, salt, pepper,
sugar, tomatoes and corn in
slow cooker.
2. Add 2 cups water, bouillon and lemon juice. Cover
and cook on low 2-3 hours
until zucchini is tender.
3. Make a paste of 1 cup
water and flour by whisking
together in small bowl.
4. Gradually pour flour
mixture into hot soup, stirring
continuously.
5. Cover and cook 30-60
minutes until thickened.
6. Add evaporated milk
and cheeses. Stir and heat
through.

Go-Along:
• Corn muffins.

African Peanut Soup

Barbara Hershey
Lititz, PA

Makes 5-6 servings

Prep. Time: 20 minutes
Cooking Time: 45 minutes

2 Tbsp. peanut oil
1 onion, chopped
1 green bell pepper, diced
  small
1 red bell pepper, diced small
2 cloves garlic, minced
28-oz. can stewed tomatoes,
  puréed
4 cups vegetable stock
⅛ tsp. hot pepper flakes, *or*
  to taste
1 Tbsp. curry powder,
  optional
¼ cup uncooked white rice
¼ cup peanut butter
salt and pepper, to taste

1. In large pot, warm the
peanut oil over medium heat.
2. Add onions, peppers
and garlic. Sauté until onion
begins to brown.
3. Add tomatoes, stock,
hot pepper flakes, and curry
powder if you wish. Simmer
uncovered over medium heat
for 30 minutes.
4. Add rice and peanut
butter. Cook, covered, for 20
minutes or until rice is done.
5. Season with salt and
pepper to taste.

Go-Along:
• Hard, crusty bread and
green lettuce salad.

Moroccan Stew

Kristi See
Weskan, KS

Mary Ann Lefever
Lancaster, PA

Makes 8 servings

Prep. Time: 15 minutes
Cooking Time: 4-6 hours
Ideal slow-cooker size: 5-qt.

1 large onion, chopped
1 Tbsp. olive oil
2 tsp. ground cinnamon
2 tsp. ground cumin
1 tsp. ground coriander
½ tsp. cayenne pepper
½ tsp. ground allspice
¼ tsp. salt
3 cups water
1 small butternut squash,
    peeled and cubed
2 medium potatoes, peeled
    and cubed
4 medium carrots, sliced
3 plum tomatoes, chopped
2 small zucchini, cut into
    1" pieces
15-oz. can garbanzo beans,
    rinsed and drained

1. In Dutch oven, sauté onions in oil until tender.

2. Add cinnamon, cumin, coriander, pepper, allspice and salt. Cook 1 minute longer.

3. Transfer to slow cooker.

4. Stir in water, squash, potatoes, carrots, zucchini and tomatoes.

5. Cook on low 4-6 hours.

6. Stir in beans. Cook 15 more minutes, or until heated through.

Variation:

Add ½ cups raisins, pinch of saffron and ¼ chopped fresh parsley about 10 minutes before end of cooking time.
Mary Ann Lefever

Go-Along:

• Hard-boiled eggs, couscous with almonds, pita bread.

If it's possible to taste a dish before you serve it, do so. It might need a little salt, a little sugar, more herbs, a splash of vinegar or Worcestershire sauce. Learn to taste and adjust, and then jot a note on your recipe about what you did.

Margaret High, Lancaster, PA

Sweet Potato Barley Soup

Renae Hege
Midville, GA

Makes 6-8 servings

Prep. Time: 15 minutes
Cooking Time: 6-8 hours
Ideal slow-cooker size: 4- or 5-qt.

3 cups water
2 cups tomato juice
14½-oz. can diced tomatoes
1 cup chopped onions
1 rib celery, diced
1 cup sliced carrots
2 cups peeled, diced sweet
    potatoes
½ cup uncooked pearl barley
1 tsp. salt
1 tsp. seasoned salt
½ tsp. pepper
¼ cup all-purpose flour
3 cups milk

1. In a 4- or 5-quart greased slow cooker, place water, juice, tomatoes, onions, celery, carrots, sweet potatoes, barley, salt, seasoned salt and pepper.

2. Cover. Cook on low 6-7 hours.

3. Combine flour with milk in a small bowl and whisk until smooth.

4. Pour into soup. Stir.

5. Cook on low an additional hour, or on high for 30 minutes. Stir occasionally.

Variation:

For a variation, omit the flour and milk at the end. Just add a little more water or tomato juice if needed.

Sweet Potato and Corn Chowder

Jean Harris Robinson
Pemberton, NJ

Makes 10-12 servings

Prep. Time: 20 minutes
Cooking Time: 45 minutes

5 Tbsp. butter
6 large sweet potatoes, peeled and cubed
2 garlic cloves, chopped, *optional*
1 large white onion, diced
2 ribs celery, diced
3 carrots, diced
2 fennel bulbs, chopped, *optional*
8 cups vegetable stock, *or* water
5 dashes vegetarian Worcestershire sauce
¼ cup dark brown sugar, packed
1 Tbsp. ground coriander
2 cups heavy cream
16-oz. can whole corn, drained
16-oz. can creamed corn
salt and pepper, to taste

1. In large stockpot, melt butter and add sweet potatoes, garlic if you wish, onion, celery, carrots, and fennel if you wish.
2. Sauté and stir for 15 minutes.
3. Add vegetable stock and bring to boil.
4. Reduce heat and simmer, covered, until vegetables are soft.
5. Turn off heat. Add Worcestershire sauce, brown sugar, coriander and cream.
6. Puree with hand blender or in stand blender. Then add corn to chowder in stockpot.
7. Gently heat soup 5-10 minutes.
8. Add salt and pepper to taste.

Tip:
A great chowder to serve at Thanksgiving and Christmas.

Carrot and Sweet Potato Puree

Susie Shenk Wenger
Lancaster, PA

Makes 4-6 servings

Prep. Time: 20 minutes
Cooking Time: 4 hours
Ideal slow-cooker size: 5- or 6-qt.

4 large sweet potatoes, peeled and chopped
3 large carrots, sliced in chunks
1 cup water
1 large onion, diced
2-3 cloves garlic, minced
1 Tbsp. olive oil
¼ cup minced fresh parsley
1 Tbsp. honey
1 Tbsp. lemon juice
½ tsp. ground cumin
⅛ tsp. ground allspice
½ tsp. salt
pepper, to taste
1-2 tsp. curry powder, according to your taste preference
15-oz. can vegetable broth
½ cup light cream
cilantro leaves, for garnish

1. Place sweet potatoes and carrots in slow cooker with 1 cup water.
2. Cover. Cook on high until soft, about 2 hours.
3. In skillet, sauté onion and garlic in olive oil until soft.
4. Add sauté to carrots and potatoes. Add parsley, honey, lemon juice, cumin, allspice, salt, pepper, curry powder, vegetable broth and cream to slow cooker.
5. Cook on low for 2 hours.
6. Puree with a hand blender or in a stand blender.
7. Ladle into bowls and garnish with cilantro leaves.

Tip:
The amount of vegetables does not need to be exact. Use what you have available.

Go-Along:
• A hearty bread or soft whole wheat rolls go well with this bowl of health.

Sweet Potato and Ginger Soup

Jenny Kempf
Bedminster, PA

Makes 4 servings

Prep. Time: 15 minutes
Cooking Time: 30 minutes

1 lb. sweet potatoes, peeled
  and cubed
2 tsp. butter
2 tsp. olive oil
3 spring onions, chopped
2 tsp. chopped garlic
2 tsp. peeled, chopped
  ginger
2 cups vegetable stock
2 Tbsp. fresh chopped
  cilantro
1 cup coconut milk
salt and pepper, to taste
cashews, for garnish

1. Boil sweet potatoes in an inch of water in soup pot until tender. Drain.
2. Heat butter and oil in soup pot. Sauté onions, garlic and ginger until soft.
3. Add sweet potatoes and stir.
4. Add stock and bring to a boil, covered. Reduce heat and simmer 10 minutes.
5. Remove from heat. Add cilantro.
6. Puree soup with hand blender or in stand blender. Return purée to soup pot.
7. Add coconut milk. Season to taste with salt and pepper. Heat through.
8. Sprinkle with cashews and serve.

Coconut-Curried Spinach Pea Soup

Allison Martin
Royal Oak, MI

Makes 12 servings

Prep. Time: 45 minutes
Cooking Time: 30 minutes

5 cups water
2 tsp. salt
8 garlic cloves, peeled
4 cups potatoes, peeled or
  unpeeled, and diced
1 Tbsp. vegetable oil
4 cups chopped onions
1½ tsp. ginger
1½ tsp. turmeric
1½ tsp. cumin
1½ tsp. coriander
½ tsp. cinnamon
½ tsp. cardamom
¼-½ tsp. cayenne,
  according to your taste
  preference
black pepper, to taste
1½ Tbsp. lemon juice
3 cups frozen peas
4 cups torn fresh spinach
14-oz. can low-fat coconut
  milk

1. Bring water and salt to a boil in a large soup pot.
2. Toss in garlic and potatoes. Cover, reduce heat to simmer and cook about 15 minutes.
3. In a separate large sauce pan, warm vegetable oil.

Add onions and sauté until translucent.
4. Stir in ginger, turmeric, cumin, coriander, cinnamon, cardamom, cayenne and black pepper.
5. Add lemon juice and 1 cup of the simmering potato liquid. Simmer for about 5 minutes.
6. Transfer spiced mixture to the pot of undrained, cooked potatoes. Add peas and spinach. Cover and cook 5 minutes.
7. Stir in coconut milk. Purée soup with an immersion blender or a potato masher until as smooth as you like. Reheat on low if necessary.

Tip:
  Combine all of your spices in a small bowl before your begin. It makes the cooking process easier to toss in a handful of spices rather than measuring each one as you go since there are so many!

Variation:
  Add cilantro on top of each serving if you wish.

Go-Along:
• Sourdough bread with butter. This soup is quite hearty in itself.

When planning a meal for guests, prepare things ahead so you can enjoy time with the guests.

Elsie Schlabach, Millersburg, OH

Velvety Butternut Soup

Carol Collins
Holly Springs, NC

Makes 4 servings

Prep. Time: 15 minutes
Cooking Time: 2-3 hours
Ideal slow-cooker size: 5-qt.

2 Tbsp. minced shallots *or* onion
2 Tbsp. olive oil
5 cups peeled, cubed butternut squash
2 cups peeled, cubed russet potatoes
4 cups vegetable broth
⅛ tsp. cayenne pepper

1. In a small frying pan, sauté shallots or onions until softened, about 5 minutes.

2. Place in slow cooker. Add squash, potatoes, vegetable broth and cayenne pepper.

3. Cover. Cook on high for 2-3 hours, until potato and squash are very tender.

4. Use an immersible or stand blender to purée until smooth. Serve.

Tip:
Buy squash already peeled and cut into cubes to save time.

Go-Along:
• Excellent dinner with quiche.

Butternut Squash Soup with Thai Gremolata

Andy Wagner
Quarryville, PA

Makes 4-6 servings

Prep. Time: 25 minutes
Cooking Time: 2-5 hours
Ideal slow-cooker size: 3½- or 4-qt.

2 lbs. butternut squash, peeled and cut into 1" pieces
2 cups vegetable broth
14-oz. can unsweetened coconut milk
¼ cup minced onions
1 Tbsp. brown sugar, packed
1 Tbsp. soy sauce
½-1 tsp. Asian chili sauce *or* crushed red pepper
2 Tbsp. lime juice
lime wedges, *optional*

Thai Gremolata:
   ½ cup chopped fresh basil *or* cilantro
   ½ cup chopped peanuts
   1 Tbsp. finely shredded lime peel

1. In a 3½- or 4-quart slow cooker, stir together squash, broth, coconut milk, onions, brown sugar, soy sauce and Asian chili sauce.

2. Cover and cook on low for 4-5 hours or on high for 2-2½ hours.

3. Meanwhile, assemble the Thai Gremolata. Mix together basil, peanuts and lime peel. Set aside.

4. Use an immersion or stand blender to carefully blend soup until completely smooth.

5. Stir in lime juice. Ladle into bowls and top with Thai Gremolata. If you wish, serve with lime wedges.

Squash and Tomato Soup

Jean Harris Robinson
Pemberton, NJ

Makes 12 servings

Prep. Time: 25 minutes
Cooking Time: 4 hours
Ideal slow-cooker size: 5-qt.

2 Tbsp. olive oil
2-3 whole garlic cloves
1 large white onion, diced
5 carrots, diced
3 ribs celery, diced
2 lbs. winter squash, peeled and cut into chunks
2 14½-oz. cans diced tomatoes
8 cups vegetable stock
½ cup chopped fresh basil leaves
½ cup chopped fresh cilantro leaves
2 Tbsp. balsamic vinegar *or* rice vinegar
salt and pepper, to taste

1. Combine olive oil, garlic, onion, carrots, celery, squash, tomatoes and stock in slow cooker.
2. Cover. Cook on low 4 hours or until vegetables are tender.
3. Add basil, cilantro, vinegar, and salt and pepper. Purée with hand blender or in stand blender.

Variations:
1. Skip the puréeing and serve the soup chunky.
2. You can also cook it on the stovetop. Sauté the vegetables in the oil first before adding the stock and tomatoes.

Go-Along:
• Crescent rolls.

Butternut Mushroom Bisque

Doug Garrett
Palmyra, PA

Makes 10 servings

Prep. Time: 45 minutes
Baking/Cooking Time: 80 minutes
Standing Time: 30 minutes

1 medium butternut squash
3 Tbsp. butter
1¼ cups chopped onions
1 lb. fresh mushrooms, cleaned and chopped
1 tsp. Italian herb seasoning
½ tsp. salt
⅛ tsp. white pepper
6 cups vegetable broth, *divided*
12-oz. can evaporated milk, *or* 1½ cups light cream
⅓ cup dry sherry

1. Slice butternut squash lengthwise. Scoop out the seeds and discard. Place cut side down in a sprayed 9 × 13 baking dish. Bake 1 hour at 325°. Remove from oven, turn over and let cool. Scoop out insides, cube and set aside. (You can do this whole process ahead of time and refrigerate the prepared squash until you need it.)
2. To make bisque, melt butter in large stockpot. Sauté onions and mushrooms, adding Italian seasoning, salt and white pepper as you sauté.
3. When mushrooms are thoroughly browned, remove from heat and transfer to blender.
4. Add about 2-3 cups broth to blender and blend mixture until smooth. Return to the stockpot.
5. Add cooked squash to blender, add remaining broth and blend until smooth. Add to stockpot.
6. Add evaporated milk and sherry to stockpot. Heat thoroughly, but do not allow to boil.
7. Adjust seasonings if needed and serve.

Variation:
Peel and cut squash into 1" cubes. Mix with mushrooms and onions. Toss with 2 Tbsp. olive oil and omit butter. Roast at 425° until squash is soft. Proceed with recipe at Step 4.

Go-Along:
• This soup, with a hearty whole-grain bread and salad, makes a good light meal.

Acorn Squash Soup with Apples and Leeks

Kathy Rodkey
Halifax, PA

Makes 2-4 servings

Prep. Time: 1 hour
Cooking Time: 45 minutes
Standing Time: 30 minutes

1 medium acorn squash, cut in half, seeded
3 cups vegetable broth
1 small apple, unpeeled, chopped
½ cup sliced leeks
½ cup fat-free half-and-half, *or* regular half-and-half
grated nutmeg, to taste

1. Place squash, cut-side down, in foil-lined baking pan.
2. Bake 30 minutes at 375°, or until flesh is tender.
3. Let cool slightly for easier handling.
4. With a spoon, scoop out squash. Place in soup pot.
5. Add broth, apples and leeks. Cover. Simmer 15 minutes, or until leeks are tender.
6. Transfer soup to blender. Add half-and-half. Puree until smooth. Do this in batches if necessary.
7. Sprinkle with nutmeg before serving.

Three-Cheese Broccoli Soup

Deb Kepiro
Strasburg, PA

Makes 4 servings

Prep. Time: 20 minutes
Cooking Time: 4-6 hours
Ideal slow-cooker size: 5-qt.

4 cups vegetable broth
2 cups 2% milk
2 10-oz. bags frozen broccoli florets
½ cup very finely minced white onion
½ tsp. black pepper
½ tsp. kosher salt
½ tsp. ground nutmeg
3 cups shredded cheese, preferably 1 cup each of Jarlsberg, Gruyere, and cheddar, *or* cheeses of your choice

1. Mix broth, milk, broccoli, onions, pepper, salt and nutmeg together in slow cooker.
2. Cook on low for 7-9 hours, or on high for 4-6 hours. The soup is done when the onions and broccoli are cooked as tender as you like them.
3. Twenty minutes or so before serving, stir in the cheese. The cheese will be stringy and will stick to the broccoli florets---that's okay!

Tip:
Mince the onion into really small pieces so you don't crunch on onion pieces after the soup is cooked.

Broccoli Chowder

Elaine Patton
West Middletown, PA

Makes 6-8 servings

Prep. Time: 15 minutes
Cooking Time: 7 hours
Ideal slow-cooker size: 5-qt.

10-oz. pkg. chopped frozen broccoli
3 cups milk
2 10¾-oz. cans condensed cheddar cheese soup
1 cup cooked, shredded potatoes (frozen hashbrowns are fine)
1 small onion, diced small
salt and pepper, to taste

1. Break apart frozen broccoli. Place in slow cooker.
2. Add milk, soup, potatoes and onion.
3. Cover. Cook on low 7 hours. Add salt and pepper as needed.

Cauliflower Soup

Elaine Vigoda
Rochester, NY

Makes 8-10 servings

Prep. Time: 15 minutes
Cooking Time: 2 hours
Ideal slow-cooker size: 6-qt.

2 lbs. frozen cauliflower
1 onion, diced
48 oz. vegetable broth
¼ cup all-purpose flour
¼ cup water
2 cups fresh cauliflower
  florets
½ cup sliced scallions
1 cup shredded Mexican
  cheese
¼ cup chopped fresh
  cilantro

1. Put frozen cauliflower and onions in slow cooker. Pour in broth.
2. In a small bowl, whisk together flour and water until smooth.
3. Slowly stir flour mixture into soup until blended.
4. Cook on high 2 hours, or until vegetables are soft.
5. Purée soup with a hand blender or in a stand blender. Return to cooker.
6. Add fresh cauliflower. Cover and cook another 30-40 minutes on high until cauliflower florets are as tender as you like them.
7. Garnish each bowl with cheese, scallions and cilantro when serving.

Tip:
  The puréed soup can be frozen after step 5. Thaw and proceed with step 6 when ready to use.

Cauliflower and Wild Rice Soup

Carolyn Baer
Conrath, WI

Makes 6-8 servings

Prep. Time: 10 minutes
Cooking Time: 30 minutes

1 medium onion, chopped
1 cup thinly sliced celery
1 cup sliced fresh
  mushrooms
½ tsp. dried thyme
pepper, to taste
half stick (4 Tbsp.) butter
½ cup all-purpose flour
4 cups vegetable broth
2 cups cooked wild rice
2 cups cooked cauliflower
  florets
1 cup half-and-half, *or*
  regular milk with 2
  Tbsp. dry milk powder

1. In a 3-quart saucepan, sauté onion, celery, mushrooms, thyme and pepper in butter until tender.
2. Sprinkle with flour. Stir to coat.
3. Gradually add broth, stirring over medium heat.
4. Cook and stir for 1-2 minutes, or until thickened.
5. Stir in rice, cauliflower and cream.
6. Simmer until heated through. Do not boil.

Plan ahead to cool soups before pureeing them. Then you can keep the lid on the blender to avoid splashes.
  Suzanne S. Nobrega, Duxbury, MA

Broccoli and Blue Brie Soup

Jean Turner
Williams Lake, BC

Makes 6 servings

Prep. Time: 25 minutes
Cooking Time: 25-30 minutes

1 onion, chopped
1 lb. broccoli, chopped
1 large zucchini, chopped
1 large carrot, chopped
1 medium potato, peeled
   or unpeeled, chopped
2 Tbsp. butter
2 Tbsp. sunflower oil
8 cups stock *or* water,
   divided
salt and ground pepper, to
   taste
3 oz. blue brie cheese,
   cubed
sliced almonds, to garnish

1. In large saucepan, place onions, broccoli, zucchini, carrots, potatoes, butter and oil.
2. Add about 3 Tbsp. of stock or water.
3. Heat vegetable mixture until sizzling, stirring frequently.
4. Cover and cook gently for 15 minutes, shaking the pan occasionally, until all the vegetables soften.
5. Add the remainder of the stock or water.
6. Season with salt and pepper. Bring to a boil.
7. Reduce heat, cover and simmer gently for about 30 minutes.

8. Strain the vegetables and reserve the liquid.
9. Purée the vegetables in a food processor or blender. Then return them to the pan with reserved liquid.
10. Bring the soup back to a very gentle boil. Stir in the cheese until it melts.
11. Garnish with a scattering of almond slices.

Tip:
Don't let the soup boil too hard after adding the cheese or the cheese will become stringy.

Variation:
Use cauliflower in place of broccoli and Stilton cheese in place of brie cheese.

Tomato Basil Bisque

Betty Detweiler
Centreville, MI

Makes 6-8 servings

Prep. Time: 10 minutes
Cooking Time: 5-8 hours
Ideal slow-cooker size: 5-qt.

32-oz. can tomato juice
32-oz. can puréed tomatoes
2 14-oz. cans diced
   tomatoes with garlic,
   onion and basil
1 Tbsp. dried basil
half stick (¼ cup) butter
2 Tbsp. minced onion
pepper to taste
2 cups heavy cream

1. Combine juice, puréed tomatoes, diced tomatoes, basil, butter, onion and pepper in slow cooker.
2. Cover. Cook on high for 5 hours or on low for 8 hours.
3. Add heavy cream. Stir. Reheat on high if you wish, but do not allow to boil.

After working hard on making a meal, remember that presentation is important. Take the clutter off the table and serve food in pretty dishes or bowls.
Teresa Martin, Strasburg, PA

Tomato Lentil Soup

Elaine Sue Good
Tiskilwa, IL

Makes 8 servings

Prep. Time: 15 minutes
Cooking Time: 6-12 hours
Ideal slow-cooker size: 5-qt.

3 carrots, sliced
1 onion, chopped
2 cloves garlic, minced
3 15-oz. cans diced
  tomatoes
2 cups vegetable broth
2 cups dry red lentils
2 Tbsp. dried basil, *or* ⅓
  cup chopped fresh basil

1. Combine carrots, onions, garlic, tomatoes, broth, lentils and basil in your slow cooker. If using fresh basil, add it about an hour before serving.
2. Cook on low for 10 hours or on high for 6 hours, until lentils are tender.

Tip:
  The amount of liquid needed for this recipe will vary depending on how hot your slow cooker heats. Check after 8 hours on low or after 4 hours on high to be sure the soup isn't cooking dry.

Spiced Tomatoes and Couscous

Rhonda Burgoon
Collingswood, NJ

Makes 4 servings

Prep. Time: 10 minutes
Cooking Time: 45 minutes

1 Tbsp. olive oil
1 large onion, chopped
2 carrots, diced
3 ribs celery, diced
3 Tbsp. harissa paste
1 tsp. ground cumin
14-oz. can chopped
  tomatoes
1-2 Tbsp. tomato paste
2 cups vegetable stock
14-oz. can garbanzo beans,
  rinsed and drained
2 Tbsp. uncooked couscous
½ small bunch parsley,
  chopped

1. Heat oil in a large pan and cook the onion, carrots and celery for a few minutes until softened.
2. Add the harissa and cumin and stir.
3. Add in tomatoes, tomato paste, stock and garbanzo beans. Stir well, then cover and simmer for 30 minutes.
4. Add the couscous and simmer for another 5 minutes. Stir in parsley just before serving.

Vegan Chili

Denise Nolt
Fleetwood, PA

Makes 8 servings

Prep. Time: 10 minutes
Cooking Time: 2-3 hours
Ideal slow-cooker size: 5-qt.

28-oz. can crushed
  tomatoes
15-oz. can light *or* dark
  kidney beans, rinsed and
  drained
15-oz. can black beans,
  rinsed and drained
15-oz. can chili beans
11-oz. can Mexi-corn
8-oz. can crushed
  pineapple
1 green bell pepper, diced
1 red bell pepper, diced
1 yellow bell pepper, diced
1 orange bell pepper, diced
1 medium red onion, diced
1 hot chili pepper, diced,
  optional
garlic, to taste
paprika, to taste
cayenne pepper, to taste
chili powder, to taste

1. Combine all ingredients in slow cooker.
2. Cook on high 2-3 hours or until vegetables are as soft as you like them. Serve with tortilla chips.

White Chili

Andrea Bjorlie
Grand Rapids, MI

Makes 6 servings

Prep. Time: 20 minutes
Cooking Time: 4 hours
Ideal slow-cooker size: 5-qt.

1 Tbsp. oil
1 onion, chopped
3 garlic cloves, minced
2 15-oz. cans Great
    Northern beans, rinsed
    and drained
15-oz. can vegetable broth
1 tsp. salt
1 tsp. ground cumin
1 tsp. dried oregano
½ tsp. black pepper
1 tsp. cayenne pepper
½ cup half-and-half
1 cup sour cream
fresh cilantro, to taste,
    optional

1. Sauté onion and garlic in oil in skillet until softened.
2. Put in slow cooker with beans, broth, salt, cumin, oregano, pepper and cayenne pepper.
3. Cook on low for 4 hours.
4. Turn heat off for a bit near serving time. Add half-and-half and sour cream. Serve garnished with cilantro, if you wish.

Black Bean Chili

Kenda Autumn
San Francisco, CA

Makes 6-8 servings

Prep. Time: 15 minutes
Cooking Time: 8 hours
Ideal slow-cooker size: 5-qt.

1 Tbsp. oil
1 onion, chopped
1 tsp. ground cumin
1 tsp. ground coriander
1 Tbsp. chili powder
1 tsp. garam masala
16-oz. can black beans,
    rinsed and drained
14-oz. can diced tomatoes
1 sweet potato, cubed
1 cup corn

1. Heat oil in saucepan. Brown onion, cumin, coriander, chili powder and garam masala.
2. Transfer sauté to slow cooker.
3. Add beans, tomatoes, sweet potato and corn.
4. Cook on low 8 hours.

Tip:
    I use this recipe as a starting point for chili. I add other vegetables in step 3 that I have on hand: butternut squash, red bell pepper and mushrooms.

Go-Along:
• Some fun chili toppings are chives, fresh cilantro, cheddar cheese and diced hot peppers.

Vegetarian Chili

Mary Ann Bowman
Ephrata, PA

Makes 10-12 servings

Prep. Time: 45 minutes
Standing Time: 15 minutes
Cooking Time: 5½ hours
Ideal slow-cooker size: 6-qt.

2 cups tomato juice
1 cup uncooked bulgur
    wheat
4 cloves garlic, crushed
1½ cups chopped onions
2-3 Tbsp. olive oil
1 cup chopped celery
1 cup diced carrots
1 tsp. ground cumin
1 tsp. dried basil
1 tsp. chili powder
dash of cayenne
salt and pepper, to taste
1 cup chopped green bell
    pepper
3 15½-oz. cans kidney
    beans, rinsed and
    drained
2 cups chopped fresh
    tomatoes
½ lemon, juiced
6-oz. can tomato paste
3 cups water

1. Heat tomato juice to boiling and pour over wheat in 6-quart slow cooker.
2. Cover and let set 15 minutes.
3. Sauté garlic and onions in olive oil in a good-sized skillet.
4. Add celery, carrots, cumin, basil, chili powder, cayenne, salt and pepper.

5. When vegetables are soft, add peppers and cook until tender.

6. Combine sautéed vegetables with wheat, beans, tomatoes, lemon juice, tomato paste and water in slow cooker.

7. Cover. Cook on low 4-5 hours.

Tip:

If chili thickens too much, add extra tomato juice or water

Go-Along:

• Serve with shredded cheese and sour cream.

Chili with Corn

Rosemarie Fitzgerald
Gibsonia, PA

Makes 8-10 servings

Prep. Time: 10-15 minutes
Cooking Time: 8-10 hours
Ideal slow-cooker size: 6-qt.

2 onions, chopped
5-6 garlic cloves, minced
2 jalapeño peppers, minced
2 10-oz. pkgs. frozen
   meatless crumbles
3 14-oz. cans diced
   tomatoes with juice
2 cups frozen corn
2 Tbsp. chili powder
1 tsp. ground cumin
1 tsp. salt
1 tsp. dried oregano
¼ tsp. cayenne pepper, *or*
   to taste

2 15-oz. cans kidney beans,
   rinsed and drained
2 15-oz. cans black beans,
   rinsed and drained
3 Tbsp. cornstarch
⅓ cup water

1. In a 6-quart slow cooker, combine onion, garlic, jalapeño peppers, crumbles, tomatoes, corn, chili powder, cumin, salt, oregano, cayenne, kidney beans and black beans.

2. Mix gently.

3. Cover. Cook on low for 8-9 hours.

4. In a small bowl, mix together cornstarch and water. Stir into slow cooker.

5. Cover and cook on high for 20-30 minutes, or until thickened.

Go-Along:

• Cornbread.

Big-Batch Vegetarian Lentil Chili

Moreen and **Christina Weaver**
Bath, NY

Makes 8-10 servings

Prep. Time: 20 minutes
Cooking Time: 5 hours
Ideal slow-cooker size: 6- or 7-qt.

4 14½-oz. cans diced
   tomatoes, *or* tomatoes
   with green chilies
2 15-oz. cans red kidney
   beans, rinsed and drained

3 cups water
1 green bell pepper, chopped
1 large onion, chopped
2 cups dry red lentils,
   rinsed and drained
¼ cup chili powder
2 Tbsp. garlic powder
8-oz. can tomato sauce
6-oz. can tomato paste
⅛ tsp. black pepper
2 cups shredded cheddar
   cheese
tortilla chips, *optional*
chipotle pepper, *optional*

1. In 6- or 7-quart slow cooker, combine tomatoes, beans, water, green pepper, onions, lentils, chili powder and garlic powder.

2. Cover. Cook on low 4 hours.

3. Stir in tomato sauce, tomato paste and black pepper.

4. Cook on low, covered, 1 more hour.

5. Serve with cheese.

6. Add tortilla chips and chipotle pepper if you wish, as toppings.

Vegetable Broth in the Slow Cooker

Margaret High
Lancaster, PA

Makes 10 cups

Prep. Time: 15 minutes
Cooking Time: 9-11 hours
Standing Time: 1 hour or longer
Ideal slow-cooker size: 6-qt.

1 yellow onion, unpeeled,
    cut in chunks
1 large potato, unpeeled,
    cut in chunks
2 carrots, unpeeled, cut in
    chunks
1 Tbsp. olive oil
3 dried mushrooms,
    such as Chinese black
    mushrooms *or* shiitake
handful fresh parsley *or* 2
    ribs celery, chopped
10 cups water
2 bay leaves
10 peppercorns
3 Tbsp. soy sauce

1. Pile onion, potato and carrot chunks on a rimmed baking sheet. Drizzle with olive oil. Mix.

2. Roast vegetables at 425° for 30 minutes, stirring once or twice. Vegetables should be fragrant and crispy brown in spots.

3. Scrape vegetables into slow cooker, being sure to get all the browned bits.

4. Add rest of ingredients to slow cooker.

5. Cover. Cook on low 8-10 hours. Allow to cool at least an hour or even longer.

6. Strain the broth through a mesh strainer, pressing on the solids in the strainer to get all the broth out. Discard solids.

7. Measure out reasonable portions (1-2 cups) and pour into containers with lids. Label. Cover.

8. Store in refrigerator for up to 1 week. Keep in freezer several months.

Variations:

1. Skip the roasting step and omit the olive oil. The broth will not be as deeply flavored or colored, but still tasty.

2. Cook the broth down with the lid off the slow cooker until it's reduced by half – now it's concentrated and takes up less storage space. Add water when you're ready to use it.

3. Add herbs to your taste, especially if you know what you're likely to use the broth for. I like to keep the broth a little under-salted and without too many herbs so it's as flexible as possible.

Add a quarter cup of mashed pumpkin to foods like chili, taco soup, or spaghetti sauce to cut down on the acidity that can cause heartburn. The pumpkin is a nutritious additive, and it doesn't obtrude on the flavors.

Debra Kilheffer, Millersville, PA

Pasta

Vegan

Homemade Spaghetti Sauce

Beverly Hummel
Fleetwood, PA

Makes 12 cups

Prep. Time: 20 minutes
Cooking Time: 4-5 hours
Ideal slow-cooker size: 6-qt.

4 qts. cherry tomatoes
1 onion, minced
2 cloves garlic, minced
1 Tbsp. oil
3 tsp. sugar
1 tsp. dried rosemary
2 tsp. dried thyme
2 tsp. Italian herb
   seasoning
1 tsp. salt
½ tsp. pepper
hot cooked spaghetti

1. Stem tomatoes, leaving the skins on. Blend until smooth in blender.
2. In a skillet, sauté onions and garlic in oil.
3. Add sauté to slow cooker. Add tomatoes, sugar, rosemary, thyme, Italian seasoning, salt and pepper.
4. Simmer on low in slow cooker until thickened, about 4-5 hours. Remove the lid for the final 30-60 minutes of cooking time if you'd like a thicker sauce.
5. Serve over spaghetti.

Olive oil is very sensitive to heat, so when using it in cooking, don't be afraid to use a cheaper brand. But keep a bottle of good quality on hand to use when the heat is off.   Bob Coffey, New Windsor, NY

Big-Batch Puttanesca Sauce

Monica Wagner
Quarryville, PA

Makes 11 cups

Prep. Time: 30 minutes
Cooking Time: 4-10 hours
Ideal slow-cooker size: 6-qt.

½ cup pitted Kalamata olives, *divided*
3 28-oz. cans diced tomatoes, undrained
6 Tbsp. tomato paste
1 large onion, chopped
4 cloves garlic, minced
¼ cup snipped fresh Italian parsley
2 Tbsp. capers, drained
2 tsp. dried basil
¼ tsp. cayenne pepper
¼ tsp. salt
¼ tsp. ground black pepper
pasta *or* rice, cooked
Parmesan cheese, shaved, *optional*

1. Chop ¼ cup Kalamata olives. Halve the other ¼ cup and set aside.
2. In 4- to 6-quart slow cooker stir together undrained tomatoes, tomato paste, onions, garlic, chopped olives, snipped parsley, capers, basil, cayenne pepper, salt and ground black pepper.
3. Cover. Cook on low 8-10 hours or high for 4-5 hours.
4. Remove half of sauce, about 5½ cups. Freeze or set aside for additional meals.
5. Turn slow cooker to high. Add halved olives to sauce in cooker. Cover. Cook 5 minutes more or until heated through.
6. Serve over hot cooked pasta or rice. Sprinkle with shaved Parmesan cheese if you wish.

Vegetarian Pasta Sauce

Dorothy Lingerfelt
Stonyford, CA

Makes 14 cups

Prep. Time: 35 minutes
Cooking Time: 5 hours
Ideal slow-cooker size: 6-qt.

3 medium onions, chopped
1 medium green bell pepper, chopped
1 medium red bell pepper, chopped
5 garlic cloves, minced
2 Tbsp. olive oil
3 medium yellow squash, chopped
3 medium tomatoes, chopped
½ tsp. salt
½ tsp. pepper
½ lb. sliced fresh mushrooms
2 28-oz. cans crushed tomatoes
6-oz. can tomato paste
2 2¼-oz. cans sliced ripe olives, drained
¼ cup chopped fresh basil
3 Tbsp. chopped fresh oregano
2 Tbsp. dried rosemary
2 tsp. dried Italian herb seasoning

1. In a skillet, sauté onions, peppers and garlic in oil until softened.
2. Pour sauté into slow cooker. Add rest of ingredients and stir. Cover.
3. Turn on high. After 3 hours, remove lid and turn to low.
4. Simmer, uncovered, 1½-2 hours, or until sauce is thickened.

Mushroom Spaghetti Sauce

Natalia Showalter
Mt. Solon, VA

Rosemary Martin
Bridgewater, VA

Makes 10 servings

Prep. Time: 20 minutes
Cooking Time: 2-4 hours
Ideal slow-cooker size: 6-qt.

⅓ cup olive oil
4 medium onions, chopped
6 garlic cloves, minced
4 large bell peppers, chopped
¾-1 lb. fresh mushrooms, sliced
4 cups tomato sauce
8 cups chunky tomatoes
1½ tsp. salt
¼ cup evaporated cane juice *or* sugar
2 Tbsp. honey
6 bay leaves
1 tsp. garlic powder
1 tsp. dried thyme
1 tsp. dried oregano
1 tsp. dried basil
1 tsp. black pepper

1 tsp. chili powder
½ tsp. ground cumin
½ tsp. cayenne pepper, *or*
to taste
2 Tbsp. dried parsley flakes

1. Place oil in saucepan over medium heat.
2. Sauté onions, garlic, peppers and mushrooms until onions are transparent, 5-7 minutes. Place in slow cooker.
3. Add rest of ingredients.
4. Simmer on low 2-4 hours.
5. Remove bay leaves before serving.

Tip:

Serve over cooked spaghetti with freshly grated Parmesan cheese.

Mushroom Manicotti

Marcia S. Myer
Manheim, PA

Makes 4 servings

Prep. Time: 30 minutes
Cooking/Baking Time: 55 minutes

1 Tbsp. oil
3 cups sliced fresh mushrooms
½ tsp. garlic powder
1 cup nonfat cottage cheese
2 egg whites
½ cup shredded mozzarella cheese
¼ cup shredded Parmesan cheese
½ tsp. dried oregano

8 manicotti shells, cooked
2 cups spaghetti sauce, *divided*

1. Heat oil in skillet. Sauté mushrooms and garlic powder until mushrooms are tender.
2. In a mixing bowl, combine cottage cheese, egg whites, mozzarella cheese, Parmesan cheese, oregano and ½ cup of cooked mushrooms.
3. Spoon ¼ cup of cheese mixture into each manicotti shell.
4. Spread ½ cup spaghetti sauce into lightly greased 2-quart baking dish.
5. Arrange filled shells in dish.
6. Top with remaining sauce and remaining cooked mushrooms.
7. Cover with foil.
8. Bake at 375° for 35 minutes.
9. Remove cover and bake 10 additional minutes.

Vegetarian Spaghetti

Jean M. Butzer
Batavia, NY

Makes 6 servings

Prep. Time: 10 minutes
Cooking Time: 2 hours
Ideal slow-cooker size: 5-qt.

1 cup chopped onions
½ cup chopped celery
1 tsp. garlic powder
3 Tbsp. canola oil
24-oz. jar meatless spaghetti sauce
15-oz. can garbanzo beans, rinsed and drained
14½-oz. can diced tomatoes with garlic and onion, undrained
1 tsp. sugar
½ tsp. salt
½ tsp. dried oregano
1 bay leaf
16-oz. pkg. spaghetti
¼ cup grated Parmesan cheese

1. In large skillet, sauté onions, celery and garlic powder in oil until tender.
2. Pour sauté into slow cooker. Add spaghetti sauce, beans, tomatoes, sugar, salt, oregano and bay leaf. Cover. Cook on low 2 hours.
3. Cook spaghetti according to package directions. Drain.
4. Discard bay leaf from sauce.
5. Top hot spaghetti with tomato sauce and cheese.

Garbanzo-Stuffed Shells

Karen Burkholder
Narvon, PA

Makes 6 servings

Prep. Time: 30 minutes
Cooking/Baking Time: 45 minutes

18 uncooked jumbo pasta
  shells
15-oz. can garbanzo beans,
  rinsed and drained
2 egg whites *or* 1 egg
15 oz. reduced-fat ricotta
  or cottage cheese
½ cup minced fresh parsley
⅓ cup grated Parmesan
  cheese
1 small onion, quartered
1 garlic clove, minced
28-oz. jar meatless
  spaghetti sauce, *divided*
1½ cups shredded
  mozzarella cheese

1. Cook pasta shells according to package directions. Drain. Set aside.
2. Place beans and egg whites in a food processor or blender. Process until smooth.
3. Add ricotta, parsley, Parmesan cheese, onions and garlic to food processor or blender. Cover and process until well-blended.
4. Pour 1¼ cups of spaghetti sauce into lightly greased 9 × 13 baking dish and set aside.
5. Divide bean mixture evenly between cooked shells. Stuff in gently.
6. Lay stuffed shells over spaghetti sauce in pan. Drizzle with remaining sauce.
7. Bake uncovered at 350° for 30 minutes.
8. Sprinkle with mozzarella cheese and bake 5-10 minutes longer, or until cheese is melted and sauce is bubbling.

Go-Along:
• Serve with leafy salad or green beans.

Spinach- and Cheese-Stuffed Shells

Marilyn Mowry
Irving, TX
Lois Hess
Lancaster, PA

Makes 6 servings

Prep. Time: 30 minutes
Cooking/Baking Time: 45 minutes

18 jumbo pasta shells
2 10-oz. pkgs. frozen
  chopped spinach, thawed
15 oz. ricotta cheese
1 cup grated Parmesan
  cheese, *divided*
2 tsp. fennel seeds
2 Tbsp. chopped fresh basil
3 cloves garlic, minced
salt and pepper, to taste
3½ cups spaghetti sauce,
  divided

1. Cook pasta shells according to package directions.
2. Drain and set aside.
3. Squeeze spinach dry. Place in mixing bowl.
4. Add ricotta cheese, ½ cup Parmesan cheese, fennel, basil, salt and pepper. Blend well.
5. Spoon ⅓ cup spaghetti sauce over bottom of lightly greased 9 × 13 baking dish.
6. Fill each pasta shell with spinach mixture.
7. Place on layer of sauce in dish. Spoon remaining sauce over filled shells.
8. Sprinkle with ½ cup Parmesan cheese.
9. Cover loosely with foil.
10. Bake at 350° for 30 minutes.

Variation:
  Omit 1 package of spinach, fennel and garlic. Add 2 cups grated mozzarella cheese, ¼ tsp. ground nutmeg, and 2 beaten eggs. Instead of filling shells, divide mixture between 12 cooked lasagne noodles. Roll up and place seam-side down on sauce. Proceed with step 7.

Lois Hess

Cheese-Stuffed Shells

Doreen Bishop
Harrisburg, PA

Mary Jane Hoober
Shipshewana, IN

Makes 10-12 servings

Prep. Time: 30 minutes
Cooking/Baking Time: 45 minutes

12-oz. box jumbo shells
4 cups ricotta *or* cottage cheese
2 cups shredded mozzarella cheese
¾ cup grated Parmesan cheese
3 eggs
1 Tbsp. chopped fresh parsley
¾ tsp. dried oregano
½ tsp. salt
¼ tsp. pepper
3½ cups spaghetti sauce, *divided*

1. Cook shells according to the box directions (there will 36-40 shells). Drain. Set aside to cool.
2. Combine ricotta, mozzarella cheese, Parmesan cheese, eggs, parsley, oregano, salt and pepper.
3. Fill each shell with about 2 Tbsp. of cheese mixture.
4. Spread a thin layer of spaghetti sauce on bottom of a lightly greased 9 × 13 baking pan.
5. Place shells in a single layer on top of sauce. Top with remainder of spaghetti sauce. Cover with aluminum foil.
6. Bake at 350° for 35 minutes or until hot and bubbly.

Tip:
I find this recipe an easy one to fix in a foil pan (so it doesn't have to be returned) and transported to a friend who is recovering from surgery or who just needs a lift for the day. It is always enjoyed and appreciated.
Mary Jane Hoober

Variations:
1. My mother-in-law taught me two tricks with this recipe:
Filled shells can be frozen individually, then put into a larger freezer bag. Get out as many as you need for a meal and bake.
Frozen shells can be cooked with spaghetti sauce on low for 5-6 hours in a slow cooker.
Doreen Bishop

2. Add 10-oz. package frozen chopped spinach, thawed, and drained to the cheese mixture.
Mary Jane Hoober

Black Bean Lasagna Rolls

Janelle Reitz
Lancaster, PA

Makes 8 servings

Prep. Time: 30 minutes
Cooking/Baking Time: 35 minutes

1 cup shredded Monterey Jack cheese, *or* cheddar cheese
15 oz. ricotta cheese
4½-oz. can chopped green chilies, drained
½ tsp. chili powder
2 Tbsp. chopped fresh cilantro
2 cups cooked black beans, drained
8 uncooked lasagna noodles
15½-oz. jar salsa

1. Combine Monterey Jack cheese, ricotta cheese, chilies, chili powder, cilantro and black beans.
2. Cook lasagna noodles according to package directions.
3. Rinse and spread on waxed paper.
4. Spread bean mixture over one side of each noodle.
5. Roll up noodles, beginning at narrow ends.
6. Place lasagna rolls, seam-side down, in a lightly greased 7 × 11 baking pan.
7. Pour salsa over rolls.
8. Cover. Bake at 350° for 25 minutes.

Follow directions carefully the first time; experiment the second! Karen Sauder, Adamstown, PA

109

Summer Squash Lasagna

Natalia Showalter
Mt. Solon, VA

Shirley Knicely
Bridgewater, VA

Makes 12 servings

Prep. Time: 30 minutes
Cooking/Baking Time: 1 hour
Standing Time: 10-15 minutes

2 medium zucchini squash, thinly sliced
2 medium yellow squash, thinly sliced
8-oz. pkg. portabello mushrooms, sliced
1 large onion, diced
1 red bell pepper, chopped
4 cups chopped tomatoes
6-oz. can tomato paste
1 Tbsp. minced garlic
1 tsp. minced fresh basil
1 Tbsp. brown sugar
½ tsp. salt
½ tsp. dried oregano
½ tsp. pepper
15 oz. ricotta cheese *or* 12 oz. cottage cheese
8-oz. pkg. cream cheese, softened
2 large eggs, beaten
1 Tbsp. minced fresh parsley
6 uncooked whole wheat lasagna noodles
2-4 cups shredded mozzarella cheese
2 cups shredded colby cheese *or* Italian cheese blend, *divided*

1. In a large kettle, place squash, mushrooms, onions and peppers.
2. Fill kettle with enough water to cover vegetables. Cover. Bring to boil and reduce heat. Simmer 5 minutes.
3. Drain. Return vegetables to kettle.
4. Add tomatoes, tomato paste, garlic, basil, sugar, salt, oregano and pepper.
5. Simmer over medium heat for 15-20 minutes.
6. In a bowl, combine ricotta, cream cheese, eggs and parsley. Set aside.
7. Spread half of hot vegetable mixture in bottom of buttered 9 × 13 baking pan.
8. Place 3 uncooked noodles on top of mixture.
9. Spread with half of ricotta mixture.
10. Sprinkle with half of the mozzarella and colby cheeses.
11. Repeat layers.
12. Bake uncovered at 350° for 40 minutes, or until hot and bubbly.
13. Let stand 10-15 minutes before cutting and serving.

Tips:
1. To save time, chop vegetables and grate cheese ahead.
2. This is a wonderful dish to take to summer picnics.

Slow-Cooker Fresh Veggie Lasagna

Deanne Gingrich
Lancaster, PA

Makes 4-6 servings

Prep. Time: 30 minutes
Cooking Time: 4-5 hours
Ideal slow-cooker size: 4-qt.

1½ cups shredded mozzarella cheese
½ cup ricotta cheese
⅓ cup shredded Parmesan cheese
1 egg, lightly beaten
1 tsp. dried oregano
¼ tsp. garlic powder
1 cup marinara sauce, *divided*, plus more for serving
1 medium zucchini, diced, *divided*
4 no-boil lasagna noodles
4 cups baby spinach, *divided*
1 cup mushrooms, sliced, *divided*

1. Combine mozzarella, ricotta, Parmesan, egg, oregano and garlic in a bowl. Set aside.
2. Spread 2 Tbsp. marinara sauce in the slow cooker.

3. Sprinkle with ½ of the diced zucchini and ⅓ of the cheese mixture.

4. Break 2 noodles into large pieces to cover cheese layer.

5. Spread 2 Tbsp. sauce, ½ of the spinach and ½ of the mushrooms over top cheese.

6. Repeat layers, ending with the cheese mixture and sauce. Press layers down firmly.

7. Cover and cook on low 4-5 hours. Allow to rest 20 minutes before cutting and serving. Serve with extra sauce.

Tip:

Don't worry about the order of layers, but end with cheese and sauce.

Spinach Lasagna

Bernice Esau
North Newton, KS

Makes 10 servings

Prep. Time: 30 minutes
Cooking/Baking Time: 75 minutes
Standing Time: 10 minutes

8 oz. uncooked lasagna noodles
2 Tbsp. olive oil
1 small onion, chopped
1 medium garlic clove, minced
16-oz. can tomatoes, undrained
2 6-oz. cans tomato paste
½ cup dry red wine
1 tsp. dried basil
½ tsp. salt
½ tsp. dried oregano
⅛ tsp. pepper
2 16-oz. containers ricotta cheese
3 large eggs, *divided*
20-oz. frozen chopped spinach, thawed and well-drained
16-oz. pkg. part-skim mozzarella cheese, sliced *or* shredded, *divided*
¼ cup grated Parmesan cheese

1. Prepare lasagna noodles as label directs. Drain. Set aside.

2. In 2-quart saucepan cook onion and garlic in hot olive oil over medium heat until tender, stirring occasionally.

3. Stir in tomatoes with liquid, tomato paste, red wine, basil, salt, oregano and pepper. Heat to boiling.

4. Reduce heat to medium-low. Partially cover and cook 15 minutes to blend flavors, stirring occasionally.

5. Meanwhile, in medium bowl, mix ricotta with 2 eggs.

6. In another bowl, mix spinach with 1 egg. Set aside.

7. Evenly spoon ¾ cup tomato sauce into a lightly greased 9 × 13 baking dish. Arrange half the lasagna noodles over sauce, overlapping to fit.

8. Spoon half the ricotta mixture over noodles in baking dish.

9. Top with half the mozzarella, half the spinach mixture and half the remaining tomato sauce.

10. Repeat layers, ending with sauce. Sprinkle with grated Parmesan cheese.

11. Cover dish with foil. Place on rimmed baking sheet.

12. Bake at 350° for 60 minutes, or until heated through and bubbling.

13. Remove from oven and let stand 10 minutes before cutting for easier serving.

Easy Black Bean Lasagna

Kristen Leichty
Ames, IA

Makes 15 servings

Prep. Time: 20-30 minutes
Baking Time: 35 minutes
Standing Time: 15 minutes

15-oz. can black beans, rinsed and drained
28-oz. can crushed tomatoes, undrained
15-oz. can fat-free re-fried beans
¾ cup chopped onions
½ cup chopped green bell peppers
¾ cup medium salsa
1 tsp. chili powder
½ tsp. ground cumin
8 oz. cottage cheese
¼ tsp. garlic powder
2 eggs
salt and black pepper, to taste
10 uncooked lasagna noodles
1½ cups shredded cheddar cheese, *divided*
1½ cups shredded mozzarella cheese, *divided*

1. In a large bowl, combine black beans, tomatoes, re-fried beans, onions, green peppers, salsa, chili powder and cumin. Mix well.
2. In a small bowl, combine cottage cheese, garlic powder, eggs, salt and black pepper.
3. Spread 1 cup of the tomato mixture in bottom of greased 9 × 13 baking dish.
4. Top with half of the uncooked noodles, overlapping slightly. Top with half of the remaining tomato mixture.
5. Spoon cottage cheese mixture over the top and top with half the shredded cheese, then the remaining noodles, tomato mixture and shredded cheese.
6. Cover with a greased sheet of aluminum foil.
7. Bake at 350° for 35 minutes. Uncover and bake additional 10 minutes.
8. Let stand 15 minutes before serving.

Tip:
This can be refrigerated for 1 day before baking. If refrigerated beforehand, add 15 minutes to baking time.

Italian Pasta Pie

Judy Hershberger
Millersburg, OH

Makes 6-8 servings

Prep. Time: 20 minutes
Cooking/Baking Time: 1 hour
Standing Time: 30 minutes

1 loaf Italian country bread, day-old and sliced ¼" thick, *divided*
1 lb. uncooked rigatoni *or* ziti pasta
half stick (4 Tbsp.) butter, *divided*
1 small onion, chopped
½ cup frozen peas
½ tsp. dried basil
pinch fennel seed
28-oz. can tomatoes, chopped
1 cup heavy cream
1 lb. mozzarella cheese, cut into ½" cubes
1 cup grated Parmesan cheese, *divided*, plus more for serving
salt

1. Grease a 10" springform pan or 4-qt. casserole.
2. Line the bottom and sides of the pan with bread slices, fitting them tightly. Reserve several bread slices for the top.
3. In a large pot of boiling, salted water, cook the pasta until al dente.
4. Meanwhile, in a large skillet, melt 2 Tbsp. butter over medium heat. Add the onions and cook until softened, about 5 minutes.
5. Stir in the peas, basil and fennel and cook for 1 minute.

6. Stir in the tomatoes and heavy cream, mixing until combined, and bring to a simmer. Set aside 1 cup of the sauce.

7. Drain the pasta, add to the sauce in the skillet and toss to coat.

8. Stir in the mozzarella and ½ cup Parmesan. Taste for salt.

9. Pour the pasta mixture into the bread-lined pan, pressing down with a wooden spoon.

10. Cover with the remaining bread slices. Sprinkle the remaining Parmesan on top and dot with the remaining 2 Tbsp. butter.

11. Bake uncovered at 375° for 40 minutes until golden and crusty. Loosely cover with foil if necessary to prevent overbrowning.

12. Let cool for about 30 minutes. Unmold the pasta pie.

13. Serve with the reserved tomato sauce and extra Parmesan.

Baked Pasta E Fagioli

Susan Kasting
Jenks, OK

Makes 4 servings

Prep. Time: 25 minutes
Cooking/Baking Time: 40 minutes

8 oz. uncooked mini penne pasta
2 Tbsp. olive oil

---

1 medium onion, chopped
2 cloves garlic, minced
1 rib celery, chopped
28-oz. can petite diced tomatoes, undrained
2 Tbsp. tomato paste
8-oz. can tomato sauce
1 tsp. dried basil
1 tsp. dried oregano
2 15-oz. cans white beans, rinsed and drained
½ cup vegetable broth
10-oz. pkg. chopped frozen spinach, thawed and squeezed dry
½ cup Parmesan cheese, *divided*

1. Cook pasta according to directions and drain.

2. In large saucepan, add oil and sauté onions, garlic and celery until tender.

3. Stir in diced tomatoes, tomato paste, tomato sauce, basil, oregano, beans and broth.

4. Bring to a boil, then simmer uncovered 15 minutes.

5. Mix together pasta, sauce, spinach and ¼ cup Parmesan cheese.

6. Place in lightly greased 3-quart glass baking dish.

7. Top with remaining cheese.

8. Bake uncovered at 350° for 25-35 minutes.

Baked Spaghetti Corn

Shelia Heil
Lancaster, PA

Makes 6-8 servings

Prep. Time: 15 minutes
Standing Time: 1 hour
Cooking Time: 3½ hours
Ideal slow-cooker size: 4-qt.

16-oz. can whole-kernel corn, undrained
16-oz. can cream-style corn
1 stick (½ cup) margarine, *or* butter, cut in chunks
2 Tbsp. chopped onions
1 cup diced cheese of your choice
1 cup uncooked broken spaghetti pieces, ½-1" long

1. Mix corn, margarine, onion, cheese, and spaghetti in 4-quart slow cooker.

2. Let stand 1 hour or longer.

3. Cover. Cook on low for 2-3 hours.

4. Remove cover. Turn to high. Cook an additional 30-35 minutes.

Drop 1 Tbsp. butter in boiling water before adding pasta or rice and it will keep food from clumping.

Leah Hersberger, Dundee, OH

Spaghetti Pizza

Ruth C. Hancock
Earlsboro, OK

Makes 6-8 servings

Prep. Time: 35 minutes
Cooking/Baking Time: 30 minutes
Standing Time: 5 minutes

¼ lb. uncooked thin spaghetti
½ cup milk
1 egg, beaten
2 Tbsp. cooking oil
½ cup chopped bell peppers
½ cup chopped onions
2 cloves garlic, chopped
15-oz. jar pizza sauce
1 Tbsp. Italian herb seasoning
4-oz. can mushrooms, drained
2 cups shredded mozzarella cheese

1. Cook spaghetti as directed on package. Drain.
2. Mix milk and egg in bowl and add cooked spaghetti. Mix well.
3. Spread over bottom of greased 9 × 13 baking pan and set aside.
4. Pour oil into skillet.
5. Add chopped peppers, onions and garlic. Stir and cook over medium heat until onions are clear.
6. Add pizza sauce and Italian seasoning. Simmer 10 minutes.
7. Spoon mixture over spaghetti mixture in pan.

Sprinkle evenly with mushrooms and cheese.
8. Bake 20 minutes uncovered at 350°.
9. Let stand 5 minutes before serving. Cut in squares to serve.

Sauerkraut Casserole

Arnola Siggelkow
Fairbank, IA

Bonnie Whaling
Clearfield, PA

Makes 4-6 servings

Prep. Time: 10 minutes
Cooking Time: 1-2 hours
Ideal slow-cooker size: 4-qt.

8-oz. pkg. noodles, cooked and drained
28-oz. can sauerkraut, drained
10¾-oz. can cream of mushroom soup
1 small onion, diced
2 Tbsp. butter, melted

1. Mix ingredients together in buttered slow cooker.
2. Cover and cook on high for 1½-2 hours.

To make your own cream of mushroom soup, please turn to pages 260-261.

Crumb-Topped Macaroni and Cheese

Carolyn Spohn
Shawnee, KS

Makes 8 servings

Prep. Time: 20 minutes
Cooking/Baking Time: 60 minutes

---

2 cups uncooked elbow macaroni
2 cups shredded sharp cheddar cheese
½ cup milk
3 Tbsp. butter, *divided*
1 egg, beaten
¾ cup sour cream
2 tsp. chopped onions, *optional*
1 cup cottage cheese
¼ cup dry bread crumbs

1. Cook macaroni according to package directions. Drain.
2. Mix macaroni, cheddar cheese, milk, 1 Tbsp. butter, egg, sour cream, onions, and cottage cheese.
3. Place in lightly greased 2-quart casserole.
4. Melt remaining 2 Tbsp. butter in skillet. Add bread crumbs. Stir and cook until crumbs are browned.
5. Sprinkle browned crumbs over casserole. Cover.
6. Bake at 350° for 30-40 minutes.
7. Uncover. Bake an additional 10 minutes to crisp up crumbs.

Go-Along:
• Crusty bread and green vegetable.

Zesty Macaroni and Cheese

Rosemarie Fitzgerald
Gibsonia, PA

Makes 4 servings

Prep. Time: 15 minutes
Cooking/Baking Time: 40 minutes

¼ lb. uncooked whole wheat elbow macaroni
1¼ cups hot milk
½ lb. cheddar cheese, shredded
6 Tbsp. dry bread crumbs *or* ¾ cup fresh crumbs
2 Tbsp. chopped fresh parsley
1 medium onion, chopped
1 green bell pepper, finely chopped
3-4 scallions, chopped, *or* more to taste
1 tsp. salt, *optional*
2 eggs, beaten
sprinkle of paprika

1. Cook macaroni until tender-firm. Drain and set aside.
2. In a large bowl, pour hot milk over cheese and crumbs.
3. Add parsley, onions, peppers, scallions and salt if you wish.
4. Stir in eggs and cooked macaroni.

5. Pour into lightly greased 3-quart casserole dish. Sprinkle with paprika.
6. Bake at 350° for 30 minutes, or until the top of the casserole is firm and golden brown.

Veggie Macaroni and Cheese

Dorothy Lingerfelt
Stonyford, CA

Makes 12 servings

Prep. Time: 30 minutes
Cooking/Baking Time: 30 minutes

1½ cups uncooked elbow macaroni
3 cups chopped broccoli
2 cups chopped cauliflower
3 carrots, thinly sliced
2 celery ribs, sliced
1 medium onion, diced
1 Tbsp. butter
¼ cup all-purpose flour
1 cup milk
3 cups shredded cheddar cheese
1 Tbsp. Dijon mustard
¼ tsp. pepper
¼ tsp. paprika

1. In a large pot of salted boiling water, cook macaroni 1-2 minutes.
2. Add broccoli, cauliflower, carrots, and celery and cook 5 more minutes.
3. Drain, but reserve 1 cup cooking water.
4. Pour vegetables and macaroni into lightly greased 9 × 13 baking pan. Set aside.
5. Meanwhile, in a saucepan, sauté onions in butter until tender.
6. Sprinkle with flour and stir until blended.
7. Over low heat, gradually stir in milk and reserved 1 cup cooking water.
8. Bring to boil over medium heat, stirring. Cook and stir for 2 minutes, or until thickened.
9. Turn off heat. Stir in cheese, mustard and pepper.
10. Pour sauce over macaroni mixture in pan. Stir to coat. Spread evenly in pan.
11. Sprinkle with paprika.
12. Bake uncovered at 350° for 15-20 minutes or until heated through.

Horseradish Macaroni and Cheese

Joan Terwilliger
Lebanon, PA

Makes 6 servings

Prep. Time: 20 minutes
Cooking/Baking Time: 40 minutes
Standing Time: 5 minutes

2¼ cups uncooked elbow macaroni
2 Tbsp. butter
¼ cup, plus 2 Tbsp., all-purpose flour
3 cups milk
1 Tbsp., plus 1 tsp., horseradish mustard
1 cup shredded cheddar *or* horseradish cheese, *divided*
½ cup shredded Swiss cheese
½ tsp. salt
pepper, to taste

1. Cook macaroni according to package directions. Drain. Set aside.
2. Melt butter in a large saucepan. Stir in flour until smooth.
3. Gradually add one cup of milk, whisking until smooth. Gradually add remaining milk, stirring constantly, and cook 10 minutes until thickened and smooth.
4. Remove from heat and stir in mustard, ½ cup cheddar cheese, Swiss cheese, salt and pepper. Stir until cheese melts.
5. Stir in cooked macaroni.
6. Put macaroni mixture in greased 7 × 11 baking dish. Sprinkle remaining cheddar on top.
7. Cover. Bake at 350° for 20 minutes.
8. Let stand, covered, for 5 minutes before serving.

Cheesy Slow-Cooker Macaroni

Michele Ruvola
Vestal, NY

Makes 6 servings

Prep. Time: 10 minutes
Cooking Time: 4-5 hours
Ideal slow-cooker size: 4-qt.

2 eggs
12-oz. can evaporated milk
1½ cups fresh milk
1 tsp. salt
½ tsp. pepper
½ lb. uncooked elbow macaroni
4 cups shredded cheddar cheese, *divided*

1. Grease inside of slow cooker with cooking spray or oil.
2. Beat eggs, evaporated milk, fresh milk, salt, and pepper in large bowl.
3. Mix in uncooked macaroni and 3 cups cheese.
4. Transfer mixture to slow cooker. Sprinkle remaining 1 cup cheese on top.
5. Cover. Cook on low 4-5 hours.

Slow-Cooker Macaroni and Cheese

Ruthie Schiefer
Vassar, MI
Natalie Butikofer
Richland Center, WI
Lena Hartzler
Belleville, PA
Doris Hoover
Penn Yan, NY

Makes 6-8 servings

Prep. Time: 15 minutes
Cooking Time: 1½-2 hours
Ideal slow-cooker size: 4-qt.

2 cups uncooked elbow macaroni
2 cups grated cheese
1½ tsp. salt
½ tsp. pepper
1½ cups evaporated milk
1 cup water

1. Mix ingredients. Place in greased 4-quart slow cooker.
2. Cook on high for 1½-2 hours or on low for 3-4 hours.

Variations:
1. Sauté the uncooked macaroni with 3 Tbsp. butter before placing in slow cooker.
Doris Hoover
Natalie Butikofer

2. You can use 4 cups cooked macaroni.
Lena Hartzler

Ricotta Gnocchi with Spinach Sauce

Judy Hershberger
Millersburg, OH

Makes 4 servings

Prep. Time: 35 minutes
Cooking/Baking Time: 40 minutes

2 Tbsp. butter
1 large onion, halved and thinly sliced
1½ cups, plus 1 Tbsp., all-purpose flour, *divided*
2 cups half-and-half
½ tsp. ground nutmeg
5 oz. baby spinach, rinsed and drained
15-oz. container ricotta cheese
3 large eggs
1 cup grated Parmesan cheese, *divided*
1 tsp. salt
½ tsp. pepper

1. Bring a large Dutch oven of salted water to a boil.

2. Meanwhile, in a large, ovenproof skillet, melt the butter over medium-low heat.

3. Add the onions and cook, stirring occasionally, until softened and golden, 10-12 minutes.

4. Add 1 Tbsp. flour and cook, stirring constantly, 2 minutes.

5. Add the half-and-half and simmer, stirring constantly, until slightly thickened, about 3 minutes.

6. Add the nutmeg. Season with salt and pepper.

7. Working in batches, stir in the spinach and cook over low heat until just wilted, 3 to 5 minutes. Cover and set sauce aside.

8. In a medium bowl, lightly beat together the ricotta, eggs, ½ cup Parmesan, the remaining 1½ cups flour, and salt and pepper. Stir until well combined.

9. Using a soup spoon, drop 10 to 12 generous spoonfuls of dough (about half the dough) into the boiling water. Cook for 3 minutes. Gently stir the gnocchi to keep from clumping together.

10. When the gnocchi rise to the surface, cook for about 3 minutes more.

11. Using a slotted spoon, transfer gnocchi to a towel-lined plate to drain. Repeat process with the remaining dough.

12. Add the cooked gnocchi to the spinach sauce and stir gently to coat.

13. Transfer mixture to a baking dish. Sprinkle with the remaining ½ cup Parmesan.

14. Broil until golden, about 3 minutes.

Linguini with Sun-Dried Tomato Pesto

Monica Wagner
Quarryville, PA

Makes 6 servings

Prep. Time: 20 minutes
Cooking Time: 15 minutes
Standing Time: 20-30 minutes

1 cup sun-dried tomatoes, drained
2 cups boiling water
1 Tbsp. olive oil *or* oil from the sun-dried tomatoes
½ cup grated Parmesan, plus more for garnish
2 medium cloves garlic
1½ cups fresh basil, tightly packed
½ tsp. salt
¼ tsp. red pepper flakes
12 oz. uncooked linguini

1. Place tomatoes in heat-proof bowl and cover with boiling water. Let sit until softened, 20-30 minutes.

2. Drain tomatoes, but reserve 1 cup tomato liquid.

3. Place tomatoes, 1 cup tomato liquid, oil, ½ cup Parmesan, garlic, basil, salt and red pepper flakes into food processor. Process until smooth.

4. Meanwhile, cook pasta as directed on package. Reserve 1 cup cooking water. Drain pasta.

5. In serving bowl toss pasta with pesto and ¾-1 cup cooking liquid, depending on desired consistency.

6. Sprinkle with some grated Parmesan.

Israeli Couscous with Vegetables

Barbara Hershey
Lititz, PA

Makes 2-4 servings

Prep. Time: 10 minutes
Cooking Time: 10 minutes
Standing Time: 30 minutes

1½ cups vegetable stock
dash of hot red pepper flakes
1 cup uncooked Israeli couscous
2 Tbsp. butter
1 tsp. dried dill weed
1 clove garlic, minced
5 mushrooms, sliced thinly
⅓ cup chopped scallions, tops included
½ cup coarsely shredded carrots

1. In medium saucepan, combine stock and red pepper.
2. Bring to boil and add couscous.
3. Turn heat off. Cover. Let stand 30 minutes.
4. In large skillet melt butter and add dill, garlic, mushrooms, scallions and carrots.
5. Sauté 5-6 minutes or until soft.
6. Add couscous to vegetable mixture. Stir gently. Serve immediately.

Pasta with Beans and Greens

Vegan

Carol Sherwood
Batavia, NY

Makes 4-6 servings

Prep. Time: 35 minutes
Cooking Time: 20 minutes

6 oz. uncooked pasta of your choice
cooking spray
6 cloves garlic, coarsely chopped
4 cups (6-oz. bag) fresh spinach, coarsely chopped
15-oz. can cannellini beans, rinsed and drained
2 cups vegetable broth

1. Cook pasta until barely al dente. Drain, reserving ½-1 cup pasta water.
2. Spray large saucepan with cooking oil.
3. Add garlic and cook over medium heat 3 minutes, until softened. Do not let garlic burn or it will taste bitter.
4. Add spinach and beans. Cook and stir 2-3 minutes or until spinach is wilted.
5. Add broth and bring to a boil.
6. Reduce heat and simmer 3 minutes.
7. Add cooked pasta and cook 2 minutes, stirring occasionally. If you want a soupier sauce, stir in some of all of the reserved pasta water.
8. Let stand 5 minutes before serving.

Tip:
I save some pasta water in case extra liquid is needed.

Whole Wheat Pasta with Vegetables and Lemon Broth

Rebekah Zehr
Lowville, NY

Makes 6 servings

Prep. Time: 30 minutes
Cooking Time: 20 minutes

½ cup sun-dried tomatoes
13-oz. box uncooked whole wheat pasta, your choice of shapes
1 cup shelled frozen edamame
10 oz. asparagus, trimmed and cut into 2½" pieces.
2 Tbsp. extra-virgin olive oil, plus more for drizzling
2 shallots *or* one small onion, finely chopped
4 cloves garlic, minced
½ tsp. red pepper flakes, *or* to taste
⅓ cup dry white wine
1 lb. kale, chopped, *or* 2 cups baby arugula
3 Tbsp. lemon juice
1 tsp. salt, *or* to taste
¼-½ cup freshly grated Parmesan cheese, *or* ricotta salata
freshly ground pepper, to taste

118

1. Soak the sun-dried tomatoes in hot water until they are soft, about 10 minutes. Drain and cut into pieces.

2. Bring a large pot of water to a boil. Add pasta. Cook al dente following package instructions, adding edamame and asparagus for the last 3-4 minutes. Drain, reserving 1 cup of cooking liquid.

3. Heat the olive oil in a large skillet. Add shallot or onion and sauté about 3-4 minutes.

4. Add garlic and cook 1 more minute.

5. Add red pepper flakes and sun-dried tomatoes. Cook and stir 1 minute.

6. Add wine. Bring mixture to a boil.

7. Add kale or arugula. Cook uncovered until liquid is reduced

8. Add lemon juice, salt, and 1 cup reserved pasta-cooking liquid.

9. Place drained pasta and vegetables in big serving dish. Pour tomato-kale mixture with its broth and seasonings over pasta.

10. Top with cheese. Drizzle with olive oil and sprinkle with more salt if you wish and freshly ground pepper.

Mushroom Goulash

Shelia Heil
Lancaster, PA

Makes 4 servings

Prep. Time: 15 minutes
Cooking Time: 1-2 hours
Ideal slow-cooker size: 4-qt.

2 4-oz. cans mushrooms
1½ cups uncooked macaroni
1 quart tomato juice
½ tsp. salt
½ tsp. dried thyme, *optional*
1 cup chopped onions
hot sauce, to taste, *optional*

1. Combine ingredients in slow cooker.

2. Cook on high 1-2 hours until macaroni is tender.

Tips:
1. Mixed vegetable juice may be used in place of tomato juice.

2. If recipe mixture seems dry, add water by the tablespoon.

Homey Mac Dinner

Vonnie Oyer
Hubbard, OR

Makes 6-8 servings

Prep. Time: 5 minutes
Cooking Time: 20 minutes

¾ cup uncooked macaroni
15½-oz. can kidney beans, rinsed and drained
1 cup cooked garbanzo beans, drained
15-oz. can vegetable broth
1 tsp. dried basil
1 tsp. vegetarian Worcestershire sauce
14½-oz. can diced tomatoes
1 clove garlic, minced
¼ cup chopped onions
¼ cup chopped green bell peppers
grated Parmesan cheese, *optional*

1. Combine all ingredients except cheese in a saucepan. Cover.

2. Cook over medium low heat until macaroni is tender, approximately 20 minutes.

3. Serve with Parmesan cheese if you wish.

Tip:
This is a great dinner to make when camping. All the cans can fit into a big pot. Cook on a camp stove or over a fire.

Asparagus Fettuccine

Melva Baumer
Mifflintown, PA

Makes 2 servings

Prep. Time: 15 minutes
Cooking Time: 15-20 minutes

4 oz. uncooked fettuccine
½ lb. fresh asparagus, cut in 1" pieces
¼ cup chopped onions
1 garlic clove, minced
1 Tbsp. butter
2 oz. cream cheese, cubed
¼ cup milk
¼ cup shredded Parmesan cheese
1½ tsp. lemon juice
¼ tsp. salt
⅛ tsp. pepper

1. Cook fettuccine according to package directions. Drain.

2. In large skillet, sauté asparagus, onions, and garlic in butter until tender.

3. Add cream cheese, milk, Parmesan cheese, lemon juice, salt and pepper.

4. Cook and stir over medium heat for 5 minutes or until cheese is melted and sauce is blended.

5. Toss fettuccine with asparagus mixture.

Linguini with Mushroom Sauce

Abigail Thompson
Millersville, PA

Makes 6 servings

Prep. Time: 10-15 minutes
Cooking Time: 25 minutes

16-oz. box linguini
¼ cup extra-virgin olive oil
¼ cup diced shallots
1 clove garlic, minced
1 lb. portabello mushrooms, sliced
¼ tsp. dried thyme
¼ tsp. ground nutmeg
salt and pepper, to taste
½ cup dry Marsala wine
1 cup vegetable stock
½ cup heavy cream
¼ cup grated Parmesan cheese
snipped fresh chives, for garnish

1. Bring a large pot of water to a boil. Once it comes to a roiling boil add a little salt and the pasta. Cook according to package directions. When done, drain and set aside.

2. While pasta is cooking, heat up a large sauté pan over medium heat and add the oil. Cook shallots and garlic for 3-4 minutes.

3. Add the mushrooms and cook until softened, about 5 minutes. Add thyme, nutmeg, salt and pepper.

4. Add the wine. Simmer over medium heat until half the liquid remains.

5. Add the vegetable stock. Stir. Simmer again until half the liquid remains.

6. Add cream and cook over low heat 5 minutes. Once thickened add the cheese and additional salt and pepper, if needed.

7. Toss the sauce with the cooked linguini and top with chives. Serve immediately.

Tip:
When you cook the mushrooms, do not add any salt or pepper until they are brown and tender. Otherwise they will not brown.

Go-Along:
• Sautéed asparagus or cooked peas.

Broccoli Alfredo

Rosanne Hankins
Stevensville, MD

Makes 2-4 servings

Prep. Time: 5 minutes
Cooking Time: 25 minutes

10¾-oz. can cream of
  mushroom soup
1 cup whole milk
½ cup grated Parmesan
  cheese
¼ cup extra-virgin olive oil
2 Tbsp. Old Bay seafood
  seasoning
10-oz. bag frozen broccoli
12 oz. whole wheat pasta,
  cooked al dente, and
  drained

1. In a saucepan, blend
soup and milk and heat for
5-8 minutes.
2. Stir in cheese, oil,
seasoning, and broccoli.
3. Simmer 10 minutes.
4. Toss with cooked pasta.

Go-Along:
• Garlic bread.

*To make your own
cream of mushroom
soup, please turn to
pages 260-261.*

Creamy Spinach Ravioli

Jessalyn Wantland
Arlington, WA

Makes 4-6 servings

Prep. Time: 5 minutes
Cooking Time: 20 minutes

2 9-oz. pkgs. refrigerated
  cheese ravioli
½ cup chive-and-onion
  cream-cheese spread
1 cup milk
¼ cup, plus 2 Tbsp., grated
  Parmesan cheese, *divided*
4 cups baby spinach leaves
2 Tbsp. chopped fresh dill
1 tsp. grated lemon peel
6-8 cherry tomatoes,
  quartered

1. Cook pasta according to
package. Drain. Set aside and
keep warm.
2. Place cream cheese
spread in large skillet. Add
milk. Cook on medium heat
2-4 minutes or until cream
cheese is melted and mixture
is well blended, stirring
frequently.
3. Add ¼ cup Parmesan
cheese, spinach, dill and
lemon peel. Mix well.
4. Add pasta to cream
cheese sauce. Toss to coat.
5. Serve topped with
tomatoes and remaining 2
Tbsp. Parmesan cheese.

Garlicky Tomatoes and Olives with Spaghetti

Lucille Amos
Greensboro, NC

Makes 6 servings

Prep. Time: 15 minutes
Cooking Time: 15 minutes

13¼ oz. uncooked
  spaghetti
3 Tbsp. olive oil, *divided*
2 cloves garlic, chopped
2 medium tomatoes,
  coarsely chopped
¾ cup pitted Kalamata
  olives, chopped
½ cup chopped fresh
  parsley
salt and pepper, to taste
½ cup crumbled feta
  cheese

1. Cook spaghetti in salted
water according to package
directions.
2. Drain and return spa-
ghetti to pan to stay warm.
3. Heat 2 Tbsp. oil in
separate skillet.
4. Add garlic and cook 1
minute.
5. Add tomatoes and olives
and cook 3 minutes or until
tomatoes are hot.
6. Add mixture to cooked
spaghetti.
7. Stir in remaining oil and
parsley.
8. Add salt and pepper. Mix
well.
9. Sprinkle each serving
with feta cheese.

Farfalle with Tomatoes, Garlic and Basil

Jennifer Hoke Bentivogli
Gordonville, PA

Makes 4 servings

Prep. Time: 5 minutes
Cooking Time: 15 minutes

16 oz. uncooked farfalle
  (bow-tie pasta)
1 Tbsp. olive oil
2 cloves garlic, crushed
2 large tomatoes, diced
½ teaspoon red pepper
  flakes, *optional*
1 Tbsp. balsamic vinegar
¼ cup finely chopped fresh
  basil, plus whole leaves
  for garnish
1 Tbsp. finely chopped
  fresh parsley
freshly grated Parmesan
  cheese, for garnish, *optional*

1. Cook farfalle according to package directions.
2. Meanwhile, heat oil in a sauté pan over medium-high heat. Add garlic and sauté for 1 minute.
3. Add tomatoes and red pepper flakes (if using) and cook for another minute.
4. Stir in balsamic vinegar. Cook uncovered for 3-4 minutes.
5. Remove from heat before the tomatoes lose their shape. Stir in chopped basil and parsley.
6. Drain and rinse farfalle. Toss farfalle with sauce in a serving bowl.
7. Garnish with whole basil leaves and Parmesan.

Rigatoni with Grilled Vegetables

Ronda Burgoon
Collingswood, NJ

Makes 4-6 servings

Prep. Time: 35 minutes
Cooking Time: 25 minutes

1 lb. uncooked rigatoni
1 baby Italian eggplant,
  sliced in ½"-thick discs
1 zucchini, halved
  lengthwise
1 medium onion, sliced
1 red bell pepper,
  quartered, cored and
  seeds removed
3 Tbsp. olive oil, *divided*
salt and freshly ground
  pepper
1 Tbsp. chopped garlic
1 tsp. Italian herb seasoning
1 tsp. crushed red pepper

1. Bring a large pot of water to a boil over high heat. Add pasta and cook until al dente, about 8 minutes. Drain and set aside.
2. Lightly brush all sides of eggplant, zucchini, onion, and bell pepper pieces with 1 Tbsp. olive oil.
3. Place on the grill or grill pan, season with salt and pepper and grill for 3 minutes per side.
4. Transfer to a cutting board. Cut all the vegetables into bite-size pieces.
5. Add remaining 2 Tbsp. olive oil to a large skillet over medium heat.
6. Add garlic, Italian herb seasoning and red pepper flakes and sauté for 1 minute.
7. Stir in the pasta, add the chopped vegetables and toss. Serve.

Variation:
  If you don't want to grill, just cut the vegetables into bite-size pieces, sauté and remove after cooking.

The cooking time on an outdoor grill may vary slightly from a grill pan, so adjust a recipe accordingly.
  Monica Wagner, Quarryville, PA

Garlic Pasta

MaryAnn Beachy
Dover, OH

Makes 4 servings

Prep. Time: 15 minutes
Cooking Time: 15 minutes

1 whole garlic bulb
⅓ cup olive *or* vegetable oil
½ cup chopped fresh
  parsley
¼ cup fresh oregano,
  chopped *or* 4 tsp. dried
  oregano
1 tsp. salt
¼ tsp. pepper
1 lb. pasta of your choice,
  cooked and drained
½ cup grated Parmesan
  cheese

1. Separate garlic into
cloves and remove papery
skins. Chop fine.

2. In a large skillet over low
heat, sauté garlic in oil until
golden brown. Remove from
heat.

3. Add parsley, oregano,
salt and pepper.

4. Toss with cooked pasta.
Stir in cheese. Serve immediately.

Parsley Pasta

Sara Neilon
Lyndonville, VT

Makes 6 servings

Prep. Time: 15 minutes
Cooking Time: 15 minutes

1 lb. uncooked pasta of
  your choice
1-1½ cups finely chopped
  fresh parsley (about 1
  large bunch)
½ cup olive oil, *divided*
1 medium onion, halved,
  and sliced in very thin
  wedges
1 red bell pepper, sliced in
  ribs
2-3 garlic cloves, minced
½ tsp. salt
¼ tsp. pepper
juice of half a lemon,
  optional
1 cup finely shredded
  Parmesan cheese, *divided*
chopped Kalamata olives,
  optional

1. Cook pasta according to
directions. Drain. Set aside,
keeping it warm.

2. Place 2 Tbsp. of olive oil
in skillet. Sauté onions and
red peppers until translucent
and lightly browned.

3. Add 1 tsp. olive oil and
mix garlic into onion mixture.
Cook until lightly fragrant,
about 1 minute.

4. In separate bowl, mix
remaining olive oil with
parsley, salt and pepper. Add
lemon juice, if you wish.

5. Mix pasta in warm bowl
with parsley and oil. Add ⅔
cup Parmesan cheese.

6. Place pasta onto plates
and serve onion/red pepper
mixture on top.

7. Sprinkle remaining
cheese on top of pasta.
Serve warm.

Tips:

1. Food processors make
quick work of chopping
parsley. Roasted red peppers
in jars also can work. Just
heat them lightly with onions.

2. Parsley is fine just tossed
with hot pasta: it stays fresher
and has more nutrients. Do
not overcook the parsley!

Rigatoni with Roasted Cauliflower and Asiago

Bob Coffey
New Windsor, NY

Makes 4 servings

Prep. Time: 15 minutes
Cooking/Baking Time: 30 minutes

3 Tbsp. olive oil, plus more for serving
1 head cauliflower, cut into bite-sized pieces
6 cloves garlic, peeled and diced
1 lb. uncooked rigatoni
1 cup bread crumbs
½ cup chopped curly parsley
½ cup shredded asiago cheese

1. Combine oil, cauliflower and garlic on a baking sheet. Roast for 20 minutes in a 400° oven, stirring occasionally.
2. Cook rigatoni according to package instructions. Drain.
3. After 20 minutes, add bread crumbs and parsley to cauliflower, stirring to coat and adding more olive oil as needed.
4. Continue roasting until bread crumbs begin to brown, about 10 more minutes.
5. Place cooked pasta on individual plates, sprinkle with asiago cheese to taste and a swirl of good-quality olive oil. Top with cauliflower mixture.

Tip:
Making sure that the cauliflower is evenly coated with bread crumbs and parsley will ensure that each bite is fantastic!

Go-Along:
• A simple spinach salad is perfect to eat alongside this dish.

Basil Vegetable Pasta

Kim Patrick
Norwood, PA

Makes 4 servings

Prep. Time: 30 minutes
Cooking Time: 30 minutes

2 cups uncooked whole wheat *or* rice pasta, any shape
2 medium zucchini
¼ cup pine nuts
1 Tbsp. olive oil
½ tsp. ground cumin
2 cups shelled edamame, cooked
¼ cup packed fresh basil
1 tsp. salt

1. Cook pasta according to package directions. Reserve ¾ cup of cooking liquid before draining.
2. Slice zucchini lengthwise into thick, long ribbons and set aside.
3. Heat olive oil in skillet, over medium heat, and toast pine nuts for 4-5 minutes.
4. Remove pine nuts to a plate.
5. In same skillet, heat cumin 1 minute until fragrant.
6. Add zucchini and ¼ cup reserved pasta liquid.
7. Simmer zucchini 3-5 minutes and set aside.
8. Blend pine nuts, edamame, basil, salt and remaining ½ cup of pasta water in food processor until smooth paste forms.
9. Place pasta and zucchini in bowl and toss with edamame paste. Serve immediately.

Edamame are soybeans, usually found in the freezer section of large supermarkets and health food stores. They are a complete protein containing all the essential amino acids. They can be served hot or cold in salads, casseroles, and soups.

Rebekah Zehr, Lowville, NY

Five-Ingredient Pasta Toss

Jennifer Freed
Harrisonburg, VA

Makes 4 servings

Prep. Time: 8 minutes
Cooking Time: 12 minutes

¼ cup extra-virgin olive oil
2 cloves garlic, crushed
8 oz. uncooked farfalle (bow-tie) pasta
15-oz. can small white beans, rinsed and drained
2 large tomatoes, chopped, with juice
¼ cup fresh basil leaves, chopped

1. Combine the olive oil and garlic in a small bowl. Set aside.
2. Cook the pasta according to package directions. Drain and set aside.
3. Place the pasta, beans, tomatoes, basil and 2 Tbsp. of the garlic olive oil in a large bowl. Toss gently until combined.
4. Serve the remaining olive oil at the table to drizzle over individual servings.

Tip:
This isn't a hot pasta dish so it's perfect for summer.

Go-Along:
• Serve with crusty bread to soak up the sauce and any leftover garlic oil.

Summer Pasta

Dawn Alderfer
Oley, PA
Peg Zannotti
Tulsa, OK

Makes 4 servings

Prep. Time: 5 minutes
Cooking Time: 15 minutes

7-oz. pkg. uncooked angel-hair pasta *or* thin spaghetti
2 small zucchini, cut into ¼" pieces
2-4 garlic cloves, minced
3 Tbsp. olive *or* vegetable oil
1½ cups chopped tomatoes
¼ cup minced fresh parsley
2 tsp. dried oregano *or* Italian herb seasoning
pinch red pepper flakes

1. Cook pasta according to package directions. Drain. Set aside, keeping it warm.
2. Meanwhile, in a large skillet, sauté zucchini and garlic in oil until zucchini is crisp-tender.
3. Add the tomatoes, parsley, oregano and red pepper flakes. Heat through.
4. Top pasta with zucchini mixture and serve.

Variation:
Prick a medium eggplant all over. Bake at 450° for 40 minutes, turning occasionally. Cool. Peel. Dice pulp. Add to skillet with tomatoes and proceed with step 3.
Peg Zannotti

It is important to not overcook pasta. Begin testing pasta for doneness at about ¾ of the lowest cooking time recommended on the package. Check each minute after that, making sure to stop cooking as soon as pasta is cooked but still firm.

Bob Coffey, New Windsor, NY

Sesame Noodles

Judy Hershberger
Millersburg, OH

Makes 4-6 servings

Prep. Time: 15 minutes
Cooking Time: 10 minutes

1 lb. uncooked capellini
(angel-hair pasta)
¼ cup low-sodium soy
sauce
2 Tbsp. tahini
2 Tbsp. toasted sesame oil
2 pinches cayenne pepper,
or to taste
2 cloves garlic, minced
1" piece gingerroot, peeled
and grated
3 scallions, sliced thinly on
an angle
1 large carrot, grated
toasted sesame seeds, to
garnish
crushed red pepper flakes,
to garnish

1. Cook pasta according
to package directions, just
until al dente. Drain and
run it under cold water until
noodles are chilled. Drain
well.
2. Meanwhile, combine
soy sauce, tahini, sesame oil,
cayenne, garlic and gingerroot
in a bowl. Whisk until dressing is smooth.
3. Pour noodles into a big
bowl with the dressing and
combine until noodles are
evenly coated with a thin
layer of sauce.
4. Add scallions and car-
rots. Mix well.

5. Pour noodles into a serving dish. Garnish with sesame
seeds and a few crushed red
pepper flakes.

Tip:
Serves 4 for a lunch or light
supper with fruit or a vegetable salad. Serves up to 8 as
a side-dish or party offering.

Pasta with Szechwan Peanut Dressing

Jenny Kempf
Bedminster, PA

Deanne Gingrich
Lancaster, PA

Makes 4 servings

Prep. Time: 15 minutes
Cooking Time: 15 minutes

½ cup peanut butter
¼ cup vegetable stock *or*
water
2 Tbsp. soy sauce
2 Tbsp. rice vinegar *or*
lemon juice
2 Tbsp. sunflower *or*
vegetable oil
1-2 cloves garlic, minced
½ tsp. dried crushed red
pepper, *or* to taste
8 oz. uncooked linguini *or*
soba noodles
2 cups broccoli florets *or*
sugar snap peas
2 cups cherry tomatoes *or*
chopped red bell peppers
chopped scallions, for
garnish

1. Whisk peanut butter and
stock until smooth
2. Stir in soy sauce, vinegar,
oil, garlic and red pepper.
3. Cook pasta in boiling
water. Add broccoli for the
last 2-3 minutes.
4. Drain pasta and broccoli.
Place in serving dish.
5. Pour sauce over pasta.
Add cherry tomatoes. Toss to
coat well.
6. Garnish with chopped
scallions.

Variation:
Add 1 tsp. dried basil to
sauce. Reduce peanut butter
to 2 Tbsp. and omit stock.
Cook sauce until boiling
before pouring over pasta.
Deanne Gingrich

Beans and Legumes

Cornbread-Topped Frijoles

Andy Wagner
Quarryville, PA

Makes 8-10 servings

Prep. Time: 20 minutes
Cooking Time: 3 hours
Ideal slow-cooker size: 5-qt.

1 medium onion, chopped
1 medium green bell
  pepper, chopped
1 Tbsp. canola oil
2 garlic cloves, minced
16-oz. can kidney beans,
  rinsed and drained
15-oz. can pinto beans,
  rinsed and drained
14½-oz. can diced
  tomatoes, undrained
8-oz. can tomato sauce
1 tsp. chili powder
½ tsp. pepper
¼ tsp. hot pepper sauce

Cornbread Topping:
  ½ cup all-purpose flour
  ½ cup yellow cornmeal
  2 tsp. sugar
  1 tsp. baking powder
  ¼ tsp. salt
  1 egg, lightly beaten
  ¾ cup skim milk
  ½ cup cream-style corn
  1½ Tbsp. canola oil

1. In a large skillet, sauté onions and green pepper in oil until tender. Add garlic; cook 1 minute longer. Transfer to a greased 5-quart slow cooker.

2. Stir in the beans, tomatoes, tomato sauce, chili powder, pepper and pepper sauce.

3. Cover and cook on high for 1 hour.

4. Meanwhile, in a large bowl, combine the flour, cornmeal, sugar, baking powder and salt.

5. In another bowl, combine the egg, milk, corn and oil. Add to dry ingredients and mix well. Spoon evenly over bean mixture.

6. Cover and cook on high 2 hours longer or until a toothpick inserted near the center of cornbread comes out clean.

I cook beans in large quantities, and after draining, lay them on cookie sheets in the freezer to individually quick-freeze. Stored in a gallon resealable bag in the freezer, it is easy to measure out the exact quantity of beans that you need whenever you want.

Roanna Martin, Morgantown, WV

Mexican Rice and Beans

Helen Schlabach
Winesburg, OH

Makes 6-8 servings

Prep. Time: 10 minutes
Cooking Time: 2-3 hours
Ideal slow-cooker size: 4-qt.

15-oz. can black beans, rinsed and drained
10 oz. package frozen whole-kernel corn
1 cup uncooked long-grain white *or* brown rice
16-oz. jar thick and chunky mild salsa
1½ cups vegetable juice cocktail
½ tsp. ground cumin
½ tsp. dried oregano
salt and pepper, to taste
¾ cup shredded cheddar cheese

1. Combine ingredients, except cheese, in greased 4-quart slow cooker.
2. Cook, covered, on high for 2-3 hours, stirring once.
3. When rice is tender, sprinkle casserole with cheese. Serve when cheese is melted.

Southwestern Rice and Beans

Marcia Kauffman
Waynesboro, VA

Makes 4-6 servings

Prep. Time: 30 minutes
Cooking Time: 3-4 hours
Ideal slow-cooker size: 4-qt.

1 medium green bell pepper, diced
1 medium onion, chopped
2 garlic cloves, minced
1 Tbsp. olive oil
14½-oz. can reduced-sodium vegetable broth
½ cup water
1 cup uncooked long-grain rice
½ tsp. ground cumin
⅛ tsp. ground turmeric
15-oz. can black beans, rinsed and drained
10-oz. can diced tomatoes and green chilies, undrained
10-oz. pkg. frozen corn, thawed

1. Combine everything in 4-quart slow cooker.
2. Cook on low, covered, until rice is done, 3-4 hours.

"Re-fried" Beans

Gail Shetler
Goshen, IN

Makes 8-10 servings

Prep. Time: 10 minutes
Cooking Time: 7-8 hours
Ideal slow-cooker size: 5-qt.

1 medium onion, peeled and halved
3 cups dry pinto beans, washed and sorted
½ fresh jalapeño pepper, seeded and chopped *or* 1 Tbsp. canned jalapeño, chopped
2-3 cloves garlic, minced
3 tsp. salt
1 tsp. black pepper
¼ tsp. ground cumin
9 cups water

1. Combine ingredients in slow cooker. Cover.
2. Cook on high for 7-8 hours.
3. Drain off a few cups of liquid. Save the liquid.
4. Mash the beans in the cooker with a potato masher. Add some of the saved liquid to reach the consistency you like.

Tips:
1. These beans will absorb more of the liquid as they cool. You might want to save the reserved liquid to reheat the leftovers.
2. These "re-fried" beans freeze very well.
3. Depending on the hotness of your peppers you may want to use more or less.

Spray the slow cooker with cooking spray to ease clean-up.
Renae Hege, Midville, GA

Meatless Mexican Lasagna

Mabel Shirk
Mt. Crawford, VA

Makes 6 servings

Prep. Time: 15 minutes
Cooking Time: 2 hours
Ideal slow-cooker size: 5-qt.

3 cups frozen corn, thawed
15-oz. can black beans, rinsed and drained
14½-oz. can diced tomatoes with basil, oregano and garlic, undrained
4-oz. can chopped green chilies
3 green onions, sliced
2 tsp. dried oregano
2 tsp. ground cumin
4 6" corn tortillas, *divided*
1½ cups shredded Mexican cheese blend, *divided*
6 Tbsp. sour cream

1. In a bowl, combine, corn, beans, tomatoes, green chilies, onions, oregano, and cumin.
2. Grease 5-quart slow cooker. Place 2 tortillas in crock.
3. Spread tortillas with half of the bean mixture.
4. Sprinkle with cheese.
5. Repeat the layers.
6. Cook on high 2 hours or until heated through.
7. Let stand for 5 minutes.
8. Garnish with sour cream.

White Beans with Sun-Dried Tomatoes

Steven Lantz
Denver, CO

Makes 4-6 servings

Prep. Time: 15 minutes
Cooking Time: 4-6 hours
Ideal slow-cooker size: 4-qt.

2 cups uncooked Great Northern beans, rinsed
2 cloves garlic, minced or pressed
1 onion, chopped
6 cups water
½ tsp. salt
⅛ tsp. pepper
1 cup chopped sun-dried tomatoes in oil, drained
2-oz. can sliced black olives, drained
½ cup grated Parmesan cheese

1. Mix all ingredients except tomatoes, olives and cheese in 4- or 5-quart slow cooker.
2. Cover and cook on high 4-6 hours or until beans are tender.
3. Mash some of the beans to thicken mixture. Stir in tomatoes and olives. Cook 20-30 minutes more, until thoroughly heated.
4. Ladle into bowls and sprinkle each with Parmesan cheese.

Savory Red Beans and Rice

Arianne Hochstetler
Goshen, IN

Makes 10-12 servings

Prep. Time: 15 minutes
Cooking Time: 5½ hours
Ideal slow-cooker size: 6-qt.

2 cups (16-oz. pkg.) dry kidney beans, sorted and rinsed
1 large green bell pepper, chopped
1 cup chopped onions
2 garlic cloves, minced
7 cups water
1½ tsp. salt
¼ tsp. pepper
2 cups uncooked instant rice
hot pepper sauce
salsa
sour cream

1. In a 4- or 6-quart slow cooker, combine beans, peppers, onions, garlic, water, salt and pepper.
2. Cover. Cook on high 4-5 hours.
3. Stir instant rice into bean mixture.
4. Cover. Cook on high an additional 15-20 minutes. Serve with hot pepper sauce, salsa and sour cream.

Tip:
I like to sauté the peppers, onions, and garlic before adding them to the slow cooker.

Go-Along:
• Corn muffins.

Black-Bean Sweet-Potato Skillet with Greens and Raspberries

Roanna Martin
Morgantown, WV

Makes 4 servings

Prep. Time: 10-15 minutes
Cooking Time: 20 minutes

2 sweet potatoes, peeled
  or unpeeled, cut in ½"
  cubes, about 3 cups
1 clove garlic, minced
1 tsp. olive oil
1½ cups cooked black beans,
  rinsed and drained
2 cups greens (kale, chard,
  spinach), roughly chopped
¼ cup water
⅔ cup raspberries, fresh *or*
  frozen
1 tsp. ground ginger
salt and pepper, to taste
apple cider vinegar, to taste

1. Place sweet potato cubes
in large skillet over medium
high heat, along with minced
garlic and oil.
2. Sauté for about 10 minutes, or until sweet potatoes
are nearly soft.
3. Add black beans. Cook
another 3 minutes or so.
4. Stir in chopped greens.
Toss in skillet along with ¼
cup water. Cover and cook
until greens are wilted, about
2-3 minutes.
5. Add raspberries, ground
ginger, salt and pepper to
taste. Stir through gently.

6. Top with a drizzle of
vinegar. Serve immediately.

Tip:
    This is a fantastically
simple one-pan meal: starch,
protein, vegetable, and even
fruit, all in the same dish!

Black Beans and Rice

Elaine Good
Lititz, PA

Makes 8 servings
Cooking Time: 23 minutes

1½ cups sliced carrots
vegetable oil
1 cup diced green bell
  peppers
1 cup diced onions
1 cup sliced celery
½ cup picante sauce
½ cup water
1 Tbsp. chili powder
1 tsp. ground cumin
1 tsp. onion powder
½ tsp. salt, *optional*
½ tsp. black pepper
⅛ tsp. red cayenne pepper
3 16-oz. cans black beans,
  rinsed and drained
3 cups hot cooked rice

1. In large kettle, sauté
carrots in vegetable oil for 3
minutes.
2. Add peppers, onions,
celery, picante sauce and water.
3. Add chili powder, cumin,
onion powder, black pepper
and red cayenne pepper.

4. Cover. Cook for 15
minutes.
5. Add beans.
6. Cook 5 more minutes.
7. Serve over hot rice.

Tip:
    Adjust spices to your pref-
erences.

Quinoa and Black Beans

Gloria Frey
Lebanon, PA

Makes 6-8 servings

Prep. Time: 15 minutes
Cooking Time: 2-3 hours
Ideal slow-cooker size: 4-qt.

1 tsp. vegetable oil
1 onion, chopped
3 cloves garlic, chopped
1 red bell pepper, chopped
¾ cup uncooked quinoa
1½ cups vegetable broth
1 tsp. ground cumin
¼ tsp. cayenne pepper
salt and pepper, to taste
1 cup frozen corn
2 15-oz. cans black beans,
  rinsed and drained
½ cup fresh cilantro,
  chopped

1. Sauté onions, garlic
and red bell pepper in oil in
skillet until softened. Place in
4-quart slow cooker.
2. Mix quinoa into it and
cover with vegetable broth.
3. Season with cumin,
cayenne pepper, salt and
pepper.

4. Cover. Cook on low 1-2 hours until quinoa is done.

5. Stir frozen corn, beans and cilantro into cooker and continue to cook on low 30-60 minutes until heated through.

Go-Along:
• Tossed salad, red beets, or red-beet eggs.

Delicious Baked Beans

Esther Bowman
Gladys, VA

Makes 6-8 servings

Prep. Time: 10 minutes
Cooking Time: 3-5 hours
Ideal slow-cooker size: 3½-qt.

28-oz. can baked beans
1 small onion, diced
1 small green bell pepper, diced
½ cup ketchup
1 Tbsp. vegetarian Worcestershire sauce
3 Tbsp. brown sugar
1 tsp. prepared mustard
2 tsp. vinegar
¼ tsp. salt

1. Mix baked beans, onions, pepper, ketchup, Worcestershire sauce, sugar, mustard, vinegar and salt together in slow cooker.

2. Cover. Cook on low 3-5 hours.

Go-Along:
• Egg salad sandwiches and tossed salad.

Country Baked Beans

Susan Guarneri
Three Lakes, WI

Makes 6 servings

Prep. Time: 20 minutes
Cooking Time: 4-6 hours
Ideal slow-cooker size: 6-qt.

1 onion, chopped
2 Tbsp. olive oil
1 apple, peeled and shredded
1 carrot, shredded
1½ cups tomato paste
1 tsp. dry mustard
3 Tbsp. cider vinegar
½ tsp. ground cumin
¼ tsp. ground nutmeg
½ tsp. black pepper
1 tsp. salt
1 Tbsp. brown sugar
1 cup vegetable broth
4-5 cups cooked beans

1. In a skillet, sauté onions in oil until golden brown.

2. Put the onions in a 4- or 5-quart slow cooker. Add rest of ingredients to slow cooker. Cover.

3. Cook on low for 4-6 hours.

Variation:
You can use canned kidney, pinto or navy beans for this recipe. A variety looks attractive!

Go-Along:
• Cheesy cornbread with vegetable crudites and dip.

Baked Beans

Julia Burkholder
Robesonia, PA
Carol Eveleth
Wellman, IA

Makes 4-6 servings

Prep. Time: 15 minutes
Cooking Time: 10-11 hours
Standing Time: 8 hours or overnight
Ideal slow-cooker size: 5-qt.

1 lb. dried navy beans
8 cups water
1 tsp. salt
2 tsp. prepared mustard
⅓ cup molasses
1 small onion, finely chopped
¼ tsp. pepper
1 cup tomato juice
¼ cup ketchup
½-1 cup brown sugar
1 Tbsp. Worcestershire sauce, *optional*
¼ tsp. liquid smoke, *optional*

1. In slow cooker, soak beans in water overnight.

2. Cook on low for 6-8 hours, until beans are almost soft. Remove some water if needed, so that water level is below surface of beans.

3. Add rest of ingredients. Stir well.

4. Replace lid. Cook on low an additional 2-3 hours.

Baked Beans For A Crowd

Susan Henne
Fleetwood, PA

Makes 24-30 servings

Prep. Time: 20-30 minutes
Cooking/Baking Time: 3-3¾
hours total
Chilling Time: 4-12 hours
Standing Time: 12 hours

3 lbs. dried Great Northern
  beans
12 quarts water, *divided*
3 26-oz. cans tomato soup
2 12-oz. jars molasses
2 cups barbeque sauce
2 cups light brown sugar
½ cup Dijon mustard
2 5-oz. pkgs. vegetarian
  bacon

1. Soak beans in 6 quarts of water for 8 to 12 hours. Drain and rinse the beans.

2. Put beans in a large stockpot and add 6 quarts of fresh water.

3. Bring beans to a boil and reduce heat to simmer. Cook, covered, for 60-70 minutes or until beans are tender but not over-cooked.

4. While the beans are cooking, mix the tomato soup, molasses, barbeque sauce, brown sugar and mustard together in a large bowl.

5. Drain beans and rinse with cold water. Return beans to pot.

6. Pour sauce over cooked beans and mix well. Refrigerate for several hours or overnight to marinate the beans.

7. Pour beans into appropriately-sized baking pans to a depth of less than 5".

8. Top pan(s) with vegetarian bacon strips.

9. Bake, uncovered, at 350° for 2-2½ hours.

Tips:

1. This recipe is great for picnics, church dinners, family gatherings, or any other large function.

2. Beans can be kept warm for long periods of time in slow cookers set on low.

3. For the molasses in this recipe, I use one bottle of Brer Rabbit Full-Flavor Molasses and one bottle of Grandma's Original Molasses.

4. For the barbeque sauce in this recipe, I use one cup of sweet and spicy BBQ sauce and one cup of honey BBQ sauce.

Variation:

To save time, canned Great Northern beans can be substituted for the dry beans. Start at step 4.

BBQ Kidney Beans

Laura Wenger
Manheim, PA

Makes 6 servings

Prep. Time: 10 minutes
Baking Time: 45 minutes

3 15-oz. cans kidney beans,
  drained
1 medium onion, chopped
2 tsp. prepared mustard
½ cup ketchup
2 Tbsp. vinegar
1 tsp. salt
3 Tbsp. brown sugar

1. Put kidney beans and onions in a greased 1½-qt. baking dish.

2. In a separate bowl, combine mustard, ketchup, vinegar, salt and sugar. Stir into the kidney beans and onions.

3. Bake, covered, at 375° for 45 minutes.

Variation:

Vary the beans if you wish, according to what you have on hand.

Go-Along:

• This makes a great topping for baked potatoes.

Soybean Loaf

Linda Gebo
Plattsburgh, NY

Makes 4-6 servings

Prep. Time: 20-25 minutes
Cooking Time: 4 hours
Standing Time: 8 hours or
* overnight*
Ideal slow-cooker size: 4-qt.

1 cup dry soybeans, soaked
  overnight
1 tsp. dried parsley
¼ tsp. garlic powder
½ tsp. salt, *optional*
¼ tsp. paprika
½ tsp. crumbled dried sage
1½ cups water
3 ribs celery, diced
1 onion, diced
2 pimientos, diced, *optional*
2.2-oz. can pitted olives,
  sliced in half
1 Tbsp. soy sauce
1 Tbsp. nutritional yeast
  flakes
½ cup bread crumbs

1. In blender, purée
soybeans, parsley, garlic
powder, salt, paprika and sage
in water.
2. Pour into bowl. Add
celery, onions, pimientos if
you wish, olives, soy sauce,
nutritional yeast flakes and
bread crumbs. Place in
4-quart slow cooker.
3. Cook covered on high for
4 hours.

Variation:
  You may bake this dish,
covered, in the oven at 350°
for 2 hours.

Black-Eyed Peas with Turnip Greens

Teri Sparks
Glen Burnie, MD

Makes 4 servings

Prep. Time: 15 minutes
Cooking Time: 30 minutes

1 turnip *or* medium potato,
  peeled and diced
¼ cup diced onion, *optional*
16 oz. vegetable broth
15-oz. can black-eyed peas,
  rinsed and drained
6 cups torn fresh turnip
  greens
salt and pepper, to taste

1. In a large saucepan,
simmer turnip or potato, with
onion if you wish, in broth
until fork-tender.
2. Add beans. Cover and
cook 5 minutes more.
3. Add turnip greens and
cook until wilted.
4. Salt and pepper, to taste.

Variation:
  This recipe is very versatile. Use what you have!
Any bean can be used
in place of peas. Kale or
spinach can replace the
turnip greens.

Go-Along:
• Serve over brown rice
or with cornbread.

Lima Beans with Sour Cream

Mary B. Sensenig
New Holland, PA

Makes 2-3 servings

Prep. Time: 5 minutes
Cooking Time: 10 minutes

2 cups cooked lima beans
2 tsp. grated onions
2 Tbsp. chopped pimento
1 Tbsp. butter
½ cup sour cream
salt and pepper, to taste

1. Combine ingredients in
saucepan.
2. Heat to simmering
over medium heat, about 10
minutes. Serve.

Haystacks

Lucille, **Rosalie** and **Dawn Martin**
Barnett, MO

Makes 4-6 servings

Prep. Time: 30 minutes
Cooking Time: 15 minutes

Cheese Sauce:
  2 cups milk
  ½ tsp. salt
  ½ tsp. ground cumin
  ¼ tsp. garlic powder
  ¼-½ tsp. cayenne pepper, to taste
  ¼ cup brown rice flour *or* **all-purpose flour**
  2 Tbsp. milk
  1-2 cups grated sharp cheddar cheese

tortilla chips
brown rice, cooked
black beans, cooked and drained
lettuce, chopped
tomatoes, chopped
onions, chopped
black olives

1. Heat milk, salt, cumin, garlic powder and cayenne pepper in a medium saucepan.
2. In a small bowl, stir together flour and 2 Tbsp. milk until smooth.
3. Add to hot milk mixture, stirring with a whisk to avoid lumps. Continue cooking over medium heat, and stirring continually, until mixture smooths and thickens.
4. Reduce heat.
5. Add cheese and stir until melted. Set aside.

6. Invite those eating to make layers on their plates of chips, rice and black beans.
7. Top with lettuce, tomatoes, onions and black olives.
8. Spoon cheese sauce over top. Eat immediately.

Curry Pilaf with Garbanzos

Janice Sams
Lancaster, PA

Makes 4 servings

Prep. Time: 20 minutes
Cooking Time: 15-20 minutes

1 cup vegetable stock
1 cup uncooked whole wheat couscous
1 Tbsp. olive oil
2 cloves garlic, minced
½ red onion, chopped
1 Tbsp. curry powder
1 Tbsp. water
½ red bell pepper, minced
1 cup cooked garbanzo beans
1 cup green peas
½ cup chopped fresh parsley
1 tsp. tamari *or* **soy sauce**
freshly ground pepper, to taste
chopped cilantro, *optional*
hot sauce, *optional*

1. In a pot with a tight-fitting lid, bring stock to boil. Pour in couscous. Cover. Let sit for 5 minutes. Fluff with a fork, and set aside.
2. Heat the oil in a large wok or skillet and cook the garlic and onions over high heat for 3 to 4 minutes, stirring frequently.
3. When the onions begin to look translucent, stir in the curry powder. Continue to cook for 1 minute.
4. Add water, bell pepper and garbanzo beans. Stir well, lower heat to medium, and cook for 5 minutes, stirring frequently.
5. Stir in peas, parsley and cooked couscous. Mix well over low heat for a couple of minutes until the couscous is hot.
6. Remove from heat. Season with tamari, freshly ground pepper, cilantro and hot sauce as you wish.

Go-Along:
• This is a quick Indian-style dish. Serve with warmed, buttered naan or pita bread, and a cool salad of thinly sliced cucumbers in yogurt, spiced with a little curry powder.

Be adventuresome with your spice cupboard. After a while you will know what tastes suit you and your family best.
Gail Shetler, Goshen IN

Chickpea Curry

Esther Nafziger
La Junta, CO

Makes 8-10 servings

Prep. Time: 25 minutes
Cooking Time: 30 minutes

2 Tbsp. oil
1 onion, diced
3 cloves garlic, minced
1-3 cups julienned carrots
1 tsp. ground ginger
1 small yellow squash, sliced
1 small zucchini, sliced
1 cup broccoli florets
½ cup frozen peas
2 Tbsp. Thai curry powder
    or paste
1 tsp. salt
1 large tomato, diced
15-oz. can coconut milk
2 15-oz. cans chickpeas
    (garbanzo beans), rinsed
    and drained
3 hot chilies, *optional*
hot rice

1. Sauté the onions, garlic and ginger together in the oil in the bottom of a large pan.
2. When the onion is just starting to get soft, add the carrots.
3. A few minutes later, add yellow squash, zucchini, broccoli and peas. Sauté until soft.
4. Add the curry powder and salt. Stir for about one minute or until the curry powder is fragrant. Add tomato and stir.
5. Add the coconut milk and chickpeas. Bring to a gentle simmer.
6. Add chilies, if using. Simmer for 5-10 minutes or until flavors are blended and vegetables are done.
7. Serve over rice.

Variation:
Cut carrots in slices if you don't have time to julienne. Also, use what vegetables you have on hand or what's in season.

Vegetable Enchiladas

Judy Houser
Hershey, PA

Makes 6-8 servings

Prep. Time: 15-20 minutes
Cooking/Baking Time: 20 minutes

2 Tbsp. vegetable oil
1 medium onion, chopped
1 medium green bell
    pepper, chopped
¼ cup chopped fresh
    cilantro
2 cups frozen corn, thawed
2 cups grated zucchini
2 cups cooked pinto beans,
    lightly mashed
1 tsp. ground cumin
1 tsp. chili powder
freshly ground black
    pepper and salt, to taste
12 corn tortillas
2 cups salsa
2 cups grated extra-sharp
    cheddar
1 cup grated Monterey Jack
    cheese

1. In a large skillet, heat the vegetable oil.
2. Sauté the onion and green pepper until just tender.
3. Add cilantro, corn and zucchini and cook about 5 minutes.
4. Add beans, cumin, chili powder, salt and pepper to vegetables. Stir thoroughly.
5. Heat tortillas in microwave for 1 minute to soften.
6. Place ⅓ cup filling in each tortilla. Roll up tortillas and place in greased 9 × 13 baking dish.
7. Pour salsa evenly over top. Sprinkle evenly with both cheeses.
8. Bake at 350° until sauce bubbles and cheese melts, about 20 minutes.

Tips:
1. I freeze grated zucchini in three-cup amounts, so that after thawing and draining, I still have a nice amount for this casserole.
2. If you like more heat add some hot sauce or use "chili hot beans."

Go-Along:
• Green salad.

Red Beans and Corn in Pitas

Leanne Yoder
Tucson, AZ

Makes 2 servings

Prep. Time: 15 minutes
Cooking Time: 25 minutes

2 Tbsp. olive oil
1 small onion, chopped
1 small green bell pepper, chopped
¾ cup canned tomatoes
1 cup corn kernels
1 cup cooked red kidney beans, drained
salt and freshly ground black pepper
2 pita breads

1. Heat the oil in a frying pan. Add the onions and bell pepper. Cover and cook gently for 10 minutes, or until the vegetables are getting tender.
2. Add the tomatoes with their juice. Mash up the tomatoes. Cook 10 more minutes.
3. Add corn and kidney beans. Cook gently for a few more minutes until hot. Season with salt and pepper.
4. Warm the pita breads under the broiler or in a toaster.
5. Cut them lengthwise in half. Gently open up each half, fill with the red-bean mixture and serve at once.

Variation:
This is also good over corn chips with chopped lettuce, cheese and sour cream.

Tasty Lentil Tacos

Betty Detweiler
Centreville, MI

Makes 6 servings

Prep. Time: 10 minutes
Cooking Time: 35 minutes

1 cup finely chopped onions
1 garlic clove, minced
1 tsp. canola oil
1 cup dried lentils, rinsed
1 Tbsp. chili powder
2 tsp. ground cumin
1 tsp. dried oregano
2½ cups vegetable broth
1 cup salsa
12 taco shells
1½ cups shredded lettuce, *divided*
1 cup chopped tomatoes, *divided*
1½ cups grated cheddar cheese, *divided*
6 Tbsp. sour cream, *divided*

1. In a large nonstick skillet, over medium-high heat, sauté the onions and garlic in oil until tender.
2. Add the lentils, chili powder, cumin and oregano. Cook and stir for 1 minute.
3. Add the broth and bring to a boil. Reduce the heat. Cover and simmer for 25-30 minutes or until the lentils are tender.
4. Uncover and cook for 6-8 minutes or until the mixture is thickened.
5. Mash lentils slightly. Stir in salsa.
6. Spoon about ¼ cup of the lentil mixture into each taco shell.

7. Top with lettuce, tomatoes, cheese and ½ Tbsp. sour cream.

Triple-Decker Tortilla

Vonnie Oyer
Hubbard, OR

Makes 6 servings

Prep. Time: 5-10 minutes
Baking Time: 15 minutes

2 cups cooked pinto beans, *divided*
1 cup salsa, *divided*
4 small flour tortillas
½ cup corn
½ cup shredded Monterey Jack *or* cheddar cheese, *divided*
avocado, sliced, *optional*
cilantro, chopped, *optional*

1. Drain, rinse and slightly mash pinto beans.
2. Grease a 9" pie plate.
3. Layer in this order: ¼ cup salsa, a tortilla, 1 cup beans, 1 tortilla, ½ cup corn, ¼ cup cheese, ¼ cup salsa, 1 tortilla, the remaining 1 cup beans, the last tortilla, and ½ cup salsa.
4. Cover with foil.
5. Bake at 450° for 12 minutes. Uncover and sprinkle with remaining ¼ cup cheese. Bake 3 minutes more.
6. Top with avocado and cilantro if you wish. Cut in wedges to serve.

Vegetarian Burrito or Taco Filling

Stephen Zoss
Metamora, IL

Makes 6 servings

Prep. Time: 15 minutes
Cooking Time: 20 minutes

2 Tbsp. olive *or* vegetable oil
1 medium onion, diced
1 red *or* green bell pepper, diced
2 cloves garlic, minced
1 jalapeño *or* small Anaheim chili pepper, diced, *optional*
2 Tbsp. taco-seasoning mix
2 tsp. ground cumin
15-oz. can black beans, rinsed and drained
15-oz. can diced tomatoes
1 medium sweet potato, peeled or unpeeled, diced
salt and pepper, to taste
tortillas

1. Heat the oil in a 10" or 12" skillet.
2. Cook the onions, bell pepper, garlic, and the chili if you wish, in the hot oil until softened.
3. Add the taco seasoning and ground cumin to the skillet. Stir to blend the spices with the onions and peppers.
4. Add the beans to the skillet.
5. Drain the tomatoes and reserve the liquid. Add the tomatoes to the skillet.
6. Add the sweet potatoes to the skillet.

7. Cook until the sweet potatoes are tender. Use the reserved tomato juice as needed to keep the vegetables moist and to prevent burning.
8. Salt and pepper to taste.
9. Roll filling up in warmed tortillas.

Go-Along:
• Any salsa, guacamole, sour cream and shredded Jack cheese.

Black Bean Burritos

Esther Nafziger
La Junta, CO
Vonnie Oyer
Hubbard, OR

Makes 6 servings

Prep. Time: 15 minutes
Standing Time: 2 hours
Cooking Time: 3 hours

1 lb. dry black beans
water
hot chilies, diced, to taste
½ cup chopped onion
⅓ cup salsa
3 cloves garlic, minced
1 tsp. dried oregano
1 tsp. chili powder
2 tsp. salt
½ tsp. black pepper
6-8 flour tortillas
lettuce, chopped
chopped tomatoes *or* salsa
1½ cups shredded cheese

1. Sort and rinse dry beans. Place in saucepan and cover with water. Cover pan.
2. Bring to a boil. Boil 2 minutes. Let sit, covered, for two hours. Drain and rinse. Return beans to cooking pot.
3. Add 3½ cups water and cook 1½ hours.
4. Add hot chilies, onions, salsa, garlic, oregano, chili powder, salt and pepper.
5. Simmer about 1 hour more or until beans are tender.
6. Spoon filling down the center of tortillas. Top with lettuce, tomatoes and cheese. Fold top and bottom of tortilla over filling and roll up to serve.

Tip:
Leftovers freeze well.

Variation:
Use 1 tsp. cumin instead of oregano. Easily make these into enchiladas by placing filled, rolled-up tortillas in greased baking pan. Sprinkle with cheese. Bake at 350° until warmed through, 8-10 minutes.

Vonnie Oyer

Go-Along:
• Spanish rice.

Salsa Lentils

Karen Stanley
Amherst, VA

Makes 4 servings

Prep. Time: 15 minutes
Cooking Time: 30 minutes

2 cups dry green lentils
4 cups water
2 Tbsp. oil
2 cups chopped onions
¼ cup chopped garlic
2 cups salsa
1-3 jalapeño peppers,
   seeded and chopped
1.25-oz. pkg. taco
   seasoning
½ tsp. salt
1 cup chopped fresh
   cilantro

1. In a saucepan, combine lentils with water. Bring to a boil, and simmer for 10 minutes.
2. In a skillet, fry onions and garlic over medium heat in oil until tender.
3. Add sauté to lentils. Add salsa, peppers, taco seasoning and salt. Stir.
4. Bring to a boil. Cover and simmer for 15 minutes on medium-low heat.
5. Add cilantro.

Tip:
   Serve over rice or with corn chips. Top with grated cheese, sour cream, chopped lettuce and diced tomatoes.

Lentils Swiss-Style

Lenore Waltner
North Newton, KS
Zoë Rohrer
Lancaster, PA
Teresa Martin
Strasburg, PA
Natalia Showalter
Mt. Solon, VA
Marcia S. Myer
Manheim, PA

Makes 6 servings

Prep. Time: 15 minutes
Cooking Time: 4-6 hours
Ideal slow-cooker size: 5-qt.

1¾ cups dry lentils, rinsed
2 cups water
1 whole bay leaf
2 tsp. salt
¼ tsp. pepper
½ tsp. dried marjoram
½ tsp. dried sage
½ tsp. dried thyme
2 large onions, chopped
2-4 cloves garlic, minced
2 cups canned tomatoes
2 large carrots, sliced
   ⅛"-thick
½ cup thinly sliced celery
1 green bell pepper,
   chopped, *optional*
¼ cup chopped fresh
   parsley
¼ cup sherry
3 cups shredded Swiss
   cheese

1. Combine lentils, water, bay leaf, salt, pepper, marjoram, sage, thyme, onions, garlic, tomatoes, carrots, celery, and green peppers if you wish, in slow cooker.
2. Cover. Cook on low 4-6 hours until lentils are soft. Remove bay leaf.
3. Stir in parsley and sherry. Sprinkle with cheese. When melted, serve.

Variations:
1. Use sharp cheddar cheese instead of Swiss.

Lenore Waltner

2. Use colby cheese and add ⅛ tsp. cayenne with the herbs.

Natalia Showalter

3. Add 4 oz. frozen spinach. Cook the lentils, water, onion, garlic, tomatoes and herbs alone for 2 hours on low before adding the other ingredients. Cook additional 2 hours on low before adding cheese on top.

Zoë Rohrer

4. To make this in the oven, combine lentils, water, herbs, onion, garlic and tomatoes in greased 9 × 13 baking dish. Cover. Bake 30 minutes at 375°. Add carrots, celery, and pepper and stir. Cover again and bake 40 more minutes. Stir in parsley. Sprinkle with cheese.

Teresa Martin

Go-Along:
• Fresh fruit and rolls.

Herbed Rice and Lentil Casserole

Peg Zannotti
Tulsa, OK

Makes 4-6 servings

Prep. Time: 15 minutes
Cooking Time: 4-6 hours
Ideal slow-cooker size: 4-qt.

2⅔ cups vegetable broth, *or* water
¾ cup dried green lentils
¾ cup chopped onions
½ cup uncooked brown rice
¼ cup dry white wine *or* water
½ tsp. dried basil
¼ tsp. dried oregano
¼ tsp. dried thyme
⅛ tsp. garlic powder
½ cup shredded Italian-mix cheese *or* cheddar cheese

1. Combine broth, lentils, onions, rice, wine, basil, oregano, thyme, garlic powder and cheese.
2. Pour into 3-quart slow cooker.
3. Cover.
4. Cook on low 4-6 hours, stirring once, until rice and lentils are tender.

Variations:
1. May add salt if you wish.
2. Top casserole with Italian-flavored panko bread crumbs and cook, uncovered, for 5-10 minutes before serving.
3. Use low-fat cheese in place of regular cheese.

Go-Along:
• Vegetarian burgers.

Lentils and Barley

Linda Yoder
Fresno, OH

Makes 3-4 servings

Prep. Time: 30 minutes
Cooking Time: 40 minutes

3 cups vegetable broth, *divided*
1 cup uncooked lentils, rinsed and drained
3 Tbsp. butter *or* olive oil
½ cup uncooked barley, rolled *or* pearl
1 large onion, chopped
1 clove garlic, minced
¼ lb. fresh mushrooms, cleaned and sliced, *optional*
1 Tbsp. vegetarian Worcestershire sauce
1 tsp. dried thyme
⅛ tsp. ground pepper
salt, to taste
2 Tbsp. chopped fresh parsley
extra-virgin olive oil for garnish

1. Heat 1½ cups vegetable broth almost to a boil and add lentils. Remove from heat, cover and set aside.
2. Heat 2-3-qt. Dutch oven or skillet. Add butter, barley, onion, garlic and, if desired, mushrooms. Cook over medium-low heat, stirring occasionally, until barley is browned and the vegetables are sautéed, about 5-6 minutes.
3. Add remaining 1½ cups vegetable broth, Worcestershire sauce, thyme and pepper and bring to a boil.
4. Add lentil-broth mixture to barley mixture. Combine.
5. Bring mixture back to boil. Reduce heat and cover tightly. Simmer 30-35 minutes, until barley and lentils are soft and most of liquid has been absorbed. If mixture becomes dry before barley and lentils are soft, add up to ½ cup additional broth or water. If needed, add salt to taste.
6. Add parsley and gently mix in. Drizzle olive oil atop for garnish and serve.

Tips:
1. If using pearl barley, you may need to increase the cooking time.
2. The olive oil garnish is the frosting on the cake for this recipe. Unless you happen not to like olive oil, be sure to include this.

Go-Along:
• Cooked green beans with dill, steamed Swiss chard with vinegar, candied sweet potatoes, and salad.

Slow-Cooked Lentils and Rice

Reba Rhodes
Bridgewater, VA

Makes 4-6 servings

Prep. Time: 20 minutes
Cooking Time: 2-3 hours
Ideal slow-cooker size: 3-qt.

1 cup dry green lentils
½ cup uncooked long-grain rice
3 tsp. dried minced onions
2 tsp. olive oil
3 cups boiling water
1 tsp. instant vegetable bouillon
2 tsp. vegetarian Worcestershire sauce
½ tsp. salt
½ tsp. pepper
1 tsp. dried thyme
10-oz. can sliced mushrooms, drained, *or* 1½ cups sliced fresh mushrooms

1. Rinse lentils.
2. Combine lentils, rice, onions, and olive oil in skillet. Sauté until rice grains begin to turn golden.
3. Pour into a 3-quart slow cooker.
4. Combine boiling water with bouillon, stirring until bouillon dissolves.
5. Add to cooker along with Worcestershire sauce, salt, pepper, thyme and mushrooms. Stir gently.
6. Cover. Cook on low 2-3 hours until lentils and rice are tender.

Go-Along:
• Serve warm with chopped lettuce and ranch dressing.

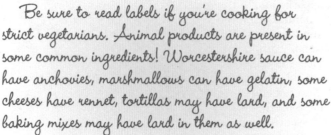

Be sure to read labels if you're cooking for strict vegetarians. Animal products are present in some common ingredients! Worcestershire sauce can have anchovies, marshmallows can have gelatin, some cheeses have rennet, tortillas may have lard, and some baking mixes may have lard in them as well.

Margaret High, Lancaster, PA

Curried Lentils

Susan Kasting
Jenks, OK

Makes 4-6 servings

Prep. Time: 20 minutes
Cooking Time: 5-6 hours
Ideal slow-cooker size: 4-qt.

2 Tbsp. olive oil
1 large onion, chopped
5 tsp. curry powder
¼ tsp. cayenne pepper
5½ cups vegetable broth
1 lb. dry lentils, rinsed
15-oz. can garbanzo beans, rinsed and drained
10-oz. pkg. frozen chopped spinach, thawed and squeezed dry
plain yogurt, for garnish

1. Heat oil in skillet and sauté onions until golden.
2. Add curry and pepper. Stir.
3. Combine broth, lentils and sautéed vegetables in 4-quart slow cooker.
4. Cover. Cook on low for 3-5 hours until lentils are almost tender.
5. Add beans and spinach. Stir.
6. Cover and cook an additional 30-45 minutes.
7. Add garnish of yogurt on individual servings.

Go-Along:
• Pita bread.

Hot Sweet Potato
Fries, page 162

Spiced Applesauce, page 192 >>

Banana Millet Muffins, page 59

Potato-Crust
Quiche, page 41

Feta Bruschetta, page 17

Carrot and Sweet
Potato Puree, page 94

Flourless Brownies,
page 259

Veggie Macaroni
and Cheese, page 115

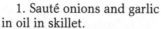

Lentil Sauce, Vegetables and Rice

Marcia S. Myer
Manheim, PA

Makes 4-6 servings

Prep. Time: 20 minutes
Cooking Time: 4-5 hours
Ideal slow-cooker size: 5-qt.

1 onion, chopped
4 large garlic cloves, minced
1 Tbsp. oil
1½ cups dry lentils
4 cups water
3 ribs celery, sliced
2 carrots, sliced
2½ cups crushed tomatoes
½ lb. zucchini, cut in half lengthwise, and sliced
1 bay leaf
1 tsp. ground coriander
1½ tsp. ground cumin
⅛ tsp. cayenne pepper
1½ tsp. salt
½ tsp. black pepper
¼ cup chopped fresh cilantro
1 lemon, juiced
2 cups hot cooked brown rice

1. Sauté onions and garlic in oil in skillet.
2. Combine with lentils, water, celery, carrots, tomatoes, zucchini, bay leaf, coriander, cumin, cayenne, salt and pepper in slow cooker.
3. Cook on low or until lentils are soft, 4-5 hours.
4. Remove bay leaf. Stir in cilantro and lemon juice.
5. Serve with brown rice.

Go-Along:
• Salad.

Red Lentil Sauce

Christie Detamore-Hunsberger
Harrisonburg, VA

Makes 4-6 servings

Prep. Time: 45 minutes
Cooking Time: 30 minutes

4½ cups water
1 cup dry red lentils
1 onion, chopped
1 cup shredded potatoes
½ cup shredded carrot
1 Tbsp. amino acids *or* soy sauce
1 tsp. dried basil
¼ tsp. dried dill weed
pepper, to taste
cooked rice, cooked quinoa, *or* toast, for serving

1. Combine water, lentils, onion, potatoes, carrot, amino acids, basil, dill and pepper in a saucepan. Cover.
2. Cook over low heat for 30 minutes or until vegetables are as soft as you like, stirring occasionally.
3. Serve over rice, whole wheat toast or quinoa for a fast meal.

Tip:
Make extra because it freezes very well.

Vegetable Moussaka

Kelly Martin
Mount Joy, PA

Makes 4-6 servings

Prep. Time: 60 minutes
Standing Time: 30 minutes
Cooking/Baking Time: 80 minutes

1 lb. eggplant, sliced
½ cup dry green lentils
2½ cups vegetable stock
1 bay leaf
water
3 Tbsp. olive oil, *divided*
1 medium onion, sliced
1 garlic clove, minced
1½ cups sliced mushrooms
14-oz. can garbanzo beans,
    rinsed and drained
14-oz. can chopped
    tomatoes
2 Tbsp. tomato paste
3 Tbsp. water
1¼ cups plain Greek yogurt
3 eggs
salt and pepper
½ cup grated cheddar
    cheese

1. Sprinkle eggplant slices with salt and place in colander. Cover and let sit for at least 30 minutes, to allow bitter juices to be extracted.

2. Meanwhile, place lentils, stock and bay leaf in a saucepan, cover with water and bring to a boil. Simmer for about 20 minutes until the lentils are just tender but not mushy. Drain thoroughly and keep warm.

3. Heat 1 Tbsp. olive oil in large saucepan. Add onions and garlic and cook, stirring for 5 minutes.

4. Stir in lentils, mushrooms, garbanzo beans, tomatoes, tomato paste, and 3 Tbsp. water.

5. Bring to boil, cover and simmer gently for 10 minutes, stirring occasionally.

6. Rinse eggplant slices, drain and pat dry.

7. Heat remaining 2 Tbsp. olive oil in frying pan and fry the slices in batches, turning once so both sides are browned, about 2 minutes per side.

8. Season the lentil mixture with salt and pepper.

9. Arrange a layer of eggplant in the bottom of a greased large, shallow, ovenproof dish. Then spoon a layer of the lentil mixture on top. Continue the layers until all the eggplant and lentil mixture are used up.

10. In a mixing bowl, beat the yogurt, eggs, salt and pepper together.

11. Pour yogurt mixture over the vegetables. Sprinkle with grated cheese.

12. Bake at 350° for about 50-60 minutes, until the topping is golden brown and bubbling. Serve immediately.

Tip:
    Leftovers keep well in the refrigerator for several days.

Go-Along:
• Hearty bread.

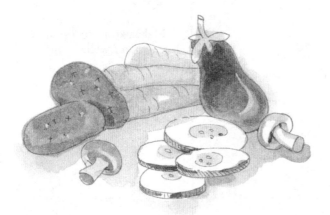

More heat is not necessarily better. The High setting on the burner is used only for limited operations. Most of the time you will be using the medium or simmer range.

Rose Stewart, Lancaster, PA

Grains

Almond Cranberry Rice Pilaf

Debra Kilheffer
Millersville, PA

Makes 4 servings

Prep. Time: 15 minutes
Cooking Time: 2-3 hours
Ideal slow-cooker size: 3-qt.

1 Tbsp. butter *or*
  margarine
¼ cup chopped onions
¼ cup chopped carrots
½ cup uncooked white rice
3 Tbsp. uncooked brown
  rice
¼ cup dried cranberries
¼ cup slivered almonds
½ cup frozen peas
1¼ cups water
1 vegetarian bouillon cube

1. Sauté onions and carrots in butter for 3 minutes.
2. Add rices and dried cranberries and sauté another minute.

3. Combine with water and bouillon in a 3-quart slow cooker. Cover.
4. Cook on low 2-3 hours until rice is tender.
5. Add peas and almonds. Cook additional 20 minutes until hot.

Tropical Rice

Lindsay Spencer
Morrow, OH

Makes 4-6 servings

Prep. Time: 10 minutes
Standing Time: 30 minutes
Cooking Time: 25 minutes

¼ cup chopped dried
  apricots
3 Tbsp. unsalted butter
1 tsp. garam masala
1 medium onion, chopped
1 cup uncooked long-grain
  white rice
2 Tbsp. lemon zest

¼ cup chopped pineapple
2 cups cold water
¼ cup snipped fresh mint
  leaves

1. Soak apricots in cold water for 30 minutes. Drain.
2. In a saucepan, melt butter and add garam masala.
3. Cook and stir 1 minute.
4. Add onion and sauté for 6 minutes.
5. Stir in rice, drained apricots, lemon zest, pineapple and water.
6. Cover. Bring to simmer. Simmer for 15-20 minutes.
7. Turn off heat. Let stand for 5 minutes.
8. Sprinkle mint over rice and serve.

Tomato Rice

Linda Tyson
Brownstown, PA

Makes 4 servings

Prep. Time: 10 minutes
Cooking Time: 25 minutes

1 onion, chopped
14½-oz. can Italian-style
    diced tomatoes
1½ cups water
2 Tbsp. butter
½ tsp. salt
1 cup uncooked long-grain
    white rice
1¼ cups grated Mexican-
    blend cheese, *divided*

1. Combine onions, toma-
toes, water, butter and salt in
a 3-quart saucepan.
2. Bring to a boil, then add
rice and stir.
3. Reduce heat to simmer
and cover. Cook for 20 minutes and remove from heat.
4. Place half of hot rice
mixture in 2½-quart microwave dish. Sprinkle with half
of the cheese. Repeat layers,
ending with cheese on top.
5. Heat in microwave for
3-5 minutes to melt cheese.

Go-Along:
• Steamed broccoli.

Wild Rice with Mushrooms

Renae Hege
Midville, GA

Makes 4 servings

Prep. Time: 15 minutes
Cooking Time: 2 hours
Ideal slow-cooker size: 4-qt.

6-oz. box long-grain-and-
    wild-rice
1 Tbsp. olive oil
2 cups water
seasoning pack from rice
10-oz. pkg. frozen chopped
    spinach, thawed
2 cups sliced fresh
    mushrooms
⅓ cup slivered almonds
2 Tbsp. olive oil
salt and pepper, to taste,
    optional

1. Pour rice into slow
cooker, greased with cooking
spray.
2. Stir in olive oil. Pour in
water.
3. Add seasoning pack from
rice package.
4. Cover. Cook on high for
1 hour.
5. Remove cover. Add
chopped spinach.
6. Cook an additional hour,
or until rice is soft.
7. Meanwhile, sauté
mushrooms and almonds in
olive oil.
8. Add salt and pepper if
you wish.
9. Stir mushroom mixture
into rice.
10. Serve.

Wild Rice Pilaf

Jenny Unternahrer
Wayland, IA

Makes 4-6 servings

Prep. Time: 15 minutes
Cooking Time: 60 minutes

1½ tsp. olive oil
½ cup uncooked brown rice
½ cup uncooked wild rice
½ cup diced carrots
½ cup diced onions
3 cups vegetable broth
½ cup uncooked long-grain
    white rice

1. In large saucepan
(preferably non-stick) sauté
brown rice, wild rice, carrots
and onions in olive oil for 10
minutes or until brown rice is
golden.
2. Add broth and bring to a
boil. Reduce heat, cover and
simmer for 25 minutes.
3. Stir in white rice. Cover
and simmer for another 25
minutes or until liquid is
absorbed. Drizzle in a little
more broth or water if the
liquid is gone and the rice is
not quite finished.

Variation:
Use all brown rice instead
of the white, but add it all in
the beginning and be sure to
watch the liquid as brown
rice absorbs liquid more
quickly than white rice. You
may need another ½ cup
broth.

Herbed Rice Pilaf

Jo Horst
Newmanstown, PA
Lucy St. Pierre
Peru, NY

Makes 6 servings

Prep. Time: 10 minutes
Cooking Time: 2 hours
Ideal slow-cooker size: 3-qt.

1 cup uncooked long-grain
  rice
1 cup chopped onions
3 Tbsp. butter
2½ cups water
1 Tbsp. vegetable bouillon
  base
¼ tsp. black pepper
¼ tsp. dried marjoram
¼ tsp. dried rosemary
3 Tbsp. fresh parsley

1. In a frying pan, cook and
stir together rice, onions and
butter until rice is brown.

2. Pour into slow cooker.
Stir in water, bouillon base,
pepper, marjoram and
rosemary.

3. Cover. Cook on high
1½-2 hours or until rice is
done. Stir once.

4. Sprinkle with parsley
just before serving.

Savory Rice

Jane Geigley
Lancaster, PA

Makes 6-8 servings

Prep. Time: 10 minutes
Cooking Time: 2-3 hours
Ideal slow-cooker size: 4-qt.

2 cups uncooked short-grain
  brown rice
5 cups water
1 Tbsp. butter
½ tsp. ground thyme
2 Tbsp. dried parsley
2 tsp. garlic powder
1 tsp. dried basil
1 tsp. salt

1. Mix rice, water, thyme,
parsley, garlic powder, basil
and salt.

2. Pour into slow cooker.
Cover.

3. Cook on high for 2-3
hours or until water is
absorbed.

Tip:
  A rice cooker may also be
used.

Go-Along:
• Gravy or a sweet and sour
sauce.

Rice, Corn and Cheese Casserole

Sara Harter Fredette
Williamsburg, MA

Makes 6-8 servings

Prep. Time: 10 minutes
Cooking Time: 3-4 hours
Ideal slow-cooker size: 4-qt.

3 cups cooked rice
15-oz. can whole-kernel
  corn, drained
1 small onion, chopped
2 cups grated sharp
  cheddar cheese
1½ cups milk
½ tsp. salt
½ tsp. chili powder
¼ tsp. pepper

1. In large bowl, combine
rice, corn, onions, cheese,
milk, salt, chili powder and
pepper.

2. Pour into greased 4-quart
slow cooker.

3. Cook on low 3-4 hours or
until set.

Variation:
  Use cream-style corn and
reduce milk to 1 cup.

Go-Along:
• Cranberry Squash.

Eating out for lunch every day will quickly consume your cash. Cook more than you need for supper the night before, and then you will have a delicious, nutritious, and quick lunch ready to take with you the next day.
Leanne Yoder, Tucson, AZ

Baked Rice

Mary Anne Cressman Musser
Lancaster, PA
Laura Wenger
Manheim, PA
Anna Musser
Manheim, PA

Makes 6 servings

Prep. Time: 10 minutes
Baking Time: 1-2½ hours

2 cups uncooked brown *or* white rice
¼ cup soy sauce
2 tsp. vegetable bouillon granules
1 tsp. onion powder
¼ tsp. pepper
¼ tsp. celery seed
1 Tbsp. dried parsley
¼ cup oil *or* butter
3 cups boiling water for white rice, 3½ cups for brown rice

1. Mix ingredients together in a 9 × 13 baking pan. Cover tightly.
2. Bake at 350° for 55-60 minutes for white rice or 1½-2 hours for brown rice.

Variations:
1. Choose your flavor twists!
2. Cook rice in vegetable broth, tomato juice, apple, orange or pineapple juice.
3. Add ½-1 tsp. curry powder, cumin, thyme, turmeric or mace to the liquid. Add a pinch of saffron.
4. Add chopped onions, garlic, celery, carrots, mushrooms or raisins to rice at the start of cooking.

5. After cooking, garnish with nuts, toasted sesame seeds or plain yogurt.
Laura Wenger

6. Serve baked rice with sweet and sour sauce. Combine and bring to boil: 3 cups sugar, 1½ cups vinegar, 3 Tbsp. chopped green bell pepper, ½ tsp. salt, 3 tsp. paprika. Boil for 5 minutes. Stir together ½ cup cold water and 3 Tbsp. cornstarch. Stir cornstarch mixture into boiling liquid, stirring constantly until thickened and clear. Serve over rice.
Anna Musser

Go-Along:
• Baked lentils, cooked veggies, any kind of salad.

Fried Rice

Anita Troyer
Fairview, MI

Makes 4 servings

Prep. Time: 20 minutes
Standing Time: 30 minutes
Cooking Time: 50 minutes

1 cup uncooked long-grain rice
2 eggs, beaten
1 cup frozen peas, thawed
¼ cup finely grated carrots
½ cup diced onions
1½ Tbsp. butter
2-3 Tbsp. soy sauce

1. Cook the rice following instructions on package, or use 2½ cups cooked rice.

2. Cool rice for 30 minutes before continuing with the recipe.
3. Scramble eggs in a small skillet over medium heat. Place scrambled eggs on cutting board. Chop into pea-sized bits.
4. Add eggs, peas, carrots and onions to cooled rice. Mix gently.
5. Melt butter in a large frying pan over medium heat.
6. Add mixed rice and veggies to pan.
7. Add soy sauce and fry 10 minutes over medium heat, turning over every 2 minutes.

Tip:
You can add other veggies to this dish to suit your taste. Do not use instant or quick rice, however.

Go-Along:
• Serve with sweet and sour sauce and egg rolls.

Mexican Rice Skillet

Zoë Rohrer
Lancaster, PA

Makes 4 servings

Prep. Time: 15 minutes
Cooking Time: 60 minutes

2 Tbsp. canola oil
1 cup uncooked brown rice
½ cup chopped onions
3 cloves garlic, minced
½ cup cold water
½ tsp. salt
1 cup boiling water
1½ cups chopped red bell
  pepper
1 cup frozen corn, thawed
⅔ cup grated cheddar cheese
4 oz. sour cream
½ cup crushed tortilla chips

1. In a heavy-bottomed pot, heat oil.
2. Add rice and stir and toast 1-2 minutes.
3. Add onions, garlic, ½ cup cold water and salt.
4. Cook, stirring constantly, until water is absorbed.
5. Add boiling water, peppers and corn to the pot.
6. Cover. Simmer 40 minutes, or until rice is tender.
7. Remove from heat.
8. Sprinkle with cheese. Cover and allow cheese to melt.
9. Serve immediately. Garnish individual servings with sour cream and crushed tortilla chips.

Go-Along:
• We like to eat this recipe with green beans or salad.

Cheese Sauce with Rice and Peas

Elva Evers
Wayland, IA
Mabel Eshelman
Lancaster, PA

Makes 4-6 servings

Prep. Time: 5-10 minutes
Cooking Time: 45 minutes

3 cups water
1½ cups uncooked brown
  rice
half stick (¼ cup) butter
¼ cup all-purpose flour
2 cups milk, warmed
1 cup diced Velveeta *or*
  shredded cheddar cheese
4-6 cups frozen peas

1. Place water and brown rice in a saucepan. Cover. After water comes to a boil, reduce the heat and simmer about 45 minutes until water is absorbed.
2. Meanwhile, to make the white sauce, melt butter over medium heat in 4-quart saucepan.
3. Add flour. Whisk until bubbly and just turning tan.
4. Warm the milk in the microwave until just warm, not steaming hot. You may also use cold milk, but you will stir and cook the sauce longer before it thickens!
5. Turn heat to low. Whisking continuously, slowly pour the warm milk into flour and butter.
6. Continue to cook and whisk over low heat until

sauce is thickened and steaming. Do not allow to boil.
7. Add cheese and stir until melted. Set aside until rice and peas are ready. If necessary, heat the white sauce again, on low heat, stirring often and not allowing to boil.
8. Heat the peas in the microwave or cook on stove until hot.
9. Serve the peas over the rice, topped with the cheesy white sauce.

Tip:
We learned to eat this while in Voluntary Service in Mantua, OH and have enjoyed ever since. Children especially enjoy this simple meal.

Elva Evers

Variations:
1. Make the white sauce in the microwave (times vary according to microwave). Melt the butter in a glass bowl. Whisk in flour and pour in cold milk. Heat in microwave for a few minutes. Whisk well. Return to microwave and heat until thick and hot, a few more minutes. Stir in cheese to melt.

Elva Evers

2. Instead of peas, use 3 cups cooked soybeans. Use a 10-oz. can of mushroom soup instead of making white sauce. Mix soybeans, mushroom soup, and cheese. Serve sauce over rice.

Mabel Eshelman

Cracked Wheat or Bulgur Pilaf

Carolyn Baer
Conrath, WI

Makes 4-6 servings

Prep. Time: 5 minutes
Cooking Time: 2 hours
Ideal slow-cooker size: 4-qt.

1 small onion, chopped
1 cup uncooked cracked
    wheat *or* bulgur
1 Tbsp. oil
½ tsp. salt
2 cups vegetable broth *or*
    stock

1. Sauté onions and wheat in oil, over medium heat, until onions are transparent and wheat is glazed.
2. Pour into slow cooker. Add salt and broth.
3. Cook, covered, on low for 2 hours or until liquid is absorbed.

Variation:
You may sauté ¼ lb. sliced mushrooms with onions and wheat in step 1. Increase oil to 3 Tbsp.

Family Favorite Quinoa Pilaf

Colleen Heatwole
Burton, MI

Makes 4-6 servings

Prep. Time: 15 minutes
Cooking Time: 30 minutes

½ cup blanched slivered
    almonds
1 cup uncooked quinoa
1½ cups vegetable stock
1 tsp. salt
1 cinnamon stick, broken
    in half
1 bay leaf
½ cup dried cranberries

1. Rinse quinoa thoroughly. Drain.
2. In saucepan, heat, stir and toast almonds until golden.
3. Add quinoa and roast until dry and turning color.
4. Add stock, salt, cinnamon and bay leaf.
5. Bring to a boil.
6. Reduce heat. Cover.
7. Simmer for 20 minutes.
8. Remove from heat and let sit 5 minutes.
9. Fluff with fork. Remove bay leaf. Stir in cranberries. Serve.

Quinoa is cooked when the grains have changed from white to transparent and the spiral-like germ has separated.
Colleen Heatwole, Burton, MI

Tip:
May be served in place of potatoes.

Variation:
For a different flavor, omit almonds, cinnamon, bay leaf and cranberries. Sauté ½ cup chopped onions in 2 Tbsp. oil. Add 2 chopped carrots, quinoa and broth. When cooked according to directions above, stir in ⅔ cup toasted walnuts and ¼ cup chopped fresh parsley.

Polenta Pepper Casserole

Shirley Hedman
Schenectady, NY

Makes 4-5 servings

Prep. Time: 20 minutes
Cooking/Baking Time: 45 minutes

1 cup cornmeal
1 cup water
1½ cups milk
½ cup plus 2 Tbsp.
    shredded asiago cheese,
    or Parmesan, *divided*
1 red bell pepper, sliced in
    long, thin strips
1 green bell pepper, sliced
    in long, thin strips
1 yellow bell pepper, sliced
    in long, thin strips
2 large carrots, thinly sliced
½-1 jalapeño pepper,
    seeded and diced
½ tsp. Italian herb
    seasoning

dash of garlic powder,
  optional
4 cups baby spinach leaves,
  loosely packed
¼ tsp. salt
¼ tsp. black pepper

1. In a saucepan, whisk together cornmeal with water and milk. Bring to boil.
2. Cook and stir 3 minutes, or until it looks like mashed potatoes. Turn off heat.
3. Stir in ½ cup cheese.
4. Spread mixture in greased 9 × 13 baking pan.
5. In large non-stick skillet, cook peppers, carrots and jalapeño pepper 8 minutes, or until tender.
6. Sprinkle with Italian seasoning and garlic powder.
7. Add spinach, salt and pepper. Cook 1-2 minutes, or until spinach is wilted.
8. Spread vegetables over cornmeal layer and sprinkle with remaining 2 Tbsp. cheese.
9. Bake at 400° for 30 minutes.

Go-Along:
• I serve this with sliced beets in an oil-vinegar dressing.

Quinoa with Broccoli and Hoisin Sauce

Margaret High
Lancaster, PA

Makes 4 servings

Prep. Time: 15 minutes
Cooking Time: 20 minutes

2 Tbsp. butter
2 small onions, cut in wedges
1 cup uncooked quinoa
2 cups water
3 Tbsp. hoisin sauce
2 Tbsp. soy sauce
1 tsp. honey
⅛ tsp. ground cloves
⅛ tsp. fennel seeds, crushed *or* ground
black pepper, to taste
2-3 cups chopped broccoli
shredded cheese, *optional*

1. Melt butter in Dutch oven. Add the onions. Cover. Cook on medium for 7 minutes without peeking.
2. Stir and flip onions. Cover again for 7 more minutes. Onions should be limp and caramelized in spots.
3. Remove from Dutch oven and set aside.
4. Meanwhile, prepare the quinoa. Place quinoa and water in small saucepan and cover. Bring to boil, turn down heat, and simmer for 15 minutes until water is gone.
5. Mix together hoisin sauce, soy sauce, honey, cloves, fennel, and pepper in a small bowl. Set aside.
6. In hot Dutch oven that the onions came out of, toss in broccoli on medium heat. Stir and cook for 2 minutes until broccoli turns bright green.
7. Add sauce mixture and cooked quinoa to Dutch oven. Stir and cook for 3-5 minutes, or until broccoli is as tender as you like it.
8. Place broccoli/quinoa mixture in serving dish. Top with caramelized onions. Garnish with cheese, if you wish.

Tip:
  It may look like a lot of steps, but it goes together quickly.

Variation:
  You can use couscous instead of quinoa if you want, but quinoa is an excellent protein and mineral source.

Go-Along:
• This is sometimes a complete lunch for us! I've also served it with a green salad with Asian dressing and pudding for dessert.

Polenta with Spicy Bean Sauce

Carolyn Spohn
Shawnee, KS

Makes 4 servings

Prep. Time: 20 minutes
Cooking Time: 20 minutes

28 oz. can crushed
   tomatoes
1 Tbsp. capers, drained,
   optional
½ tsp. hot pepper sauce, *or*
   to taste
14-oz. can black beans,
   rinsed and drained
1 small onion, chopped
1 clove garlic, minced
1½ cups yellow cornmeal
4 cups water, *divided*
¾ tsp. salt
1½ Tbsp. butter
½ cup grated Parmesan
   cheese
2 Tbsp. chopped parsley *or*
   cilantro

1. In non-stick pan, combine tomatoes, capers if you wish, hot pepper sauce, beans, onions and garlic.
2. Cover. Heat 8-10 minutes.
3. To make polenta, in separate saucepan heat 3 cups water to boiling.
4. In a glass measuring cup, combine cornmeal and 1 cup water.
5. Slowly pour cornmeal mixture into boiling water, whisking continuously. Add salt.
6. Cook and stir over low heat 15 minutes, or until it pulls away from side of pan.
7. Turn off heat. Stir in butter and cheese. Mix well.
8. Place mound of polenta on each plate.
9. Make indentations with spoon and fill with bean mixture.
10. Sprinkle with parsley.

Go-Along:
• Green vegetable, fruit, yogurt.

Barley with Mushrooms

Rosemary Martin
Bridgewater, VA
Mabel Eshelman
Lancaster, PA

Makes 4-6 servings

Prep. Time: 15 minutes
Cooking Time: 3-4 hours
Ideal slow-cooker size: 3-qt.

¾ cup uncooked pearl barley
½ cup diced onions
1 clove garlic, minced
2 Tbsp. butter
14½-oz. can vegetable broth
4-oz. can mushrooms, with
  juice, *or* 3 cups chopped
  fresh mushrooms
½ cup slivered almonds,
  optional
pinch cayenne
  pepper or black
  pepper, to taste
⅓ cup shredded
  sharp cheddar
  cheese, *optional*

1. In a skillet, sauté barley, onions and garlic in butter until barley browns.
2. Pour into slow cooker. Add broth, mushrooms, almonds and cayenne.
3. Cover. Cook on high for 3-4 hours, until barley is tender.
4. Remove lid. Sprinkle with cheese.

Tip:
  May be baked, covered, at 350° for 75 minutes.

Garden Ratatouille with Barley

Nancy Leaman
Bird-in-Hand, PA

Makes 4-6 servings

Prep. Time: 30 minutes
Standing Time: 2-10 minutes
Cooking/Baking Time: 40 minutes

1 medium eggplant
1 large butternut squash
1 medium onion, chopped
2 cloves garlic, minced
2 bell peppers, diced
2 cups chopped fresh
  tomatoes
1½ Tbsp. minced fresh
  basil
1 tsp. dried tarragon
1 tsp. dried marjoram
1 tsp. sea salt
1 tsp. coarse black pepper
3 Tbsp. olive oil
1 cup sliced black olives,
  optional
2 cups cooked barley
2 cups shredded Parmesan
  cheese
1 cup vegetable broth
1 cup crushed cheese
  crackers, *optional*

1. Peel the eggplant, chop into 1"-size cubes and soak in salt water for 2-10 minutes.
2. Peel the butternut squash and chop into 1" cubes.
3. In a skillet, sauté the onion, garlic and peppers until softened. Set aside.
4. In a saucepan with a little water, cook the butternut squash until lightly tender, about 10 minutes.

5. Drain the eggplant and rinse off. Drain.
6. Mix the butternut squash, tomatoes, basil, tarragon, marjoram, sea salt, pepper, eggplant, sautéed veggies and optional black olives. Place into a lightly greased 9 × 13 casserole.
7. Stir in cooked barley, Parmesan cheese and broth. Mix gently.
8. Optional: top with 1 cup crushed cheese crackers before baking.
9. Bake at 350° for 20 minutes. Do not overcook or the veggies will get mushy.

Go-Along:
• A good selection of breads, tossed salad of mixed greens.

Herbed Risotto

Kim Patrick
Norwood, PA

Makes 4 servings

Prep. Time: 60 minutes
Cooking Time: 1½ hours

3 cups vegetable broth,
  divided
1 Tbsp. unsalted butter
2 Tbsp. olive oil
3 garlic cloves, chopped
2 medium shallots,
  chopped
1 cup uncooked short-grain
  brown rice
10 oz. frozen squash purée,
  thawed
¼ cup freshly grated
  Parmesan cheese

½ tsp. salt
¼ tsp. freshly ground
  pepper
¼ cup chopped fresh basil
  leaves

1. Bring broth to a simmer in medium saucepan over moderate heat.
2. Reduce heat and keep warm.
3. Combine butter and oil in large saucepan over moderate heat.
4. Add garlic and shallots and cook 3 minutes, until softened.
5. Add rice and cook 2 minutes, stirring until translucent.
6. Add 1 cup warm broth to rice and cook over moderate heat, stirring constantly, until broth is nearly absorbed.
7. Continue to add the remainder of the broth, one cup at a time. Cook and stir until broth is absorbed.
8. When rice is cooked through, but firm, add squash and Parmesan cheese.
9. Stir until cheese is melted.
10. Season with salt and pepper and sprinkle with basil.

Go-Along:
• We eat this with a nice salad, and it is a light, tasty meal.

Summer Risotto

Doreen Bishop
Harrisburg, PA

Makes 6 servings

Prep. Time: 40 minutes
Cooking Time: 30 minutes

half stick (¼ cup) butter
1 Tbsp. olive oil
1½ cups uncooked arborio
  rice
¾ cup diced green onions
1 Tbsp. freshly chopped
  garlic
5 cups hot vegetable broth,
  divided
12 oz. fresh green beans,
  trimmed and halved
8 oz. portabello
  mushrooms, sliced
6 medium Roma tomatoes
3 Tbsp. chopped fresh basil
½ tsp. pepper
Parmesan cheese, grated

1. Melt butter with oil in large skillet until sizzling.
2. Add rice, green onions and garlic. Cook over medium heat, stirring occasionally until onions are soft, 3-4 minutes.
3. Add one cup of hot broth, green beans and mushrooms. Stir until the broth is absorbed.
4. Keep adding broth one cup at a time, allowing it to absorb each time.
5. Stir in tomatoes, basil and pepper. Continue cooking until liquid is absorbed and tomatoes are heated through.
6. Top with grated Parmesan cheese.

Variation:
Can substitute with 1 Tbsp. jarred minced garlic, 14½-oz. can diced tomatoes, or 1 Tbsp. dried basil.

Stuffed Peppers

Angela Newcomer Buller
Beavercreek, OH

Makes 4-6 servings

Prep. Time: 30 minutes
Cooking/Baking Time: 45-50 minutes

4-5 green bell peppers
15-oz. can black beans,
  drained
2 cups cooked brown rice
1 cup shredded cheddar
  cheese
1 Tbsp. chili powder
pinch of ground cumin
24-oz. can tomato sauce
2 cloves garlic, minced
1 tsp. dried oregano
1 tsp. dried basil

1. Cut tops off peppers and remove seeds and white ribs.
2. In a bowl, combine beans, rice, cheese, chili powder and cumin.
3. Spoon the mixture evenly into the peppers, pushing gently if needed.
4. Place peppers in a casserole dish. Cover.
5. Bake at 350° for 45-50 minutes.
6. While the peppers are baking, pour tomato sauce in saucepan and add the garlic, oregano and basil.
7. Heat on low until hot. Serve sauce with peppers.

Tip:
For a lovely presentation, cut the peppers in half on the plate and spoon the tomato sauce over top.

Go-Along:
• This recipe is excellent with homemade bread and an oil-based dipping sauce. We like to end the meal with a nice rich, chocolate dessert.

Delicious Cabbage Rice Casserole

June Hackenberger
Thompsontown, PA

Makes 8 servings

Prep. Time: 40 minutes
Cooking/Baking Time: 1 hour

12 cups shredded cabbage
4 cups cooked brown rice
2 cups sliced fresh
  mushrooms
half stick (¼ cup) butter
5 Tbsp. flour
2 tsp. salt
1 tsp. dry ground mustard
¼ tsp. pepper
3 cups milk
1 cup shredded sharp
  cheese

1. Place cabbage in large stockpot. Add water to come half-way up on cabbage. Boil 5 minutes. Drain.
2. Place cooked rice in a greased 9×13 pan.
3. Top with cabbage.
4. In a saucepan, sauté mushrooms in butter until tender. Stir in flour, salt, dry mustard and pepper.
5. Stir in milk. Cook and stir until thickened.
6. Pour white sauce over cabbage and rice.
7. Sprinkle with cheese.
8. Bake at 350° for 30 minutes.

Vegetable Rice Pie

Bethany Martin
Bethel, PA

Makes 6 servings

Prep. Time: 30 minutes
Cooking/Baking Time: 50 minutes

1½ cups cooked rice
1 cup grated Parmesan
  cheese, *divided*
½ cup mayonnaise, *divided*
⅔ cup finely chopped
  onions, *divided*
1 cup broccoli florets
1 cup cauliflower florets
1 cup chopped carrots
3 Tbsp. all-purpose flour
1 cup milk
¼ tsp. salt
⅛ tsp. pepper

1. Combine rice, ½ cup cheese, ¼ cup mayonnaise and ⅓ cup onions.
2. Press into greased 9" deep-dish pie pan.
3. In a saucepan, cook broccoli, cauliflower, carrots and remaining ⅓ cup onions in small amount of water until crisp-tender. Drain. Set aside.
4. In saucepan, mix flour and remaining mayonnaise.
5. Add milk, salt and pepper. Cook and stir over medium heat 3-5 minutes, until mixture is hot and thickened.
6. Stir in vegetables. Pour mixture into rice crust.
7. Sprinkle with remaining ½ cup cheese.
8. Bake at 350° for 30-40 minutes.
9. Let stand 10 minutes before serving.

Quick Southwestern Veggies and Rice

Kristi See
Weskan, KS

Makes 4 servings

Prep. Time: 5 minutes
Cooking Time: 10 minutes

12-oz. pkg. frozen
  vegetarian meat
  crumbles, *optional*
10¾-oz. can condensed
  tomato soup
12-oz. pkg. frozen
  southwest corn
1 cup water
1 tsp. ground cumin
¼ tsp. salt
¼ tsp. garlic pepper
1 cup uncooked instant
  rice
1 cup shredded Monterey
  Jack cheese

1. In a saucepan, bring to boil vegetable meat crumbles, tomato soup, corn, water, cumin, salt and garlic pepper.
2. Stir in rice.
3. Remove from heat. Cover and let stand 5-7 minutes or until rice is tender.
4. Sprinkle with cheese.

Go-Along:
• Fresh bread and tossed salad.

Little Broccoli Rice Casseroles

Danae Mast
Millersburg, OH

Makes 4 servings

Prep. Time: 30 minutes
Cooking/Baking Time: 10 minutes

2 cups milk
1 cup water
1 cup uncooked long-grain converted rice
3 cups broccoli
cooking spray
½ cup chopped onions
½ cup chopped celery
¼ cup chopped mushrooms
½ cup chopped green bell pepper
¼ cup cream cheese
¼ tsp. salt
¼ tsp. black pepper
¼ cup grated Parmesan cheese

1. Combine milk and water in saucepan. Bring to a boil.
2. Add rice. Cover and cook 10 minutes.
3. Add broccoli. Cook 5 minutes. Drain. Discard liquid.
4. Coat a skillet with cooking spray. Add onions, celery, mushrooms and bell pepper. Sauté 5 minutes over medium-high heat.
5. Add cream cheese. Stir until cheese melts.
6. Remove from heat. Stir in rice, broccoli, salt and pepper.
7. Spoon 1 cup rice mixture into each of 4 10-oz. ramekins coated with cooking spray.
8. Sprinkle each ramekin with 1 Tbsp. Parmesan.
9. Bake at 375° for 10 minutes or until cheese melts.

Broccoli Hot Dish

Lucy St. Pierre
Peru, NY

Makes 8 servings

Prep. Time: 15 minutes
Cooking/Baking Time: 45 minutes

14-oz. pkg. frozen broccoli cuts
2 cups cooked rice
⅓ cup (5⅔ Tbsp.) butter, *divided*
2 slices whole wheat bread, cubed
1 medium onion, diced
3 Tbsp. flour
1 tsp. salt
¼ tsp. pepper
3 cups milk
shredded cheddar cheese

1. Cook broccoli according to package directions. Drain.
2. Spread rice in bottom of greased 9 × 13 baking pan.
3. Add broccoli on top.
4. In saucepan, melt butter.
5. Remove 2 Tbsp. melted butter and toss with bread cubes. Set aside.
6. Sauté onion in remaining butter for 5 minutes.
7. Add flour, salt, pepper and milk. Cook and stir over medium heat until thickened.
8. Pour sauce over rice and broccoli.
9. Sprinkle bread cubes over top.
10. Bake at 350° for 30 minutes.
11. Sprinkle with cheddar cheese. Serve when melted.

Brown Rice Vegetable Casserole

Judy Buller
Bluffton, OH

Makes 8 servings

Prep. Time: 20-30 minutes
Cooking/Baking Time: 1½ hours

3 cups vegetable broth
3 Tbsp. soy sauce
2 Tbsp. butter
1½ cups raw brown rice
2 cups chopped onions, *divided*
½ tsp. dried thyme
3 Tbsp. olive oil
1 medium carrot, cut in thin sticks
1 cup sliced zucchini
1 cup sliced yellow squash
1 cup broccoli florets
1 cup cauliflower florets
1 medium red bell pepper, cut in strips
2 garlic cloves, minced
1 cup cashews
2 cups shredded cheddar cheese

1. Combine broth, soy sauce and butter in a saucepan and bring to boil.

2. Place rice, 1 cup onion and thyme in greased, 3-quart casserole dish.

3. Pour broth mixture over rice. Cover with foil.

4. Bake at 350° for 65-70 minutes.

5. Place oil in large skillet.

6. Add carrots, zucchini, yellow squash, broccoli, cauliflower, peppers, garlic and remaining 1 cup onions.

7. Sauté until crisp-tender.

8. Spoon veggie mixture over cooked rice.

9. Cover. Bake at 350° for 10 minutes.

10. Remove cover. Sprinkle with cashews and shredded cheese.

11. Return to oven for 5-7 minutes, until cheese is melted.

Variation:

Any veggies can be used to sauté. Use what is in season. I place carrots in first and add less dense vegetables after a few minutes.

Go-Along:
• Fresh fruit and crusty whole-grain rolls.

Millet Loaf
Deb Bucher
Lisbon Falls, ME

Makes 10-15 servings

Prep. Time: 30 minutes
Standing Time: 45 minutes
Cooking/Baking Time: 90 minutes

6 cups water
3 cups uncooked millet
3 cups uncooked quick oats
1 cup powdered milk, *optional*
2 cups grated sharp cheese, *divided*
¾ cup sunflower seeds
½ cup chopped onions
3 eggs
1½ cups milk
1½ tsp. soy sauce *or* tamari
6 tsp. lemon juice
29-oz. can tomato sauce
½ tsp. dried basil
¼ tsp. dried oregano
dash hot sauce, *optional*

1. In a saucepan, bring water to boil. Add millet. Stir a few times until water returns to boil.

2. Cover. Turn heat to low. Simmer for about 30 minutes until water is absorbed and millet is soft.

3. Pour cooked millet into mixing bowl to cool at least 45 minutes.

4. When millet is cool, add oats, powdered milk if you wish, 1 cup cheese, sunflower seeds and onions.

5. In a blender, blend eggs, milk, soy sauce and lemon juice. Blend well and then stir into millet mixture.

6. Pour into a greased 9 × 13 pan. Bake at 350° for 45 minutes.

7. Mix tomato sauce with herbs and optional hot sauce. Pour it over the millet mixture.

8. Sprinkle with remaining 1 cup cheese.

9. Return to oven. Bake an additional 15 minutes.

Tips:

1. You can prepare this ahead of time up to step 5. Refrigerate.

2. You can use broth instead of milk and omit the cheese for dairy-sensitive persons.

Go-Along:
• A green salad and a cooked vegetable.

Place a full baking casserole on a cookie sheet just in case juice cooks out over the casserole dish.
Nancy Leaman, Bird-in-Hand, PA

Vegetable Loaf

Evelyn Page
Gillette, WY

Makes 8 servings

Prep. Time: 30 minutes
Baking Time: 45 minutes

1 cup ground peanuts
1 cup bread crumbs
1 cup cooked rice
1 cup cooked peas
1 cup cooked mashed
   carrots
1 cup diced tomatoes

1. In mixing bowl, mix ingredients well.
2. Pat into casserole dish.
3. Bake at 400° for 45 minutes.

Tip:

I use leftovers for this recipe, freezing them in 1-cup bags until I have all the components.

Variation:

This may be served with white sauce. Add ½ cup tomatoes to the white sauce.

Ghanaian Rice Meal

Mary Hackenberger
Thompsontown, PA

Makes 10-12 servings

Prep. Time: 30 minutes
Cooking Time: 1 hour 20 minutes

9 cups water
4 cups uncooked brown
   rice
5 Tbsp. oil, *divided*
1 green bell pepper,
   chopped
3 carrots, chopped
1 large onion, chopped
6 eggs, lightly beaten
1 tsp. salt
⅛ tsp. black pepper
32 oz. tomato purée
1 large onion, thinly sliced
2 cloves garlic, minced
1-2 vegetable bouillon
   cubes
2 tsp. hot sauce, or to taste
½ tsp. chili powder
1 scant tsp. salt
1½ tsp. sugar

1. Cook rice in water over low heat until water is absorbed, about 1 hour. You want 15 cups cooked rice.
2. Heat 2 Tbsp. oil in skillet. Sauté green pepper, carrots and chopped onion until softened.
3. Add eggs, 1 tsp. salt and pepper. Scramble and cook until done.
4. Mix with cooked rice.
5. In a saucepan, combine tomato purée, sliced onions, garlic, bouillon cubes, hot sauce, chili powder, 1 scant tsp. salt, sugar and remaining 3 Tbsp. oil. Bring to a boil. Turn down heat. Simmer uncovered for 20 minutes.
6. Serve hot sauce over rice.

Savory Yeast Gravy

Margaret Wenger Johnson
Keezletown, VA

Makes 1½ cups

Prep. Time: 5 minutes
Cooking Time: 10-15 minutes

2 Tbsp. butter
2 Tbsp. whole wheat flour
2 Tbsp. nutritional yeast,
   powder *or* flakes
1 cup vegetable stock,
   water, *or* milk
¼ tsp. salt

1. Melt butter in saucepan. Stir in flour and yeast. The mixture will be dry and crumbly.
2. Continue to cook and stir this over medium heat for 3 minutes.
3. Add the stock slowly. Cook, stirring constantly, over medium heat until sauce starts to boil and thicken. Stir in salt. If a thinner sauce is desired, stir in more stock.

Variation:

To make simple yeast butter, melt ½ cup butter and add 2-3 Tbsp. nutritional yeast. Serve as a sauce for vegetables, or refrigerate and spread on your toast in the morning.

Go-Along:
• Good on top of rice, steamed vegetables, or mashed potatoes - anytime vegetarians want some gravy!

Artichoke Stuffing
Laura Peachey
Goshen, IN

Makes 8-10 servings

Prep. Time: 35 minutes
Cooking/Baking Time: 25-35 minutes

1 lb. sourdough bread, cut into ½" cubes
½ lb. fresh mushrooms, sliced
2 ribs celery, chopped
1 medium onion, diced
3-4 cloves garlic, minced
2 Tbsp. butter
2 6½-oz. jars marinated artichoke hearts, drained and artichokes chopped
½ cup grated Parmesan cheese
1 tsp. poultry seasoning
1 egg
14½-oz. container vegetable broth

1. Place bread cubes in two 10 × 15 baking pans.
2. Bake for 15 minutes at 350°, or until lightly browned.
3. In a large skillet, sauté mushrooms, celery, onions and garlic in butter over medium heat until tender.
4. Stir in artichokes, Parmesan cheese and poultry seasoning.
5. Transfer to a large bowl and stir in bread cubes.
6. Whisk egg and broth in a separate bowl until blended.
7. Pour over bread mixture and mix well.
8. Transfer to a greased, 3-quart baking dish.
9. Cover. Bake at 350° for 20 minutes.
10. Remove cover and bake 5-15 minutes longer or until well browned.

Go-Along:
• Serve with a salad.

Anona's Chestnut Stuffing
Donna Conto
Saylorsburg, PA

Makes 12-14 servings

Prep. Time: 30 minutes
Cooking Time: 5 hours
Ideal slow-cooker size: 5-qt.

2 sticks (1 cup) butter
2 cups chopped onions
2 cups chopped celery
1½ tsp. salt
½ tsp. pepper
¼ cup chopped fresh parsley
12-13 cups bread cubes
2 cups chopped peeled chestnuts
3¼-4½ cups vegetable broth
2 eggs, beaten

1. Melt butter in saucepan.
2. Sauté onions and celery until soft, about 5 minutes.
3. Remove from heat. Add salt, pepper, parsley, bread cubes and chestnuts.
4. Add broth and eggs and mix well.
5. Pour into lightly greased slow cooker.
6. Cover. Cook on high 1 hour. Then cook on low for 4 hours.
7. Stir every hour to prevent sticking on bottom of slow cooker.

Keep stale bread for croutons, bread puddings, bread crumbs, and stuffing/dressing.
Karen Stanley, Amherst, VA

Easy Stuffing

Mary Lou Nagy
Maytown, PA

Makes 6 servings

Prep. Time: 30 minutes
Cooking Time: 3-4 hours
Ideal slow-cooker size: 4-qt.

½ cup diced celery
½ cup diced onion
¾ stick (6 Tbsp.) butter
6 eggs
2 tsp. salt
dash of pepper
10¾-oz. can cream of
   mushroom soup
1 cup milk
6 cups day-old bread cubes

1. Put diced celery, onions and butter in a skillet and sauté until soft and browned, 5-10 minutes.
2. In mixing bowl mix eggs, salt, pepper, soup and milk together.
3. Add sautéed vegetables to the bowl. Add bread cubes.
4. Mix until bread is completely coated.
5. Place the mixture into greased slow cooker.
6. Cook covered on low 3-4 hours.

Go-Along:
• Great for any festive meal.

Pineapple Casserole

Eunice Kauffman
Alto, MI

Makes 6-8 servings

Prep. Time: 5 minutes
Cooking Time: 1¼-2¼ hours
Ideal slow-cooker size: 3- or 4-qt.

2 20-oz. cans pineapple
   chunks, undrained
5 Tbsp. flour
½ cup sugar
½ cup shredded sharp
   cheese
1½ cups cracker crumbs
1 stick (½ cup) butter,
   melted

1. Pour pineapple and its juice in greased 3- or 4-quart slow cooker.
2. Mix flour and sugar and spread over pineapple.
3. Sprinkle cheese over casserole. Cover.
4. Cook on high 1-2 hours until bubbling.
5. Mix crackers and butter and scatter over top.
6. With lid off, continue to cook 15 minutes.

Mom's Pineapple Filling

Susan Henne
Fleetwood, PA

Makes 4 servings

Prep. Time: 20 minutes
Baking Time: 1 hour

1 stick (½ cup) butter,
   softened
4 eggs
20-oz. can crushed
   pineapple, undrained
6-7 slices of bread, cubed
cinnamon

1. Combine butter, eggs and pineapple in a blender and mix well.
2. Put cubed bread in a large bowl and pour blender mixture over top. Mix well.
3. Place mixture in 1½-quart greased baking dish. Sprinkle cinnamon on top.
4. Bake at 325° for 60 minutes or until firm and golden brown on top.
5. Let stand 5 minutes before serving.

Go-Along:
• This filling is a tasty treat my mom usually serves at Christmas and Easter dinners, but it can be served at any time with any meal.

To make your own cream of mushroom soup, please turn to pages 260-261.

Vegetables and Fruits

A Meal on a Sweet Potato

Rhoda Atzeff
Lancaster, PA

Makes 4 servings

Prep. Time: 10-15 minutes
Baking Time: 1½-1½ hours

4 medium sweet potatoes
12 oz. small frozen
  Brussels sprouts, thawed
2 Tbsp. olive oil
½ cup chopped pecans
½ cup dried cranberries
½ cup crumbled feta *or*
  blue cheese

1. Place sweet potatoes on baking sheet. Jag potatoes all over with a fork. Bake in 350° oven for 1 hour or until soft.
2. Meanwhile, sauté Brussels sprouts in a skillet in olive oil over medium heat, just until tender. (If you can't find small Brussels sprouts, use regular-sized ones, but cut them in half.)
3. Make a straight cut through the length of each baked sweet potato (but not cutting through the bottom skin). Push down gently on the cut, spreading it open, and mashing the potato just slightly.
4. Pile the Brussels sprouts, pecans, dried cranberries and cheese evenly on top of each sweet potato.
5. Return sweet potatoes to baking sheet and then into the hot oven. Bake at 375° for 15-30 minutes, or until heated through.

Tip:
  You can toast the pecans. You can also use walnuts or cashews if you wish.

Go-Along:
• A green salad and apple-sauce with cinnamon.

Keep your pantry stocked with basic ingredients for a simple meal. Make it when you have unexpected guests or you are tired.

Rhoda Nissley, Parkesburg, PA

Twice-Baked Sweet Potatoes

Susan Guarneri
Three Lakes, WI

Makes 4 servings

Prep. Time: 20 minutes
Baking Time: 75 minutes

4 medium-large sweet
   potatoes
2 Tbsp. butter, softened
⅓ cup orange juice
1½ tsp. salt
1 small ripe banana,
   mashed
½ cup vegetarian mini-
   marshmallows
¼ cup chopped pecans

1. Wash and scrub sweet potatoes.
2. Prick with fork.
3. Bake at 375° for 45-60 minutes, or until tender.
4. When baked, remove from oven and cut lengthwise.
5. Scoop out pulp, keeping skin intact.
6. In a bowl, mash pulp with butter, orange juice, salt, banana, marshmallows and pecans.
7. Spoon into sweet potato shells. Place in baking dish.
8. Cover with aluminum foil to prevent scorching.
9. Return to oven and bake an additional 12-15 minutes.

Tip:
   Choose sweet potatoes that are uniform in size.

Go-Along:
• Green salad with orange or mandarin segments and vinaigrette dressing.

Sweet Potato Soufflé

Marie Skelly
Bayshore, NY
Edwina Stoltzfus
Narvon, PA
Polly Winters
Lancaster, PA
Mary Lou Nagy
Maytown, PA
Lynn Higgins
Marion, OH

Makes 6-8 servings

Prep. Time: 20 minutes
Cooking Time: 2 hours
Ideal slow-cooker size: 3-qt.

Filling:
   3 cups cooked, mashed
      sweet potatoes, or yams
   1 cup white sugar
   ½ tsp. salt
   2½ Tbsp. butter, melted
   2 eggs
   ½ cup milk
   1 tsp. vanilla

Topping:
   ½ cup light brown sugar
   2½ Tbsp. flour
   ½ cup chopped pecans
   2½ Tbsp. butter, melted
   ½ cup grated coconut

1. For filling, mix sweet potatoes, sugar, salt, butter, eggs, milk and vanilla together.
2. Pour into small greased slow cooker. Cook on high 1½ hours.
3. For topping, mix brown sugar, flour, pecans, butter and coconut together.
4. Sprinkle over sweet potato mixture. With lid off, cook another 15-20 minutes.

Tips:
1. Canned sweet potatoes or yams may be used in place of fresh.
2. Bake at 350° for 50 minutes instead of putting in the slow cooker.

Lynn Higgins

Asian
Sweet Potatoes

Margaret High
Lancaster, PA

Makes 4-6 servings

Prep. Time: 15 minutes
Baking Time: 40-55 minutes

3 large sweet potatoes,
   peeled or not, chopped
   coarsely into 1" chunks
1 Tbsp. sesame oil
2 Tbsp. brown sugar
2 Tbsp. mirin, *or* sweet
   sherry
2 Tbsp. minced garlic,
   optional
3 Tbsp. soy sauce
¼ cup water
2-4 Tbsp. sesame seeds

1. Place cut-up sweet
potatoes in large baking pan
with sides in single layer.
2. Mix together oil, sugar,
mirin, garlic if you wish, soy
sauce and water.
3. Pour over sweet potatoes
and mix gently.
4. Cover. Bake at 400° until
nearly done, approximately
30-40 minutes.
5. Uncover and bake 10-15
minutes more.
6. Sometime during baking,
put a handful of sesame seeds
on a small tray and put them
in the oven to toast for 10
minutes.
7. Sprinkle sweet potatoes
with sesame seeds. Serve hot
or at room temperature.

Go-Along:
• Spring rolls.

Moroccan Sweet
Potato Medley

Pat Bishop
Bedminster, PA

Makes 6 servings

Prep. Time: 20 minutes
Cooking Time: 2¼-3¼ hours
Ideal slow-cooker size: 4-qt.

2 tsp. olive oil
1 medium onion, sliced
2 cloves garlic, minced
1½ tsp. ground coriander
1½ tsp. cumin
¼ tsp. cayenne pepper
2 medium sweet potatoes,
   peeled, cut into ½" slices,
   and cooked, *or* canned
   sweet potatoes, drained
14-oz. can stewed tomatoes
¾ cup uncooked bulgur
2¼ cups water
15-oz. can garbanzo beans,
   rinsed and drained
½ cup raisins
1 cup cilantro leaves

1. Sauté onion in oil in small
skillet until onion is tender.
2. Combine with garlic,
coriander, cumin, cayenne
pepper, sweet potatoes,
tomatoes, bulgur and water
in 4-quart slow cooker.
3. Cover. Cook on low
2-3 hours, or until water is
absorbed.
4. Stir in beans, raisins, and
cilantro. Cook 15 more minutes.
5. Serve.

Tip:
Adjust the amount of cay-
enne pepper to suit your taste.

Bourbon
Sweet Potatoes

Dorothy Vandeest
Memphis, TN

Makes 8 servings

Prep. Time: 15 minutes
Baking Time: 1 hour

3½ lbs. sweet potatoes
½ cup packed brown sugar
2 Tbsp. bourbon
coarse salt and ground
   pepper, to taste
3 Tbsp. butter, at room
   temperature

1. Peel and cut sweet
potatoes in 1"-thick wedges,
lengthwise.
2. Arrange potatoes in
greased 9 × 13 baking pan.
3. Add sugar and bourbon
and toss to combine.
4. Season with salt and
pepper.
5. Bake at 350° for 1 hour,
or until potatoes are as soft as
you like them. Toss halfway
through baking time.
6. Stir in butter before
serving.

Sweet Potatoes with Fruit

Melinda Wenger
Middleburg, PA

Makes 4 servings

Prep. Time: 20-30 minutes
Cooking Time: 2-3 hours
Ideal slow-cooker size: 4-qt.

4 medium sweet potatoes, peeled and sliced thin
1 large green apple, peeled and diced
½ cup raisins
2 Tbsp. maple syrup
½ cup orange juice

1. Place sweet potatoes in slow cooker.
2. Top with diced apples and raisins.
3. Drizzle with maple syrup.
4. Pour orange juice over all.
5. Cover.
6. Cook on high for 2-3 hours, or until sweet potatoes are tender.

Hot Sweet Potato Fries

Bob Coffey
New Windsor, NY

Makes 4 servings

Prep. Time: 10-15 minutes
Baking Time: 25 minutes

4 large sweet potatoes, peeled and cut into steak-fry strips
2 tsp. kosher salt
1 tsp. cayenne pepper
3 Tbsp. olive oil
3 Tbsp. maple syrup
½ cup reduced-fat sour cream

1. In a good-sized bowl, toss cut potatoes with salt, cayenne and olive oil.
2. Spread potatoes evenly on large baking sheet with sides. Roast for 25 minutes at 400°, tossing 2-3 times during the baking time.
3. Meanwhile, stir syrup into sour cream in a small bowl, mixing thoroughly.
4. Dip baked fries into sauce and enjoy!

Tip:
Good quality maple syrup makes a big difference in this recipe; try to buy local if you can. For perfectly shaped fries, consider splurging and get a French-fry cutter, available at most home stores for under $20. An olive-oil mister will also help evenly coat the fries.

Go-Along:
• This dish is a perfect side for a sandwich.

Slow-Cooker Sweet Potatoes

Charmaine Caesar
Lancaster, PA

Makes 4 servings

Prep. Time: 5 minutes
Cooking Time: 2-4 hours
Ideal slow-cooker size: 4- or 5-qt.

4 sweet potatoes *or* yams
1 Tbsp. butter, melted
2 Tbsp. honey
cinnamon to taste

1. Poke holes in potatoes with a sharp-tined fork. Wrap in foil. Place in slow cooker.
2. Cook on high in slow cooker for 2-4 hours, or until done.
3. To serve, remove potatoes from foil. Cut a small slit in the top of each potato. Squeeze the ends gently so the potato opens.
4. In a small bowl, mix butter, honey and cinnamon together.
5. To serve, top potatoes with butter-honey-cinnamon mixture.

Roasted Garlic Sweet Potatoes

Tricia Stoltzfus
Lancaster, PA

Makes 6-8 servings
Prep. Time: 10-15 minutes
Baking Time: 20-30 minutes

3 large sweet potatoes, *or* one peeled butternut squash, cut in bite-size cubes, enough to make 6 cups of the cubed vegetables
4 cloves garlic
1 carrot
1 Tbsp. butter, melted
1 Tbsp. grapeseed *or* olive oil
salt, to taste
pepper, to taste

1. Place cut-up sweet potatoes or squash into good-sized mixing bowl. Slice in garlic and carrot.
2. Toss vegetables with butter and oil.
3. Lightly salt and pepper the vegetables.
4. Spoon ingredients into a lightly greased 9 × 13 glass baking dish.
5. Bake at 450° for 20-30 minutes, or until vegetables are soft.

Honey-Roasted Parsnips, Sweet Potatoes and Apples

Gloria Yurkiewicz
Washington Boro, PA

Makes 4 servings
Prep. Time: 20 minutes
Baking Time: 1 hour

1½ cups parsnips, peeled and cubed
1 large sweet potato, peeled and cubed
2 firm red apples, cored and sliced thick
1 Tbsp. canola oil
1 Tbsp. honey
2 Tbsp. soy sauce
¼ tsp. ground ginger

1. Mix parsnips, sweet potatoes and apples in greased casserole dish.
2. In a microwave-safe bowl, mix oil and honey. Warm in microwave on high for 10 seconds.
3. Mix soy sauce and ginger into honey/oil. Pour sauce over vegetables and apples. Toss to coat.
4. Cover. Bake at 400° for 1 hour.

Go-Along:
• Green bean casserole, carrot-pineapple-raisin slaw.

Cabbage and Potatoes

Deb Kepiro
Strasburg, PA

Makes 4 servings
Prep. Time: 15 minutes
Cooking Time: 3-6 hours
Ideal slow-cooker size: 5-qt.

1 small head cabbage, cut into thin slices
12-14 baby potatoes, cut into 1" chunks
10-12 whole cloves garlic
¼ cup olive oil
2 Tbsp. balsamic vinegar
1 tsp. kosher salt
½ tsp. black pepper

1. Put cabbage, potatoes and garlic cloves in slow cooker.
2. Add oil, vinegar, salt and pepper.
3. Toss with hands or a spoon to coat thoroughly.
4. Cover. Cook on high for 3 hours or low for 4-6 hours. The vegetables are done when the potatoes and cabbage are both as tender as you like them.

Tip:
The cabbage will get a little caramelized and crispy around the edges where it touches the crock walls. That's okay — it tastes good!

Mashed Potatoes in the Slow Cooker

Barbara Miller
Boyertown, PA

Makes 6 servings

Prep. Time: 15 minutes
Cooking Time: 4-6 hours
Ideal slow-cooker size: 5-qt.

3 lbs. potatoes
1½ cups water
1 tsp. salt
¾ stick (6 Tbsp.) butter, softened
1 cup heated milk, or more if needed

1. Peel potatoes and cut in 1" chunks.
2. Place potatoes, water and salt in slow cooker.
3. Cover. Cook on low 4-6 hours.
4. Drain and mash potatoes.
5. Fold in butter.
6. Add milk while stirring.

Tip:
   This recipe can be held in a slow cooker for 2 hours after mashing.

Go-Along:
• Peas, fruit salad.

Cheese Scalloped Potatoes and Carrots

Rachel Gingrich
Myerstown, PA
Lena Hostetter
East Earl, PA

Makes 10 servings

Prep. Time: 30 minutes
Baking Time: 40 or more minutes

2½ lbs. potatoes, peeled and sliced thin
5 medium carrots, sliced thin
1½ cups onions, sliced
2 cups boiling water
2 tsp. salt, *divided*
3 Tbsp. butter
2 Tbsp. flour
⅛ tsp. pepper
1½ cups milk
1½ cups shredded cheddar cheese, *divided*

1. In a large Dutch oven, combine potatoes, carrots, onions, water and 1 tsp. salt. Bring to a boil.
2. Reduce heat, cover and cook for 10 minutes.
3. In a saucepan, melt butter. Remove from heat and stir in flour, remaining 1 tsp. salt and pepper until smooth.
4. Gradually stir in milk. Bring to a boil over medium heat, stirring constantly. Cook and stir for 2 minutes, until mixture thickens.
5. Stir in 1 cup cheese. Reduce heat and stir until cheese melts.
6. Drain the vegetables. Layer half the vegetables in a greased 9 × 13 baking dish. Top with half of the cheese sauce. Repeat layers.
7. Sprinkle remaining shredded cheese over top. Cover.
8. Bake at 375° for 30 minutes.
9. Uncover. Bake 10 more minutes, or until potatoes are tender.

When preparing mashed turnips, potatoes or cauliflower, experiment with what you have. Try cream cheese instead of butter, or ranch dressing instead of milk!

Teri Sparks, Glen Burnie, MD

Company Potato Casserole

Rachel Yoder
Dundee, OH

Makes 8 servings

Prep. Time: 30 minutes
Cooking Time: 2-3 hours
Ideal slow-cooker size: 3-qt.

5 cups potatoes, peeled,
  cubed and cooked
1½ cups sour cream
1¼ cups shredded Swiss
  cheese, *divided*
½ cup shredded carrots
¼ cup chopped onions
2 Tbsp. minced fresh
  parsley
1 tsp. salt
½ tsp. dried dill weed
¼ tsp. black pepper
¼ tsp. paprika

1. In a large bowl, combine
the sour cream, 1 cup cheese,
carrots, onions, parsley, salt,
dill weed and pepper.
2. Gently mix potatoes into
mixture.
3. Transfer to 3-quart slow
cooker.
4. Sprinkle with paprika
and remaining cheese.
5. Cook on low 2-3 hours,
or until bubbly.

Tip:
Cube the potatoes small.

Go-Along:
• Salad and corn.

Cheese Potatoes

Jalisa Brubaker
Myerstown, PA

Makes 8-10 servings

Prep. Time: 30 minutes
Cooking Time: 1 hour
Ideal slow-cooker size: 4- or 5-qt.

half *or* whole stick (¼-½
  cup) butter
⅓ cup chopped onions
1 Tbsp. prepared mustard
¼ tsp. pepper
1 cup milk
¼-½ lb. mild, creamy
  cheese of your choice,
  cubed
1 tsp. salt
6 medium potatoes,
  cooked, cooled, peeled
  and shredded

1. Melt butter in skillet.
2. Cook onions in skillet
until tender.
3. Mix rest of ingredients
together in slow cooker. Add
onions and butter.

4. Cover. Cook on high
1 hour, or until potatoes are
hot through.

Tips:
1. These freeze well before
or after baking.
2. To prepare potatoes for
Step 3 above, place in kettle
and cover with water. Cover
saucepan. Bring to a boil
and cook unto potatoes can
easily be poked with a fork.
Allow to cool. Potatoes will
peel easily by tugging on the
peels with a knife. Refrigerate
potatoes until thoroughly
chilled. Then shred.

Go-Along:
• Cooked green beans with
brown butter.

*To make your own
hash browns, please
turn to page 261.*

Baked Potatoes Supreme

Susan Guarneri
Three Lakes, WI

Makes 4 servings

Prep. Time: 20 minutes
Baking Time: 75 minutes

4 large russet potatoes
½ stick (4 Tbsp.) butter, *divided*
1 cup shredded carrots
2 Tbsp. chopped onions
½ tsp. dill weed
1½ tsp. salt
⅓-⅔ cup sour cream

1. Wash and scrub potatoes. Prick all over with a fork.
2. Bake at 425° for 45-60 minutes, or until tender.
3. Meanwhile, heat 2 Tbsp. butter in skillet.
4. Add carrots, onions, dill weed and salt. Cook on low for 10 minutes.
5. When potatoes are finished baking, remove from oven and cool slightly.
6. Cut lengthwise.
7. Scoop out pulp, keeping skins intact.

8. In a good-sized mixing bowl, mash pulp. Beat in sour cream and remaining 2 Tbsp. butter.
9. Stir in carrot mixture.
10. Spoon into potato shells.
11. Return to 425° oven and bake an additional 15 minutes.

Tip:
Choose large, uniform potatoes and wrap them in aluminum foil before baking.

Go-Alongs:
• Cheese and broccoli topping.
• Extra sour cream.

Golden Parmesan Potatoes

Natalie Butikofer
Richland Center, WI

Janeen Troyer
Fairview, MI

Makes 6 servings

Prep. Time: 15-20 minutes
Baking Time: 1 hour

5⅓ Tbsp. (⅓ cup) butter
¼ cup flour
¾ tsp. salt
¼ cup grated Parmesan cheese
¼ tsp. pepper
6 large potatoes, peeled or not, and cut in wedges
chopped parsley, for garnish

1. Turn oven to 375°. Cut butter into chunks and distribute over bottom of 9×13 baking pan. Place in oven to melt while oven preheats.
2. In a plastic bag, combine flour, salt, cheese and pepper.
3. Moisten potato wedges with water. Shake in bag, a few at a time, coating well. Place in baking pan, in single layer as much as possible.
4. Bake for 1 hour until golden brown, turning potatoes over once.
5. Sprinkle with parsley just before serving.

Tip:
Use red potatoes, unpeeled, if you can find them.

Seasoned Oven Fries

Rosie Glick
Perry, NY

Makes 6 servings

Prep. Time: 10 minutes
Baking Time: 20-30 minutes

6 medium baking potatoes
2 Tbsp. butter, melted
2 Tbsp. vegetable oil
2 tsp. seasoned salt

1. Cut each potato lengthwise into thirds.
2. Cut each of those portions into thirds.
3. In a large resealable bag, combine butter, oil and salt.
4. Add potatoes slices to the bag, a few at a time. Shake to coat. Repeat until all slices have been coated.
5. As you finish coating the potatoes, place them on a greased baking sheet with sides in a single layer.
6. Bake, uncovered, at 450° for 20-30 minutes, or until crispy on the outside and tender on the inside. Turn potatoes once while baking.

Tip:
You can add extra seasoning to the potatoes after you've placed them on the baking sheet.

Oven Fried Potatoes

Mrs. Anna Gingerich
Apple Creek, OH
Verna Stutzman
Navarre, OH

Makes 6 servings

Prep. Time: 15-20 minutes
Baking Time: 1 hour

6 medium potatoes, peeled
and cut into ¾" cubes
2 Tbsp. flour
2 Tbsp. grated Parmesan
cheese
1 tsp. salt
½ tsp. garlic powder
½ tsp. paprika
¼ tsp. pepper
3 Tbsp. oil

1. Combine flour, cheese, salt, garlic powder, paprika and pepper in bag.
2. Add cubed potatoes, a portion at a time, and shake to coat.
3. Pour oil in 10 × 15 × 1 baking pan.
4. As you finish coating potatoes, place potatoes in pan in a single layer, as much as possible.
5. Bake, uncovered, at 375° for 1 hour, basting with oil mixture every 15 minutes.

(Tilt the pan so you can scoop up some of the oil and spoon it over the potatoes.)
6. Turn potatoes over for last 15 minutes of baking.

Variation:
You can also cut the potatoes lengthwise to create fries. And you can use cornmeal in place of flour.

Go-Along:
• Tossed salad or coleslaw.

Peel potatoes ahead of time and cover with cold water to prevent them from turning brown.

Natalie Butikofer, Richland Center, WI

Potato Roquefort Gratin

Janice Sams
Lancaster, PA

Makes 6-8 servings

Prep. Time: 20-25 minutes
Baking Time: 1½-2 hours

2 large garlic cloves, cut in
  half lengthwise
1 tsp. unsalted butter *or*
  olive oil
3-3½ lbs. small russet *or*
  new potatoes, scrubbed
  and sliced about ¼"
  thick
salt and freshly ground
  pepper to taste
pinch of freshly grated
  nutmeg
4½ cups skim milk
2 eggs, beaten
½ lb. Roquefort cheese,
  crumbled

1. Rub inside of large oval gratin/casserole dish with the cut garlic and brush with the butter or olive oil. Rub again with the garlic.
2. Slice the garlic thin into a large mixing bowl. Slice potatoes into same bowl. Season with salt, pepper and grated nutmeg.
3. In a separate bowl, beat together the milk and eggs. Stir in the Roquefort.
4. Pour over potatoes and garlic. Toss to combine.
5. Turn into gratin dish.
6. Bake uncovered at 400° for 1½ to 2 hours, until the top is golden and crusty

and the potatoes are tender. During the first hour, every 20 minutes or so, remove the casserole from the oven and break up the top layer of potatoes that is getting dry and crusty, give the potatoes a stir and return to the oven. Serve hot.

Tip:
  If the gratin is getting golden and crusty but still needs more baking time, cover top with foil.

Go-Along:
• A salad of lettuces and sliced tomatoes with a good vinaigrette makes this a tasty meal.

Corny Garlic Mashed Potatoes

Moreen and **Christina Weaver**
Bath, NY

Makes 6-8 servings

Prep. Time: 50-60 minutes
Baking Time: 25 minutes

1 whole garlic bulb
1 Tbsp. olive oil
8 medium red potatoes,
  peeled or unpeeled and
  cut into chunks
1 stick (½ cup) butter, cut
  into chunks
1 cup sour cream
2 Tbsp. milk
1 Tbsp. minced fresh
  parsley
3 green onions, thinly sliced

11-oz. can whole-kernel
  corn, drained
salt and pepper, to taste
1½ cups shredded cheddar
  cheese

1. Remove outer skin from garlic. Do not peel or separate cloves.
2. Brush with olive oil.
3. Wrap in heavy-duty foil.
4. Bake at 425° for 30-35 minutes.
5. Cool for 10-15 minutes.
6. Cut off top of garlic head, leaving root-end intact.
7. Squeeze softened garlic into a large bowl and set aside.
8. Meanwhile, in saucepan, cook potatoes in water for 15-20 minutes.
9. Drain. Add to garlic.
10. Add butter, sour cream, milk and parsley. Mash.
11. Add onions, corn, salt and pepper. Mix well.
12. Spoon into greased 7 × 11 × 2 baking pan.
13. Sprinkle with cheese.
14. Bake, uncovered, at 350° for 25 minutes.

Asparagus Potato Bake

MaryAnn Beachy
Dover, OH

Makes 5 servings

Prep. Time: 15-20 minutes
Baking Time: 60 minutes

5 medium potatoes
2 medium onions
10-12 asparagus spears
1 tsp. salt
½ tsp. pepper
½ stick (¼ cup) butter
4 slices of your favorite cheese

1. Peel and slice potatoes. Place in lightly greased 9 × 13 baking dish.
2. Dice onions and sprinkle over potatoes.
3. Arrange asparagus spears on top, or cut up asparagus if you wish and scatter over top.
4. Season with salt and pepper. Dot with butter.
5. Cover tightly and bake at 350° for 45-60 minutes, or until potatoes are tender.
6. Lay cheese slices on top and let melt before serving.

Tip:
Use fresh or frozen asparagus.

Roasted Asparagus

Barbara Hoover
Landisville, PA

Makes 3-4 servings

Prep. Time: 10 minutes
Baking Time: 10 minutes

1 lb. fresh asparagus
2 Tbsp. olive oil
2 tsp. sesame oil
¼ tsp. salt
¼ tsp. black pepper
1-2 Tbsp. sesame seeds

1. Trim any tough, woody stems from asparagus. Place asparagus on an ungreased large baking sheet.
2. Combine the olive oil and sesame oil in a small bowl. Spoon mixture over asparagus. Sprinkle with salt and pepper. Toss asparagus to coat and arrange in a single layer on the baking sheet.
3. Roast at 400° until tender, about 10 minutes. Turn the baking sheet front to back and end to end halfway through roasting.
4. Meanwhile, toast the sesame seeds in a large skillet over medium heat, stirring constantly until golden, 1-2 minutes. Sprinkle seeds over roasted asparagus. Serve immediately.

Tip:
For extra flavor, add 2 tsp. balsamic vinegar to olive and sesame oil in Step 2 before roasting.

Asparagus Stir-Fry

Sharon Yoder
Doylestown, PA

Makes 4-5 servings

Prep. Time: 20 minutes
Cooking Time: 15 minutes

⅓ cup water
2 Tbsp. cornstarch
1 tsp. sugar
¼ tsp. ground ginger
⅓ cup soy sauce
3 Tbsp. vegetable oil
3 cups asparagus, cut in 1" pieces
1 carrot, thinly sliced
1 zucchini, or yellow squash, thinly sliced
1 medium onion, sliced ¼" thick and separated into rings
1 tsp. minced garlic
3 cups cooked brown rice

1. Combine the water, cornstarch, sugar, ginger and soy sauce and stir. Set aside.
2. Heat oil over high heat in a large skillet.
3. Add asparagus, carrot, zucchini or squash, onion and garlic. Stir constantly until vegetables are crisp-tender, about 7-8 minutes.
4. Add soy sauce mixture, stirring constantly until mixture boils and thickens.
5. Serve over rice.

Tip:
Sometimes I use a different vegetable mix, depending on the vegetables I have available in the garden or refrigerator.

Country Market Cauliflower

Susie Shenk Wenger
Lancaster, PA

Makes 6 servings

Prep. Time: 20 minutes
Cooking Time: 2-4 hours
Ideal slow-cooker size: 5- or 6-qt.

1 cup uncooked brown rice
2 cups water
1 Tbsp. butter
1 Tbsp. olive oil
juice of 1 lemon
8 oz. fresh baby bella
  mushrooms, sliced
1 large Vidalia or candy
  sweet onion, chopped
½ cup red *or* yellow bell
  pepper
1 large head cauliflower,
  cut in pieces
3 cloves garlic, crushed
1 tsp. dried basil
salt and pepper, to taste
½ cup grated Parmesan
  cheese

1. Cook 1 cup uncooked rice in water according to package directions. Set aside.
2. Meanwhile, in a good-sized skillet, sauté mushrooms, onions and bell pepper in olive oil and butter with the lemon juice.
3. Place cauliflower, garlic, basil, salt and pepper in a greased 5- or 6-quart slow cooker.
4. Stir in cooked rice and sautéed vegetable mixture.
5. Cook on low, covered, for 2-4 hours, or until cauliflower is as tender as you like it.
6. Top with Parmesan cheese just before serving, while still hot.

Go-Along:
• Serve with side fruit salad for a delicious luncheon.

Mashed Cauliflower

Ellie Oberholtzer
Ronks, PA

Makes 6-8 servings

Prep. Time: 10 minutes
Cooking Time: 15 minutes

1 large head cauliflower
1-2 Tbsp. butter
½ cup warm milk
½ tsp. salt
¼ tsp. pepper

1. Chop cauliflower coarsely.
2. Place in covered saucepan with a little water. Boil cauliflower until soft, 10-15 minutes. Drain.
3. Puree cauliflower in blender. Place in serving dish.
4. Add butter, milk, salt and pepper. Stir well.

Tips:
1. Serve instead of mashed potatoes.
2. You can use a potato masher instead of the blender.

Variations:
1. Roast the cauliflower instead of steaming it.
2. Add garlic cloves, cheese, or other seasonings your family likes in mashed potatoes.

Italian Broccoli

Linda Gebo
Plattsburgh, NY

Makes 4 servings

Prep. Time: 25-30 minutes
Cooking Time: 10-15 minutes

1 large head of broccoli
1 clove garlic
½ cup water
1 Tbsp., or more, vegetable
  broth
salt and pepper, to taste
2-oz. jar pimientos

1. Remove leaves and peel lower part of broccoli stalks. Cut into florets and ½" slices.
2. Steam cut-up broccoli and whole garlic clove in water for about 4 minutes. Discard garlic and add broth.
3. Salt and pepper to taste.
4. Cover and cook over low heat 10 to 15 minutes, or until broccoli is tender. You may need to add more broth if skillet gets dry.
5. Sprinkle with pimientos and serve.

Broccoli and Corn Casserole

Mary Martins
Fairbank, IA

Makes 4-5 servings

Prep. Time: 20-30 minutes
Baking Time: 30 minutes

4 cups fresh broccoli, chopped
16-oz. can whole-kernel corn, drained
1 Tbsp. minced onion
½ tsp. salt
¼ tsp. pepper
1 stick (½ cup) butter, melted
1½ cups snack crackers, crushed

1. Steam broccoli for 3-4 minutes. Then plunge into cold water to stop the cooking.
2. In a large bowl, gently mix together broccoli, corn, onion, salt and pepper. Set aside.
3. In another bowl, mix butter and snack crackers.
4. Add half of cracker mixture to broccoli mixture.
5. Place in greased 1½-quart baking dish.
6. Spread remaining crumbs on top.
7. Bake at 350° for 30 minutes.

Go-Along:
• Salad and mashed potatoes.

Green Bean Tomato Sauté

Becky S. Frey
Lebanon, PA

Makes 4-6 servings

Prep. Time: 20-30 minutes
Cooking Time: 30 minutes

1-2 Tbsp. olive oil
1 large onion, coarsely chopped
2 cups sliced fresh mushrooms
14½-oz. can diced tomatoes
1 quart frozen green beans
4-oz. can green chilies, chopped
1-oz. envelope dry ranch dressing mix
1 Tbsp. liquid smoke, *or* to taste

1. Pour olive oil into skillet and sauté onion over low heat, covered, until onion is caramelized. Stir occasionally.
2. Add mushrooms. Increase heat to medium and stir continually until they begin to give up their moisture.
3. Add tomatoes, green beans, chilies, ranch dressing and liquid smoke.
4. Cook until beans are as tender as you like them.

Vegan

Barbecued Green Beans

Janette Fox
Honey Brook, PA

Makes 4-6 servings

Prep. Time: 20 minutes
Cooking Time: 3 hours
Ideal slow-cooker size: 3½-qt.

1 quart green beans, trimmed
1 cup water
¾ cup ketchup
⅓ cup brown sugar
1½ tsp. prepared mustard

1. Cook green beans with water, covered, until green beans are crisp-tender. Drain, but save the liquid.
2. Mix ketchup, brown sugar, mustard, cooked green beans and ½ cup bean liquid in 3- or 4-quart slow cooker.
3. Cover. Cook on low for 3 hours.

Build your menu around vegetables and fruits when they are in season — they tend to be less expensive.
Susan Heil, Strasburg,, PA

Herbed Green Beans with Tomatoes

Doreen Miller
Albuquerque, NM

Makes 6-8 servings

Prep. Time: 45 minutes
Cooking Time: 25 minutes

2 Tbsp. olive oil
1 garlic clove, minced
⅓ cup green onions, thinly sliced
1 Tbsp. minced fresh basil *or* 1 tsp. dried basil
1 Tbsp. minced fresh oregano *or* 1 tsp. dried oregano
½ tsp. salt
4 medium fresh tomatoes, peeled and chopped
4 cups fresh green beans, cut into 2" pieces
1 cup water

1. In a large frying pan, sauté garlic in olive oil for 1 minute. Do not allow to brown.
2. Add green onions, basil and oregano. Cook a few minutes.
3. Add salt, tomatoes, green beans and water. Cook uncovered until beans are as tender as you like them, 10-20 minutes.

Variation:
Canned beans and tomatoes may be substituted for fresh ones. Reduce cooking time and do not add water.

Green Beans with Sesame Seeds

Anita Troyer
Fairview, MI

Makes 2 servings

Prep. Time: 20 minutes
Cooking Time: 10 minutes

8 oz. fresh green beans
¼ cup sesame seeds
2 tsp. sugar
1 Tbsp. soy sauce
1 Tbsp. instant vegetable bouillon

1. Trim ends of beans.
2. Cook in boiling water for 4 minutes, or until they are tender to your liking.
3. Drop hot beans in cold water to stop the cooking and preserve their color. Drain well and cut in half or thirds.
4. Grind the sesame seeds in a mortar, leaving some seeds whole. If you do not have a mortar and pestle, roughly chop the seeds on a cutting board with a knife.
5. Stir in the sugar, then add soy sauce and bouillon. Mix well.
6. Add sauce to beans. Serve at room temperature or reheat.

Lemon Garlic Green Beans

Dorothy Lingerfelt
Stonyford, CA

Makes 4 servings

Prep. Time: 10 minutes
Cooking Time: 10-13 minutes

2 garlic cloves, minced
2 tsp. olive oil
1 lb. fresh green beans, trimmed and broken in pieces
1 Tbsp. lemon juice
1 Tbsp. lemon zest
¼ tsp. ground pepper
⅛ tsp. salt

1. In large skillet, cook garlic in oil over medium heat for 30 seconds.
2. Add green beans.
3. Cook and stir frequently for 10-13 minutes, until as tender-crisp as you like them.
4. Stir in lemon juice, lemon zest, pepper and salt.

Mustard Green Beans

Renee Hankins
Narvon, PA

Makes 2 servings

Prep. Time: 10 minutes
Cooking Time: 10 minutes

½ lb. fresh green beans,
   trimmed
2 tsp. butter
2 tsp. coarsely ground
   mustard

1. In a covered saucepan,
boil green beans in small
amount of water until crisp-
tender.
2. Drain. Remove green
beans to serving dish and
cover with pan lid.
3. In saucepan, melt butter.
Add mustard and stir well.
4. Pour hot green beans
back into saucepan with the
butter sauce. Mix well. Pour
sauced green beans into serving dish and serve.

Tip:
   Nuts and sunflower seeds
may be added.

Asian Green Beans

Norma Musser
Womelsdorf, PA

Makes 8 servings

Prep. Time: 20 minutes
Cooking Time: 10 minutes

1½ lbs. fresh green beans,
   ends trimmed
6 medium mushrooms,
   quartered
1 medium onion, halved
   and thinly sliced
2 Tbsp. butter
1 Tbsp. brown sugar
1 Tbsp. sesame oil
1 Tbsp. soy sauce
2 cloves garlic, minced
½ tsp. crushed red pepper

1. Cook beans in covered
saucepan with a little water
until soft, about 7-10 minutes.
2. Meanwhile, in another
pan, sauté mushrooms and
onion in butter.
3. Turn heat to low. Add
sugar, oil, soy sauce, garlic
and red pepper. Stir and cook
until heated through.
4. Drain beans. Combine
beans with sauce. Serve hot.

Tip:
   Set all ingredients out
before mixing.

Go-Along:
• Pasta.

California Blend Bake

Edna Good
Richland Center, WI

Makes 3-4 servings

Prep. Time: 5-7 minutes
Cooking Time: 1-3 hours
Ideal slow-cooker size: 3-qt.

½ cup long-grain rice,
   uncooked
1⅛ cups water
1 lb. California blend
   frozen vegetables
1 tsp. onion salt
dash of salt, *optional*
½ cup shredded cheese of
   your choice

1. Mix together rice, water,
vegetables, onion salt and
salt. Place in lightly greased
3-quart slow cooker.
2. Cover. Cook on high 1-3
hours,or until vegetables and
rice are cooked to your liking.
3. Cover the top of the
vegetables with cheese.
Return lid and continue
cooking, about 10 minutes,
until cheese is melted.

*Save water from cooking vegetables as a base
for soup later.*
A. Catherine Boshart, Lebanon, PA

Hot Tomato Curry

Norma Musser
Womelsdorf, PA

Makes 2 servings

Prep. Time: 30 minutes
Cooking Time: 45 minutes

1 lb. fresh tomatoes
2 Tbsp. vegetable oil
¼ tsp. mustard seeds
¼ tsp. cumin seeds
2 bay leaves
⅓ cup finely chopped
    onions
½ tsp. ground ginger
2 cloves garlic
½ tsp. curry powder
½ tsp. turmeric
1 tsp. salt
¼ cup water
½-¾ cup plain yogurt
2 hard-boiled eggs,
    chopped, *optional*

1. Peel tomatoes and dice.
Set aside.
2. Heat oil in a skillet.
Stir in mustard seeds, cumin
seeds, bay leaves and onions.
Cook until golden brown.
3. Add ginger, garlic, curry
powder and turmeric. Cook
for a few minutes until flavors
blend.
4. Add tomatoes, salt and
water. Cover and simmer for
35 minutes. Remove from
heat and let cool.
5. Serve over rice. Top
individual servings with a
dollop of plain yogurt.
6. If you wish, crumble
hard-boiled eggs over top.

Taos Posole

Colleen Konetzni
Rio Rancho, NM

Makes 8 servings

Prep. Time: 10 minutes
Cooking Time: 2-2½ hours
Ideal slow-cooker size: 4-qt.

2 16-oz. cans hominy,
    drained
1 cup grated cheddar
    cheese
½ cup chopped green
    chilies
1 clove garlic, minced
2 cups sour cream

1. Mix hominy, cheese,
chilies and garlic.
2. Place in greased slow
cooker.
3. Cook on high for 2-2½
hours.
4. Fifteen minutes before
end of cooking time, stir in
sour cream. Cover.
Continue cook-
ing on low
until heated
through.

Saucy Succotash

Andy Wagner
Quarryville, PA

Makes 6-8 servings

Prep. Time: 15 minutes
Cooking Time: 2½-6 hours
Ideal slow-cooker size: 3½- or
*   4-qt.*

16-oz. package frozen corn,
    thawed
16-oz. package frozen lima
    beans, thawed
14¾-oz. can cream-style
    corn
1 cup red sweet pepper,
    chopped
1 cup smoked Gouda
    cheese, shredded
½ cup chopped onions
2 tsp. cumin seeds
¼ cup water
8-oz. carton light sour
    cream

1. In slow cooker, combine
corn, lima beans, cream-style
corn, sweet pepper, cheese,
onions and cumin seeds.
Pour the water over all.
2. Cover and cook on
low for 5 to 6 hours or
on high for 2½ to 3
hours.
3. Gently stir in
sour cream. Let
stand for 10
minutes
before
serving.

Slow-Cooker Creamed Corn

Andy Wagner
Quarryville, PA

Makes 10-12 servings

Prep. Time: 10 minutes
Cooking Time: 2-6 hours

1-lb. package frozen corn
   kernels
8-oz. package cream
   cheese, cubed
half stick (¼ cup) butter
½ cup milk
1 Tbsp. sugar
salt and pepper, to taste

1. In a slow cooker, combine corn, cream cheese, butter, milk and sugar. Season with salt and pepper to taste.
2. Cook on high for 2-4 hours, or on low for 4-6 hours.

Baked Corn

Leilani Slabaugh
Apple Creek , OH

Makes 8 servings

Prep. Time: 10-15 minutes
Cooking Time: 4-6 hours
Ideal slow-cooker size: 4-qt.

2 eggs
1 stick (½ cup) butter,
   melted
1 cup sour cream
14¾-oz. can cream-style
   corn
15¼-oz. can whole-kernel
   corn, mostly drained
8½-oz. box cornmeal
   muffin mix

1. In medium bowl, beat eggs.
2. Mix in butter and sour cream.
3. Add corn and mix well.
4. Add cornmeal mix and mix.
5. Pour into greased 4-quart slow cooker.
6. Cover. Cook on high for 4 hours or low 6 hours.

Tip:
   I double this recipe for church gatherings.

Variation:
   You can also bake this in a greased casserole for 35-40 minutes at 350°.

Corn Casserole

Natalie Butikofer
Richland Center, WI

Makes 4-6 servings

Prep. Time: 5 minutes
Cooking/Baking Time: 30 minutes

1-lb. package cream-style
   corn
1 cup milk
1 egg, well beaten
1½ cups cracker crumbs,
   divided
¼ cup minced onion
3 Tbsp. chopped pimento
¾ tsp. salt
dash of pepper
2 Tbsp. butter, melted

1. In a saucepan, combine corn and milk. Heat on medium heat until steaming hot.
2. In a small bowl, beat the egg well.
3. Stirring continuously and quickly, pour beaten egg slowly into hot milk and corn. Remove from heat.
4. Add 1 cup cracker crumbs, onion, pimento, salt and a dash of pepper. 5. Mix well. Pour into greased 8" baking dish.
5. Combining remaining ½ cup cracker crumbs with the melted butter. Sprinkle cracker crumbs over the top of the corn mixture.
6. Bake at 350° for 25-30 minutes or until bubbly around the edges.

Variation:
   Top with ½ cup shredded cheese instead of buttered cracker crumbs.

Cheesy Corn Bake

Susan Kasting
Jenks, OK

Makes 3-4 servings

Prep. Time: 10 minutes
Baking Time: 30 minutes

2 Tbsp. butter
2 Tbsp. flour
½-1 tsp. hot sauce,
  depending on how much
  heat you like
½ cup milk
½ cup sour cream
15¼-oz. can whole-kernel
  corn, drained
½ cup shredded cheddar
  cheese
½ cup crushed tortilla chips

1. Melt butter in a saucepan.
2. Stir in flour and hot sauce.
3. Cook until smooth and bubbles appear.
4. Remove from heat and stir in milk and sour cream.
5. On low heat, stir until mixture thickens and almost boils.
6. Add corn and cheese and mix well.
7. Spoon into greased 1-quart casserole dish.
8. Top with crushed chips.
9. Bake at 350° for 30 minutes.

Variation:
  Sauté a little chopped onion in the butter before adding the flour and hot sauce.

Go-Along:
• Green salad, Mexican bean dishes.

Corn Fritters

Mary Brubacker
Barnett, MO
Anna Stoltzfus
Honey Brook, PA
Linda Yoder
Fresno, OH
Trudy Guenter
Vanderhoof, BC
Julia Burkholder
Robesonia, PA
Janet Derstine
Telford, PA
Leesa Demartyn
Enola, PA

Makes 10-12 fritters

Prep. Time: 10 minutes
Cooking Time: 20 minutes

2 cups grated fresh corn
2 eggs, beaten
¼ cup flour
1 tsp. salt
⅛ tsp. pepper
1 tsp. baking powder
2 Tbsp. cream
4 Tbsp. shortening

1. In a mixing bowl, mix corn, eggs, flour, salt, pepper, baking powder and cream.
2. In frying pan, melt shortening.
3. Drop corn mixture, by spoonfuls, into hot shortening over medium-high heat.
4. Turn fritters when the edges begin to brown and fritters start to "set." Flip and fry on other side until brown. Add more shortening to pan as needed between batches.
5. Remove to a platter when done and cover loosely, or put in a warm oven until all fritters have been fried.
6. Serve hot with ketchup, maple syrup or thin slices of sharp cheese.

Tip:
  1. If the batter is too thin, add more flour.
Julia Burkholder

Variations:
  1. Add a little chopped onion, if your family likes it.
  2. Add marjoram, sage, oregano, thyme and garlic powder to taste.
Linda Yoder

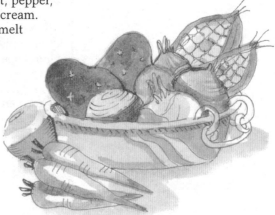

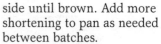

Oven-Fried Eggplant

Susan Heil
Strasburg, PA

Makes 4 servings

Prep. Time: 15 minutes
Cooking Time: 24 minutes

½ cup non-fat mayonnaise
1 tsp. vinegar
1 Tbsp. minced onion
12 slices eggplant, ½" thick
⅓ cup fine dry bread
    crumbs
⅓ cup grated Parmesan
    cheese
½ tsp. Italian seasoning

1. Combine mayonnaise,
vinegar and onion in a small
bowl. Spread the mixture on
both sides of the eggplant
slices.
2. In a shallow bowl,
combine bread crumbs,
cheese and Italian seasoning.
Coat each piece of eggplant
with this dry mixture.
3. Place the coated eggplant
slices on a greased cookie
sheet.
4. Bake at 425° for 12
minutes. Turn the slices and
bake another 12 minutes.
Serve hot.

Go-Along:
• This is a nice side dish for
an Italian pasta meal.

Broiled Eggplant

Elaine Good
Lititz, PA

Makes 2-6 servings

Prep. Time: 10 minutes
Cooking Time: 10 minutes

1 eggplant
extra-virgin olive oil
tomatoes, sliced
fresh mozzarella cheese
fresh basil
salt
balsamic vinegar

1. Cut eggplant into
½"-thick slices.
2. Brush slices with olive
oil.
3. Place on baking sheet
and broil on both sides
until golden brown, about 3
minutes per side.
4. Top with sliced tomatoes,
cheese and basil.
5. Return to broiler for 1-2
minutes until cheese melts,
watching carefully to be sure
the cheese doesn't burn.
6. Sprinkle with salt and
drizzle with balsamic vinegar.
Serve immediately.

Go-Along:
• Pasta, green salad.

Eggplant Casserole

Lavina Hochstedler
Grand Blanc, MI

Makes 4-6 servings

Prep. Time: 15 minutes
Cooking Time: 3-4 hours
Ideal slow-cooker size: 3½- or 4-qt.

4 cups eggplant, diced
½ tsp. salt
⅓ cup milk
10¾-oz. can mushroom soup
1 egg, slightly beaten
½ cup chopped onions
1¾ cups herb seasoned
    stuffing, *divided*
2 Tbsp. butter, melted
1 cup grated sharp cheese

1. In a saucepan, cook
eggplant in salted water until
tender, approximately 5-6
minutes. Drain.
2. In a large bowl, combine
milk and mushroom soup.
3. Stir in drained eggplant,
egg, onions and ¾ cup stuffing.
4. Toss lightly to mix. Spoon
into a greased slow cooker.
5. Crush the remaining
stuffing (1 cup) and toss with
butter.
6. Sprinkle over casserole
and top with cheese.
7. Cook on low for 3-4
hours.

Go-Along:
• Mashed potatoes, lettuce
salad, fruit.

*You can cook eggplant ahead of time and freeze
for future needs.*
Janet Derstine, Telford, PA

177

Eggplant Tomato Casserole

Dorothy Reise
Westminster, MD

Makes 6 servings

Prep. Time: *20 minutes*
Cooking Time: *2¼ hours*
Ideal slow-cooker size: *4-qt.*

1 medium eggplant, peeled, sliced into ½"-thick slices
salt, to taste
1 large tomato, sliced
1 medium onion, sliced
¾ stick (6 Tbsp.) butter, melted, *divided*
½ tsp. dried basil
½ cup dry bread crumbs
4 slices mozzarella cheese, each cut into thirds
2 Tbsp. grated Parmesan cheese

1. Place eggplant in colander. Set colander on dinner plate.
2. Sprinkle with salt. Toss. Let stand 30 minutes.
3. Rinse and drain well.
4. In lightly greased 4-quart slow cooker, layer eggplant, tomato slices and onion slices.
5. Drizzle with 4 Tbsp. butter. Sprinkle with basil.
6. Cover. Cook on high 2 hours.
7. Toss crumbs with remaining butter.
8. Place mozzarella cheese pieces over vegetables.
9. Sprinkle with buttered bread crumbs and Parmesan cheese. Cook uncovered for an additional 15 minutes.

Tip:
This recipe can be prepared several hours ahead and cooked when needed.

Go-Along:
• Spinach salad and corn.

Batilgian, an Armenian Recipe

Donna Treloar
Muncie, IN

Makes 4-6 servings

Prep. Time: *15-20 minutes*
Cooking Time: *3 hours*
Ideal slow-cooker size: *5- or 6-qt.*

1 large Spanish onion, diced
5 Tbsp. olive oil, *divided*
4 celery ribs, cut in 1" pieces
2 cups fresh green beans, trimmed, cut in 2" pieces
3 bay leaves
3 garlic cloves, pressed
2 Tbsp. finely chopped fresh basil *or* 2 tsp. dry basil
1 large eggplant, cubed
salt and pepper, to taste
28-oz. can tomatoes with juice
2 Tbsp. fresh lemon juice
2 Tbsp. capers, *optional*

1. In a large skillet, sauté onions in 3 Tbsp. oil.
2. Add celery. Cover and cook 5 minutes.
3. Add green beans, bay leaves, garlic and basil. Cover and cook 7 minutes.
4. Transfer mixture to 5- or 6-quart slow cooker. Add cubed eggplant on top of vegetables.
5. Sprinkle with salt and pepper. Drizzle 2 Tbsp. oil over all.
6. Top with tomatoes and juice.
7. Cover. Cook on low 3 hours, stirring gently once or twice.
8. Add lemon juice, and capers if you wish, just before serving.

Go-Along:
• A hearty, crusty bread dipped in olive oil.

When different flavors in a dish have had time to blend for a day, the result may be better than when you first prepared the dish. Rose Stewart, Lancaster, PA

Eggplant Parmesan

Jackie Finstad
New Ulm, MN

Makes 4 servings

Prep. Time: 30 minutes
Baking Time: 15-20 minutes

1 large eggplant, peeled
    and sliced into ½"-thick
    rounds
salt
½ cup bread crumbs
½ cup grated Parmesan
    cheese
1 Tbsp. garlic powder
1 egg
¼ cup water
1 cup tomato sauce
½ cup part-skim
    mozzarella cheese

1. Place the eggplant in a single layer on a kitchen towel. Generously sprinkle salt on top and place another towel on top. Allow to sit for 30 minutes (this pulls out excess liquid as well as the bitterness).

2. Lightly rinse eggplant of salt and pat dry.

3. Mix together bread crumbs, Parmesan cheese and garlic powder in a shallow bowl.

4. In another shallow bowl, beat egg with water.

5. Dip eggplant slices in egg-water wash, then in bread-crumb mixture.

6. Place coated slices on cookie sheet generously coated with cooking spray.

7. Bake at 450° for 15-20 minutes, turning over halfway through cooking time, or until browned and crispy.

8. Put a spoonful of sauce on each round, top with cheese and return to oven until cheese is melted.

Tip:
Add additional herbs as you like to the tomato sauce.

Peachy Carrots

Bonnie Lahman
Broadway, VA

Makes 8 servings

Prep. Time: 15 minutes
Cooking Time: 10 minutes

1 lb. carrots, sliced
⅓ cup peach preserves
1 Tbsp. butter
pinch of salt

1. Cook carrots in covered saucepan in small amount of water until as crisp-tender as you like them, 5-10 minutes. Drain. Return carrots to pan.

2. Over low heat, add peach preserves, butter and salt. Mix gently.

3. When thoroughly mixed and heated through, serve.

Go-Along:
• Baked potato, green beans, beets, apple salad, stuffed eggs.

Zippy Glazed Carrots

Irene Zimmerman
Lititz, PA

Makes 4 servings

Prep. Time: 15 minutes
Cooking Time: 12-15 minutes

2 Tbsp. butter
¼ cup brown sugar
2 Tbsp. prepared mustard
¼ tsp. salt
1 Tbsp. parsley flakes
3-4 cups cooked, sliced, hot
    carrots, drained

1. Cook carrots in covered saucepan in small amount of water until as crisp-tender as you like them, 5-10 minutes. Drain. Return carrots to pan.

2. In a small pan, mix and heat butter, sugar, mustard and salt.

3. Add parsley and pour over hot carrots.

Tip:
Don't overcook the carrots.

Go-Along:
• Mashed potatoes and coleslaw.

Golden Carrot Loaf

Wanda Dyck
Burns Lake, BC

Makes 4-6 servings

Prep. Time: 25 minutes
Baking Time: 1 hour

2 Tbsp. minced onions
3 Tbsp. butter
1 cup bread crumbs
2 eggs, beaten
2 cups cooked carrots,
  mashed
1½ cups milk
½ tsp. salt
¼ tsp. pepper

1. Sauté onions in butter until tender.
2. Mix onions, bread crumbs, eggs, carrots, milk, salt and pepper together in a bowl.
3. Place in greased 1½-quart baking dish.
4. Bake at 350° for 1 hour.

Baked Carrot Ring

Lois Mae E. Kuh
Penfield, NY

Elaine Vigoda
Rochester, NY

Makes 8 servings

Prep. Time: 25 minutes
Cooking/Baking Time: 1 hour
  18 minutes

2 lbs. carrots, sliced
1 stick (½ cup) butter,
  softened
⅔ cup flour
⅓ cup sugar
3 eggs, beaten, *optional*
hot cooked peas *or* rice

1. Cook carrots, covered, in a small amount of water until tender, about 15-18 minutes. Drain.
2. Puree carrots in a food processor or blender.
3. Add butter, flour, sugar, and eggs if you wish. Mix until well blended.
4. Pour mixture into a well-greased 6-cup mold or bundt pan.
5. Bake at 375° for 1 hour, or until set.
6. Invert the mold onto a plate. Fill the center with hot peas or rice.

Baked Butternut Squash

Susan Guarneri
Three Lakes, WI

Makes 4 servings

Prep. Time: 15 minutes
Baking Time: 45 minutes

1 large butternut squash
¼ tsp. cinnamon
¼ tsp. nutmeg
½ cup brown sugar
1 stick (½ cup) melted
  butter
2 tsp. lemon juice

1. Use a vegetable peeler to pare squash. Cut it in half lengthwise. Use a spoon to scrape out seeds and fibers. Cut squash into 1" cubes.
2. Place squash cubes in 2-quart casserole dish.
3. Sprinkle with cinnamon, nutmeg, and brown sugar.
4. Drizzle with butter and lemon juice.
5. Bake, uncovered, at 375° for 45 minutes, stirring once halfway through.

Go-Alongs:
• Wild rice with soy nuggets.
• Brussels sprouts with garlic and red pepper.

Build your menu around vegetables and fruits when they are in season — they tend to be less expensive.
Susan Heil, Strasburg, PA

Filled Acorn Squash

Teresa Martin
Strasburg, PA

Makes 4 servings

Prep. Time: 20 minutes
Baking Time: 65 minutes

**2 medium acorn squash,
  about 1¼ lbs. each,
  halved and seeded**
2 tsp. olive oil
**½ tsp. freshly ground
  pepper,** *divided*
**15-oz. can black beans,
  rinsed and drained**
½ cup pine nuts, toasted
**1 large tomato, coarsely
  chopped**
2 scallions, thinly sliced
1 tsp. ground cumin
**2 oz. reduced-fat shredded
  Monterey Jack cheese**

1. Grease rimmed baking sheet.
2. Brush cut sides and cavity of squash with oil. Sprinkle with ¼ tsp. pepper. Place cut-side down on baking sheet. Don't pierce shell with fork.
3. Bake at 425° for 30-40 minutes.
4. Meanwhile, mix beans, toasted pine nuts, tomato, scallions, cumin and remaining ¼ tsp. pepper in medium bowl.
5. Turn baked squash cut-side up. Spoon heaping ½ cup of bean mixture into each halved squash, pressing down gently to fill cavity.

6. Bake another 15 minutes. Remove from oven and sprinkle filling evenly with cheese. Bake 5-7 minutes until cheese is melted and golden brown.

Tip:
   I enjoy serving this recipe in the fall when I can buy squash at our local farmers market or roadside stands where they are plentiful and inexpensive. This dish is also high in protein and fiber and low in fat.

Dinner in a Pumpkin

Becky Harder
Monument, CO

Makes 6 servings

Prep. Time: 1 hour
Baking Time: 1 hour

1 medium round pumpkin
¼ cup honey
¼ cup brown sugar, *divided*
2 Tbsp. butter, melted
¼ tsp. salt
¼ tsp. pepper
⅓ cup chopped onions
**¼ cup chopped red and
  green bell peppers**
1 cup chopped celery
¼ cup soy sauce
1 cup orange juice
**2 Tbsp. freshly chopped
  parsley**
**1 cup chopped fresh
  mushrooms**
**10¾-oz can vegetarian
  vegetable stock**
½ cup sliced almonds

½ tsp. ground ginger
4 cups cooked wild rice
2 cups cooked brown rice
olive oil

1. Cut top from pumpkin and save. Scoop out seeds.
2. Combine honey, 2 Tbsp. brown sugar and butter.
3. Brush on inside of pumpkin. Set aside.
4. In a saucepan, mix salt, pepper, onions, red and green peppers, celery, soy sauce, orange juice and remaining brown sugar.
5. Cover. Simmer 10 minutes.
6. Add parsley, mushrooms, stock, almonds, ginger and rices. Stir.
7. Transfer mixture into pumpkin.
8. Replace pumpkin top. Brush pumpkin with olive oil and place on foil-lined baking sheet.
9. Bake at 375° for 1 hour on lowest rack of oven.

Tip:
   If there is extra rice mixture after filling pumpkin cavity, place it in a greased casserole and bake alongside pumpkin.

Go-Along:
• Bread and baked apples.

Apple-Stuffed Acorn Squash

Sharon Yoder
Doylestown, PA

Makes 2 servings

Prep. Time: 20 minutes
Baking Time: 65 minutes

1 medium acorn squash
2 Tbsp. melted butter,
 divided
1 baking apple
1 Tbsp. lemon juice
salt
2 Tbsp. brown sugar
¼ tsp. cinnamon

1. Cut squash in half horizontally. Remove seeds.
2. Place squash cut-side down on a rimmed baking sheet. Add ¼" to ½" water and bake at 375° for 35 minutes.
3. Peel, core and chop apple while squash is baking. Add lemon juice to chopped apple and stir to coat.

4. Remove squash from oven. Turn cut side up and brush cut surfaces and cavity with 1 Tbsp. melted butter.
5. Sprinkle lightly with salt.
6. Divide chopped apple evenly into squash cavities.
7. Combine brown sugar and cinnamon and sprinkle over apples. Drizzle remaining butter over apples.
8. Empty water from baking sheet. Place filled squash in baking dish.
9. Reduce heat to 350° and bake 30 additional minutes.

Tip:
You can easily double or triple this recipe.

Cranberry Squash

Sara Harter Fredette
Williamsburg, MA

Makes 4-6 servings

Prep. Time: 20 minutes
Baking Time: 45 minutes

1½ lbs. winter squash,
 peeled and diced
1 cup fresh cranberries
1 small apple, chopped
juice and peel of 1 orange
1½ Tbsp. honey
1 Tbsp. butter, melted
salt, to taste

1. Place squash, cranberries and apple in baking pan large enough to spread squash in single layer.
2. Mix orange juice and peel with honey, butter and salt.
3. Pour over squash.
4. Cover with foil.
5. Bake at 350° for 35 minutes. Remove foil. Bake 10 more minutes until squash is tender.

Go-Along:
• Rice, Corn, and Cheese Casserole.

Zucchini Bake

Gloria Julien
Gladstone, MI

Makes 6-8 servings

Prep. Time: 45 minutes
Cooking Time: 2-4 hours
Ideal slow-cooker size: 4-qt.

6 cups thinly sliced zucchini
1 medium onion, chopped
2 Tbsp. minced garlic
¼ tsp. pepper
¼ tsp. celery seed
1 tsp. dried basil
1 cup sour cream
10¾-oz. can cream of
  celery soup
1 cup shredded carrots
⅓ cup (5⅓ Tbsp.) melted
  butter
2 cups dry stuffing mix *or*
  bread cubes, toasted
1 cup shredded cheddar *or*
  Parmesan cheese, *divided*

1. Mix together zucchini,
onions, garlic, pepper, celery
seed, basil, sour cream, celery
soup and carrots in a large bowl.
2. In a separate bowl, mix
melted butter with stuffing mix.
3. Spread half of the
stuffing mixture in a greased
4-quart slow cooker.
4. Spoon vegetable mixture
over top.
5. Sprinkle with ½ cup
cheese.
6. Place remaining stuffing
mixture on top. Sprinkle with
remaining cheese. Cover.
7. Cook on low 2-4 hours.

Go-Along:
• Salad, bread or buns, and
cranberry chutney.

Zucchini Carrot Medley

Elaine Good
Lititz, PA

Makes 4 servings

Prep. Time: 10 minutes
Cooking Time: 10 minutes

3 cups diced zucchini
3 cups shredded carrots
2 tsp. cooking oil
3 Tbsp. water
¼ tsp. dried oregano
¼ tsp. dried thyme
dash salt and pepper
2 Tbsp. butter

1. In a saucepan, sauté
squash and carrots in oil for a
few minutes. Add water.
2. Add oregano, thyme,
salt, pepper and butter. Stir.
3. Cook over low heat until
tender.

Zucchini Pizza-Style

Marcella Roberts
Denver, PA

Makes 6 servings

Prep. Time: 10 minutes
Cooking Time: 30 minutes

2-3 medium-large zucchini,
  both yellow and green,
  unpeeled
15-oz. can stewed tomatoes
1 cup grated mozzarella
  cheese

1. Slice zucchini in ½"-1"-
thick slices.
2. Layer in a greased 9 × 13
baking pan, alternating colors.
3. Pour stewed tomatoes
evenly over top. Sprinkle with
cheese.
4. Bake uncovered at
350° for 30 minutes, or until
bubbly.

*When zucchini is in season, shred it into 2-cup
amounts for future recipes. Freeze until needed.*

Betty Moore, Avon Park, FL

Zucchini "Crab" Cakes

Carolyn Leaman
Strasburg, PA

Makes 4-6 servings

Prep. Time: 15 minutes
Cooking Time: 7 minutes per cake

2½ cups shredded zucchini
2 Tbsp. grated onions
1 Tbsp. minced parsley
1½ tsp. Old Bay seasoning
dash garlic powder
⅛ tsp. black pepper
⅓ cup seasoned bread crumbs
2 Tbsp. mayonnaise
1 egg

1. Mix all ingredients together well in a medium-sized bowl.
2. Heat a greased skillet over medium high heat.
3. Drop zucchini mixture by spoonfuls into skillet to form little pancakes.
4. Fry 4 minutes. Flip and fry other side for 3 more minutes, or until crispy brown.
5. Place zucchini cakes on baking sheet in 200° oven to keep warm until serving.

Go-Along:
• Sliced fresh tomatoes, coleslaw, baked beans.

Roasted Harvest Vegetables

Gloria Yurkiewicz
Washington Boro, PA
Barbara Landis
Lititz, PA
Marcia S. Myer
Manheim, PA

Makes 4 servings

Prep. Time: 15 minutes
Baking Time: 45 minutes

1 cup parsnips, peeled or not, and chopped
1 cup turnips, peeled or not, and chopped
1 cup potatoes, peeled or not, and chopped
1 cup carrots, peeled or not, and chopped
1 cup onions or leeks, chopped
2-3 Tbsp. olive oil
1 tsp. salt
½ tsp. pepper
2-3 Tbsp. balsamic vinegar

1. Combine parsnips, turnips, potatoes, carrots and onions in a good-sized mixing bowl.
2. Drizzle vegetables with olive oil. Season with salt and pepper.
3. Spoon into lightly greased 9 × 13 baking dish. Cover.
4. Bake at 350° for 45 minutes or until vegetables are as tender as you like them.
5. During the last 15 minutes of baking, stir in balsamic vinegar.

Variations:
1. You can also roast halved mushrooms, whole garlic cloves, chopped celery, halved Brussels sprouts, cubed zucchini and cubed eggplant.
Barbara Landis

2. Add a tablespoon of mixed herbs: basil, oregano, and parsley to Step 2.

Go-Along:
• Tossed salad, green beans, corn.

You can scrub parsnips with a stiff brush rather than peeling them. Gloria Yurkiewicz, Washington Boro, PA

Colorful Oven Vegetables

Kathy Bless
Fayetteville, PA

Makes 10-12 servings

Prep. Time: 15 minutes
Baking Time: 45 minutes

5⅓ Tbsp. (⅓ cup) butter, cut into chunks
½ tsp. dried thyme
¼-½ tsp. salt
¼ tsp. pepper
3 cups cauliflower florets
1½ cups julienned carrots
½ large onion, chopped
2 cups broccoli florets

1. Place butter in jelly-roll or 9×13 baking pan.
2. Place in oven set at 375° to melt.
3. Stir in thyme, salt and pepper.
4. Add cauliflower, carrots and onions.
5. Toss to coat with butter mixture.
6. Bake at 375° for 25 minutes. Stir.
7. Stir in broccoli florets.
8. Bake 20 minutes more, or until vegetables are tender-crisp.

Vegetable Stir-Fry with Peanut Sauce

Kelly Martin
Mount Joy, PA

Makes 4 servings

Prep. Time: 20 minutes
Cooking Time: 15-20 minutes

Peanut Sauce:
½ cup vegetable broth
¼ cup peanut butter
¼ cup low-sodium soy sauce
3 Tbsp. brown sugar
2 Tbsp. rice vinegar
2 tsp. peeled, grated fresh ginger
2 tsp. chili paste with garlic
4-6 cloves garlic, minced

Stir Fry:
8 oz. uncooked linguini
1 lb. firm tofu, drained and cubed
1 Tbsp. extra-virgin olive oil
1 large onion, chopped
2 large carrots, peeled and diced into bite-sized pieces
1 cup snow peas, trimmed
1 small head broccoli, cut into bite-sized pieces
8 oz. sliced fresh mushrooms

1. Combine all sauce ingredients in a saucepan. Cook over medium heat for five minutes or until smooth, stirring frequently. Keep warm.

2. Cook pasta according to package directions, but add tofu for final minute. Drain. Set aside and keep warm.
3. Prepare all vegetables by slicing, trimming, peeling, dicing and chopping.
4. Heat oil in a large skillet or wok. Stir-fry onions, carrots, snow peas and broccoli until beginning to soften.
5. Stir in mushrooms and continue stir-frying until all vegetables become crisp-tender.
6. When vegetables are done cooking, add sauce and pasta to vegetables, gently tossing to combine.
7. Remove from heat and serve.

Tips:
1. Any vegetable combination works in this stir-fry. Feel free to make any substitutions for vegetables you have on hand.
2. Do not overcook the vegetables or they will get mushy!

Easy Stir-Fry

Abby Diller
Delphos, OH

Makes 3-4 servings

Prep. Time: 5 minutes
Cooking Time: 15 minutes

2 Tbsp. honey
2 Tbsp. vinegar
2 Tbsp. orange juice
4 tsp. soy sauce
1½ tsp. cornstarch
2 Tbsp. oil
16-oz. bag frozen stir-fry
 vegetables
2 cups hot cooked rice

1. In small bowl mix together honey, vinegar, orange juice, soy sauce and cornstarch. Set aside.
2. Pour oil into large skillet. Heat to medium-high.
3. Add vegetables and cook for 5 minutes, stirring frequently.
4. Add sauce mixture to skillet and cook until thick and bubbly, stirring continuously.
5. Serve over hot rice.

Thai Veggie Curry

Christen Chew
Lancaster, PA

Makes 4-5 servings

Prep. Time: 30 minutes
Cooking Time: 5-6 hours
Ideal slow-cooker size: 3½- or 4-qt.

1 Tbsp. olive oil
2 large carrots, thinly sliced
1 medium onion, chopped
3 cloves garlic, chopped
2 Tbsp. curry powder
1 tsp. ground coriander
1 tsp. cayenne pepper
2 large potatoes, peeled
 and diced
15½-oz. can garbanzo
 bean, rinsed and drained
14½-oz. can diced
 tomatoes, undrained
2 cups vegetable stock
½ cup frozen green peas,
 thawed
½ cup unsweetened
 coconut milk
salt, to taste

1. Heat oil in large skillet. Stir in carrots, onions and garlic. Cook until tender.
2. Stir in curry powder, coriander and cayenne until vegetables are well coated.
3. Transfer veggies to slow cooker.
4. Stir in potatoes, garbanzo beans, tomatoes and stock. Cover.
5. Cook on low 5-6 hours.
6. Just before serving, stir in the peas and coconut milk. Season with salt to taste.
7. Serve over cooked rice.

Nepal Vegetable Curry

Lois Stoltzfus
Honey Brook, PA

Makes 4 servings

Prep. Time: 15 minutes
Cooking Time: 30 minutes

2 Tbsp. oil
1 onion, sliced
¼ tsp. salt
1-2 garlic cloves, minced
½ tsp. turmeric
¼ tsp. ground cumin
¼ tsp. ground ginger
½-1 Tbsp. curry powder, to
 taste
hot pepper flakes, *optional*
2 cups diced, unpeeled
 potatoes
2 cups chopped cabbage
2 cups chopped tomatoes
 or canned chunks
⅓ cup chopped fresh
 cilantro

1. In wok or large saucepan, sauté onions in 2 Tbsp. oil.
2. Add salt, garlic, turmeric, cumin, ginger, curry powder, and hot pepper flakes if you wish. Stir for a few minutes.
3. Add potatoes, cabbage and tomatoes. Cover. Simmer for approximately 20 minutes or until vegetables are tender.
4. Stir in cilantro just before serving, or sprinkle on top for garnish.

Go-Along:
• Serve over rice and with Naan Bread.

Aloo Gobi with Peas

Stephen Zoss
Metamora, IL

Makes 8 servings

Prep. Time: 20 minutes
Cooking Time: 30 minutes

2 Tbsp. vegetable *or* olive oil
1 tsp. cumin seeds
1 large onion, diced
1 bunch fresh cilantro, chopped, with stalks and leaves separated
2 tsp. turmeric
1 tsp. salt
14½-oz. can diced tomatoes, drained, with liquid reserved
⅛-¼ tsp. hot chili sauce, to taste
2 tsp. chopped garlic
1 tsp. chopped fresh ginger
3 medium potatoes, thoroughly washed and cut into large dice
16-oz. bag frozen cauliflower
1 tsp. fenugreek seeds, crushed, *optional*
1 cup frozen peas
2 tsp. garam masala

1. Heat the oil in a large saucepan or skillet.
2. Add the cumin seeds and chopped onions. Stir to mix. Cook until the onion is translucent.
3. Add the cilantro stalks and half the leaves, the turmeric and salt.
4. Add the drained tomatoes and hot sauce, to taste, and stir together.
5. Add the garlic and ginger and mix together.
6. Stir in the potatoes and cauliflower. Add a little of the reserved tomato liquid so the mixture does not stick to the pan. Stir the mixture until the potatoes and cauliflower are thoroughly coated.
7. If you wish, stir in the fenugreek seeds.
8. Cover and simmer until the cauliflower and potatoes are tender. Add more of the tomato liquid if the mixture becomes dry.
9. Stir in the frozen peas and garam masala. Cook for 5 minutes or so, or until the peas are heated through.
10. Stir in the remaining cilantro leaves.
11. Remove from heat. Keep warm until time to serve.

Tips:
1. When fresh cauliflower, tomatoes and peas are available, be sure to use them.
2. I think the flavors are better if the dish is refrigerated overnight and warmed the next day.

Caramelized Onions

Teresa Martin
Strasburg, PA

Makes 3 cups

Prep. Time: 10 minutes
Cooking Time: 30 minutes

1 Tbsp. butter
4 medium red onions, sliced
salt and black pepper, to taste
2 Tbsp. balsamic vinegar

1. Heat the butter in a large saucepan over medium-low heat. Add the sliced onions and a few pinches of salt.
2. Stir frequently until the onions have gone from translucent to a light caramel color, about 20-25 minutes.
3. Add the vinegar and a few pinches of black pepper.
4. Cook for another 3-4 minutes, stirring continually.

Go-Along:
• Use them as a topping for homemade pizza, eggs, or on panini sandwiches.

Don't be afraid to try a new recipe. You never know, it could be your new family favorite!

Jenny Unternahrer, Wayland, IA

Ol' Fashioned Onion Rings

Judy Hershberger
Millersburg, OH

Makes 3 servings

Prep. Time: 15 minutes
Cooking Time: 3 minutes

1 qt. oil for frying, or more
    as needed
1 large onion, cut into
    ¼"-thick slices
1¼ cups all-purpose flour
1 tsp. baking powder
1 tsp. salt
1 egg
1 cup milk, or more as
    needed
¾ cup dry bread crumbs
seasoned salt, to taste

1. Heat the oil in a deep fryer to 365°F.
2. Separate the onion slices into rings, and set aside. In a small bowl, stir together the flour, baking powder and salt.
3. Dip the onion slices into the flour mixture until they are all coated. Set aside.
4. Whisk the egg and the milk into the flour mixture using a fork. Dip the floured rings into the batter to coat, then place on a wire rack to drain until the batter stops dripping. The wire rack may be placed over a sheet of aluminum foil for easy clean up.
5. Spread the bread crumbs out on a plate or shallow dish. Place rings one at a time into crumbs and scoop the crumbs up over the rings to coat. Give it a hard tap as you remove it from the crumbs. The coating should cling very well.
6. Deep-fry the rings a few at a time for 2-3 minutes, or until golden brown. Season with seasoned salt and serve.

Mushrooms in Red Wine

Donna Lantgen
Arvada, CO

Makes 4 servings

Prep. Time: 5 minutes
Cooking Time: 4-6 hours
Ideal slow-cooker size: 3-qt.

1 lb. whole fresh
    mushrooms, cleaned
4 cloves garlic, minced
¼ cup chopped onions
1 Tbsp. olive oil
1 cup red wine
½ tsp. salt
⅛ tsp. pepper
¼ tsp. dried thyme

1. Mix ingredients in slow cooker.
2. Cover. Cook on low 4-6 hours.

Go-Along:
• Pasta.

Mushroom Gravy

Judy Houser
Hershey, PA

Trudy Guenter
Vanderhoof, BC

Makes 4 cups

Prep. Time: 10 minutes
Cooking Time: 15 minutes

½ cup chopped onions
2 cups sliced fresh
    mushrooms
2 Tbsp. oil *or* butter
2 Tbsp. flour
1¼ cups warm water
2 Tbsp. soy sauce
salt and pepper, to taste
½ cup sour cream, *optional*

1. In skillet, sauté onions and mushrooms in butter or oil until onion is soft and transparent.
2. Stir in flour. The mixture should be dry. Whisk and stir a few minutes.
3. Whisk in water very slowly, stirring to dissolve any lumps of flour. Add soy sauce, salt and pepper.
4. Cook over low heat, stirring until thickened, approximately 10 minutes.
5. Add sour cream if you wish. Serve over mashed potatoes, eggs, rice or pasta.

Tip:
    Replace water with vegetable stock and omit soy sauce.

Cabbage Rolls

Mabel Shirk
Mt. Crawford, VA

Makes 4 servings

Prep. Time: 30 minutes
Cooking/Baking Time: 35-45 minutes

4 large outer cabbage leaves
1 cup chopped cabbage
1 Tbsp. butter
½ cup chopped onions
½ tsp. nutmeg
½ tsp. salt
⅛ tsp. pepper
dash hot pepper sauce, *optional*
10½-oz. can tomato soup, *divided*
2 cups cooked brown rice, *divided*

1. Cook cabbage leaves and chopped cabbage in a large pot of water for 3 minutes. Drain. Separate whole leaves from chopped. Set both aside.
2. In skillet, sauté onions in butter over medium heat until limp. Turn off heat.
3. Stir in nutmeg, salt, pepper, pepper sauce if you wish, half of the soup, and 1 cup rice. Mix.
4. Lay out the 4 soft cabbage leaves. Divide rice mixture evenly among cabbage leaves.
5. Roll up and fasten with toothpicks.
6. Spread remaining rice in lightly oiled baking dish. Spread cooked chopped cabbage over it. Arrange cabbage rolls on top.
7. Pour remaining tomato soup over top.

8. Cover. Bake at 375° for 35-45 minutes.

German Cabbage Au Gratin

Ruthie Schiefer
Vassar, MI

Makes 10 servings

Prep. Time: 20 minutes
Cooking/Baking Time: 30-35 minutes

1 head cabbage, cut in wedges
water
½ cup crushed crackers
1 stick (½ cup) butter, melted
1 cup milk
2 eggs, beaten
1 tsp. salt
⅛ tsp. pepper
⅛ tsp. celery seed
dash cayenne
1 small onion, chopped
1 garlic clove, minced, *or*
  ¼ tsp. garlic powder
1 cup grated cheddar cheese
paprika

1. Cook cabbage in water until tender. Drain well.
2. Pour into greased 9 × 13 baking pan.
3. In a mixing bowl, mix crackers, butter, milk, eggs, salt, pepper, celery seed, cayenne, onion and garlic. Spoon over cabbage.
4. Sprinkle with cheese. Sprinkle with paprika.
5. Bake at 325° for 30-35 minutes or until mixture sets and cheese is brown.

6. Let stand 5 minutes before cutting.

Tip:
  This recipe can be made a day ahead and baked just before serving.

Go-Along:
• Mashed potatoes, sautéed green beans.

Cabbage with Noodles

Leona Slabaugh
Apple Creek, OH

Makes 2-3 servings

Prep. Time: 30 minutes
Cooking Time: 30 minutes

1 cup uncooked noodles
2 Tbsp. butter
⅓ cup finely chopped onions
2½ cups finely chopped cabbage
¾ tsp. caraway seeds

1. Cook noodles according to package directions, omitting salt. Set aside.
2. In a skillet, heat butter. Add onions and fry for a few minutes.
3. Add cabbage and stir-fry until cabbage is tender.
4. Add drained noodles and caraway seeds. Stir together and heat through.

Go-Along:
• Add a glass of milk and a baked apple and the meal is complete nutritionally.

Stir-Fry Cabbage

Esther Bowman
Gladys, VA

Makes 4-6 servings

Prep. Time: 10 minutes
Cooking Time: 15 minutes

2 Tbsp. butter
1 small onion, chopped
1 clove garlic, minced
4 cups shredded cabbage
½ cup coarsely shredded
  carrots
⅛ tsp. paprika
1 tsp. salt
dash pepper
2 tsp. soy sauce

1. Melt butter in large skillet or wok.
2. Briefly stir-fry onions and garlic, then add cabbage and carrots. Stir-fry over medium heat about 5 minutes or until vegetables are tender-crisp.
3. Add paprika, salt, pepper and soy sauce and mix well. Serve at once.

Tip:
   Garnish with chopped peanuts for some extra crunch.

Baked Cabbage Casserole

Nancy Leaman
Bird-in-Hand, PA

Makes 10 servings

Prep. Time: 30 minutes
Cooking/Baking Time: 50 minutes

1 small head cabbage
  sliced thin, about 6 cups
1-2 carrots, peeled and
  shredded
1 tart apple, peeled and
  chopped
1 tsp. sea salt
1 Tbsp. olive oil
1 small onion, chopped
1 medium green bell
  pepper, chopped
1 garlic clove, chopped
1 Tbsp. spicy brown
  mustard
1 Tbsp. horseradish
1 cup vegetable broth
½ cup maple syrup
½ cup cornstarch
16-oz. can Italian tomato
  chunks with basil and
  oregano
2 fresh tomatoes, chopped
1 tsp. dried oregano
2 tsp. fennel seed
1 tsp. dried hot pepper
  flakes
1 cup crushed olive oil and
  herb flatbread crackers
1 cup dill Havarti cheese *or*
  Swiss cheese, *optional*

1. Combine cabbage, carrots and apples in saucepan. Add an inch of water and sea salt. Cover and cook for 10 minutes or until tender. Drain.
2. Put in a greased 9 × 13 baking dish.
3. In the same saucepan, sauté onions, green peppers and garlic in olive oil until tender.
4. In a small bowl, whisk together mustard, horseradish, vegetable broth, maple syrup and cornstarch. Add this mixture to the sautéed veggies. Cook and stir until thickened, about 10 minutes.
5. Add tomatoes, oregano, fennel seed and hot pepper flakes. If this mixture is too juicy, you can add a little more cornstarch by first spooning out about ¼ cup juice, adding 1-2 Tbsp. cornstarch and stirring with a fork to mix well. Then add back to the tomato mixture.
6. Pour the spicy tomato mixture over top of the cabbage in the baking dish.
7. Top the casserole with crushed cracker crumbs and cheese, if you wish.
8. Bake at 350° for 30 minutes.

Go-Along:
• Mixed green salad with apples, walnuts and shredded Parmesan cheese.

Homestyle Cabbage

Sandra Haverstraw
Hummelstown, PA

Makes 6 servings

Prep. Time: 20-25 minutes
Cooking/Baking Time: 30 minutes

1 medium head cabbage
2 Tbsp. butter
1 Tbsp. sugar
1 medium onion, thinly sliced
1 medium green *or* yellow bell pepper, cut in thin rings
28-oz. can diced tomatoes, *or* stewed tomatoes
½ tsp. salt
⅛ tsp. pepper
1 cup shredded cheddar cheese

1. Cut cabbage into 6 wedges, removing core.
2. Place cabbage in small amount of water in pot.
3. Cover. Cook 10 minutes. Drain.
4. Place in greased 9 × 13 baking pan.
5. In saucepan, melt butter.
6. Add sugar, onions and green pepper rings.
7. Cook over medium heat until veggies are tender.
8. Add tomatoes, salt and pepper. Stir.
9. Pour sauce over cabbage.
10. Bake at 350° for 20-30 minutes.
11. Sprinkle with cheese during last 5 minutes of baking.

Sautéed Tofu with Spinach

Donna Treloar
Muncie, IN

Makes 2 servings

Prep. Time: 5 minutes
Cooking Time: 5 minutes

6 oz. firm fresh tofu
2 Tbsp. extra-virgin olive oil
1 clove garlic, minced
8 oz. fresh spinach, washed
2 Tbsp. balsamic vinegar

1. Cut tofu in thin strips.
2. Heat oil in large saucepan.
3. Sauté tofu strips until brown on one side.
4. Stir in garlic and turn the tofu strips as you do so.
5. Toss in spinach and vinegar. Cover saucepan.
6. Cook for 1 minute or until spinach wilts.
7. Remove from heat and serve.

Tip:
I like to spray this dish with liquid aminos seasoning just before serving.

Party Beets with Pineapple

Kathie Holden
Bradford, PA

Makes 3-4 servings

Prep. Time: 10 minutes
Cooking Time: 10 minutes

16-oz. can sliced beets, drained
1 Tbsp. butter
1 Tbsp. lemon juice
¼ tsp. salt
8-oz. can pineapple tidbits, drained, with syrup reserved
1 Tbsp. cornstarch

1. In saucepan, combine beets, butter, lemon juice and salt.
2. Stir in drained pineapple tidbits.
3. Cook over medium heat until hot.
4. Meanwhile, stir cornstarch into pineapple syrup until a smooth paste forms.
5. Stir cornstarch paste into mixture in saucepan. Continue stirring until smooth and thickened.

Invest in a spoon-shaped silicone scraper that can withstand high temperatures. This works well when you need to stir in non-stick pans.

Becky S. Frey, Lebanon, PA

Spiced Applesauce

Andy Wagner
Quarryville, PA

Makes 8 servings

Prep. Time: 20 minutes
Cooking Time: 6½-8½ hours
Ideal slow-cooker size: 5-qt.

8 apples, peeled, cored and
   thinly sliced
⅓ cup water
¼-¾ cup brown sugar,
   packed, to taste
½ tsp. pumpkin pie spice

1. Combine the apples and water in a slow cooker. Cook covered on low for 6-8 hours.
2. Stir in the brown sugar and pumpkin pie spice. Continue cooking another 30 minutes.

Tip:
   Adjust sugar depending on how sweet your apples are.

Hot Fruit Casserole

Sharon Wantland
Menomonee Falls, WI

Kathleen Rogge
Alexandria, IN

Judy Wantland
Menomonee Falls, WI

Makes 10 servings

Prep. Time: 10 minutes
Cooking Time: 60 minutes
Ideal slow-cooker size: 4- or 5-qt.

16-oz. can applesauce
16-oz. can apricot halves,
   drained
16-oz. can pear halves,
   drained
16-oz. can sliced peaches,
   drained
16-oz. can white cherries,
   drained, pitted
16-oz. can pineapple
   chunks, drained
⅓ cup brown sugar, *divided*
½ tsp. cinnamon, *divided*
¼ tsp. nutmeg, *divided*
¾ stick (6 Tbsp.) butter

1. In slow cooker, arrange layers of applesauce, apricots, pears, peaches, cherries, and pineapple with brown sugar, cinnamon and nutmeg between each layer.
2. Dot with butter.
3. Cook on high 1 hour, covered.

Variation:
   Reduce butter to 2 Tbsp. Use a can of apples instead of applesauce. Reserve ½ cup syrup from drained peaches. Mix it with 2 Tbsp. cornstarch. Stir mixture into hot fruit just before end of cooking time to thicken.

   Kathleen Rogge

Ambrosia Salad

Susan Henne
Fleetwood, PA

Makes 12-16 servings

Prep. Time: 15 minutes
Chilling Time: 4-12 hours

2 20-oz. cans pineapple
   chunks, drained
3 15-oz. cans mandarin
   oranges, drained
3 cups flaked coconut
3 generous cups miniature,
   vegetarian marshmallows
2¼ cups sour cream

1. Put all ingredients into a medium mixing bowl.
2. Gently mix together to combine ingredients.
3. Chill for several hours or overnight. Serve.

Tip:
   This recipe is great for picnics, church meals and family gatherings.

Sunny Fruit Fiesta

Joanne Ruth
Oley, PA

Makes 6 servings

Prep. Time: 20-30 minutes
Chilling Time: 1 hour

1 cantaloupe, halved,
　seeded
½ honeydew melon, seeded
¼ cup sugar
¼ cup fresh lime juice
2 Tbsp. lemon juice
1½ tsp. grated lime peel
1 cup fresh strawberries,
　sliced
1 cup red seedless grapes

1. Scoop flesh from
cantaloupe and honeydew
with melon scoop, making
little balls. Set aside. Reserve
hollowed-out melon halves for
serving, if you wish.
2. In large glass bowl,
combine sugar, lime juice,
lemon juice and lime peel.
3. Stir well to dissolve
sugar.
4. Add reserved melon
balls, strawberries and grapes.
Stir very gently.
5. Cover bowl with plastic
wrap and refrigerate for 1
hour. Stir one or two times.
6. Spoon mixture into
serving bowls or hollowed-out
melon halves. Serve immediately.

Tip:
　This is great served at a
summer picnic.

Tasty Orange Salad

Sally Grun
O'Fallon, MO

Makes 4 servings

Prep. Time: 20 minutes

4 small navel oranges
½ small red onion, cut
　in half lengthwise and
　thinly sliced
½ cup pitted green olives,
　coarsely chopped
1 Tbsp. chopped fresh, flat-
　leaf parsley
1 tsp. olive oil
¼ tsp. pepper
⅛ tsp. salt

1. Cut one orange in half.
Juice it to get ½ cup juice.
2. Peel other three oranges
and divide into sections. If
time permits, remove the
flesh from the white mem-
branes.
3. Gently stir together
orange sections, onions, olives
and parsley in a medium
bowl.
4. In a small bowl, combine
reserved ½ cup juice, oil,
pepper and salt. Stir well with
a whisk.
5. Pour over orange/olive
mixture and gently toss. Serve
immediately or cover and
chill until ready to serve.

Fruit Salad

Lucy St. Pierre
Peru, NY

Makes 8 servings

Prep. Time: 15 minutes
Chilling Time: 1 hour

2 pints strawberries,
　divided
2 bananas
1 cup white grapes
1 cup red grapes
8-oz. can pineapple
　chunks, drained
¼ cup powdered sugar
6 oz. orange juice

1. Slice 1 pint strawberries
and bananas into large bowl.
2. Add grapes and pine-
apple.
3. Place 1 pint strawberries,
powdered sugar and orange
juice in blender.
4. Blend until smooth.
5. Combine sauce with
fruit mixture and chill at least
1 hour.

*Wash and clean strawberries right before use.
They keep longer unwashed.* Susan Heil, Strasburg, PA

Grapes Juanita

Jeanette Oberholtzer
Lititz, PA

Makes 8 servings

Prep. Time: 10 minutes
Chilling Time: 2 hours

2 lbs. seedless grapes
1 cup sour cream
½ cup brown sugar
grated orange rind

1. Wash and stem grapes.
2. Combine grapes and sour cream.
3. Chill for 2 hours.
4. Just before serving, stir and then sprinkle with brown sugar.
5. Garnish with grated orange rind.

Banana Split Salad

Jackie Stefl
Lower Fairport, NY

Makes 1 serving

Prep. Time: 10 minutes

banana
16-oz. container cottage cheese
fresh fruit in season, *or* sugared frozen fruit, thawed
sugar
3 maraschino cherries, *optional*

1. Peel banana. Slice banana lengthwise.
2. Place on salad plate.
3. Add three scoops of cottage cheese over top of banana to look like scoops of ice cream on a banana split.
4. Cover with 3 kinds of fresh fruit or frozen fruit.
5. If you wish, place cherry on top of each scoop.

Tip:
If making ahead, sprinkle banana with lemon juice so that it does not discolor. Use ice cream scoop for cottage cheese.

Go-Along:
• Fruit or oatmeal scones and nut bread.

Fruit Salad with Yogurt and Nuts

Laraine Good
Bernville, PA

Makes 2 servings

Prep. Time: 10 minutes

1 apple, cored and cut into small bites
1 pear, cored and cut into small bites
2 Tbsp. chopped almonds
2 Tbsp. chopped walnuts
2 Tbsp. chopped pecans
1 cup plain yogurt

1. Mix apple, pear and nuts together.
2. Stir in yogurt. Serve immediately.

Tip:
Use sweetened yogurt and serve salad as dessert.

Use as many fresh ingredients as possible.

Doug Garrett, Palmyra, PA

Eggs, Dairy, and Cheese

Swiss Chard Scramble

Elaine Good
Lititz, PA

Makes 3 servings

Prep. Time: 15 minutes
Cooking Time: 15 minutes

1 Tbsp. olive oil
1 small sweet onion, chopped
2 garlic cloves, chopped *or* pressed
4-6 Swiss chard leaves, chopped
¼ cup chopped fresh basil, oregano, *or* parsley
6 eggs, beaten
½ cup grated Parmesan, Romano, *or* asiago cheese
¼ tsp. salt
coarsely ground pepper, to taste

1. Heat oil in large skillet.
2. Add onion and garlic and sauté for 5 minutes.

3. Add chard and basil, oregano or parsley. Sauté until wilted, about 2 minutes.
4. Add eggs, cheese, salt and pepper.
5. Cook, stirring until eggs are set.

Spinach Casserole

Susan Segraves
Lansdale, PA

Makes 8 servings

Prep. Time: 15 minutes
Cooking Time: 2¼ hours
Ideal slow-cooker size: 3-qt.

2 10-oz. pkgs. frozen chopped spinach, cooked and drained
3 eggs, beaten
4 oz. cream cheese
half stick (¼ cup) butter
¾ cup milk
dash pepper
dash nutmeg

3 tsp. dried minced onion
1½ cups crushed wheat crackers
½ cup shredded cheddar cheese

1. Place spinach in medium saucepan with small amount of water. Cook for several minutes until hot. Drain.
2. Add cream cheese and butter. Stir over low heat until melted. Add milk, pepper, nutmeg and onion.
3. In a small bowl, mix crushed crackers and cheese.
4. Place half of spinach mixture in a greased 3-quart slow cooker.
5. Top with half the crumbs. Pour remaining spinach over top.
6. Cover and cook on low for 2 hours.
7. Top with remaining crumbs and cheese. Cook uncovered an additional 15 minutes.

Tip:
Reheats well. May be served as a main dish or side dish.

195

Spinach Bake

Esther Porter
Minneapolis, MN

Makes 4 servings

Prep. Time: 10-15 minutes
Cooking Time: 2-3 hours
Ideal slow-cooker size: 3-qt.

10-oz. pkg. frozen chopped
  spinach
¾ cup grated mild cheese
  of your choice
½ tsp. garlic salt
1 Tbsp. diced onion
⅓ cup uncooked instant
  rice
1 egg, beaten
1 cup milk

1. Thaw spinach. Then
squeeze out as much of the
moisture as you can. Place
spinach in a mixing bowl.
2. Add grated cheese, garlic
salt, onion, and rice.
3. Mix well and add egg
and milk to rice mixture.
4. Place in buttered 3-quart
slow cooker.
5. Cook on low for 2-3
hours, or until set in the
middle.

Go-Along:
• Baked sweet potatoes or
baked squash.

Creamed Fresh Spinach

Betty Moore
Avon Park, FL

Makes 4 servings

Prep. Time: 10 minutes
Cooking Time: 15 minutes

2 lbs. fresh baby spinach
half stick (¼ cup) butter,
  cubed,
¼ cup flour
1 cup heavy whipping
  cream
1 cup milk
2 Tbsp. finely chopped
  onion
salt and pepper, to taste

1. Wash and trim spinach.
Leave on the water that clings
to the spinach.
2. Place in large stockpot.
3. Steam over medium heat
4 minutes, or until just wilted.
4. Drain and chop. Set
aside.
5. In large saucepan, melt
butter over medium heat.
6. Stir in flour until smooth.
7. Add cream and milk. Stir
continually until thickened.
8. Stir in onion, salt and
pepper.
9. Add spinach and heat
thoroughly.

Creamed Spinach

Mary Reichert
O' Fallon, MO

Makes 4 servings

Prep. Time: 10 minutes
Cooking Time: 2-3 hours
Ideal slow-cooker size: 3-qt.

2 10-oz. boxes frozen
  spinach, thawed and
  drained
1 envelope onion soup mix
1 cup sour cream
8-oz. can water chestnuts,
  chopped, *optional*
1 cup shredded cheddar
  cheese

1. In a mixing bowl, mix
spinach, onion soup mix
and sour cream. Add water
chestnuts if using. Blend well.
2. Spray 3-quart slow
cooker with cooking spray.
Add spinach mixture and top
with cheese.
3. Cook on low 2-3 hours,
until bubbly.

Tomato Herb Mini Frittatas

Nancy Leaman
Bird-in-Hand, PA

Makes 8 servings
Makes 4-5 cups

Prep. Time: 10 minutes
Baking Time: 30 minutes

12 large eggs
1 cup half-and-half *or* whole milk
½ tsp. sea salt
½ tsp. pepper
2 Tbsp. chopped fresh basil
2 Tbsp. chopped fresh parsley
1 tsp. chopped fresh oregano
1 pt. grape tomatoes, halved
1½ cups shredded Italian 3-cheese blend, *divided*

1. Process eggs, half-and-half, salt and pepper in a blender.
2. Mix together basil, parsley and oregano in a small bowl.
3. Place 8 lightly greased 4" ramekins on 2 baking sheets.
4. Layer tomatoes, 1 cup cheese and herb mixture into the ramekins, dividing these ingredients equally.
5. Pour the egg mixture over top and sprinkle with the remaining ½ cup cheese, again dividing among the ramekins.
6. Bake at 450° for 7 minutes, placing 1 baking sheet on the middle oven rack and the other on the lower oven rack. Switch baking sheets and bake 7 to 8 more minutes, or until set.
7. Remove the top baking sheet from oven. Transfer bottom sheet to middle rack and bake 1-2 minutes or until lightly brown.

Variation:

It is fun to use the ramekins. However, it may be easier and more practical for many settings to use a larger baking dish. Prepare recipe as directed, substituting a lightly greased 9 × 13 baking dish for the ramekins and increasing bake time to 18-20 minutes or until set.

Go-Alongs:

• Mixed green salad tossed with olive oil, lemon juice, salt and pepper dressing.
• Lightly steamed asparagus spears, lightly seasoned with olive oil, salt and pepper. I lay these across the top of the frittata when I serve it.

Tomato Galette

Renee Hankins
Narvon, PA

Makes 2 servings

Prep. Time: 15 minutes
Cooking Time: 30 minutes

1 refrigerated pie crust
½ cup ricotta cheese
¼ cup goat cheese
2 tsp. pesto
¼ lb. tomatoes, sliced
1 egg, slightly beaten

1. Roll pie dough out in a circle and place on baking sheet.
2. Mix ricotta and goat cheese. Spread over crust, leaving 1½" border.
3. Spread pesto over cheese. Lay tomatoes on top.
4. Fold edges of dough over and leave center exposed.
5. Brush egg on top of dough.
6. Bake at 425° for 30 minutes.

Use small amounts of leftover vegetables in omelets or frittatas. Norma Musser, Womelsdorf, PA

Tomato Pesto Frittata

Rebekah Zehr
Lowville, NY

Makes 4-6 servings

Prep. Time: 10 minutes
Cooking Time: 15 minutes

3-5 scallions, chopped
2 Tbsp. olive oil
2-3 fresh tomatoes, chopped
6 eggs
1 Tbsp. half-and-half
salt and pepper, to taste
¼ cup slivered fresh basil, *divided*
3 oz. feta cheese, crumbled
2 Tbsp. coarsely chopped pine nuts

1. In large oven-proof skillet, sauté scallions in olive oil for 2-3 minutes.
2. Add tomatoes and cook until heated through, about 3-5 minutes. Turn off heat but leave vegetables in skillet.
3. Whisk together eggs, half-and-half, salt and pepper in a bowl. Stir in 2 Tbsp. of slivered basil.
4. Pour egg mixture evenly over tomato/scallion mixture. Do not mix.
5. Turn heat on to medium-low to cook eggs. Do not scramble but gently tilt skillet and lift edges of cooked egg with a spatula. This will let the uncooked egg run to the bottom of the pan. Cook for about 5 minutes, or until eggs begin to set.
6. Turn off heat and sprinkle top with feta, pine nuts and rest of basil.
7. Place under broiler until nuts begin to brown, about 3-5 minutes.
8. Remove from oven and cut into pie shaped wedges.

Tip:
This dish can be served any time of day. It is great as a main dish for a Sunday brunch or as a quick, healthy dinner.

Go-Along:
• Great with crusty toast.

Tomato Pie

Michele Shenk
Manheim, PA

Makes 8 servings

Prep. Time: 30-45 minutes
Baking Time: 20-30 minutes

3-4 tomatoes, diced
salt and pepper to taste
½ cup mayonnaise
1 cup shredded sharp cheddar cheese
1 cup shredded Colby Jack cheese
1 Tbsp. dried chives
1 Tbsp. dried basil
9" pie crust, baked

1. Place tomatoes on paper towels to absorb moisture.
2. Remove tomatoes to a bowl and sprinkle with salt and pepper.
3. In separate bowl, combine mayonnaise, cheeses, chives and basil.
4. Carefully fold in tomatoes.
5. Pour into pie crust.
6. Bake at 400° for 20-30 minutes.

Go-Along:
• Tossed salad and crusty rolls

Amish Corn Pie

MaryLynn Miller
Reinholds, PA

Makes 8 servings

Prep. Time: 30 minutes
Baking Time: 30-40 minutes

pastry for a double-crust
   9" pie
3 cups fresh *or* frozen corn
1½ cups diced raw potatoes
3 hard-boiled eggs, diced
salt and pepper, to taste
2 Tbsp. flour
milk
2 Tbsp. chopped onion,
   optional

1. Line a casserole or 9"
deep-dish pie pan with pastry.
Set aside portion for top crust.
2. Combine corn, potatoes
and eggs. Pour into pastry-
lined dish.
3. Sprinkle with flour. Add
enough milk to barely cover
vegetables.
4. Cover with top pastry.
Pinch edges firmly together
to seal. Cut several slits (or
decorations!) in top crust.
5. Bake at 425° for 30-40
minutes, until crust is
browned and milk is bubbly
throughout.

Crustless Quiche

Mary Jones
Marengo, OH

Makes 9-12 servings

Prep. Time: 15 minutes
Baking Time: 45 minutes
Standing Time: 5 minutes

1 stick (½ cup) butter
½ cup all-purpose flour
6 eggs
1 cup milk
1 tsp. baking powder
½ tsp. garlic salt
1 lb. Monterey Jack cheese,
   shredded
3 oz. cream cheese,
   softened
2 cups cottage cheese

1. Melt butter in small
saucepan.
2. Add flour and cook,
stirring until smooth.
3. Remove from heat.
4. In a mixing bowl, beat
eggs and add milk, baking
powder, garlic salt, Monterey
Jack cheese, cream cheese,
cottage cheese and flour
mixture.
5. Beat again.
6. Pour into greased 9 × 13
baking pan.
7. Bake at 350° for 40-45
minutes or until set in the
middle. Allow to stand 5
minutes before cutting and
serving.

Variation:
   Gluten-free flour may be
used.

Crustless Spinach Quiche

Barbara Hoover
Landisville, PA

Barbara Jean Fabel
Waussau, WI

Makes 8 servings

Prep. Time: 10 minutes
Cooking Time: 4-6 hours
Ideal slow-cooker size: 3-qt.

2 10-oz. pkgs. frozen
   chopped spinach,
   squeezed dry
2 cups cottage cheese
half stick (¼ cup) butter,
   cut into pieces
1½ cups sharp cheese,
   cubed
3 eggs, beaten
¼ cup flour
1 tsp. salt

1. Combine ingredients
thoroughly.
2. Pour into a greased slow
cooker. Cover.
3. Cook on low 4-6 hours.

Variations:
1. Recipe may be doubled
for a 5-qt. slow cooker.
2. Omit cottage cheese.
Add 1 cup milk, 1 tsp. baking
powder, and raise the quantity of flour to 1 cup. Reserve
cheese and sprinkle on top.
   Barbara Jean Fabel

Turkish Crustless Quiche

Tina Campbell
Lancaster, PA

Makes 8-10 servings

Prep. Time: 10 minutes
Baking Time: 35-40 minutes

1 lb. feta cheese, crumbled
1½ cups plain yogurt
3 eggs
1 lb. zucchini, grated
4 cloves garlic, minced
4-oz. can green chilies, drained
2-4 Tbsp. minced fresh dill, *or* to taste
2-4 Tbsp. minced fresh parsley, *or* to taste
2-4 Tbsp. minced fresh mint, *or* to taste
½ cup pine nuts
salt and pepper, to taste

1. Combine feta, yogurt and eggs in a food processor or blender and process until well blended.
2. In a mixing bowl, combine zucchini, garlic, chilies, dill, parsley, mint, pine nuts, salt and pepper.
3. Pour egg mixture into other ingredients. Mix with a spoon.
4. Pour into greased 9 × 13 baking dish, or 10" pie dish.
5. Bake at 350° for 35-40 minutes, or until center is firm.

Low-Fat Veggie Quiche

Samantha Seifried
Lancaster, PA

Makes 6 servings

Prep. Time: 15 minutes
Baking Time: 60 minutes

4 spring onions, sliced thinly
½ cup halved grape tomatoes
½ cup sliced mushrooms
1 Tbsp. olive oil
6-oz. container plain, non-fat Greek yogurt
1⅓ cups egg substitute
1⅓ cups skim milk
salt and pepper, to taste
10" unbaked pie crust
½ cup shredded low-fat cheese, cheddar *or* Colby Jack

1. Sauté onions, tomatoes and mushrooms in olive oil for 5 minutes.
2. Drain on paper towel.
3. In a mixing bowl, whisk together yogurt, egg substitute, milk, salt and pepper.
4. Sprinkle tomatoes, mushrooms and onions on bottom of pie shell.
5. Sprinkle cheese on top of veggie layer.
6. Pour egg mixture over everything.
7. Place on cookie sheet. Bake at 350° for one hour, or until knife inserted in center comes out clean.

Go-Along:
• Serve with hashbrowns or a tossed salad.

Garden Medley Quiche

Lois Hess
Lancaster, PA

Makes 8 servings

Prep. Time: 15 minutes
Baking Time: 40-45 minutes

10 eggs
½ cup all-purpose flour
1 tsp. baking powder
1 tsp. onion powder
½ tsp. garlic powder
half stick (4 Tbsp.) butter,
  melted
3 cups cottage cheese,
  divided
1 cup fresh spinach,
  cooked and chopped *or*
  10 oz. frozen chopped
  spinach, thawed and
  squeezed dry
½ red bell pepper, chopped
½ green *or* yellow pepper,
  chopped
1 bunch green onions,
  chopped
12 oz. shredded cheddar
  cheese

1. In a blender or food processor combine eggs, flour, baking powder, onion powder, garlic powder, butter and 1 cup of the cottage cheese. Blend well.
2. Pour blended mixture into a large bowl and add remaining cottage cheese, spinach, peppers, green onions and shredded cheese. Mix all ingredients thoroughly.
3. Divide mixture between two greased 10" pie pans.

4. Bake at 350° for 40-45 minutes, or until set.

Tip:
  A versatile dish for breakfast, lunch or dinner.

Go-Along:
• A green salad to complement the lunch/dinner option.

Broccoli Quiche

Debra Kauffman
Pequea, PA

Makes 8 servings

Prep. Time: 20 minutes
Baking Time: 50 minutes

Pie Crust:
  1 cup flour
  ¾ tsp. salt
  ¼ cup peanut oil
  2-3 Tbsp. milk *or* cold
    water

Quiche:
  3 cups chopped broccoli
  ½ cup shredded cheddar
  ½ cup shredded Swiss
    cheese
  1½ cups milk
  4 eggs
  1 Tbsp. flour
  1 Tbsp. butter, melted
  pinch of salt and pepper

1. To make crust, stir together flour and salt in bowl. Add oil and milk on top. Stir slightly with a fork until barely mixed. Do not over-stir.
2. Form into a loose ball. Roll out into a circle between two pieces of waxed paper.
3. Lift off top sheet of waxed paper. Gently center crust over 10" pie plate. Remove other sheet of waxed paper. Crimp edges of pie crust.
4. Bake empty pie crust at 350° for 7 minutes.
5. Remove. With a fork, prick bottom and sides. Bake another 5 minutes.
6. Put chopped broccoli in pie dish. Sprinkle with cheeses.
7. Mix milk, eggs, flour, butter, salt and pepper in a small bowl. Pour over broccoli and cheese.
8. Bake at 375° for 40 minutes, or until set in center.

Go-Along:
• I like to serve homemade rolls.

In my experience, it is best to buy good-quality knives and pots and pans. You will use these nearly every day for the rest of your life.

Carolyn Leaman, Strasburg, PA

Cauliflower Herb Squares

Mary Reichert
O' Fallon, MO

Makes 6 servings

Prep. Time: 35 minutes
Baking Time: 20 minutes

1 medium head
  cauliflower, broken
  into florets
1 cup grated carrots
2 Tbsp. olive oil
¼ cup chopped onions
1 cup chopped green bell
  pepper
1 cup shredded cheddar
  cheese
⅔ cup skim milk
3 eggs
½ cup buttermilk baking
  mix
1 tsp. dried marjoram
1 tsp. dried rosemary
salt and pepper, to taste

1. Coat a 9 × 9 glass baking dish with cooking spray.
2. Steam cauliflower in a small amount of water, just until tender. Drain.
3. Place cauliflower and carrots in baking dish.
4. Heat oil in a non-stick skillet over medium heat. Add onions and bell pepper. Sauté until tender, about 3 minutes. Add to baking dish.
5. Sprinkle cheese over vegetables.
6. Combine milk, eggs, baking mix, marjoram, rosemary, salt and pepper in mixing bowl. Mix briefly with fork.
7. Pour over veggies and cheese.
8. Bake at 400° for 20 minutes, or until top is browned and center is set.

Broccoli Tofu Strata

Arianne Hochstetler
Goshen, IN

Makes 8 servings

Prep. Time: 20 minutes
Chilling Time: 4-12 hours
Baking Time: 50-55 minutes
Standing Time: 10 minutes

1½ cups broccoli florets,
  or 10-oz. pkg. frozen
  broccoli
½ cup chopped onion
6 slices day-old rye *or*
  wheat bread, cubed
1 cup shredded Monterey
  Jack cheese
12 oz. tofu, drained and
  cubed
2 cups skim milk
2 eggs
⅛ tsp. ground red pepper

1. In medium saucepan, cover and cook broccoli and onion in small amount of boiling water for 5-7 minutes. Drain.
2. Arrange bread cubes and broccoli mixture in bottom of 9 × 9 baking pan.
3. Sprinkle with cheese.
4. In blender or food processor, blend tofu, skim milk, eggs and ground red pepper on low speed until smooth.
5. Pour over bread and broccoli mixture.
6. Cover and chill several hours or overnight.
7. Bake, uncovered, at 325° for 50-55 minutes, or until knife inserted in center comes out clean.
8. Let stand 10 minutes before slicing and serving.

Go-Along:
• Spinach strawberry or cranberry salad.

Any questions that you have while cooking can be answered using the Internet. Just type in your question and sometimes there are even pictures to go with the answer! I have been cooking for over 50 years and I still have questions.

Marilyn Widrick, Adams, NY

Broccoli Custard

Judy Wantland
Menomonee Falls, WI

Makes 4 servings

Prep. Time: 20 minutes
*Cooking/Baking Time: 40-50
minutes*

1¼ cups milk
10-oz pkg. frozen broccoli
3 eggs, lightly beaten
½ tsp. salt
½ tsp. nutmeg
½ cup grated cheese

1. Heat milk to boiling in small saucepan. Set aside to cool to lukewarm.
2. Meanwhile, cook broccoli for 3 minutes in small amount of water. Drain.
3. Mix eggs with salt and nutmeg.
4. Add cooled milk and cheese to eggs, beating constantly.
5. Pour into greased 8 × 8 glass baking dish. Add broccoli.
6. Bake at 350° for 40-50 minutes, or until knife inserted in center comes out clean. Serve hot.

Baked Creamed Eggs

Marilyn Widrick
Adams, NY

Makes 8 servings

Prep. Time: 15 minutes
Baking Time: 20-30 minutes

8 eggs, hard-boiled and cut
  in half lengthwise
half stick (¼ cup)
  margarine, *or* butter
¼ cup all-purpose flour
2 cups milk
¾ tsp. salt
⅛ tsp. pepper
⅛ tsp. garlic powder
¼ tsp. dry mustard
1 cup grated sharp cheddar
  cheese
½ cup grated Parmesan
  cheese

1. Place eggs cut side down in a 9 × 13 greased baking dish.
2. In a saucepan, melt the margarine. Add the flour. Cook, stirring for 2-3 minutes until bubbly and tan.
3. Add the milk gradually, whisking. Stir and cook over low heat until mixture thickens. Turn off heat.
4. Season with salt, pepper, garlic powder and dry mustard.
5. Add the cheddar cheese and stir until melted.
6. Pour the sauce over the eggs and sprinkle top with the Parmesan cheese.
7. Bake for 20-30 minutes at 350° until bubbling and top is golden brown.

Tip:
  Lovely topped with sliced mushrooms, peppers, and chunks of fresh tomato.

Go-Along:
• Serve with favorite style of potato, salad, and bread and butter.

Corn Tortilla and Eggs

Donna Lantgen
Arvada, CO

Makes 4 servings

Prep. Time: 5 minutes
Cooking Time: 15 minutes

½ cup chopped *or* broken
  corn tortillas
1 Tbsp. butter
6 eggs
½ cup favorite salsa
½ cup shredded cheddar
  cheese

1. In skillet, fry tortillas in butter until crispy.
2. Add eggs and scramble until cooked.
3. Stir in salsa and cheese.

Go-Along:
• Toast or English muffins.

Sunshine Casserole

Abigail Zuck
Manheim, PA
Bonnie Lahman
Broadway, VA
Rosene Zimmerman
Ephrata, PA

Makes 8-10 servings

Prep. Time: 30-40 minutes
Cooking Time: 3-4 hours
Ideal slow-cooker size: 4-qt.

2 cups shredded carrots
2 cups cooked rice
2 cups cream-style corn,
  or whole-kernel corn,
  drained
2 eggs
1½ cups sharp cheese,
  cubed
¼ cup milk
1 Tbsp. butter *or*
  margarine, melted
¼ tsp. dry mustard
  powder, *optional*
¼ cup minced onion
½ tsp. salt
¼ tsp. pepper

1. Combine all ingredients
in buttered slow cooker.
2. Cook covered on low 3-4
hours.

Variations:
1. Can be cooked on high for
1 hour. Uncover and cook 15-30
more minutes or until set.
2. Omit corn and add additional cup of grated carrots.
Bonnie Lahman

Chili Rellenos Casserole

Darla Sathre
Baxter, MN
Becky Harder
Monument, CO
Elena Yoder
Albuquerque, NM
Donna Suter
Pandora, OH

Makes 6 servings

Prep. Time: 10 minutes
Cooking Time: 1½ hours
Ideal slow-cooker size: 3-qt.

6 eggs, beaten slightly
1½ cups low-fat cottage
  cheese
20 buttery crackers,
  crushed
4-oz. can chopped green
  chilies
¾ cup shredded cheddar
  cheese, *divided*
¾ cup shredded Monterey
  Jack cheese, *divided*

1. Combine eggs, cottage
cheese, crackers, chilies and
half the cheddar and Mon-
terey Jack cheeses.
2. Pour into greased 3-quart
slow cooker.
3. Cook on high for 1 hour
and 15 minutes. Check to see
if it's set. If not, allow to cook
another 15 minutes and then
check again.
4. Remove lid and sprinkle
with remaining cheese.
5. Cook until cheese melts.
6. Let stand for 5 minutes
before serving.

Variations:
1. Omit the chopped green
chilies and use 18-20 mild
chili peppers. Don't grate
the cheese—instead, cut it in
sticks and stuff each chili pepper. Place peppers in bottom
of greased slow cooker and
pour egg mixture over top.
Top with more grated cheese
if you wish.
Elena Yoder
Becky Harder

2. Use poblano peppers
and roast them first under the
broiler. Peel off the blackened
skin and proceed with Variation #1.
Donna Suter

3. Instead of the slow
cooker, place in greased 9 × 13
baking pan. Bake at 350° for
35-45 minutes.
Becky Harder

Go-Along:
• Sour cream and Spanish
rice. Hominy, salad, and tortillas. Rice and beans, salad.

Huevos Rancheros

Pat Bishop
Bedminster, PA

Makes 6 servings

Prep. Time: 10 minutes
Cooking Time: 35 minutes

3 Tbsp. oil
1 green bell pepper,
  chopped
1 large onion, chopped
2 cloves garlic, chopped
2 large tomatoes, chopped,
  or 2 cups stewed
  tomatoes, drained
½ cup tomato sauce
½ tsp. salt
1-2 Tbsp. chili powder,
  depending on your taste
  preference
½ tsp. ground cumin
½ tsp. dried oregano
6 eggs
6 slices mozzarella cheese
cooked rice

1. Pour oil in skillet and
sauté peppers, onions and
garlic until tender.
2. Add tomatoes, tomato
sauce, salt, chili powder,
cumin and oregano.
3. Cook 20 minutes over
medium heat, uncovered,
stirring occasionally.
4. Carefully break eggs
into hot sauce, keeping them
separate from each other.
5. Cover each egg with a
slice of cheese.
6. Cover skillet and poach
eggs over low heat for 3-5
minutes, or until eggs are to
the firmness you like.
7. Serve over cooked rice.

Curried Eggs
with Rice

Kathy Hertzler
Lancaster, PA

Makes 4 servings

Prep. Time: 20 minutes
Cooking Time: 40 minutes

2 cups uncooked brown
  rice
2 Tbsp. vegetable *or* olive
  oil
1 large onion, chopped
4 garlic cloves, minced
1 Tbsp. minced fresh
  ginger
salt and pepper, to taste
1 Tbsp. curry powder
3 cups marinara sauce
8 hard-boiled eggs, peeled,
  quartered
½ cup light sour cream
2 scallions, thinly sliced
1 lime, cut in 8 wedges

1. Cook rice according to
package directions.
2. In large skillet, over
medium heat, sauté onions,
garlic, ginger, salt and pepper
for 6 minutes.
3. Add curry and cook 1
minute.
4. Add marinara sauce and
simmer 5 minutes.
5. Add quartered eggs. Stir
gently to avoid breaking eggs.
6. Serve curried eggs over
rice.
7. Garnish with sour
cream, scallions and lime
wedges.

Tip:
  A quality marinara sauce or
homemade sauce makes the
taste and appearance better.

Go-Along:
• Tossed salad.

Southwestern Hash

Zoë Rohrer
Lancaster, PA

Makes 5 servings

Prep. Time: 10 minutes
Cooking Time: 35-40 minutes

4 cups chopped, unpeeled
  potatoes
2 Tbsp. butter
¼ cup chopped red or
  green bell pepper
¼ cup chopped onion
1 tsp. salt
1-2 tsp. chili powder
2 cups cooked kidney
  beans, drained
2 cups frozen corn, thawed
5 eggs
¾ cup grated cheddar
  cheese

1. In a saucepan, cook potatoes in boiling salt water until soft. Set aside.
2. In large skillet, melt butter over low heat and sauté pepper and onion.
3. Stir in salt, chili powder, potatoes, beans and corn.
4. Heat mixture until warmed. Stir often.
5. In separate skillet, fry eggs sunny-side up. Set aside.
6. Dish potato hash into 5 soup bowls.
7. Sprinkle with cheese and top each bowl with an egg. Serve immediately.

Tip:
  If I'm not serving a green vegetable on the side, I will add frozen spinach or Swiss chard at the end of cooking time.

Go-Along:
• Fresh green salad.

Cheesy Rice Casserole

Charlotte Burkholder
East Petersburg, PA

Makes 2-4 servings

Prep. Time: 10 minutes
Baking Time: 40 minutes

2 cups cooked rice
1 green bell pepper,
  minced, *optional*
1 bunch parsley, minced
1 cup plain yogurt
1 cup tofu
½ cup shredded sharp
  cheese
1 egg
1 small onion, chopped

1. Mix rice, bell pepper, and parsley in lightly greased 9×13 baking dish.
2. Combine yogurt, tofu, cheese, egg and onion in a blender and blend well.
3. Pour over rice mixture. Cover.
4. Bake at 350° for 30 minutes. Remove cover. Bake an additional 10 minutes.

Pickled Beets & Eggs

Marilyn Kurtz
Willow Street, PA

Makes 12 servings

Prep. Time: 15 minutes
Cooking Time: 12-15 minutes
Chilling Time: 24 hours

2 14½-oz. cans beets, sliced
½ cup brown sugar
½ cup vinegar
1 tsp. salt
1 Tbsp. prepared mustard
12 large eggs, hard-boiled, peeled

1. Drain the juice from the beets. Heat the juice with brown sugar until it dissolves.
2. Remove from heat and add vinegar, salt and mustard.
3. Slice the beets into ¼" strips. Add to beet juice.
4. Place the eggs in a large jar. Pour beets and juice over them. Cover and refrigerate for 24 hours before serving.

Tips:
1. The eggs are easier to shell if they are refrigerated for at least an hour before peeling.
2. To serve, slice the eggs in half and arrange on a plate with the beet strips.

Go-Along:
• They are great along with other salads at a picnic!

Best Deviled Eggs

Judith Horst
Newmanstown, PA

Makes 12 servings

Prep. Time: 15 minutes

12 hard-boiled eggs, peeled
½ cup mayonnaise
1 tsp. dried parsley flakes
½ tsp. dried chives
½ tsp. ground mustard
½ tsp. dried dill weed
¼ tsp. salt
¼ tsp. paprika, plus more for garnish
⅛ tsp. pepper
⅛ tsp. garlic powder
2 Tbsp. milk
fresh parsley, to garnish

1. Slice eggs in half lengthwise. Remove yolks and set whites aside.
2. In a small bowl, mash yolks.
3. Add mayonnaise, parsley flakes, chives, mustard, dill weed, salt, paprika, pepper, garlic powder and milk. Mix well.
4. Divide mixture evenly among whites.
5. Garnish with parsley and paprika.

Mustard Eggs

Karen L. Gingrich
Bernville, PA

Makes 12 servings

Prep. Time: 10 minutes
Cooking Time: 10 minutes
Chilling Time: 2 days or more

2 Tbsp. prepared mustard
1 cup sugar
1 tsp. salt
1 tsp. celery seed
1 tsp. mustard seed
6 whole cloves, *optional*
2 onions, sliced, *optional*
2 cups apple cider vinegar
12 hard-boiled eggs, peeled

1. In saucepan, mix mustard, sugar, salt, celery seed, mustard seed, cloves and onions if you wish, and vinegar.
2. Simmer 10 minutes.
3. Place eggs in large heat-proof container. Pour hot marinade over peeled eggs.
4. Let set in refrigerator until colored, at least 2 days.
5. Serve whole or halved.

Tip:
To serve, I like to devil the yolks, sprinkle with paprika and dot with olives or pickles.

Broccoli Pie

Tamera Baker
Lafayette, IN

Makes 6-8 servings

Prep. Time: 15 minutes
Baking Time: 35-40 minutes

2 cups chopped, cooked broccoli
⅓ cup chopped onion
⅓ cup shredded carrots
⅓ cup chopped green *or* red bell pepper
¾ cup shredded sharp cheese
3 eggs, beaten
1½ cups milk
1 cup biscuit baking mix
1 tsp. salt

1. Arrange broccoli in greased 9" square baking dish.
2. Layer over the broccoli the onion, carrots, green pepper and cheese.
3. In a bowl, beat together eggs, milk, baking mix and salt. Pour evenly over vegetables.
4. Bake at 375° for 35-40 minutes.

Tip:
The broccoli can be exchanged for asparagus, zucchini, or mushrooms. This is a great way to use up leftover cooked veggies.

Variation:
Sauté the onion, carrots, and bell pepper first if you like a softer texture.

Artichoke Parmesan Quiche

Kaye Taylor
Florissant, MO

Makes 6-8 servings

Prep. Time: 15-20 minutes
Baking Time: 45-55 minutes

9" unbaked pie shell
½ cup grated Parmesan cheese, plus additional for garnish
14-oz. can artichoke hearts, drained
1¼ cups shredded Swiss cheese
3 oz. cream cheese, softened
½ tsp. ground nutmeg
⅛ tsp. salt
1 cup, plus 2 Tbsp., evaporated milk
3 eggs

1. Prick bottom and sides of pie shell with fork.
2. Bake at 450° for 7-8 minutes or until lightly browned.
3. Sprinkle ½ cup Parmesan cheese over pie crust.
4. Squeeze liquid from artichokes, blot dry and chop finely.
5. Sprinkle artichokes over Parmesan cheese.
6. Add Swiss cheese over artichokes.
7. In small bowl, beat cream cheese, nutmeg and salt.
8. Gradually beat in milk and one egg at a time, beating well after each egg. Beat until frothy.
9. Pour over filling in pie pan.
10. Bake at 400° for 40-45 minutes or until golden brown and set in the middle.
11. Sprinkle liberally with additional Parmesan cheese before serving.

Tip:
It is best to use a glass pie pan to bake crust.

Salads

California Salad

Kathy Rodkey
Halifax, PA

Makes 4 servings
Prep. Time: 30 minutes

½ cup orange juice
2½ Tbsp. lime juice
1 tsp. salt
¼ tsp. black pepper
½ tsp. chili powder
8 cups baby arugula
2 navel oranges, peeled, diced
1 avocado, pitted, cut in 1" pieces

1. In a bowl, whisk together orange juice, lime juice, salt, pepper and chili powder.
2. Mound arugula on 4 plates.
3. Top with oranges and avocado.
4. Sprinkle with dressing just before serving.

Variations:
1. Change it up:
2. Add 2 red grapefruit, sectioned; 1 cup cooked brown rice; 2 Tbsp. dried cranberries.
3. To each plate, add 2 Tbsp. soft, crumbled goat cheese; 1 medium pitted and chopped date; 1 tsp. sliced toasted almonds.

Fennel and Apple Green Salad

Jean Harris Robinson
Pemberton, NJ

Makes 4 servings
Prep. Time: 30-40 minutes
Standing Time: 30 minutes

1½ cups diced cucumbers, from 1 medium-sized cuke
½ tsp. salt
3 Tbsp. extra-virgin olive oil
3 Tbsp. rice vinegar

1 fennel bulb, cored and diced, *or* 1½ cups
2 Red Delicious apples, cored and finely diced, *or* 2 cups
3 cups torn Romaine lettuce
¼ cup diced onion, *optional*
½ cup chopped walnuts
4 oz. crumbled feta cheese

1. Combine cucumber and salt in a colander and set over a bowl for 15 minutes.
2. Whisk oil and vinegar in large bowl.
3. Add drained cucumbers, fennel and apples.
4. Let stand for up to 30 minutes to blend.
5. Add lettuce, onions if you wish, and walnuts. Toss gently.
6. Divide salad between 4 plates. Top with feta cheese.

Grilled Vegetable Salad

Jana Beyer
Harrisonburg, VA

Makes 6-8 servings

Prep. Time: 20 minutes
Cooking Time: 10 minutes

1 red onion, sliced
1 eggplant, sliced
2 red bell peppers, cut into rings
1 medium zucchini, sliced
1 medium yellow squash, sliced
10-15 asparagus spears
¼ cup olive oil
salt, to taste
freshly ground pepper, to taste
4-6 cups torn mixed greens
¼ cup balsamic vinegar
¼ cup chopped fresh basil

1. Brush onions, eggplant, peppers, zucchini, squash and asparagus with oil. Sprinkle with salt and pepper.
2. Grill onion, eggplant and peppers 8-10 minutes over medium heat, until vegetables are softened and have grill marks.
3. Grill zucchini, squash and asparagus for 5-6 minutes.
4. Set aside to cool to room temperature or put on the salads while hot.
5. Divide greens between 6-8 salad plates. Arrange grilled vegetables on top of greens.
6. Drizzle with balsamic vinegar. Sprinkle with basil. Serve immediately.

Salad Louise

Barbara Grannemann
Gerald, MO

Makes 12 servings

Chilling Time: 1-2 hours
Prep. Time: 30 minutes

8-oz. can sliced water chestnuts, drained
15-oz. can bean sprouts, drained
8-10 cups mixed greens
1 carrot, shredded
4 eggs, hard-boiled and chopped
5-oz. can chow mein noodles
⅓ cup white vinegar
1 cup vegetable oil
1 tsp. vegetarian Worcestershire sauce
½ large red onion, chopped
1 tsp. salt
¾ cup sugar

1. Place cans of water chestnuts and bean sprouts in refrigerator to chill for 1-2 hours. Chill greens and hard-boiled eggs.
2. Drain water chestnuts and bean sprouts. Add to greens in large mixing bowl. Add carrots, eggs and chow mein noodles. Mix.
3. Blend vinegar, oil, Worcestershire sauce, onions, salt and sugar in a blender until creamy and sugar is dissolved.
4. Put dressing on right before serving.

Spinach Salad with Poppy Seed Dressing

Laraine Good
Bernville, PA

Makes 4 servings

Prep. Time: 10 minutes

4-5 cups fresh spinach, washed, dried and torn
1 cup shredded cheddar cheese
1 cup cheese-and-garlic croutons
3 eggs, hard-boiled and chopped
¼ cup olive oil
2 Tbsp. mayonnaise
2 Tbsp. sugar
2 Tbsp. vinegar
¼ tsp. dry mustard
¼ tsp. salt
1 tsp. grated onion
½ tsp. poppy seeds

1. In salad bowl, combine spinach, cheese, croutons and egg.
2. Mix rest of ingredients together in a small bowl to make salad dressing. Whisk well.
3. Pour dressing over salad and toss just before serving.

Spinach Salad

Dorothy Reise
Westminster, MD

Makes 8-10 servings
Prep. Time: 30 minutes

1 lb. fresh spinach,
  washed, dried
1 head red-leaf lettuce,
  washed, dried
1 pint fresh strawberries,
  washed
14-oz. can mandarin
  oranges, drained
¼ cup sugar
1 tsp. salt
1 tsp. dry mustard
1 Tbsp. onion juice
½ cup vinegar
1 cup salad oil
1 Tbsp. poppy seeds
1 cup large-curd cottage
  cheese

1. Tear spinach and lettuce.
2. Place in large salad bowl.
Add strawberries and oranges.
3. In separate bowl mix
sugar, salt, mustard, onion
juice, vinegar, oil and poppy
seeds. Whisk well.
4. Toss half of dressing
with greens and fruit.
5. Add remaining dressing
to cottage cheese and mix well.
6. Add to greens and fruit
and serve immediately.

Tip:
  Do not toss salad with dressing until ready to serve. Greens
do not hold crispness for a long
time. Dressing may be stored
in refrigerator for one week.

Tossed Salad with Candied Almonds

Kathy Hertzler
Lancaster, PA

Makes 6 servings
Prep. Time: 30 minutes
Cooking Time: 5 minutes

1 large head Romaine
  lettuce
3 Tbsp. white sugar, *divided*
¼ cup sliced almonds
2 celery ribs, chopped
2 green onions, sliced
¼ cup vegetable oil
2 Tbsp. white wine vinegar
1 Tbsp. snipped parsley
¼ tsp. salt
2 dashes hot pepper sauce
11-oz. can mandarin
  oranges, drained

1. Tear lettuce in bite-size
pieces.
2. Sprinkle 1 Tbsp. sugar
into dry non-stick pan.
3. Sprinkle almonds on top.
4. Heat and stir over
medium heat until sugar
melts.
5. Remove from heat. Place
nuts on plate and set aside to
cool. Break into pieces when
cooled.
6. Mix celery and green
onions with lettuce.
7. Mix oil, remaining 2
Tbsp. sugar, wine vinegar,
parsley, salt and hot pepper
sauce in food processor.
8. Toss over salad.
9. Add mandarin oranges
and almonds.

Tip:
  Toss dressing just before
serving or salad will become
soggy.

Tropical Salad with Crunchy Pecans

Julie Landes
Harleysville, PA

Makes 4-6 servings

Prep. Time: 30 minutes
Cooking Time: 10 minutes

¼ cup olive oil
¼ cup balsamic vinegar
2 Tbsp. plus ½ cup sugar, *divided*
¼ tsp. salt
¼ tsp. pepper
¼ tsp. hot sauce, *or* to taste
1 cup pecans
10 oz. mixed greens *or* Romaine lettuce
2 cups cubed fresh pineapple
2 kiwis, skins removed, sliced and quartered
11-oz. can mandarin oranges, drained
16 red grapes, halved

1. Combine oil, vinegar, 2 Tbsp. sugar, salt, pepper and hot sauce. Set dressing aside.

2. In a heavy saucepan over medium heat, combine pecans and ½ cup sugar, stirring constantly until sugar is melted.

3. Quickly spread sugared pecans onto a cookie sheet lined with waxed paper. Let cool.

4. Assemble salad in a glass trifle bowl. Make layers with lettuce, pineapple, kiwi, oranges and grapes.

5. Top with sugared pecans.

6. Serve the dressing on the side.

Tip:

Both dressing and nuts can be prepared ahead of time. Dressing can be tossed with the salad, but serve immediately and know that leftovers will not keep.

Cranberry Apple Salad

Mary Hackenberger
Thompsontown, PA

Makes 6-10 servings

Prep. Time: 20-25 minutes
Baking Time: 4-7 minutes
Standing Time: 20-30 minutes

½ cup slivered almonds
10 oz. torn mixed baby greens
1 medium red apple, cored and diced
1 medium green apple, cored and diced
1 cup freshly grated Parmesan cheese
½ cup dried cranberries
1 cup fresh cranberries
½ cup sugar
½ cup cider vinegar
¼ cup frozen apple juice concentrate, thawed
1 tsp. salt
1 tsp. dry ground mustard
½ tsp. dried minced onion
1 cup oil

1. Spread almonds on a baking sheet. Bake at 350° for 4-7 minutes, watching closely to be sure they get a little tan, but not burnt. Set aside to cool for 20-30 minutes.

2. Divide salad greens among 6-10 individual bowls.

3. In a medium bowl, toss together apples, cheese, dried cranberries and cooled almonds. Spoon evenly over greens.

4. Put fresh cranberries, sugar, vinegar, juice, salt, mustard and onion in a blender. Process briefly.

5. Slowly and steadily add oil while processing. Blend until smooth.

6. Drizzle salad with desired amount of dressing. Store any unused dressing in the refrigerator.

7. Serve salads immediately.

Signature Salad

Abigail Thompson
Millersville, PA

Makes 4 servings

Prep. Time: 15-20 minutes
Cooking Time: 5 minutes

2 cups baby spinach
4 cups mixed salad greens
¼ cup chopped pecans, toasted
¼ cup chopped almonds, toasted
¼ cup chopped walnuts, toasted
½ cup dried cranberries
¼ cup dried cherries
½ cup chopped red bell pepper
1 Gala apple, cored and chopped
1 cup cottage cheese, *divided*
12-oz. bottle strawberry balsamic dressing

1. In a large bowl mix together spinach and mixed greens with the pecans, almonds, walnuts, cranberries, cherries, bell pepper and apple.
2. To serve, divide into 6-8 individual salad bowls. Top each serving with 2 heaping tablespoons of cottage cheese and drizzle with dressing.

Go-Along:
• Whole wheat bread, toasted, topped with a thin layer of ricotta cheese and a thin layer of strawberry jam.

Spring Greens with Roasted Rhubarb and Parmesan Crisps

Bob Coffey
New Windsor, NY

Makes 4 servings

Prep. Time: 20 minutes
Baking Time: 30 minutes
Standing Time: 20 minutes
Chilling Time: 1 hour or more

2 cups chopped fresh rhubarb
¼ cup honey
8 Tbsp. Parmesan cheese
2 Tbsp. champagne vinegar, *or any other white wine vinegar*
4 Tbsp. olive oil
sugar to taste
¾-1 lb. fresh greens *or spring mix*, washed

1. In a large casserole dish combine rhubarb and honey. Roast at 400° for 20 minutes or until rhubarb is tender. Set aside to cool.
2. Line a baking tray with parchment paper sprayed with cooking spray.
3. Place Parmesan cheese on paper in four round piles, spaced evenly apart. Bake at 400° for 10-15 minutes or until just browned and crispy. Once done, set aside to cool.
4. Once rhubarb is roasted, drain liquid. Chill rhubarb at least 1 hour.
5. Whisk together vinegar, olive oil and sugar to taste, adding in pinch increments and tasting.
6. When ready to serve, divide greens among 4 salad plates.
7. Add rhubarb, drizzle with dressing and top with cheese crisps. Serve immediately.

Tips:
1. Roasting with honey is messy, so I use a disposable tray from the Dollar Store.
2. The Parmesan crisps and roasted rhubarb can be prepared up to a day in advance. Assemble the salad at the last minute.

Use kitchen scissors to chop rhubarb.
Leah Hersberger, Dundee, OH

Cheddar Almond Salad

June Hackenberger
Thompsontown, PA

Makes 6-8 servings

Prep. Time: 15 minutes
Baking Time: 5-7 minutes

½ cup slivered almonds
9 cups torn Romaine
   lettuce
1 cup shredded cheddar
   cheese
¼ cup sugar
2 Tbsp. vinegar
2 Tbsp. honey
½ tsp. onion powder
½ tsp. celery seed
½ tsp. ground dry mustard
½ tsp. paprika
¼ tsp. salt
½ cup oil

1. Spread almonds on baking sheet in a single layer. Toast in oven at 350° until lightly browned, about 5-7 minutes. Cool.
2. Divide lettuce and cheese among 6-8 salad plates.
3. In blender, combine sugar, vinegar, honey, onion powder, celery seed, mustard, paprika and salt. Blend well.
4. While still processing, gradually add oil in a steady stream. Blend until well mixed.
5. Drizzle over salads. Sprinkle with toasted almonds.

24 Hour Salad

Elaine Martin
Palmerston, ON

Makes 12 servings

Prep. Time: 15 minutes
Chilling Time: 12-24 hours

1 head Romaine lettuce
1½ cups cauliflower florets
1 red onion, sliced
½ cup grated Parmesan
   cheese
2 Tbsp. sugar
1 cup mayonnaise

1. Tear lettuce into bite-sized pieces. Place in a bowl.
2. Layer cauliflower and onions on top.
3. Mix Parmesan cheese, sugar and mayonnaise together.
4. Spread on top of vegetables. Cover. Refrigerate for 12 hours and up to 24 hours.
5. Toss before serving.

Tex-Mex Salad

Barb Yoder
Angola, IN

Makes 4 servings

Prep. Time: 15 minutes

½ head iceburg lettuce,
   chopped
1 cup cooked black beans,
   drained
¼ cup chopped fresh
   cilantro
½ cup canned *or* frozen
   corn, drained
½ cup shredded cheese
1 small onion, chopped
½-1 cup salsa
tortilla chips

1. In bowl, mix lettuce, beans, cilantro, corn, cheese and onions.
2. Add salsa as dressing.
3. Serve with tortilla chips.

Croutons

Natalie Butikofer
Richland Center, WI

Makes 6 servings
Makes 1 cup

Prep. Time: 5 minutes
Baking Time: 20-25 minutes
Standing Time: 30 minutes

1 Tbsp. vegetable *or* olive oil
1 garlic clove, minced
1 cup cubed day-old bread
pinch onion salt

1. Pour the oil into an 8" square baking pan. Stir in garlic.
2. Bake at 325° until garlic is lightly browned, about 3-4 minutes.
3. Add bread and onion salt. Stir to coat.
4. Bake 15-20 minutes longer or until bread is lightly browned, stirring occasionally.
5. Cool at least 30 minutes. Store in air-tight container.

Tip:
A quick garnish for a plain old lettuce salad or cream soup!

Herb Vinaigrette

Judy Koczo
Plano, IL

Makes ⅔ cup

Prep. Time: 5 minutes

6 Tbsp. cider vinegar
6 Tbsp. oil
2 Tbsp. finely chopped onion
1 tsp. salt
½ tsp. dried chives
½ tsp. dried tarragon
½ tsp. dried dill weed

1. Mix ingredients together thoroughly in a small bowl.
2. Pour over lettuce when ready to serve.

Variation:
Add a little sugar if you like a sweet-sour dressing.

Pesto Salad Dressing

Jennifer Kuh
Bay Village, OH

Makes 1 cup

Prep. Time: 5 minutes

½ cup pesto
3 Tbsp. balsamic vinaigrette
2 tsp. prepared mustard

1. Mix pesto, vinaigrette and mustard.
2. Store in refrigerator, tightly covered. Serve over salads or use as a dip with bread.

If your household includes both vegetarians and non-vegetarians, try offering dishes that allow each person to choose from a variety of ingredients to create their own dish. This built-in menu flexibility leads to less grumbling and more happy consumers. Some examples include build-your-own burritos, haystacks, tacos, baked potatoes with toppings, salad supper and sandwiches. Be sure to provide both meat and non-meat protein options such as beans or nuts for people to choose from.
Leanne Yoder, Tucson, AZ

French Dressing Mix

Marla Folkerts
Geneva, IL

Makes 1¼ cups
Prep. Time: 10 minutes

¼-½ cup sugar
1½ tsp. paprika
1 tsp. dry mustard
1½ tsp. salt
⅛ tsp. onion powder
¾ cup vegetable oil
¼ cup vinegar

1. Combine sugar, paprika, dry mustard, salt and onion powder in small bowl.
2. Place in a glass container and store in a cool, dry place. Use within 6 months.
3. To make salad dressing, combine mix with vegetable oil and vinegar. Whisk well. Serve over lettuce.

Tip:
Package dry mix in a pretty jar, write the mixing directions and recipe on a tag, and give as a gift.

Variation:
1 Tbsp. celery seed used in place of paprika.

Celery Seed Salad Dressing

Mary Hackenberger
Thompsontown, PA

Joanne Ruth
Oley, PA

Makes 4½-5 cups
Prep. Time: 10 minutes

1 large onion, chopped
1⅓ cups sugar
1 Tbsp. salt
1½ tsp. pepper
1½ Tbsp. celery seed
3 Tbsp. prepared mustard
6 Tbsp. mayonnaise
1 cup vinegar
3 cups oil

1. Combine onion, sugar, salt, pepper, celery seed, mustard, mayonnaise and vinegar in a blender.
2. Slowly and steadily add oil while processing. Sugar should be dissolved and onion should be totally puréed.
3. The dressing keeps well in the refrigerator for several months.

Tip:
This dressing is perfect to top a salad of lettuce, chopped tomatoes, cheese, hard-boiled eggs and croutons.

Variation:
Omit mayonnaise. Use 3 tsp. dry mustard instead of prepared mustard.

Joanne Ruth

Honey Mustard Dressing

Rae Ann Henry
Conestoga, PA

Naomi Cross
Owenton, KY

Makes ¼ cup
Prep. Time: 5 minutes

¼ cup mayonnaise
1-2 Tbsp. prepared mustard
1 Tbsp. honey
2 tsp. fresh lemon juice

In a small bowl whisk together all ingredients. Store covered in the refrigerator.

Variation:
Add a dash of paprika or garlic powder if you wish.

Tofu Mayonnaise

Janice Sams
Lancaster, PA

Makes 1 cup

Prep. Time: 10 minutes

6 oz. soft tofu, well drained
2 Tbsp. prepared salad
  dressing *or* mayonnaise,
  optional
⅓ cup olive oil
1 small clove garlic
2 tsp. Dijon mustard
2½ tsp. fresh lemon juice
  or vinegar
¼ tsp. salt
pepper, to taste

1. Put tofu in food processor with the salad dressing, if using it, and oil. Puree until smooth. Scrape down the sides.
2. Add garlic, mustard, lemon juice and ¼ tsp. salt. Puree until smooth.
3. Taste for salt and season with a little pepper. Scrape into a bowl and refrigerate, covered. Keeps up to five days.

Tip:
  Omit the prepared salad dressing/mayonnaise to keep this recipe totally vegan. No need to buy vegan mayo!

Cucumber Salad with Cumin

Kim Patrick
Norwood, PA

Makes 6 servings

Prep. Time: 30 minutes

2 Tbsp. mayonnaise
juice of 1 lemon
zest of 1 lemon
1 tsp. cumin seed, toasted
1-2 tsp. sugar
¼ tsp. salt
2 peeled cucumbers,
  seeded and sliced

1. Whisk mayonnaise, lemon juice, lemon zest, cumin seed, sugar and salt together.
2. Toss over sliced cucumbers.

Go-Along:
• Serve with garbanzo burgers.

Old-Fashioned Cucumber Salad

Laraine Good
Bernville, PA

Makes 4 servings

Prep. Time: 10 minutes
Chilling Time: 30 minutes

2 large cucumbers, peeled
  and sliced
2 Tbsp. sliced onion
¼ cup milk
1½ Tbsp. vinegar
dash of salt
1 Tbsp. sugar
¼ cup mayonnaise

1. Combine cucumbers and onions in a dish.
2. In another bowl, mix milk, vinegar, salt, sugar and mayonnaise. Stir well. Pour over veggies.
3. Refrigerate 30 minutes before serving.

Variation:
  Add 1 Tbsp. dried dill weed.

I keep olive oil on my counter in a salad dressing dispenser.
  Gloria Frey, Lebanon, PA

Marinated Sliced Tomatoes

Dawn Alderfer
Oley, PA

Makes 6 servings

Prep. Time: 10 minutes
Chilling Time: 3-12 hours

6 medium tomatoes, sliced
⅔ cup vegetable oil
¼ cup vinegar
¼ cup minced fresh parsley
1 Tbsp. sugar
2 tsp. fresh marjoram *or* ¾
   tsp. dried marjoram
1 tsp. salt
¼ tsp. pepper

1. Place tomatoes in a large bowl.
2. Combine oil, vinegar, parsley, sugar, marjoram, salt and pepper in a container with a tight-fitting lid. Shake well.
3. Pour over tomatoes. Chill for several hours or overnight, spooning dressing over tomatoes at least twice.
4. To serve, use a slotted spoon to lift tomatoes out of marinade. Lay on a platter.

Go-Along:
• Great as a side at a summer picnic.

Mai Family's Carrot and Red-Beet Salad

Susan Henne
Fleetwood, PA

Makes 4-6 servings

Prep. Time: 15-20 minutes
Chilling Time: 1-2 hours

3 carrots
1 raw red beet
2" piece fresh gingerroot
2 Tbsp. olive oil
1½ Tbsp. lemon juice *or*
   apple cider vinegar
1½ Tbsp. raw honey
½ bunch fresh cilantro,
   chopped

1. Scrub carrots and red beet with a vegetable brush.
2. Peel red beet. Carrots may be peeled, if you wish.
3. Shred carrots and red beet in a food processor, or use a manual grater.
4. Press gingerroot to extract juice. You should have 1 tsp. ginger juice.
5. Mix carrots, red beet, oil, lemon juice, honey and ginger juice together in a medium bowl.
6. Refrigerate mixture for 1 to 2 hours.
7. Add cilantro to salad just before serving. Mix well and serve.

Red-Beet Salad

Mary Ann Bowman
Ephrata, PA

Makes 6-8 servings

Prep. Time: 15 minutes

1 quart pickled red beets,
   drained, diced
1 cup finely diced celery
¼ cup finely chopped
   onions
4 hard-boiled eggs, peeled
   and chopped
¾ cup salad dressing *or*
   mayonnaise
minced fresh parsley, for
   garnish

1. Drain red beets. Place in serving bowl.
2. Add celery, onions and eggs.
3. Add salad dressing. Sprinkle with minced parsley.

Tips:
1. Add more or less salad dressing.
2. This salad looks nice on a bed of salad greens, too.

Elegant Beets

Susan Segraves
Lansdale, PA

Makes 6 servings
Makes 3 cups

Prep. Time: 15 minutes
Baking Time: 8 minutes
Chilling Time: 3 hours

½ cup coarsely chopped
  walnuts
2 15-oz. cans sliced beets
2 Tbsp. apple cider vinegar
1½ tsp. Dijon mustard
½ tsp. sugar
¼ cup olive oil
½ cup crumbled blue
  cheese
parsley sprigs, for garnish

1. Spread walnuts on
baking sheet. Toast walnuts at
350° for 8 minutes. Set aside.
2. Drain beets and place in
shallow serving dish.
3. Mix vinegar, mustard,
sugar and olive oil by vigorously shaking in a jar with a
tight-fitting lid.
4. Add dressing to beets
and toss well. Cover. Marinate
in refrigerator for at least 3
hours.
5. Just before serving, top
with toasted walnuts and blue
cheese. Garnish with parsley.

Thai Carrot Salad with Peanuts

Janice Sams
Lancaster, PA

Makes 4 servings

Prep. Time: 20-25 minutes
Standing Time: 15-20 minutes

¼ cup rice vinegar
3 Tbsp. fresh lime juice
1 Tbsp. fresh orange juice
1 Tbsp. grated orange zest
1 Tbsp. chopped fresh
  cilantro
3 Tbsp. pure maple syrup
¼ tsp. red chili flakes, *or* to
  taste
salt, to taste
black pepper, to taste
3 cups grated carrots
1 cup chopped peanuts
fresh mint, finely chopped,
  as garnish

1. In a food processor,
blend vinegar, lime juice,
orange juice, zest, cilantro and
maple syrup.
2. Add chili flakes, adding
them a little at a time, to taste
for hotness. Add salt and
pepper if you wish.
3. Place carrots in salad
bowl. Add half the dressing,
saving the rest for another
use.
4. Marinate the salad for
15-20 minutes before serving.
5. Garnish with chopped
peanuts and mint.

Variation:
Serve in lettuce cups for
attractive presentation. Use

the top half of a romaine lettuce heart.

Go-Alongs:
• This is good with a vegetarian curry served with rice.
• It's also a good side dish
with veggie burgers, in place
of slaw.

Carrot and Raisin Salad

Judy Newman
St. Marys, ON

Makes 4 servings
Makes 4 cups

Prep. Time: 15 minutes

¼ cup mayonnaise
¼ cup apple juice
2 cups shredded carrots
1 apple, shredded
¾ cup raisins

1. Mix mayonnaise and
apple juice in serving bowl.
Add carrots and apples. Stir
gently.
2. Cover and chill until
serving time.
3. Add raisins and serve.

Sweet 'n' Hot Carrots & Zucchini

Marilyn Kurtz
Willow Street, PA

Makes 4-6 servings

Prep. Time: 25 minutes
Cooking Time: 5 minutes
Chilling Time: 3-4 hours

½ cup sugar
½ cup white wine vinegar
¼-½ tsp. dried crushed red
  pepper
1 garlic clove, minced
2 carrots
2 medium zucchini, about
  2" in diameter

1. Whisk together sugar, vinegar, red pepper and garlic until sugar dissolves.
2. Peel carrots and slice into ⅛"-thick discs. Then cut into ¼"-long strips. There should be 2 cups.
3. Cook in boiling water for 2 minutes, then drain.
4. Add to vinegar mixture and refrigerate for several hours.
5. Slice zucchini the same way as the carrots. There should be 2 cups.
6. Do not cook the zucchini so it stays crunchy. Add zucchini to vinegar mixture just before serving.

Tip:
A nonfat salad that has some kick to it!

Go-Along:
• Great with cheese pizza!

Potluck Salad

Betty Moore
Avon Park, FL

Makes 8-10 servings

Prep. Time: 20 minutes
Chilling Time: 12 hours

1 medium head
  cauliflower, cut in florets
1 bunch broccoli, cut in
  florets
2 cups cherry tomatoes
2 medium carrots, sliced
6-oz. can pitted small ripe
  olives, drained
1 cup Italian vinaigrette
  dressing
1-oz pkg. Italian salad
  dressing mix
1 cup crumbled feta cheese

1. In large bowl, combine cauliflower, broccoli, tomatoes, carrots and olives.
2. In separate bowl, combine Italian dressing and dressing mix. Beat well.
3. Pour over vegetables and toss to coat.
4. Cover. Refrigerate overnight.
5. Toss again before serving.
6. Stir in feta cheese.

Broccoli Salad

Elaine Vigoda
Rochester, NY

Makes 4 servings

Prep. Time: 15 minutes
Chilling Time: 1 hour

4 cups fresh broccoli
  florets, coarsely chopped
½ cup dried cranberries
½ cup finely chopped
  sweet Vidalia onion
3 Tbsp. red wine vinegar
¼ cup sugar
¼ cup olive oil
¼ cup mayonnaise
1 Tbsp. prepared mustard
½ cup dry roasted peanuts

1. Combine broccoli, dried cranberries and onions in a large bowl.
2. In a separate bowl, whisk together vinegar, sugar, oil, mayonnaise and mustard.
3. Toss dressing with salad.
4. Chill for 1 hour.
5. Add peanuts just before serving.

Save counter space by mounting brackets on the wall under the top cabinets and hang baskets holding your spatulas and wooden spoons from them. They save space and keep utensils readily accessible.

Doreen Bishop, Harrisburg, PA

Vegetable Salad

Bonnie Lahman
Broadway, VA

Makes 10 servings

Prep. Time: 30 minutes
Cooking Time: 10 minutes
Standing Time: 30 minutes
Chilling Time: 12 hours

1½ cups frozen mixed
 vegetables
1 cup diced celery
½ medium onion, diced
1 small green bell pepper,
 diced
2 cups cooked dark red
 kidney beans, rinsed and
 drained
1 cup sugar *or* Splenda
3 Tbsp. flour
½ cup water
½ cup vinegar
3 Tbsp. prepared mustard
½ tsp. salt

1. In a saucepan, cook
mixed vegetables and bring to
a boil. Boil one minute.
2. Drain. Plunge in cold
water to cool. Drain well.
3. Add celery, onions, bell
pepper and beans to drained
vegetables.
4. To make dressing, whisk
sugar, flour, water, vinegar,
mustard and salt in saucepan.
5. Cook dressing over
medium heat. Cook and stir
until it boils and thickens.
6. Cool at least 30 minutes.
7. Mix cooled dressing
with vegetables. Refrigerate
overnight.

Tips:
 1. You can cook the dressing in the microwave.
 2. This recipe may also be
used as relish.

Go-Along:
• Baked potato or mashed
potatoes. Baked apples.

Confetti Bean Salad

Betty Moore
Avon Park, FL

Makes 12 servings

Prep. Time: 15 minutes
Chilling Time: 12 hours

16-oz. can kidney beans,
 rinsed and drained
15-oz. can garbanzo beans,
 rinsed and drained
15-oz. can black beans,
 rinsed and drained
15-oz. can whole-kernel
 corn, drained
½ cup minced fresh parsley
 or cilantro
½ cup diced orange *or* red
 bell pepper
½ cup diced green bell
 pepper
¼ cup diced onions
1 small jalapeño pepper,
 seeded, finely chopped
2 garlic cloves, minced
½ cup red wine vinegar
¼ cup olive oil *or* canola oil
1 tsp. chili powder
½ tsp. sugar

1. In a large bowl, combine
beans, corn, parsley, red
pepper, green pepper, onions,
jalapeño pepper and garlic.
2. Pour vinegar, oil, chili
powder and sugar into a jar.
3. Closely tightly. Shake to
mix.
4. Pour over bean mixture
and toss to mix.
5. Cover. Refrigerate
overnight.
6. Serve with slotted spoon.

Tip:
Great for family gatherings
or potluck meals.

Puerto-Rican Bean Salad

Tamera Baker
Lafayette, IN

Makes 4 servings

Prep. Time: 15 minutes
Chilling Time: 2 hours

15-oz. can black beans,
 rinsed and drained
15-oz. can pinto beans,
 rinsed and drained
1-1½ cups frozen corn
1 green bell pepper, chopped
1 red onion, chopped
1 rib celery, chopped
½ bunch fresh parsley,
 chopped
½ bunch cilantro, chopped
juice from 1 lime
zest from 1 lime, *optional*
2 Tbsp. olive oil
2 Tbsp. vinegar
½ tsp. salt
1 Tbsp. sugar *or* stevia
¾ tsp. chili powder
¼ tsp. dried oregano

1. Combine black beans,
pinto beans, corn, pepper,
onions, celery, parsley and
cilantro. Mix well.
2. Combine lime juice,
optional zest, oil, vinegar,
salt, sugar, chili powder and
oregano. Mix well.
3. Add oil mixture to beans.
Refrigerate at least 2 hours
before serving.

Feta and Vegetable Rotini Salad

Betty Moore
Avon Park, FL

Makes 8 servings

Prep. Time: 20 minutes
Cooking Time: 10-15 minutes

3 cups uncooked tri-colored
 rotini
1 cup cherry tomatoes,
 halved, *or* grape
 tomatoes
½ cup sliced black olives
1 cup unpeeled, chopped
 cucumber
1 small onion, finely
 chopped
½ cup zesty Italian
 dressing
1 cup crumbled feta cheese

1. Cook rotini according
to package directions. Drain.
Rinse with cold water until
cooled. Drain well.
2. In bowl, toss rotini,
tomatoes, olives, cucumbers
and onions.
3. Add dressing. Toss to
mix.
4. Add feta cheese and mix
well.
5. Cover and refrigerate
until serving time.

Variation:
You can add shredded car-
rots or sliced radishes, too.

Spinach Pasta Salad

Donna Reinford
Smoketown, PA

Makes 10-12 servings

Prep. Time: 30 minutes
Cooking Time: 15 minutes

4 cups spiral pasta,
 uncooked
4 cups torn fresh spinach
2½ cups sliced celery
2 cups halved green grapes
1 cup trimmed, halved
 fresh snow peas
1 medium tomato,
 chopped
3 green onions, sliced
½ cup vegetable oil
¼ cup sugar
2 Tbsp. vinegar
2 Tbsp. minced fresh
 parsley
1 tsp. salt
1 tsp. lemon juice
½ tsp. onion, finely
 chopped

1. Cook pasta according
to package directions. Drain.
Place under running cold
water until cool. Drain well.
2. In a large bowl, combine
spinach, pasta, celery, grapes,
peas, tomato and green
onions.
3. In a small bowl, whisk
together oil, sugar, vinegar,
parsley, salt, lemon juice and
½ tsp. onions.
4. Pour over salad and toss
to coat. Serve immediately.

Linguini Salad

Carol Sherwood
Batavia, NY

Makes 6-8 servings

Prep. Time: 30 minutes
Cooking Time: 10-15 minutes
Chilling Time: 1-12 hours

1 lb. uncooked linguini
8-oz. bottle zesty Italian
   salad dressing
half of a 2.6-oz. bottle
   Salad Supreme seasoning
½ small red onion, diced
1 green bell pepper, diced
2 small cucumbers, diced

1. Boil linguine until al dente. Drain.
2. Mix linguine, salad dressing, salad seasoning and onions.
3. Marinate at least 1 hour or overnight.
4. Toss with peppers and cucumbers just before serving.

Tip:
   To make your own version of Salad Supreme Seasoning, mix 1½ tsp. sesame seeds, 1 tsp. paprika, ¾ tsp. salt, ½ tsp. poppy seeds, ½ tsp. celery seed, ¼ tsp. garlic powder, ¼ tsp. coarsely ground black pepper, dash cayenne pepper, 2 Tbsp. grated Romano cheese. Store in refrigerator in tightly covered jar. Use the entire batch to equal the half-jar called for in this recipe, if you wish.

Bedspring Salad

Mary Reichert
O' Fallon, MO

Makes 6-8 servings

Prep. Time: 20 minutes
Cooking Time: 10-15 minutes
Chilling Time: 3 hours

3 green onions, sliced
1 carrot, grated
1 cucumber, diced
½ green bell pepper, diced
1-lb. box uncooked spiral
   pasta
1 cup mayonnaise
2 Tbsp. lemon juice
1 Tbsp. vinegar
1½ Tbsp. French dressing
2 Tbsp. milk
1 tsp. sugar, *optional*
1 tsp. salt
pepper, to taste

1. Mix together onions, carrot, cucumber and green pepper. Refrigerate.
2. Cook pasta according to package directions. Drain.
3. In a small bowl, mix mayonnaise, lemon juice, vinegar, French dressing, milk, optional sugar, salt and pepper.
4. Pour dressing over pasta and refrigerate at least 3 hours.
5. Right before serving, add veggies.

Variation:
   The amount of veggies can be more or less, according to your taste.

Macaroni Salad

Lucille, Rosalie and **Dawn Martin**
Barnett, MO

Makes 8-10 servings

Prep. Time: 30 minutes

1 lb. box macaroni, cooked,
   drained and cooled
6 hard-boiled eggs, peeled
   and chopped
1 rib celery, diced
1 onion, diced
2 carrots, shredded
1 Tbsp. vinegar
1 Tbsp. prepared mustard
¼ tsp. salt
½ cup sugar
3 Tbsp. milk
1 cup salad dressing *or*
   mayonnaise

1. Mix cooked macaroni, eggs, celery, onions and carrots in a large bowl.
2. In a separate bowl, combine vinegar, mustard, salt, sugar, milk and salad dressing.
3. Add to macaroni mixture.

Tip:
   This can be made a day before serving.

Shredded Potato Salad

Kris Zimmerman
Lititz, PA

Makes 16-18 servings

Prep. Time: 40 minutes
Cooking Time: 30 minutes
Chilling Time: 4 hours

14 medium *or* large
  potatoes, to equal 12
  cups grated
12 eggs, hard-boiled and
  chopped
1½ cups chopped onions
1½ cups chopped celery
⅓ cup grated carrots
3 cups mayonnaise
3 Tbsp. vinegar
3 Tbsp. prepared mustard
4 tsp. salt
2 cups sugar
½ cup milk

1. Peel potatoes. Cook in water to cover in large saucepan until soft. Drain. Set aside to cool and then refrigerate, at least 4 hours.

2. Coarsely shred potatoes with grater or a food processor grating attachment. You should have 12 cups grated potatoes.

3. Put shredded potatoes, eggs, onions, celery and carrots in large bowl.

4. Mix together mayonnaise, vinegar, mustard, salt, sugar and milk in medium bowl. Pour dressing over potatoes.

Tip:
It is important that the potatoes are shredded rather than cubed.

To make your own hash browns, please turn to page 261.

Potato Salad

Sherry Kauffman
Minot, ND

Makes 6-8 servings

Prep. Time: 20-30 minutes
Cooking Time: 25 minutes
Standing Time: 2-4 hours
Chilling Time: 1 hour

6 large red *or* white
  potatoes, to equal 6 cups
  cubed potatoes
10 hard-boiled eggs,
  chopped
¼ cup chopped green
  onions
1 cup salad dressing *or*
  mayonnaise
½ cup sour cream
2 Tbsp. finely chopped
  sweet *or* dill pickles
2 Tbsp. sweet *or* dill pickle
  juice
1 tsp. salt
¼ tsp. pepper

1. Cook potatoes with skins on in large pot of boiling salted water for 25 minutes. Drain.

2. Peel potatoes while they are warm. Set aside to cool 2-4 hours.

3. Cube potatoes.

4. Combine, eggs, onions, salad dressing, sour cream, pickles, pickle juice, salt and pepper.

5. Pour over potatoes.

6. Chill 1 hour before serving.

Cornbread Salad

Eunice Kauffman
Alto, MI

Melissa Miller
Bedford, PA

Betty Detweiler
Centreville, MI

Laraine Good
Bernville, PA

Sandra Haverstraw
Hummelstown, PA

Makes 8-10 servings

Prep. Time: 20 minutes
Baking Time: 15-20 minutes for
cornbread
Chilling Time: 2 hours

prepared 9 × 9 pan
  cornbread, *divided*
15½-oz. can pinto beans,
  drained, *divided*
1-2 bell peppers, chopped,
  divided
4 medium tomatoes,
  chopped, *divided*
1-2 large onions, chopped,
  divided
½ cup chopped sweet
  pickle, drained, with
  juice reserved
2 cups shredded cheese,
  divided
1 cup mayonnaise
black pepper, to taste

1. Crumble half of cornbread into large bowl.
2. Layer half the beans, half the peppers, half the tomatoes, half the onions and half the pickle on top of cornbread.
3. Add 1 cup cheese.
4. Repeat layers.

5. Mix mayonnaise, ¼ cup pickle juice and pepper. Spread on top of salad bowl contents.
6. Sprinkle with remaining cup of cheese.
7. Cover. Chill at least 2 hours before serving.

Variations:

1. Layer all the ingredients, ending with dressing on top. Mix before serving. Omit cheese.
      Eunice Kauffman

2. Before assembling the salad, cut the prepared cornbread into cubes. Spread on baking sheet. Bake at 400° for 10 minutes, stirring once. Cool and proceed with salad.
      Sandra Haverstraw

3. Add 1 cup sour cream and an envelope of dry ranch dressing mix to the dressing. Omit sweet pickles and pickle juice.
      Betty Detweiler

4. Add 2 16-oz. cans corn, drained.
      Laraine Good

5. Add 4½-oz can chopped green chilies, ⅛ tsp. ground cumin, ⅛ tsp. dried oregano, and ⅛ tsp. dried sage to the cornbread before baking.
      Melissa Miller

To make your own prepared cornbread, please turn to page 261.

Macaroni Coleslaw

Barbara Miller
Boyertown, PA

Makes 16 servings

Prep. Time: 20 minutes
Cooking Time: 10 minutes
Chilling Time: 1 hour

7-oz. pkg. uncooked ring
  macaroni *or* ditalini
16-oz. pkg. coleslaw mix
2 medium onions, finely
  chopped
2 celery ribs, finely chopped
1 medium cucumber,
  finely chopped
1 medium green bell
  pepper, finely chopped
8-oz. can water chestnuts,
  drained and chopped
1½ cups reduced-fat
  mayonnaise *or* salad
  dressing
⅓ cup sugar
¼ cup cider vinegar
½ tsp. salt
¼ tsp. pepper

1. Cook macaroni according to package directions. Drain and rinse in cold water. Drain again.
2. Transfer to large bowl.
3. Add coleslaw mix, onions, celery, cucumber, green pepper and water chestnuts.
4. In small bowl, whisk mayonnaise, sugar, vinegar, salt and pepper together.
5. Pour over salad. Toss to coat.
6. Cover. Refrigerate for 1 hour.

Coleslaw

Bonnie Lahman
Broadway, VA

Makes 8-10 servings
Prep. Time: 25 minutes

1 medium head cabbage,
  shredded
1 carrot, shredded
1 small onion, grated
1 cup mayonnaise
⅓-½ cup sugar
2 Tbsp. vinegar
1 Tbsp. Dijon mustard
¼ tsp. salt

1. In salad bowl, mix cabbage, carrot and onions.
2. In separate small bowl, mix mayonnaise, sugar, vinegar, mustard and salt.
3. Pour over cabbage mixture. Mix gently.

Tip:
  If you prefer a salad with less juice, add dressing just before serving.

Go-Along:
• Macaroni and cheese and mashed potatoes.

Vegetable Cabbage Slaw

Edna Good
Richland Center, WI

Makes 6-8 servings

Prep. Time: 30 minutes
Chilling Time: 2 hours

2 cups shredded cabbage
1 cup chopped celery
1 carrot, shredded
1 cucumber, thinly sliced
1 green bell pepper,
  chopped
1 small onion, chopped
  fine
4-6 radishes, thinly sliced,
  optional
¼ cup sugar
1 tsp. salt
½ tsp. dry mustard
¼ cup cream
3 Tbsp. vinegar *or* lemon
  juice

1. Combine cabbage, celery, carrot, cucumber, pepper, onions and radishes. Mix well.
2. Mix sugar, salt, mustard, cream and vinegar or lemon juice in a small bowl.
3. Gently stir into vegetables. Chill at least 2 hours before serving.

Mustard Coleslaw

Betty Moore
Avon Park, FL

Makes 24 servings
Prep. Time: 20 minutes

2 medium heads cabbage,
  shredded, *or* 2 1-lb. bags
  shredded cabbage
1 medium onion, diced
1 medium green bell
  pepper, diced
1 large carrot, shredded
1 celery rib, finely chopped
¾ cup prepared mustard
¾ cup cider vinegar
½ cup soup cream
½ cup ketchup
¼ cup mayonnaise
1 Tbsp. salt
½ tsp. cayenne pepper
1¼ cups sugar

1. In large bowl, combine cabbage, onions, pepper, carrot and celery.
2. In separate bowl, mix mustard, vinegar, sour cream, ketchup, mayonnaise, salt and cayenne pepper. Blend well.
3. Stir in sugar and mix.
4. Pour desired amount of dressing over vegetables and toss to coat. Refrigerate any leftover dressing.
5. Refrigerate coleslaw until serving time.
6. Serve with slotted spoon.

Sauerkraut Salad

Pauline J. Morrison
St Marys, ON
Wilma Haberkamp
Fairbank, IA
Arnola Siggelkow
Fairbank, IA

Makes 10-12 servings

Prep. Time: 15 minutes
Cooking Time: 10 minutes
Standing Time: 30 minutes
Chilling Time: 24 hours

28-oz. jar sauerkraut,
  drained
4-oz. can chopped pimento
1 cup diced celery
1 large onion, sliced
1 green bell pepper, diced
⅔ cup vinegar
⅓ cup water
½ cup cooking oil
½ cup sugar

1. Mix sauerkraut, pimento, celery, onions, and pepper lightly.
2. In a saucepan, mix vinegar, water, oil and sugar. Heat to boiling.
3. Cool at least 30 minutes.
4. Pour vinegar mixture over vegetables and toss lightly. Cover tightly.
5. Refrigerate 24 hours before serving.

Tip:
  This recipe can be stored in the refrigerator for three weeks or longer.

Pickled Beets

Peggy Howell
Hinton, WV

Makes 8-10 servings

Prep. Time: 5-10 minutes
Cooking Time: 5-10 minutes

3 15-oz. cans sliced beets
½ cup sugar
½ cup vinegar
1 tsp. allspice
salt and pepper, to taste

1. Mix beets, sugar, vinegar and allspice in large pot. Add salt and pepper if you wish.
2. Cover pot. Bring to a boil. Turn off the heat but leave the pot on the burner to cool down.
3. Serve warm or cold. Store in refrigerator.

Tips:
  1. Goes with anything. Will keep in the fridge for a long time, but it will probably be eaten first!
  2. Marinate peeled hard-boiled eggs along with the beets after they have cooled down.

Pickled Cukes

Mary Kathryn Yoder
Harrisonville, MO

Makes 18-24 servings

Prep. Time: 30 minutes
Chilling Time: 24 hours

7 cups thinly sliced
  cucumbers
2 tsp. salt
1 cup sliced onions
1 cup sugar
1 cup vinegar
½ tsp. celery seed

1. Mix cucumbers, salt, onions, sugar, vinegar and celery seed.
2. Refrigerate.
3. Stir before serving or freezing.

Sweet Zucchini Pickles

Don Pakis
Wellsville, NY

Makes 12-15 servings

Prep. Time: 30 minutes
Cooking Time: 20-25 minutes
Standing Time: 1 hour
Chilling Time: 4 days

3 small zucchini squash,
  thinly sliced
1 medium onion, chopped
1 large sweet red pepper,
  cut into ¼" strips
1 Tbsp. salt
1 cup sugar
¾ cup white vinegar
¾ tsp. mustard seed
¾ tsp. celery seed
¼ tsp. ground dry mustard

1. In a large bowl, combine zucchini, onion, red pepper and salt.
2. Cover and refrigerate for one hour. Drain off the liquid that has accumulated.
3. In a large saucepan, combine sugar, vinegar, mustard seed, celery seed and mustard. Bring to a boil.
4. Add zucchini mixture. Return to boil.
5. Remove from heat. Allow to cool at room temperature for at least an hour.
6. Refrigerate in airtight containers for at least 4 days before serving. The pickles may be stored in the refrigerator for up to 3 weeks.

Lentil Rice Salad

Stephen Zoss
Metamora, IL

Makes 4-6 servings

Prep. Time: 15 minutes
Cooking Time: 30 minutes
Chilling Time: 12 hours

½ cup dry lentils
1½ cups water
2 cups cooked rice
1 medium tomato,
  chopped
¼ cup finely chopped green
  bell pepper
2 Tbsp. chopped celery
1 medium onion, chopped
¾ cup Italian salad
  dressing

1. Cook the lentils in the water until tender. Drain and allow to cool.
2. Mix the lentils, rice, tomato, pepper, celery, onions and dressing together.
3. Cover. Chill at least 12 hours to allow the flavors to blend.

Tip:
Use leftover rice to make the preparation time quicker.

Elegant French Lentil Salad

Carol Collins
Holly Springs, NC

Makes 4 servings

Prep. Time: 10 minutes
Cooking Time: 20 minutes
Chilling Time: 1 hour

1 cup dried green French
  lentils
2 cups water
¼ cup minced shallots *or*
  red onion
¼ cup chopped fresh
  chives
3 cloves garlic, minced
salt and pepper, to taste
3 Tbsp. extra-virgin olive oil
1 Tbsp. balsamic vinegar
1 tsp. Dijon mustard

1. Cook lentils in medium saucepan of boiling salted water until lentils are tender but still firm to the bite, about 20 minutes. Drain and cool.
2. Add shallots or red onion, chives, garlic, salt and pepper to the cooled lentils.
3. Whisk oil, vinegar and mustard together. Pour over salad and mix.

Tip:
This dressing is also excellent on salad greens. You can double the dressing recipe; just remember the ratio of oil to vinegar is always 3 to 1.

Mediterranean Lentil and Bulgur Salad

Rebekah Zehr
Lowville, NY

Makes 4 servings

Prep. Time: 5-10 minutes
Cooking Time: 30 minutes
Standing Time: 2 hours

¼ cup dry lentils
2 cups water, *divided*
½ cup dry bulgur wheat
½ cup Italian salad dressing
¼ cup lemon juice
½ Tbsp. chopped fresh mint
1 tsp. dry mustard
1 Tbsp. hot sauce, *or* to taste
1½ cups cubed cucumbers
1½ cups diced tomatoes
¾ cups green onions, sliced
¼ cup fresh parsley, chopped
⅓ cup feta cheese, crumbled
4-6 cups torn Romaine lettuce

1. Cook lentils in ½ cup water until tender, about 30 minutes. Chill.
2. Place bulgur in heat-proof bowl. Pour 1½ cups boiling water over it. Cover. Allow to sit for up to an hour, until water is absorbed and bulgur is fluffy. Drain any excess water. Chill cooked bulgur.
3. Combine dressing, lemon juice, mint, mustard and hot sauce in a quart canning jar. Screw on lid. Shake vigorously.
4. In a serving bowl, mix together lentils, bulgur, cucumbers, tomatoes, onions, parsley and cheese. Add vinaigrette from jar.
5. Divide lettuce between 4 salad plates. Serve lentil mixture on beds of lettuce.

Tip:

To save prep time, cook lentils and bulgur ahead of time. Mix dressing ingredients and refrigerate. When you need a quick, nutritious meal, this can go on the table with minimum energy. Great at the end of a busy day.

Go-Along:

• Good with a nice warm creamy soup such as tomato or broccoli.

Black Lentil and Couscous Salad

Moreen and **Christina Weaver**
Bath, NY

Makes 6 servings

Prep. Time: 20 minutes
Cooking Time: 25 minutes

½ cup dry black lentils
5 cups water, *divided*
¾ cup uncooked couscous
¾ tsp. salt, *divided*
1 cup quartered cherry tomatoes
⅓ cup finely chopped red onions
⅓ cup finely chopped cucumbers
¼ cup chopped fresh parsley *or* 1 tsp. dried
1 tsp. grated lemon rind
3 Tbsp. fresh lemon juice
2 Tbsp. extra-virgin olive oil

1. Rinse lentils with cold water and drain.
2. In large saucepan, combine lentils with 4 cups water. Bring to boil, covered.
3. Reduce heat and simmer 20 minutes, or until tender.
4. Drain and rinse with cold water. Drain again.
5. Meanwhile, in medium saucepan, bring 1 cup water to boil.
6. Gradually stir in couscous and ¼ tsp. salt.
7. Remove from heat. Cover. Let stand 5 minutes. Fluff couscous with fork.
8. Add lentils, remaining salt, tomatoes, onions, cucumbers, parsley, lemon rind, lemon juice and olive oil. Stir gently.
9. Serve chilled or at room temperature.

Couscous Salad

Betty Detweiler
Centreville, MI

Makes 4 servings

Prep. Time: 30 minutes
Cooking Time: 10 minutes
Chilling Time: 2-3 hours

1½ cups vegetable broth
3 tsp. soy sauce, *divided*
1 tsp. plus 2 Tbsp. olive oil, *divided*
1 cup uncooked couscous
2 green onions, sliced
1 large red bell pepper, chopped
1½ cups sugar snap peas *or* snow peas
1 cup broccoli florets
¼ cup lemon juice
¼ tsp. pepper
¼ cup slivered almonds, toasted
1 Tbsp. sesame seeds, toasted

1. Combine vegetable broth, 1 tsp. soy sauce and 1 tsp. olive oil in a small saucepan and bring to a boil.

2. Place uncooked couscous in a large heatproof serving bowl and stir in boiling broth. Cover and let stand 5-8 minutes. Fluff with a fork.

3. Stir in the green onions and red sweet pepper. Cover and refrigerate until chilled, 2-3 hours or longer.

4. Place peas in saucepan with ½" water. Bring to boil and steam peas 1 minute. Add broccoli and steam 2 more minutes.

5. Immediately rinse peas and broccoli with cold water to stop cooking. Drain.

6. Combine in a small bowl the lemon juice, remaining 2 Tbsp. olive oil, remaining 2 tsp. soy sauce and pepper. Add to the chilled couscous mixture and mix gently.

7. Gently stir in peas and broccoli.

8. Immediately before serving mix in the almonds and sesame seeds.

9. Serve chilled or at room temperature.

Wheatberry Salad

Elaine Hostetler
Goshen, IN

Makes 4 servings

Prep. Time: 15 minutes
Standing Time: 8 hours or overnight
Cooking Time: 60 minutes

1 cup uncooked wheatberries
½ cup cooked kidney beans
3 medium tomatoes
3 green onions, chopped
3 celery ribs, chopped
¼ cup olive oil
2 Tbsp. red wine vinegar
1 clove garlic, minced
1 tsp. paprika
pepper, to taste

1. Soak wheatberries overnight in 3 cups water. Cook wheatberries 45-60 minutes until soft and water is gone.

2. Allow to cool at least 30 minutes.

3. Mix wheatberries, kidney beans, tomatoes, onions and celery together.

4. In a jar with a lid, mix the oil, vinegar, garlic, paprika and pepper vigorously.

5. Pour over the salad and mix gently. Serve room temperature or chilled.

Tip:
This salad keeps well so it can be made in advance and kept in the refrigerator until needed.

Go-Along:
• Serve on a bed of lettuce.

Wild Rice Salad with Grapes and Almonds

Gloria Yurkiewicz
Washington Boro, PA

Makes 6-8 servings

Prep. Time: 30 minutes
Cooking Time: 30 minutes
Standing Time: 1 hour
Chilling Time: 2 hours

2 6-oz. boxes long-grain
   and wild rice
1 Tbsp. vegetable oil
½ cup mayonnaise
2 Tbsp. honey
2 Tbsp. lemon juice
2 Tbsp. vinegar
⅓ cup chopped fresh
   parsley
⅓ cup sliced green onions
salt and pepper, to taste
2 cups halved grapes, green
   and red
½ cup sliced almonds,
   toasted

1. Cook rice according to directions on box, omitting butter.
2. Toss cooked rice with oil to coat. Let cool at least 1 hour. Cover and refrigerate for 2 hours.
3. Whisk mayonnaise, honey, lemon juice and vinegar in a large bowl until smooth.
4. Stir in parsley, green onions, salt and pepper.
5. Add grapes, almonds and dressing to rice. Toss until well coated. Serve chilled.

Tip:
This recipe may be prepared ahead of serving time and chilled in refrigerator.

Go-Along:
• Baked lima beans and green-bean salad.

Calico Rice Salad

Shirley Hedman
Schenectady, NY

Makes 8 servings

Prep. Time: 20 minutes

3 cups cooked white *or*
   brown rice, cooled
2 cups fresh *or* frozen corn
15-oz. can black beans,
   rinsed and drained
¾ cup diced green, red,
   and yellow bell peppers
½ cup sliced scallions
½ cup chopped cilantro
¼ cup sliced green
   pimento-stuffed olives
2 Tbsp. extra-virgin olive
   oil
4 Tbsp. lime juice
salt and pepper, to taste

1. Combine rice, corn, beans, peppers, scallions, cilantro and olives.
2. Mix well.
3. In a small bowl, combine oil, lime juice, salt and pepper.
4. Add oil mixture to rice mixture and mix well. Serve warm, cold or at room temperature.

Roasted cherry tomatoes are a wonderful way to prepare and preserve a surplus of garden cherry tomatoes. They can be frozen, thawed and used in many recipes. They taste delicious on pizza, in salads and in any warm sandwich. Rebekah Zehr, Lowville, NY

231

Fresh Corn and Rice Salad

Melissa Raber
Millersburg, OH

Makes 4-6 servings

Prep. Time: 20 minutes
Cooking Time: 10 minutes

4 ears fresh corn, husked
  and cleaned
1½ cups cooked, cooled
  rice
1 pint cherry tomatoes,
  halved
1 cup torn fresh arugula
1 small red onion, cut in
  thin wedges
1 jalapeño pepper, seeded
  and thinly sliced
2 Tbsp. rice vinegar *or* red
  wine vinegar
2 Tbsp. olive oil
salt and pepper, to taste

1. Cook corn in boiling,
lightly salted water for 3 minutes. Remove corn. Run under
cold water till cool enough to
handle. Drain well.
2. Cut corn off the cob in
planks.
3. In a serving bowl, combine rice, tomatoes, arugula,
onions, and jalapeño pepper.
Add corn on top.
4. Drizzle with vinegar and
oil. Season to taste with salt
and pepper. Serve at room
temperature.

Quinoa Salad

Linda Yoder
Fresno, OH

Makes 4 servings

Prep. Time: 30 minutes
Cooking Time: 20-25 minutes
Chilling Time: 30 minutes

1 cup uncooked quinoa,
  regular *or* red
2 cups water
¼ tsp. salt
½ cup green beans, cut to
  bite-sized pieces
⅛ tsp. salt
½ cup sliced fresh
  mushrooms
3 Tbsp. olive oil, *divided*
1 medium onion, sliced
  into rings
1 medium red bell pepper,
  coarsely chopped
½ cup shredded carrots
½ cup coarsely chopped
  walnuts
3 Tbsp. fresh lemon juice
2 Tbsp. vegetable broth
1 small garlic clove, minced
2 tsp. minced fresh dill
2 tsp. minced fresh mint
¼ tsp. salt, *or* to taste
¼ tsp. pepper
4 Romaine lettuce leaves

1. Using warm running
water, rinse quinoa well in a
fine-mesh sieve until little or
no saponin (the bitter "soap"
on quinoa) foam forms.
2. Bring 2 cups water and
¼ tsp. salt to boil in small
saucepan. Stir in quinoa and
return to boiling. Reduce heat
and cover, simmering about
15 minutes or until tender.

Uncover, remove from heat
and cool.
3. Prepare and steam the
green beans until crisp-tender.
Sprinkle with ⅛ tsp. salt.
Cool.
4. In medium skillet sauté
mushrooms in 2 Tbsp. olive
oil just until tender. Cool.
5. In a large bowl combine
beans, mushrooms, onion
rings, peppers, carrots,
walnuts and quinoa.
6. In a bowl combine
lemon juice, broth, remaining
1 Tbsp. oil, garlic, dill, mint,
salt and pepper. Whisk.
7. Pour on just enough
dressing to coat the salad and
toss gently. Add salt or pepper
as needed.
8. Turn quinoa salad into a
salad bowl lined with romaine
leaves. Chill about 30 minutes
before serving.

Tips:
1. Since red quinoa seems
to have less saponins that give
a bitter taste, it needs less
rinsing. For this reason and
because of its attractive color,
I use "Inca Red" quinoa.
2. This is a cool, colorful,
refreshing and filling dish
for a hot summer day, with
a minimum of cooking and a
maximum of color and flavor.

Go-Alongs:
• Whole grain bread with
honey or jam.
• Potato or sweet potato
"steak fries."
• Lightly browned summer
and zucchini squash, with
onion rings and minced garlic.

Pineapple Quinoa Salad with Sweet Curry Vinaigrette

Jennifer Hoke Bentivogli
Gordonville, PA

Makes 4 servings

Prep. Time: 10 minutes
Cooking Time: 15 minutes
Chilling Time: 1-2 hours

½ cup uncooked quinoa
2 cups water
3 Tbsp. canola oil
2 Tbsp. apple cider vinegar
2 Tbsp. honey
2½ tsp. curry powder
1 clove garlic, crushed
pinch salt
1½ cups pineapple tidbits, drained
⅓ cup red onion, diced
½ cup carrot, shredded
¼ cups cilantro, finely chopped, plus more for garnish, *optional*

1. Rinse quinoa well.
2. Place quinoa and water in saucepan. Bring to a simmer, covered. Simmer about 15 minutes. Drain any excess water. Fluff with a fork. There should be about 2 cups cooked quinoa.
3. Chill or cool quinoa before making salad.
4. Combine oil, vinegar, honey, curry powder, garlic and salt together in a small bowl and whisk together until completely combined. Set aside.
5. In a large bowl, combine quinoa, pineapple, onions, carrot and cilantro. Toss together.
6. Add about half of the vinaigrette and fold together until well mixed. Check for flavor and add the rest of the vinaigrette as needed.
7. Garnish with cilantro if you wish. Serve chilled or at room temperature.

Go-Along:
• Serve on its own as a main dish, as a picnic side, or on a bed of fresh greens.

Apple Salad

Susan Henne
Fleetwood, PA

Makes 12 servings

Prep. Time: 20 minutes
Chilling Time: 4-12 hours

6 apples, cored and chopped
1 cup golden raisins
¾ cup dried cranberries
½ cup chopped walnuts
½ cup chopped pecans
salad dressing *or* mayonnaise

1. Mix apples, raisins, dried cranberries, walnuts and pecans together in a medium mixing bowl.
2. Add enough salad dressing to coat the mixture.
3. Refrigerate for several hours or overnight and serve.

Variation:
Dark raisins can be substituted for the golden raisins.

Peanut Butter Waldorf Salad

Rhonda Freed
Croghan, NY

Makes 4-6 servings

Prep. Time: 15 minutes

⅓ cup salad dressing *or*
   mayonnaise
3 Tbsp. milk
¼ cup creamy peanut
   butter
1 large Red Delicious apple,
   diced
1 large Yellow Delicious
   apple, diced
¼ cup chopped celery
1 cup raisins
1 cup chopped walnuts

1. In a small bowl, mix salad dressing, milk and peanut butter together with a whisk.
2. Mix apples, celery, raisins and walnuts in a large bowl.
3. Pour dressing on top and lightly toss to coat.

Waldorf Salad

Arianne Hochstetler
Goshen, IN

Makes 8 servings

Prep. Time: 20 minutes

1 lb. green seedless grapes
2 large red apples, cored
   and chopped
½ cup seedless raisins
2 celery ribs, diced fine
½ cup low-fat mayonnaise
½ cup vanilla *or* orange
   yogurt
¼ cup chopped walnuts
3-4 green outer leaves
   from Romaine lettuce,
   chopped

1. Wash and halve grapes.
2. In large salad bowl, combine grapes, apples, raisins and celery.
3. In small cup, stir mayonnaise and yogurt together.
4. Pour over fruit and stir to mix.
5. Add nuts.
6. Serve salad on bed of chopped lettuce.

Tip:
   Apples should not be prepared ahead of time since they'll turn brown.

Go-Along:
• Cheese ball and whole wheat crackers

Desserts

Applesauce Cake with Streusel Topping

Crystal Trost
Singers Glen, VA

Makes 16-20 servings

Prep. Time: 20 minutes
Baking Time: 45-60 minutes
Standing Time: 30-60 minutes

1 stick (½ cup) plus 2 Tbsp. butter, softened, *divided*
¾ cup sugar
½ cup molasses
2 eggs, well beaten
2 cups all-purpose flour
½ cup whole wheat pastry flour
1 tsp. cinnamon
½ tsp. cloves
½ tsp. nutmeg
½ tsp. salt
1 tsp. baking soda
1½ cups unsweetened applesauce
1-2 cups chopped cranberries *or* ½ cup chopped nuts

¼ cup rolled oats
¼ cup brown sugar

1. Cream ½ cup butter. Add sugar and molasses and continue to beat until fluffy.
2. Add eggs and beat thoroughly.
3. In another bowl, sift flours, cinnamon, cloves, nutmeg, salt and baking soda together.
4. Add dry ingredients to creamed butter mixture alternately with applesauce, beating thoroughly after each addition.
5. Fold in cranberries or nuts.
6. Pour into greased tube pan.
7. In a food processor, combine oats, sugar and remaining 2 Tbsp. butter. Pulse to combine. Sprinkle on top of cake.
8. Bake at 350° for 45-60 minutes or until pick inserted in middle comes out clean.
9. Cool in pan for 10 minutes and then invert on rack to cool.

Tip:
The topping replaces the icing, so when the cake cools it is ready to serve.

Go-Along:
• A cup of hot tea!

Chopped Apple Cake

Sherri McCauley
Lakeway, TX

Makes 8 servings

Prep. Time: 15 minutes
Baking Time: 30-35 minutes

**3-4 medium apples,
  unpeeled, chopped
1 cup sugar
1½ cups all-purpose flour
1 tsp. baking soda
½ tsp. cinnamon
½ cup oil
1 egg, beaten
½ cup chopped nuts
½ cup raisins**

1. Put apples in a bowl with sugar. Stir.
2. In another bowl, sift flour, baking soda and cinnamon together.
3. Blend oil and beaten egg into apples.
4. Add dry ingredients all at once and blend well.
5. Stir in nuts and raisins. Mix well.
6. Spread batter in a greased 8 × 8 square baking pan.
7. Bake at 350° for 30-35 minutes, or until tester inserted in middle comes out clean.

Tips:
1. Use an apple slicer to save time on cutting the apples. Feel free to use your favorite nuts to make this recipe your own.

2. If there is any cake left over, store it in the refrigerator for a refreshing treat later.

Go-Along:
• This cake tastes great warm with some vanilla ice cream on top!

William Tell's Cake

Marlene Graber
Sparta, WI

Makes 12 servings

Prep. Time: 40 minutes
Baking Time: 50 minutes
Standing Time: 10 minutes

**8-oz. pkg. cream cheese,
  softened
2 cups sugar, *divided*
4 eggs, divided
1 cup canola oil
2 cups all-purpose flour
2 tsp. baking powder
2 tsp. cinnamon
1 tsp. salt
¼ tsp. baking soda
2 cups peeled, chopped
  apples
1 cup shredded carrots
½ cup chopped nuts**

Icing:
  **½ cup brown sugar,
    packed
  half stick (¼ cup) butter
  2 Tbsp. milk
  ½ cup confectioners
    sugar
  ½ tsp. vanilla extract
  ¼ cup chopped nuts,
    *optional***

1. In small bowl, beat cream cheese, ¼ cup sugar, and 1 egg. Set aside.
2. In large bowl, beat oil with remaining 1¾ cups sugar and 3 eggs.
3. Combine flour, baking powder, cinnamon, salt and baking soda. Add to oil mixture and beat.
4. Stir in apples, carrots and nuts.
5. Pour half the batter into a greased and floured 10" fluted bundt pan.
6. Pour cream-cheese mixture evenly over top. Gently pour the remaining batter on top.
7. Bake at 350° for 50-60 minutes, or until toothpick inserted into cake at several places comes out clean.
8. Cool for 10 minutes before inverting onto serving plate.
9. To make icing, in saucepan, bring brown sugar, butter, and milk to boil. Cook and stir for 1 minute.
10. Remove from heat. Stir in confectioners sugar and vanilla.
11. Drizzle over cake, and then sprinkle with nuts if you wish.

Variation:
  Try this sauce instead of the drizzled icing:
  1 stick (½ cup) butter, ½ cup sugar, ½ cup firmly packed brown sugar, ½ cup whipping cream. Cook and stir together till mixture comes to a boil. Stir in 1 tablespoon vanilla. Sprinkle cake with confectioners sugar, and serve warm sauce alongside with ladle.

Gingerbread

Natalia Showalter
Mt. Solon, VA

Makes 9-12 servings

Prep. Time: 10 minutes
Baking Time: 30-35 minutes

1 stick (½ cup) butter,
  softened
⅓ cup brown sugar
2 eggs
¾ cup sorghum molasses
2 cups all-purpose flour
1½ tsp. baking soda
½ tsp. salt
1½ tsp. ground ginger
1 tsp. ground cloves
1 cup boiling water

1. In a bowl, mix butter,
brown sugar, eggs, molasses,
flour, baking soda, salt, ginger,
and cloves.
2. Carefully stir in hot
water.
3. Place in greased 9 × 13
baking pan.
4. Bake at 350° for 30-35
minutes, or until toothpick
inserted in center comes out
clean.

Tip:
Serve warm with lemon
sauce (see next recipe) or
whipped cream.

Lemon Sauce

Natalia Showalter
Mt. Solon, VA

Makes 1½ cups

Prep. Time: 5 minutes
Cooking Time: 10 minutes

½ cup sugar
2 Tbsp. cornstarch
1 cup water
⅛ tsp. salt
2 Tbsp. lemon juice
2 Tbsp. butter
5 drops lemon oil, *optional*

1. Combine sugar, corn-
starch, water and salt in a
saucepan.
2. Cook and stir over low
heat until thick and clear.
3. Remove from heat.
4. Add lemon juice, but-
ter and lemon oil. Stir until
blended.

Tip:
Serve over gingerbread.

Raspberry Angel Food Cake

Mary Jane Musser
Manheim, PA

Makes 10-12 servings

Prep. Time: 25 minutes
Baking Time: 40 minutes
Standing Time: 1-2 hours

16-oz. box angel food cake
  mix
6-oz. container raspberry
  yogurt
⅓ cup confectioners sugar
12 oz. frozen whipped
  topping, thawed
fresh raspberries, for
  garnish
mint leaves, for garnish

1. Prepare cake mix according to package directions.
2. Bake in tube pan. Cool.
Slice cake in half horizontally
to make 2 layers.
3. Combine yogurt, sugar,
and whipped topping.
4. Spread one cup over
bottom. Top with second
layer. Frost outside of cake
with rest of yogurt mixture.
Garnish with raspberries and
mint leaves.
5. Cover. Refrigerate cake
1-2 hours before slicing to
serve.

Tres Leches Cake with Chile-Cocoa Whipped Cream

Allison Martin
Royal Oak, MI

Makes 16 servings

Prep. Time: 1 hour
Baking Time: 35 minutes
Standing Time: 20 minutes
Chilling Time: 12 hours

vegetable oil
2 cups all-purpose flour, plus more for pan
½ tsp. salt
1 tsp. baking powder
1 stick (½ cup) unsalted butter, at room temperature
1 cup sugar
5 eggs
1½ tsp. vanilla extract
1 cup half-and-half
14-oz. can sweetened condensed milk
12-oz. can evaporated milk
1-oz. square semi-sweet baking chocolate
½ pt. heavy cream
⅛ tsp. cayenne pepper
¼ tsp. cinnamon

1. Lightly oil and flour a 9 × 13 baking pan.
2. In a small mixing bowl, whisk together flour, salt and baking powder. Set aside.
3. With a stand mixer or another large mixing bowl and hand mixer, beat the stick of butter until creamed.
4. Slowly add sugar to butter, continuing to mix on high for about a minute.
5. Add one egg at a time to the mixing bowl, while beating at a medium speed until every egg has been mixed into the batter.
6. Add vanilla extract and mix to combine.
7. Slowly add the flour mixture and mix until just combined.
8. Pour and scrape batter into floured baking pan.
9. Bake at 350° for 20-25 minutes, or until cake tests done. Flip cake out of pan onto cooling rack.
10. Take a fork or a toothpick and poke holes all over the top of the hot cake—corners, middle and sides.
11. Let cool for 20 minutes.
12. Meanwhile, in a medium-sized mixing bowl whisk together half-and- half, sweetened condensed milk and evaporated milk.
13. Transfer cooled cake back to the baking dish. Pour all of the milk mixture over the cake. This should soak into the cake within 3-4 minutes.
14. Cover with plastic wrap and set in the refrigerator overnight.
15. When ready to serve, make the whipped cream topping. Melt baking chocolate in a microwave-safe dish for about a minute, until soft and mostly melted from the inside.
16. Stir. Set aside to cool.
17. In a deep mixing bowl, pour heavy cream, cayenne pepper and cinnamon. Beat on high until stiff peaks form.
18. Add about ¼ cup whipped cream to the dish with the cool, melted chocolate, folding it together until combined.
19. Add the chocolate mixture to the larger bowl of whipped cream. Swirl chocolate through the whipped cream using a table knife, until marbleized.
20. Just before serving each piece of chilled cake, top with whipped cream.

Keep a cake covered so it doesn't dry out.
Elva Mae Martin, Ephrata, PA

Triple Chocolate Cake and Sauce

Kris Zimmerman
Lititz, PA

Makes 8 servings

Prep. Time: 5 minutes
Cooking Time: 6-8 hours
Ideal slow-cooker size: 4-qt.

18-oz. box chocolate cake
  mix
2 cups sour cream
3-oz. box instant chocolate
  pudding mix
¾ cup chocolate chips
¾ cup oil
4 eggs
1 cup water

1. Spray slow cooker with non-stick spray.
2. Combine cake mix, sour cream, pudding mix, chocolate chips, oil, eggs and water in slow cooker. Stir.
3. Cook on low 6-8 hours.

Tip:
  Serve warm with ice cream. It's like a hot fudge brownie sundae!

Go-Along:
• Ice cream.

Chocolate Peanut Butter Slow-Cooker Cake

Jennifer Freed
Harrisonburg, VA

Makes 12 servings

Prep. Time: 20 minutes
Cooking Time: 2-2½ hours
Ideal slow-cooker size: 4-qt.

1 cup flour
1¼ cups sugar, *divided*
¼ cup plus 3 Tbsp. cocoa
  powder, *divided*
1½ tsp. baking powder
½ cup milk
2 Tbsp. butter *or*
  margarine, melted
1 tsp. vanilla
2 cups boiling water
½ cup peanut butter

1. In a large mixing bowl, combine the flour, ½ cup sugar, 3 Tbsp. cocoa powder and baking powder.
2. Whisk in the milk, butter and vanilla, and mix until smooth.
3. Pour into a lightly greased slow cooker.
4. Combine the ¾ cup sugar and ¼ cup cocoa powder.
5. In a separate bowl, combine the boiling water and peanut butter and whisk till smooth.
6. Add to the cocoa and sugar mixture and mix until well combined. Pour over the batter in the slow cooker. Do not stir.
7. Cover. Cook on high for 2-2½ hours, until top is set and slightly puffy.
8. Use a spoon to dish from the slow cooker. Serve warm with ice cream.

Tip:
  This is cake and sauce together!

Chocolate Praline Torte

Edna Good
Richland Center, WI

Makes 14-16 servings

Prep. Time: 35 minutes
Baking Time: 1 hour
Standing Time: 1 hour

1 cup brown sugar
1 stick (½ cup) butter
2 cups heavy whipping
   cream, *divided*
¾ cup chopped pecans
18¼-oz. pkg. chocolate
   cake mix
¼ cup confectioners sugar
¼ tsp. vanilla
chocolate curls, *optional*

1. In a saucepan, combine brown sugar, butter and ¼ cup cream. Stir over low heat just until butter is melted.
2. Divide evenly between two 9" round greased cake pans. Sprinkle with pecans. Set aside.
3. Prepare cake mix according to package directions. Divide batter evenly between the 2 pans, pouring carefully over the pecan mixture.
4. Bake at 325° for 35-40 minutes or until a toothpick inserted in center of cake comes out clean.
5. Cool in pans 10 minutes. Invert onto wire racks and carefully remove cakes from pans to cool completely.
6. Make topping when cakes are cool. For topping, beat remaining 1¾ cups cream in mixing bowl until soft peaks form. Gradually add sugar and vanilla, beating until stiff.
7. Place one cake layer, pecan-side up on serving plate. Spread with half of cream topping.
8. Place second cake layer on top and spread with remaining topping. Top with chocolate curls, if desired.

Tip:

Purchased whipped topping can be substituted for the topping ingredients in this recipe.

Chocolate Date Cake

Sharon Easter
Yuba City, CA

Makes 10-12 servings

Prep. Time: 20 minutes
Baking Time: 30-35 minutes
Standing Time: 30 minutes

1 cup boiling water
1 cup chopped dates, *or*
   raisins
1 tsp. baking soda
1 cup sugar
1 cup mayonnaise
2 cups all-purpose flour
3 Tbsp. unsweetened cocoa
   powder
1 tsp. cinnamon
1 tsp. vanilla
1 cup chopped nuts

1. Place dates and baking soda in a medium mixing bowl.
2. Pour boiling water over dates and baking soda. Let cool.
3. Meanwhile, in a mixing bowl, cream sugar and mayonnaise.
4. Stir in flour, cocoa powder, cinnamon, vanilla and nuts.
5. Add date mixture.
6. Pour into lightly greased 9×13 baking pan.
7. Bake at 350° for 30-35 minutes, or until tester inserted in middle comes out clean.

Variations:

1. Pour into tube pan and bake at 350° for 50-55 minutes, or pour into layer pans and bake at 350° for 25-30 minutes.
2. Frost with cream cheese icing if desired. Also pretty dusted with confectioners sugar.

Coconut Buttermilk Pound Cake

Janie Canupp
Millersville, MD

Makes 20 servings

Prep. Time: 30 minutes
Baking Time: 1 hour 35 minutes

1 cup shortening
3 cups sugar
6 eggs
½ tsp. salt
¼ tsp. baking soda
1 cup buttermilk
3 cups all-purpose flour
2 tsp. lemon flakes *or* lemon zest
1 cup shredded coconut

1. In blender or food processor, mix shortening and sugar until well blended.
2. Add eggs, one at a time, and blend well after each one.
3. Mix salt, baking soda, and buttermilk together in a separate bowl.
4. Add buttermilk mixture alternately with flour to egg mixture.
5. Beat well after each addition.
6. Stir in lemon and coconut.
7. Place batter in greased and floured tube pan.
8. Bake at 325° for 1 hour and 35 minutes, or until cake tests done.

Hawaiian Wedding Cake

Lucille, Rosalie and **Dawn Martin**
Barnett, MO

Makes 12-15 servings

Prep. Time: 25 minutes
Baking Time: 40 minutes
Standing Time: 2 hours

1 cup milk
18-oz. pkg. yellow cake mix
3-oz. pkg. instant vanilla pudding
8 oz. cream cheese, softened, cut in cubes
20-oz. can crushed pineapple, drained
8-oz. container whipped topping
flaked coconut, *optional*

1. Put milk in small saucepan. Heat until steaming and just breaking into a simmer. Remove from heat. Set aside to cool.
2. Bake cake according to package directions in 9 × 13 baking pan.
3. Cool completely.
4. Beat cooled milk and pudding together and slowly add cream cheese. Mix until smooth.
5. Spread on cooled cake.
6. Layer pineapple over pudding mixture.
7. Top with whipped topping.
8. Sprinkle with coconut.

Waldorf School Birthday Cake

Leanne Yoder
Tucson, AZ

Makes 12 servings

Prep. Time: 30 minutes
Baking Time: 35-45 minutes

1 cup oil
1 cup honey
1⅔ cups vanilla yogurt
4 tsp. vanilla
1 tsp. baking soda
2 cups pastry flour
2 cups whole wheat flour

1. Mix together the oil, honey, yogurt and vanilla in a large mixing bowl.
2. In another good-sized bowl, sift the dry ingredients together.
3. Mix the dry ingredients into the wet ingredients, until everything is evenly blended.
4. Pour batter into an oiled bundt or tube pan.
5. Bake for 35-45 minutes at 350° until golden brown. Cool.

Tip:
A wholesome alternative to the sugary cake with ice cream that is so often served at festive occasions.

Go-Along:
• Serve with heavy whipping cream and slices of the birthday celebrant's favorite fresh fruit or berries. Or serve warm, in a bowl with milk or cream.

Buttermilk Banana Pineapple Cake

Susie Shenk Wenger
Lancaster, PA

Makes 14-16 servings

Prep. Time: 20 minutes
Baking Time: 25-45 minutes
Standing Time: 1-2 hours

2¼ cups all-purpose flour
¼ cup flax meal *or* oat
    bran
1 tsp. cinnamon
½ tsp. ginger
1¼ cups sugar
1½ tsp. baking powder
1 tsp. baking soda
½ tsp. salt
1 cup mashed bananas
    (about 3 whole bananas)
¾ cup crushed pineapple,
    drained
¾ cup buttermilk
1 stick (½ cup) softened
    butter
1 tsp. vanilla
2 eggs

Frosting:
    5 Tbsp. butter, softened
    8-oz. pkg. cream cheese,
      softened
    1 tsp. vanilla
    1½ cups confectioners
      sugar
    ½ cup chopped pecans,
      toasted
    sprinkle of cinnamon

1. Grease and lightly flour baking pans — either one 9 × 13 pan or two round 9" pans.

2. In large bowl, mix flour, flax meal, cinnamon, ginger, sugar, baking powder, baking soda and salt.

3. In separate bowl, place banana, pineapple, buttermilk, butter and vanilla. Mix with an electric mixer for 2 minutes. Stir in eggs.

4. Stir together the two mixtures until just mixed.

5. Pour into prepared pan(s).

6. Bake at 350° for 25 minutes if using 2 round 9" pans. Increase time to 45 minutes if using a 9 × 13 pan. Bake until toothpick inserted in middle comes out clean.

7. Cool.

8. For frosting, combine butter, cream cheese, vanilla and confectioners sugar.

9. Spread on cake.

10. Top with pecans and a sprinkle of cinnamon.

Tips:

1. This is a very dense cake. Make sure the toothpick comes out clean in the center or the cake will be too wet.

2. I put ripe bananas in my freezer and when I have 3 or 4, I am ready to make this cake.

Peach Dessert

Lois Stoltzfus
Honey Brook, PA

Makes 12-14 servings

Prep. Time: 10 minutes
Baking Time: 40-45 minutes

1 quart *or* 29-oz. can sliced
    peaches
1 box brittle *or* yellow cake
    mix
1 stick (½ cup) butter,
    melted
½ cup flaked coconut
½ cup chopped pecans

1. Place peaches and juice in 9 × 13 baking pan.

2. Spread dry cake mix over fruit.

3. Pour melted butter on top. Sprinkle with coconut and pecans.

4. Bake at 350° for 40-45 minutes, or until toothpick inserted in center comes out clean.

Tip:

A substitute for cake mix: 1½ cups sugar, 2¼ cups all-purpose flour, 2½ tsp. baking powder, ½ tsp. salt. You can reduce the sugar if you wish. You can also replace some of the all-purpose flour with whole wheat pastry flour.

Go-Along:
• Ice cream.

Maple Peach Crumble Pie

Judy Newman
St. Marys, ON

Makes 8 servings

Prep. Time: 30 minutes
Baking Time: 45-50 minutes

½ cup flour
½ cup maple sugar *or* brown sugar
½ tsp. cinnamon
¼ cup butter-flavored shortening
3 eggs
1 Tbsp. lemon juice
¼ cup maple syrup
2 20-oz. cans peaches, sliced and drained
⅓ cup sliced almonds
9" unbaked pie shell

1. In a small mixing bowl, combine flour, sugar and cinnamon.
2. Cut in shortening with a pastry cutter. Set aside.
3. To make filling beat eggs, lemon juice and syrup together in a medium mixing bowl.
4. Fold in peaches.
5. Pour into pie shell. Top with flour mixture and almonds.
6. Bake at 375° for 45-50 minutes, or until set and lightly browned.

Oatmeal Coconut Pie

Karen L. Gingrich
Bernville, PA

Makes 6-8 servings

Prep. Time: 10 minutes
Baking Time: 45-50 minutes

2 eggs
½ cup white sugar
½ cup brown sugar
1 stick (½ cup) melted butter
1 tsp. vanilla
1 cup milk
¾ cup rolled oats
1 cup shredded coconut
9" unbaked pie shell

1. In a bowl, mix eggs, sugars, butter, vanilla, milk, oats and coconut.
2. Pour into unbaked pie shell.
3. Bake at 350° for 45-50 minutes, or until set in the middle.

Go-Along:
• This tastes like pecan pie. Serve warm with ice cream or milk.

Quick Apple Pie

Vivian Benner
Dayton, VA

Makes 6 servings

Prep. Time: 30 minutes
Baking Time: 30-35 minutes

5 Macintosh apples, peeled and sliced
1 Tbsp. plus 1 cup sugar, *divided*
1 tsp. cinnamon
1 stick (½ cup) butter, softened
1 egg, beaten
1 tsp. vanilla
1 cup flour
½ cup chopped nuts
whipped cream *or* ice cream, *optional*

1. In a large bowl, combine apples, 1 Tbsp. sugar and cinnamon.
2. Transfer to a greased 9" pie plate.
3. In a small bowl, cream the butter and 1 cup sugar with an electric mixer.
4. Beat in egg and vanilla.
5. Add flour. Mix well until blended.
6. By hand, stir in the nuts.
7. Spread mixture over apples.
8. Bake at 350° for 30-35 minutes, or until apples are tender and crust is brown.
9. Serve warm with whipped cream or ice cream.

Always put a pinch of love in each recipe!
Bonnie Lahman, Broadway, VA

Creamy Apple Pie

Mary Hackenberger
Thompsontown, PA

Makes 8 servings

Prep. Time: 45 minutes
Baking Time: 45 minutes

1 stick (½ cup) plus 1 Tbsp. butter, at room temperature, *divided*
¾ cup plus 2 Tbsp. sugar, *divided*
1 tsp. vanilla, *divided*
1 cup flour
8-oz. pkg. cream cheese, at room temperature
1 egg
4 cups thinly sliced apples, peeled or unpeeled
½ tsp. cinnamon
½ cup chopped pecans

1. To make crust, use an electric mixer to beat 1 stick butter, ¼ cup sugar and ½ tsp. vanilla in mixing bowl.
2. Gradually add flour, until mixture forms soft dough.
3. Press into bottom and up sides of a deep-dish 9" pie pan.
4. In a mixing bowl, use an electric mixer to beat cream cheese, 2 Tbsp. sugar, egg and remaining ½ tsp. vanilla.
5. Spread cream cheese mixture evenly over crust.
6. By hand, gently mix together apples, cinnamon, and remaining ½ cup sugar.
7. Layer apple filling evenly over cream-cheese filling.
8. Dot with remaining one tablespoon butter. Sprinkle with nuts.
9. Make a loose tent of foil to cover pie while baking.
10. Bake at 400° for 15 minutes. Lower heat to 350° and bake an additional 20 minutes. Remove foil tent. Bake 10 minutes longer, or until apples are done.

Frosty Mocha Pie

Leah Hersberger
Dundee, OH

Makes 8-10 servings

Prep. Time: 25 minutes
Chilling Time: 4 hours
Standing Time: 15 minutes

4 oz. cream cheese, at room temperature
¼ cup sugar
¼ cup unsweetened baking cocoa
1 tsp. instant coffee granules
⅓ cup milk, at room temperature
1 tsp. vanilla extract
12 oz. frozen whipped topping, thawed
9" graham-cracker crust
chocolate syrup for garnish, *optional*
crushed candy bars for garnish, *optional*

1. In large mixing bowl, beat cream cheese, sugar and cocoa with an electric mixer until smooth.
2. In a small bowl, dissolve coffee in milk.
3. Stir coffee mixture and vanilla into cream cheese mixture.
4. Gently fold in whipped topping.
5. Pour into crust.
6. Cover. Freeze for 4 hours.
7. Remove from freezer 15 minutes before serving.
8. Drizzle with chocolate syrup and sprinkle with crushed candy bars if you wish.

Tip:
This can be made ahead and kept in the freezer for up to a week, tightly covered.

Variation:
Add 8 ounces instead of 4 ounces of cream cheese if you wish.

Pecan Pumpkin Pie

Nancy Leatherman
Hamburg, PA

Makes 8 servings

Prep. Time: 15 minutes
Baking Time: 50 minutes

3 eggs, slightly beaten
1 cup sugar
½ cup corn syrup
1 cup cooked pumpkin
¼ tsp. salt
1 tsp. vanilla
½ tsp. cinnamon
9" unbaked pie shell
1 cup chopped pecans

1. In a mixing bowl, mix eggs and sugar.
2. Add syrup, pumpkin, salt, vanilla and cinnamon.
3. Beat well.
4. Pour into 9" pie shell.
5. Sprinkle with pecans.
6. Bake at 425° for 15 minutes.
7. Reduce heat to 350° and bake 30 minutes, or until set in the middle.

Lemon Pie a la Mode

Joyce Nolt
Richland, PA

Makes 8 servings

Prep. Time: 20 minutes
Cooking Time: 20 minutes
Standing Time: 30-60 minutes
Chilling Time: 3-5 hours

⅓ cup (5⅓ Tbsp.) butter
⅓ cup lemon juice
¾ cup sugar
pinch of salt
3 eggs, beaten
10" baked pie crust
1 quart vanilla ice cream, softened
2-3 cups frozen whipped topping thawed, *or* whipped cream

1. Prepare a double boiler (or place a heatproof bowl over a saucepan of simmering water; the bowl should fit with no gap and without touching the water).
2. Place butter in top of double boiler to melt.
3. When butter is melted, add lemon juice, sugar and pinch of salt.
4. Stirring constantly, slowly add beaten eggs.
5. Cook in double boiler until mixture is thick and smooth, stirring constantly.
6. Remove from heat. Set aside to cool to room temperature, 30-60 minutes.
7. Spoon into pie crust. Cover. Freeze for 2-4 hours, or until firm.
8. Remove from freezer and top with softened ice cream and whipped topping. Cover tightly.
9. Return to freezer for at least an hour before serving.

Tip:
Use chopped nuts, toasted coconut, or a drizzle of chocolate syrup to garnish if you wish.

One of the best ways I know of to simultaneously improve your household members' nutritional status, nurture the environment, and stimulate a local micro-business is to join your local community-supported agriculture (CSA) movement. CSA farms across the nation provide a weekly delivery of sustainably grown produce to subscribing consumers. The locally and organically grown fruits and vegetables that we receive from the Tucson CSA, together with their accompanying recipes, have introduced delicious variety to our family's table.

Leanne Yoder, Tucson, AZ

Lemon Cheesecake

Meg Suter
Goshen, IN

Makes 8 servings

Prep. Time: 20-25 minutes
Baking Time: 50-55 minutes
Standing Time: 1 hour
Chilling Time: 2-24 hours

1¼ cups crushed graham
   crackers (about 10 whole
   crackers)
¾ cups crushed gingersnaps
   (about 15 cookies)
¼ cup sugar
5 Tbsp. buttery spread
4½ tsp. egg substitute
6 Tbsp. water
24 oz. non-dairy cream
   cheese, softened and cut
   in small cubes
1 cup sugar
½ tsp. vanilla
4-6 Tbsp. fresh lemon juice
2 Tbsp. lemon zest
fresh strawberries for
   serving, *optional*

1. In a food processor,
crush graham crackers and
gingersnaps. Add sugar and
buttery spread. Pulse until
mixed.

2. Press into a lightly oiled
9-inch springform pan.

3. Bake crust at 350° for
10 minutes, until golden. Set
aside to cool.

4. Using electric hand
mixer in a large bowl, whip
egg substitute and water
together until thick and
creamy.

5. Beat in cream cheese for
30 seconds—don't go longer!

6. Beat in sugar, vanilla,
lemon juice and lemon zest
just until smooth. Don't over-
beat—this will cause cracking
on the surface during baking.

7. Pour batter into crust.
Smooth top with a spatula.

8. Bake at 350°, until
center barely jiggles when
pan is tapped, 50-55 minutes.
It is fine if it puffs up a bit
and turns golden brown; it
will settle as it cools.

9. Cool completely in pan
on rack for at least one hour.

10. Refrigerate for at least
two hours, but preferably 24
hours, before serving. This is
lovely garnished with strawberries when ready to serve.

No-Bake Chilled Cherry Pie

Frances L. Kruba
Dundalk, MD

Makes 8 servings

Prep. Time: 20 minutes
Chilling Time: 4 hours

15-oz. can sweetened
   condensed milk
juice of 2 lemons
zest of 1 lemon
¼ cup sugar
14½-oz. can red cherries,
   drained
1 cup chopped nuts
2 cups whipped cream,
   divided
10" graham-cracker pie
   crust *or* 9" deep-dish
   graham-cracker pie crust

1. In a mixing bowl, mix
milk, lemon juice, lemon zest
and sugar.

2. Add cherries and nuts.

3. Fold in 1 cup whipped
cream. Pour into pie crust.

4. Top with remaining
1 cup whipped cream. Cover.

5. Refrigerate 4 hours
before serving.

Apricot Crisp

Teresa Martin
Strasburg, PA

Makes 6 servings

Prep. Time: 25 minutes
Cooking Time: 3½-4 hrs
Ideal slow-cooker size: 4-qt.

½ cup quick oats
⅓ cup brown sugar, packed
¼ cup all-purpose flour
¼ cup wheat germ, toasted
¼ cup finely chopped
  almonds
½ tsp. salt
2 Tbsp. cold butter
2 Tbsp. milk
1 Tbsp. sugar
¾ tsp. ground ginger
2 14-oz. cans apricot halves
  in juice, drained
¾ tsp. almond extract
1 tsp. chopped crystallized
  ginger, *optional*
frozen yogurt, *optional*

1. Combine oats, brown
sugar, flour, wheat germ,
almonds and salt in a medium
bowl. With 2 knives or a
pastry cutter, cut in butter
until mixture resembles
coarse crumbs.

2. Gradually add milk,
tossing lightly with fork, just
until mixture resembles fine
crumbs.

3. Mix granulated sugar
and ginger in medium bowl.

4. Add apricots and almond
extract. Toss to coat. Transfer
apricot mixture to greased
slow cooker.

5. Sprinkle with crumb
topping. Lightly spray with
nonstick spray.

6. Cover. Cook on high
until topping is crisp and
begins to brown, about
3½-4 hours.

7. Top with frozen vanilla
yogurt and crystallized ginger
if you wish

Texas Peach Cobbler

Edna Good
Richland Center, WI

Makes 9 servings

Prep. Time: 20 minutes
Baking Time: 50 minutes

6 Tbsp. butter
1¼ cups all-purpose flour
¾ cup, plus 2 Tbsp., sugar,
  divided
2 tsp. baking powder
⅛ tsp. salt
dash cinnamon
1 tsp. vanilla, *divided*
1 cup milk
4 cups peaches, peeled and
  sliced
1 tsp. lemon juice

1. Turn oven on to 350°.
Place butter in 8 × 8 baking
dish. Place dish in oven to
melt butter.

2. In mixing bowl, combine
flour, sugar, baking powder, salt,
cinnamon, ½ tsp. vanilla and
milk. Stir just until combined.

3. Spoon batter over melted
butter. Do not mix!

4. In a bowl, combine
peaches, 1 Tbsp. sugar, lemon
juice and remaining ½ tsp.
vanilla.

5. Spoon peach mixture
over batter, gently pressing
peaches into batter.

6. Bake at 350° for 40
minutes.

7. Sprinkle with remaining
1 Tbsp. sugar and bake 10
minutes longer.

Build your menu around vegetables and fruits when they are in season — they tend to be less expensive.
Susan Heil, Strasburg, PA

247

Aunt Annabelle's Fruit Cobbler

Shirley Unternahrer
Wayland, IA

Makes 12 servings

Prep. Time: 15-20 minutes
Baking Time: 45 minutes

6 cups diced rhubarb,
   blueberries, blackberries,
   or cherries
2½ cups sugar, *divided*
2 cups plus 2 Tbsp. all-
   purpose flour, *divided*
1 tsp. salt
⅓ cup canola oil
2 tsp. baking powder
1 cup milk
2 Tbsp. flour
scant 2 cups boiling water

1. Spread fruit across bottom of greased 9 × 13 baking pan.
2. In a mixing bowl, mix 1 cup sugar, 2 cups flour, salt, oil, baking powder and milk. Mix until smooth.
3. Pour evenly over fruit.
4. Next mix remaining 1½ cups sugar with remaining 2 Tbsp. flour.
5. Sprinkle mixture over dough.
6. Slowly and evenly pour boiling water over top. Do not stir!
7. Bake at 375° for 40-50 minutes, until lightly browned.

Variation:
   You can use fruit such as peaches, but then reduce fruit amount to 5 cups instead of 6.

Go-Along:
• Top with ice cream or milk, or milk substitute.

Pineapple Bread Pudding

Janie Canupp
Millersville, MD

Makes 10 servings

Prep. Time: 15 minutes
Cooking Time: 2-3 hours
Ideal slow-cooker size: 4-qt.

2 Tbsp. flour
⅓ cup sugar
3 eggs
2 8-oz. cans chunky
   pineapple, with juice
6 slices bread
5⅓ Tbsp. (⅓ cup) butter

1. Mix flour, sugar and eggs until smooth. Stir in pineapple and juice. Set aside.
2. Break bread in small chunks and place in greased slow cooker.
3. Melt butter and pour over bread.
4. Pour pineapple mixture over bread.
5. Cover and cook on low for 2-3 hours, until brown and firm.

Tip:
   Good for breakfast, too!

Fruit Pudding

Betty Sue Good
Broadway, VA

Makes 6 servings

Prep. Time: 15 minutes
Baking Time: 45 minutes

1 cup sugar
2 eggs
¾ tsp. soda
½ cup sour cream *or* plain
   yogurt
½ tsp. salt
1¾ cups all-purpose flour
2 cups canned fruit, drained

1. Mix sugar and eggs in a large bowl.
2. In a separate bowl mix soda and sour cream together. Add to egg mixture, along with salt and flour. Mixture will be stiff.
3. Gently stir in fruit.
4. Pour into 7½ × 11 greased baking pan.
5. Bake at 350° for 45 minutes.

Tip:
   Substitute whole wheat pastry flour for part or all of the all-purpose flour.

Go-Along:
• Serve warm with cream or ice cream.

Fruit Mixture Crisps

Willard Swartley
Elkhart, IN

Makes 6-8 servings

Prep. Time: 30 minutes
Baking Time: 40 minutes

2 cups sour cherries,
  peaches *or* rhubarb
3 cups mulberries *or*
  blackberries, *or* 2 cups
  strawberries
½-¾ cup sugar, according
  to your taste preference
¾ cup water
3 Tbsp. cornstarch *or*
  minute tapioca
1¾ cups quick oats
1 cup flour
¾ cup brown sugar
½ tsp. baking soda
3 Tbsp. butter, softened
½ cup chopped walnuts

1. Pit the sour cherries. Cut up chosen fruits.

2. In a saucepan over low heat, cook the chosen fruits, sugar, water and cornstarch until thickened.

3. Pour into a greased 2-quart casserole dish.

4. Mix together oats, flour, brown sugar, baking soda, butter and nuts. Sprinkle over top of casserole dish.

5. Bake at 350° for 30 minutes, or until top is slightly browned and edges are bubbling.

Go-Along:
• Serve warm, topped with frozen yogurt or ice cream.

1-2-3 Apple Crisp

Lavina Hochstedler
Grand Blanc, MI

Makes 8 servings

Prep. Time: 15 minutes
Baking Time: 35-45 minutes

8 apples, peeled and cored
1½ cups brown sugar
1 cup all-purpose flour
1 cup quick *or* rolled oats
1 tsp. cinnamon
1 tsp. nutmeg
1 stick (½ cup) butter,
  softened

1. Lightly grease a 9 × 13 glass baking pan.

2. Cut apples into slices and layer in bottom of pan.

3. In a medium bowl, mix together brown sugar, flour, oats, cinnamon and nutmeg.

4. Cut in butter with a pastry blender until crumbly.

5. Sprinkle mixture over apples.

6. Bake at 375° for 35-45 minutes, or until the top is browned.

Tip:
Because of using a glass pan, I often like to cook this in the microwave for 10-15 minutes before I put the crumbs on. It shortens the baking time in the oven. Bake just until the topping browns, about 15-20 minutes.

Go-Along:
• Serve with ice cream or whipped topping. This follows a bowl of soup well!

Apple Cranberry Crisp

Charlotte Burkholder
East Petersburg, PA

Makes 8 servings

Prep. Time: 25 minutes
Baking Time: 60-75 minutes

8 large baking apples
8 oz. fresh *or* frozen
    cranberries
juice of 1 lemon
¾ cup brown sugar,
    packed, *divided*
2½ tsp. cinnamon, *divided*
2 Tbsp. whole wheat flour
1¾ cups rolled oats
⅓ cups canola oil

1. Peel, core and slice apples into a bowl. Add cranberries and lemon juice. Set aside.

2. Mix ¼ cup brown sugar, 1 tsp. cinnamon and whole wheat flour. Stir into apple mixture.

3. Put into a 8 × 10 greased baking pan

4. To make topping, mix rolled oats, remaining 1½ tsp. cinnamon, and remaining ½ cup brown sugar. Then add oil and mix until crumbly. Sprinkle over apples.

5. Cover with foil. Bake at 350° for 30 minutes. Remove foil and bake 30-45 minutes longer, until apples are soft.

Variation:
Before adding topping, sprinkle with walnuts and raisins.

Go-Along:
• Serve warm with ice cream or whipped cream.

Barbara's Apple Bubble

Mabel Eshelman
Lancaster, PA

Makes 8 servings

Prep. Time: 30 minutes
Baking Time: 1 hour

4 cups water
1 cup sugar
1 Tbsp. butter *or* margarine
1 tsp. cinnamon
3 cups all-purpose flour
2 tsp. salt
4 tsp. baking powder
2 Tbsp. shortening
¾ cup milk
4 cups sliced apples
½ cup brown sugar

1. In a small pan, bring water, sugar, butter, and cinnamon to a boil. Pour into greased 9 × 13 baking pan.

2. In a bowl, combine flour, salt, baking powder, shortening and milk to form dough.

3. On floured surface, roll dough into 12 × 18 oblong shape.

4. In a bowl, mix apples and brown sugar. Spread on dough.

5. Roll jelly-roll fashion, starting with a long side. Pinch seam to seal.

6. Cut roll into 1" slices with a sharp knife and lay flat in syrup in baking pan.

7. Cover. Bake at 375° for 30 minutes.

8. Remove cover and bake an additional 30 minutes.

9. Serve warm with milk.

Tip:
This is a good stand-in for apple dumplings.

Glazed Cinnamon Apples

Monica Wagner
Quarryville, PA

Makes 8-9 servings

Prep. Time: 10 minutes
Cooking Time: 2-3 hours
Ideal slow-cooker size: 5-qt.

6 large apples, peeled, cored and cut into 8 wedges
1 Tbsp. fresh lemon juice
½ cup sugar
½ cup light brown sugar, packed
2 Tbsp. flour
1 tsp. cinnamon
¼ tsp. nutmeg
6 Tbsp. butter, melted
vanilla ice cream
crumbled oatmeal *or* gingersnap cookies, *optional*

1. Place apples in the slow cooker; drizzle with lemon juice.
2. Mix sugar, brown sugar, flour, cinnamon and nutmeg in a medium bowl. Sprinkle mixture over apples. Stir gently to coat apples.
3. Drizzle with butter. Place lid on slow cooker.
4. Cook on low for 3 hours, or high for 2 hours, until apples are done.
5. Carefully remove the lid to allow the steam to escape. Serve warm apples topped with ice cream. Top with crumbled cookies if you wish.

Rhubarb Crunch

Kathryn Yoder
Minot, ND

Makes 10 servings

Prep. Time: 20 minutes
Baking Time: 35-40 minutes

2 cups whole wheat flour
¾ cup quick *or* rolled oats
1 cup brown sugar, packed
1½ sticks (¾ cup) butter, melted
1 tsp. cinnamon
1 cup sugar
2 Tbsp. cornstarch
1 cup water
1 tsp. vanilla
4 cups diced rhubarb

1. In a bowl, mix flour, oats, brown sugar, butter and cinnamon until crumbly.
2. Press ½ of crumbs in 9 × 9 baking dish. Set aside.
3. In medium saucepan, mix sugar, cornstarch, water and vanilla.
4. Bring to rolling boil.
5. Add rhubarb and cook 2 minutes.
6. Pour rhubarb mixture over crumb crust.
7. Sprinkle remaining crumbs on top of rhubarb mixture.
8. Bake at 350° for 35-40 minutes.
9. Cut in squares and serve.

Tip:
This may be served hot or cold, but is best served the day its made.

Go-Along:
• Eat in a bowl with milk, cream, whipped topping or ice cream.

Use kitchen scissors to chop rhubarb.
Leah Hersberger, Dundee, OH

Rhubarb Custard Dessert with Streusel

Ruthie Schiefer
Vassar, MI

Makes 12-15 servings

Prep. Time: 35 minutes
Baking Time: 1 hour 15 minutes

Crust:
2 cups all-purpose flour
½ cup confectioners sugar
¼ tsp. salt
2 sticks (1 cup) butter, softened

Custard Filling:
6 cups diced rhubarb
4 eggs, slightly beaten
1½ cups sugar
½ tsp. salt
3 Tbsp. all-purpose flour

Streusel Topping:
1 stick (½ cup) butter, softened
1 cup sugar
⅔ cup flour
dash cinnamon

1. With pastry blender, cut together flour, powdered sugar, salt and butter.
2. Press into 9 × 13 baking pan.
3. Bake at 325° for 15 minutes.
4. Spread rhubarb on crust.
5. In a mixing bowl, beat eggs, sugar, salt and flour. Pour over rhubarb.
6. With pastry blender, cut together butter, sugar, flour and cinnamon.
7. Sprinkle over top of pan.
8. Bake at 350° for 1 hour, or until top is lightly brown and knife inserted in center comes out clean.

Pumpkin Pie Pudding

Michele Shenk
Manheim, PA

Makes 6-8 servings

Prep. Time: 20-30 minutes
Cooking Time: 6-7 hours
Ideal slow-cooker size: 3- or 4-qt.

15-oz. can pumpkin
12-oz. can evaporated milk
¾ cup sugar
½ cup buttermilk baking mix
2 eggs, beaten
2 Tbsp. butter, melted
2½ tsp. pumpkin pie spice
2 tsp. vanilla
frozen whipped topping, thawed
cinnamon, for garnish
nutmeg, for garnish

1. In greased slow cooker, combine pumpkin, milk, sugar, baking mix, eggs, butter, spice and vanilla.
2. Cook covered on low 6-7 hours.
3. Serve with whipped topping sprinkled with cinnamon and nutmeg.

Tip:
A great fall recipe.

Chocolate Mousse

Meg Suter
Goshen, IN

Makes 8 servings

Prep. Time: 10 minutes
Cooking Time: 1-2 minutes
Chilling Time: 2-4 hours

2 12-oz. bags dairy-free semi-sweet chocolate chips
15-oz. container silken tofu

1. Place chocolate chips in microwaveable bowl. Microwave in 30-second increments, stirring and checking each time until chocolate is melted.
2. Combine melted chocolate and tofu in a blender. Blend until smooth.
3. Refrigerate in serving bowl or individual glass dishes until well chilled. Serve.

Tip:
This works well in a graham-cracker pie crust.

Raspberry Brownie Dessert

Bev Weaver
Logan, OH

Makes 15-18 servings

Prep. Time: 20 minutes
Baking Time: follow package directions
Standing Time: 1 hour
Chilling Time: 2 hours

19-oz. box fudge brownie mix
2 cups heavy whipping cream, *divided*
3.3-oz. instant white chocolate pudding mix
21-oz. can raspberry pie filling

1. Prepare and bake brownies according to package directions. Cool completely.
2. Combine 1 cup heavy whipping cream and pudding mix in a bowl. Stir for 2 minutes, or until very thick.
3. In another bowl, beat remaining cream with electric mixer until stiff peaks form.
4. Fold whipped cream into pudding.
5. Carefully spread over brownies. Spread top with pie filling.
6. Cover and refrigerate for at least 2 hours before cutting.

Jimmy Carter Dessert

Melissa Cramer
Lancaster, PA

Makes 12-15 servings

Prep. Time: 20 minutes
Baking Time: 20 minutes
Standing Time: 30 minutes
Chilling Time: 4-12 hours

1 stick (½ cup) margarine *or* butter
1 cup all-purpose flour
1 cup chopped peanuts
8 oz. pkg. cream cheese, at room temperature
1 cup confectioners sugar
8 oz. frozen whipped topping, thawed, plus extra for garnish
⅓ cup peanut butter
3-oz. pkg. instant vanilla pudding
3-oz. pkg. instant chocolate pudding
2½ cups cold milk
peanuts, for garnish

1. Melt margarine in microwave in microwave-safe bowl. Mix in flour and peanuts.
2. Press mixture into 9 × 13 baking pan to form crust.
3. Bake at 350° for 20 minutes. Cool for at least 30 minutes.
4. In a mixing bowl, mix cream cheese, confectioners sugar, whipped topping and peanut butter. Spread lightly onto cooled crust.
5. Combine vanilla pudding mix, chocolate pudding mix and cold milk. Beat with electric mixer until thickened. Spread over cream cheese mixture.
6. Top with additional whipped topping and peanuts as you wish for garnish.
7. Chill at least 4 hours or overnight before serving.

Lay a piece of foil over the top of just-baked brownies and cakes as they cool. This will keep them moist.

Mary Ryder, Mount Joy, PA

253

Chocolate Pudding

Diana Kampnich
Croghan, NY

Makes 6 servings

Prep. Time: 5 minutes
Cooking Time: 10-15 minutes
Standing Time: 30 minutes

1 cup sugar
6 Tbsp. unsweetened
   baking cocoa powder
½ cup cornstarch
dash salt
5½ cups milk
half stick (¼ cup) butter
2 tsp. vanilla

1. Mix all ingredients in a medium saucepan.
2. Cook on medium heat, whisking constantly. Cook for 10-15 minutes, until it reaches a thickness you like.
3. Pour into serving bowl. Serve warm after cooling for 30 minutes, or chilled after several hours in the fridge.

Peach Sherbet Popsicles

Leanne Yoder
Tucson, AZ

Makes 10 servings

Prep. Time: 20 minutes
Chilling Time: 4 hours

2 egg whites
pinch of salt
6 Tbsp., plus ½ cup, sugar,
   divided
3 cups fresh peach purée
½ cup sugar
⅛ tsp. almond flavoring
1 cup milk

1. Use electric mixer to beat egg whites until foamy. Add salt. Continue beating until soft peaks form.
2. Add 6 Tbsp. sugar, one tablespoon at a time, beating well after each addition.
3. In a separate mixing bowl, mix together puréed peaches, ½ cup sugar, almond flavoring and milk. Fold peach mixture into egg whites.
4. Pour into popsicle molds and freeze at least 4 hours.

Pink Clouds

Angela Diem
Denmark, SC

Makes 8-12 servings

Prep. Time: 15 minutes
Chilling Time: 4 hours
Standing Time: 10 minutes

8-oz. pkg. cream cheese
½ cup sugar
10-oz. container frozen
   strawberries, thawed
2 bananas, sliced
3-oz. can crushed
   pineapple
8-oz. container whipped
   topping

1. In a mixing bowl, cream together cream cheese and sugar until fluffy.
2. Combine strawberries, bananas and pineapple in blender and blend until chopped.
3. Add cream cheese and sugar to blender. Blend. Pour back into mixing bowl.
4. Gently fold in whipped topping. Be sure it is well mixed.
5. Divide mixture between two lightly greased loaf pans. Cover tightly.
6. Freeze for at least 4 hours before serving. When ready to serve, remove pans from freezer and thaw 10 minutes.
7. Serve in slices or scoops.

Strawberry-Banana Freeze

Judy Houser
Hershey, PA

Makes 2 servings

Prep. Time: 5 minutes

1 cup frozen unsweetened
  strawberries
1 cup frozen banana chunks

Process strawberries and banana in food processor until creamy and well blended. Serve immediately.

Tip:
I like to buy very ripe bananas when they are on sale, peel them and cut in chunks and freeze. This is a delightful no-sugar-added dessert that is an excellent substitute for ice cream.

Jam Sandwich Surprises

Dorothy Vandeest
Memphis, TN

Makes 35-40 cookies

Prep. Time: 45 minutes
Chilling Time: 15 minutes
Baking Time: 7 minutes
Standing Time: 30-50 minutes

3¼ cups all-purpose flour
1½ tsp. baking powder
½ tsp. salt

2½ sticks (1¼ cups) butter,
  softened
1 cup sugar
1 large egg
1 Tbsp. milk
2½ tsp. vanilla extract
12 oz. fruit jam
2 tsp. confectioners sugar

1. Combine flour, baking powder and salt in a bowl.
2. In a separate large bowl, beat butter and sugar with electric mixer, on medium speed, until light and fluffy.
3. Beat in egg, milk and vanilla.
4. Add and beat in flour mixture until smooth.
5. Divide dough in half. Roll out each half to ½" thickness between 2 sheets of parchment paper.
6. Chill 15 minutes.
7. Cut dough into 2" round cookies. Place on parchment-paper-lined baking sheets.
8. Bake at 375° for 7 minutes.
9. Cool on wire racks.
10. Meanwhile, put jam in small saucepan. Cook jam over medium heat until thickened and reduced one-quarter in volume (to about 8 ounces).
11. Cool jam completely.
12. Sandwich 1 tsp. jam between 2 cookies.
13. Dust with confectioners sugar.

Best-Ever Sugar Cookies

Jenna Yoder
Floyd, VA

Makes 30 servings

Prep. Time: 30-40 minutes
Baking Time: 6 minutes

¾ cup shortening
1 cup sugar
2 eggs
1 tsp. almond extract
1 tsp. baking powder
½ tsp. salt
2¼ cups all-purpose flour
powdered sugar for rolling
  out dough

1. Using an electric mixer, beat together shortening, sugar, eggs, extract, baking powder and salt.
2. Add flour.
3. Roll out dough ⅜" thick on powdered-sugar-covered counter.
4. Use cookie cutters to cut cookies. Place on greased cookie sheets.
5. Bake at 350° for 6 minutes. Remove immediately to wire racks to cool.

Tip:
Very good with a little icing and festive sprinkles.

Line a cookie sheet with parchment paper to make it easy to remove cookies from pan.

Janice Sams, Lancaster, PA

Peanut Butter Chocolate Chip Oatmeal Cookies

Lavina Hochstedler
Grand Blanc, MI

Makes 36 cookies

Prep. Time: 15 minutes
Baking Time: 10 minutes

⅔ cup, plus 2 Tbsp.,
  crunchy peanut butter
4 Tbsp. canola oil
2 cups light brown sugar
⅔ cup soy milk, regular *or*
  vanilla-flavored
2 tsp. pure vanilla
1 cup whole wheat flour
1 cup all-purpose flour
1 tsp. baking soda
1 tsp. salt
2 cups oats, rolled *or* quick
1⅓ cups dairy-free
  semi-sweet chocolate
  chips

1. In a large mixing bowl, stir together peanut butter, oil, brown sugar, soy milk and vanilla.
2. In a small bowl, thoroughly stir together flour, baking soda and salt.
3. Stir dry ingredients into batter.
4. Stir in oats and chocolate chips.
5. Drop batter by rounded tablespoons onto Silpat- or parchment-lined baking sheet.
6. Bake at 375° for 10 minutes, or until set.
7. Let cool on rack for 5 minutes.

Tip:
  Good for a snack or a dessert.

Go-Along:
• A glass of juice or cup of coffee.

Honey Pecan Cookies

MaryAnn Beachy
Dover, OH

Makes 48 cookies

Prep. Time: 20 minutes
Baking Time: 13 minutes

1 stick (½ cup) butter,
  softened
½ cup shortening
1½ cups sugar, plus more
  for rolling dough
½ cup honey
2 eggs
2 Tbsp. lemon juice
4 cups all-purpose flour
2½ tsp. baking soda
½ tsp. ground cloves
1 tsp. cinnamon
½ tsp. ginger
½ tsp. salt
1 cup chopped pecans

1. Cream butter, shortening and sugar together in mixing bowl until fluffy.
2. Add honey, eggs and lemon juice, and beat well.
3. In a separate bowl, combine flour, baking soda, cloves, cinnamon, ginger and salt. Gradually add to creamed mixture.
4. Fold in pecans.
5. Shape dough into 1" balls. Roll in sugar.
6. Place on ungreased baking sheets.
7. Bake at 350° for 12-13 minutes, or until light brown. Do not overbake.
8. Cool slightly before removing from baking sheets.

When making cookies, use a cool cookie sheet. Sprinkle flour on the sheet. Flour stops cookies from spreading thin. Charmaine Caesar, Lancaster, PA

Cranberry Oatmeal Cookies

Penny Blosser
Beavercreek, OH

Makes 36 cookies

Prep. Time: 15 minutes
Baking Time: 9-11 minutes

---

2 sticks (1 cup) butter, softened
1 cup granulated sugar
¾ cup brown sugar, firmly packed
2 large eggs
1 tsp. vanilla extract
1 cup all-purpose flour
¾ cup whole wheat flour
1 tsp. baking powder
1 tsp. baking soda
1 tsp. salt
3 cups quick oats
1 cup dried cranberries

1. Combine butter, sugars, eggs and vanilla with an electric mixer for 1-2 minutes, or until well blended.
2. In another bowl, whisk together flours, baking powder, baking soda and salt.
3. Add to creamed butter mixture.
4. Stir in oats and cranberries.
5. Drop by 2 tablespoonfuls of cookie dough onto greased baking sheet.
6. Bake 9-11 minutes at 350°.
7. Let cool on wire rack.

Go-Along:
• Ice Cream.

Date Balls

Miriam Detweiler
Hickory, NC

Makes 32 cookies

Prep. Time: 20 minutes
Cooking Time: 5 minutes
Chilling Time: 1-2 hours

½ tsp. salt
1 stick (½ cup) butter *or* margarine
1 cup chopped dates
1 cup sugar
1 egg
½ cup chopped nuts
2½ cups crispy rice cereal
confectioners sugar, *optional*

1. In a saucepan, mix salt, butter, dates, sugar and egg together. Boil until thickened, about 2 minutes.
2. Add nuts and crispy rice cereal.
3. Cool.
4. Form into balls, about 2 tablespoons per ball. Roll in confectioners sugar if you wish.
5. Store in refrigerator.

Vegan

Fruit & Nut Chocolate Balls

Vivian Benner
Dayton, VA

Makes 24 balls

Prep. Time: 20-30 minutes
Cooking Time: 5 minutes

---

48 dried prunes, pitted
48 whole almonds
2 cups dairy-free semi-sweet chocolate chips
2 Tbsp. creamy peanut butter

1. Stuff each prune with an almond.
2. Melt chocolate chips in a microwave-safe bowl or double boiler.
3. Add peanut butter. Mix well.
4. Dip prunes in chocolate mixture. Place on waxed paper to harden. Store in refrigerator.

Go-Along:
• Good with salty snacks.

Can't-Leave-These-Alone Bars

Marlene Zimmerman
Bradford, PA

Makes 18-20 bars

Prep. Time: 15 minutes
Baking Time: 20-25 mintues

18¼-oz. box white cake
    mix
2 eggs
⅓ cup oil
14-oz. can sweetened
    condensed milk
1 cup semi-sweet chocolate
    chips
half stick (¼ cup) butter

1. Combine dry cake mix, eggs and oil.
2. With floured hands, press ⅔ of the mixture into greased 9×13 baking pan.
3. Combine milk, chocolate chips and butter in a microwave-safe bowl.
4. Microwave in 30-second increments until melted, stirring and checking each time. Stir until smooth.
5. Pour over crust in pan.
6. Drop remaining cake mixture on top by spoonfuls.
7. Bake at 350° for 20-25 minutes.
8. Cool. Then cut into bars to serve.

Go-Along:
• Fruit.

Oatmeal Marmalade Bars

Kathryn Yoder
Minot, ND

Makes 16-20 bars

Prep. Time: 15 minutes
Baking Time: 15-17 minutes

4 cups quick oats
1 cup brown sugar
1 tsp. salt
1½ sticks (¾ cup) butter *or*
    margarine
1½ cups chopped walnuts
1 cup shredded coconut
¾ cup orange marmalade

1. In a bowl, combine oats, sugar and salt.
2. Cut in butter with two knives or a pastry cutter.
3. Stir in walnuts, coconut and orange marmalade.
4. Press into greased 10×15 jelly-roll baking pan.
5. Bake 15-17 minutes at 350°, or until nicely browned.
6. Cool. Cut into bars to serve.

Variation:
Any jam or preserve can be substituted for marmalade.

Caramel Nut Bars

Rae Ann Henry
Conestoga, PA

Makes 36 bars

Prep. Time: 20 minutes
Baking Time: 25 minutes
Chilling Time: 1-2 hours

1 cup quick-cooking oats
1 cup brown sugar, packed
1 cup flour
1½ sticks (¾ cup) butter,
    melted
½ tsp. baking soda
¼ tsp. salt
14-oz. package caramels,
    unwrapped
⅓ cup milk
1 cup semi-sweet chocolate
    chips
½ cup chopped walnuts

1. Combine oats, sugar, flour, butter, baking soda and salt in a bowl.
2. Sprinkle 1¼ cups of mixture into a greased 9×13 baking pan. Do not press down.
3. Bake at 350° for 10 minutes. Set aside.
4. Meanwhile, in the top of a double boiler or in a microwavable bowl, cook and stir caramels and milk until melted and smooth
5. Pour over baked crust. Top with chocolate chips and nuts.
6. Sprinkle with remaining oat mixture.
7. Bake at 350° for 10 minutes. Cool on wire rack.
8. Refrigerate for 1-2 hours to set the caramel. Cut into bars.

Zucchini Brownies

Laraine Good
Bernville, PA
Debra Kilheffer
Millersville, PA

Makes 12 brownies

Prep. Time: 20 minutes
Baking Time: 35 minutes

1 egg
1 tsp. vanilla
½ cup oil
¾ cup sugar
¾ cup brown sugar
1 cup flour
¾ cup whole wheat flour
⅓ cup unsweetened cocoa
   powder
½ tsp. baking soda
¼ tsp. salt
½ cup sour cream *or* plain
   yogurt
2-3 cups finely grated zucchini, peeled or unpeeled
1 cup chocolate chips
½ cups chopped pecans *or*
   walnuts

1. Combine egg, vanilla, oil, sugar and brown sugar in a bowl.
2. In a separate bowl combine flour, whole wheat flour, cocoa powder, baking soda and salt.
3. Add to egg mixture alternately with the sour cream, stirring each time.
4. Add zucchini.
5. Pour into a greased 9 × 13 baking pan. Sprinkle with chocolate chips and pecans.
6. Bake at 350° for 35 minutes, or until tester inserted in middle comes out clean.
7. Cool. Cut into bars.

Flourless Peanut Butter Bars

Jenna Yoder
Floyd, VA

Makes 16 servings

Prep. Time: 10 minutes
Baking Time: 20 minutes

1 cup peanut butter
2 medium eggs
1 cup sugar
1 tsp. baking soda
1 tsp. vanilla extract
¾ cup chocolate chips

1. Mix peanut butter, eggs, sugar, baking soda and vanilla together.
2. Add chocolate chips.
3. Put in greased 9 × 9 baking pan.
4. Bake at 350° for 20 minutes, or longer if you like well-done cookies.
5. Cool. Then cut into bars.

Flourless Brownies

Juanita Weaver
Johnsonville, IL

Makes 16 brownies

Prep. Time: 10-15 minutes
Cooking/Baking Time: 30-35 minutes

1¼ cups semi-sweet
   chocolate chips
15-oz. can garbanzo beans,
   well drained
2 eggs
2 Tbsp. instant coffee
   powder
½ cup brown sugar, packed
⅛ tsp. salt
2 Tbsp. light olive oil
1½ tsp. vanilla
½ cup chopped nuts

1. Melt chocolate chips in microwave in microwave-safe bowl.
2. Stir until smooth and set aside.
3. Place beans, eggs, coffee powder, sugar and salt in food processor.
4. Process until smooth.
5. Stir in oil, vanilla, and chocolate.
6. Spread in greased 9 × 9 baking dish.
7. Sprinkle with nuts.
8. Bake at 350° for 30-35 minutes.
9. Cool. Then cut into bars.

Tip:
Do not over-bake.

Go-Along:
• Slushy applesauce or fresh fruit salad.

From-Scratch Replacement Recipes

When I first began making cookbooks, I was a purist. No canned cream soups for me, whether I was working on cookbooks or making dinner. I resolutely turned any reference to canned creamed soups into a multi-step process, which wasn't too bad if I took a magazine along to the stove or the microwave. I would do Steps 1-4 (on next page); then I'd whip out the magazine while I stirred. It made the time fly.

But when I became a mom, I began to compromise on a few things. It was a little harder to hold a wiggly child than it was to read a magazine while I stirred up a creamy soup.

Then I heard from other people who were juggling things that didn't always allow them to stand and read while stirring. So I switched and began to permit canned soups in recipes.

If you like to know exactly what you are eating, and if you have the time, I applaud your making cream soups and bases from scratch. Here is a recipe for doing this on the stove-top or in the microwave.

If you're tight time-wise, or aren't sure you want to make the extra effort to create a creamy soup or base, you'll find canned cream soups in the ingredient lists of many recipes in this cookbook. Because my first intent is to make sure you can make a meal at home and serve it to your friends and family, no matter how full or chaotic your life is.

Homemade Cream of Mushroom Soup –on the stove

Makes about 1¼ cups (10 oz.)

3 Tbsp. butter
¼ cup mushrooms, chopped
1 Tbsp. onion, chopped
3 Tbsp. flour
1 cup milk (skim, 1%, 2%, *or* whole)

1. In a small saucepan, melt butter.
2. Sauté mushrooms and onion in butter until tender. Stir frequently.
3. Add flour and stir until smooth. Cook over low heat for a minute or so to cook off the raw flour taste.
4. Continuing over low heat, gradually add milk, stirring the whole time.
5. Stir frequently to keep soup from sticking. When soup begins to bubble, stir continuously until it thickens to a creamy consistency.

Homemade Cream of Mushroom Soup – in the microwave

Makes about 1¼ cups (10 oz.)

3 Tbsp. butter
¼ cup mushrooms, chopped
1 Tbsp. onion, chopped
3 Tbsp. flour
1 cup milk (skim, 1%, 2%, *or* whole)

1. In a 1- or 2-qt. microwave-safe container, melt 3 Tbsp. butter on high for 30 seconds.
2. Stir chopped mushrooms and onions into melted butter.
3. Microwave on high for 1 minute, or just enough to make the vegetables tender.
4. Stir in flour until well blended.
5. Microwave on high for 1 minute, just enough to overcome the raw flour taste.
6. Gradually stir in milk until as well blended as possible.
7. Microwave on Power 5 for 45 seconds.
8. Stir until well blended.
9. Microwave on Power 5 for another 45 seconds. The mixture should be starting to bubble and thicken.
10. Stir again until well blended.
11. If the mixture isn't fully bubbling and thickened, microwave on high for 20 seconds.
12. Stir. If the mixture still isn't fully bubbling and thickened, microwave on high for 20 more seconds.
13. Repeat Step 12 if needed.

Note:

If your microwave is fairly new and powerful, you will probably have a creamy soup by the end of Step 8 or 10 below. If you're working with an older, less powerful, microwave, you will likely need to go through Step 12, and maybe Step 13.

To make cream of celery soup, substitute ¼ cup finely chopped celery for the ¼ cup chopped mushrooms.

Homemade Cornbread Mix

Makes the equivalent of an 8½-oz. box of Jiffy Cornbread Mix

⅔ cup flour
½ cup cornmeal
3 Tbsp. sugar
1 Tbsp. baking powder
¼ tsp. salt
2 Tbsp. oil

Variation:

To make muffins from this mix, add:

1 egg
⅓ cup milk

1. Stir just until combined.
2. Fill muffin cups half-full.
3. Bake at 400° for 15-20 minutes, or until toothpick inserted in center of muffins comes out clean.

Homemade Frozen Hash Browns

1. Bake potatoes until tender.
2. Cool.
3. Grate coarsely.
4. Freeze.

Equivalent Measurements

dash = little less than ⅛ tsp.

3 teaspoons = 1 Tablespoon

2 Tablespoons = 1 oz.

4 Tablespoons = ¼ cup

5 Tablespoons plus 1 tsp. = ⅓ cup

8 Tablespoons = ½ cup

12 Tablespoons = ¾ cup

16 Tablespoons = 1 cup

1 cup = 8 ozs. liquid

2 cups = 1 pint

4 cups = 1 quart

4 quarts = 1 gallon

1 stick butter = ¼ lb.

1 stick butter = ½ cup

1 stick butter = 8 Tbsp.

Beans, 1 lb. dried = 2-2½ cups (depending upon the size of the beans)

Bell peppers, 1 large = 1 cup chopped

Cheese, hard (for example, cheddar, Swiss, Monterey Jack, mozzarella), 1 lb. grated = 4 cups

Cheese, cottage, 1 lb. = 2 cups

Chocolate chips, 6-oz. pkg. = 1 scant cup

Crackers (butter, saltines, snack), 20 single crackers = 1 cup crumbs

Herbs, 1 Tbsp. fresh = 1 tsp. dried

Lemon, 1 medium-sized = 2-3 Tbsp. juice

Lemon, 1 medium-sized = 2-3 tsp. grated rind

Mustard, 1 Tbsp. prepared = 1 tsp. dry or ground mustard

Oatmeal, 1 lb. dry = about 5 cups dry

Onion, 1 medium-sized = ½ cup chopped

Pasta

Macaronis, penne, and other small or tubular shapes, 1 lb. dry = 4 cups uncooked

Noodles, 1 lb. dry = 6 cups uncooked

Spaghetti, linguine, fettucine, 1 lb. dry = 4 cups uncooked

Potatoes, white, 1 lb. = 3 medium-sized potatoes = 2 cups mashed

Potatoes, sweet, 1 lb. = 3 medium-sized potatoes = 2 cups mashed

Rice, 1 lb. dry = 2 cups uncooked

Sugar, confectioners, 1 lb. = 3½ cups sifted

Whipping cream, 1 cup unwhipped = 2 cups whipped

Whipped topping, 8-oz. container = 3 cups

Yeast, dry, 1 envelope (¼ oz.) = 1 Tbsp.

Substitute Ingredients
for when you're in a pinch

For one cup **buttermilk**—use 1 cup plain yogurt; or pour 1⅓ Tbsp. lemon juice or vinegar into a 1-cup measure. Fill the cup with milk. Stir and let stand for 5 minutes. Stir again before using.

For 1 oz. **unsweetened baking chocolate**—stir together 3 Tbsp. unsweetened cocoa powder and 1 Tbsp. butter, softened.

For 1 Tbsp. **cornstarch**—use 2 Tbsp. all-purpose flour; or 4 tsp. minute tapioca.

For 1 **garlic clove**—use ¼ tsp. garlic salt (reduce salt in recipe by ⅛ tsp.); or ⅛ tsp. garlic powder.

For 1 Tbsp. **fresh herbs**—use 1 tsp. dried herbs.

For ½ lb. **fresh mushrooms**—use 1 6-oz. can mushrooms, drained.

For 1 Tbsp. **prepared mustard**—use 1 tsp. dry or ground mustard.

For 1 **medium-sized fresh onion**—use 2 Tbsp. minced dried onion; or 2 tsp. onion salt (reduce salt in recipe by 1 tsp.); or 1 tsp. onion powder. Note: These substitutions will not work for sautéing.

For 1 cup **sour milk**—use 1 cup plain yogurt; or pour 1 Tbsp. lemon juice or vinegar into a 1-cup measure. Fill with milk. Stir and then let stand for 5 minutes. Stir again before using.

For 2 Tbsp. **tapioca**—use 3 Tbsp. all-purpose flour.

For 1 cup canned **tomatoes**—use 1⅓ cups diced fresh tomatoes, cooked gently for 10 minutes.

For 1 Tbsp. **tomato paste**—use 1 Tbsp. ketchup.

For 1 Tbsp. **vinegar**—use 1 Tbsp. lemon juice.

For 1 cup **heavy cream**—add ⅓ cup melted butter to ¾ cup milk. *Note: This will work for baking and cooking, but not for whipping.*

For 1 cup **whipping cream**—chill thoroughly ⅔ cup evaporated milk, plus the bowl and beaters, then whip; or use 2 cups bought whipped topping.

For ½ cup **wine**—pour 2 Tbsp. wine vinegar into a ½-cup measure. Fill with vegetable broth. Stir and then let stand for 5 minutes. Stir again before using.

Vegan Recipe Index

Index

Index

Index

Index

Index

Index

Oranges
  Ambrosia Salad, 192
  California Salad, 209
  Gift of the Magi Bread, 55
  Orange Bran Flax Muffins, 60
  Spinach Salad, 211
  Tasty Orange Salad, 193
  Thai Carrot Salad with Peanuts, 219
  Tossed Salad with Candied Almonds, 211
  Tropical Salad with Crunchy Pecans, 212
Oven-Fried Eggplant, 177
Oven Fried Potatoes, 167
Overnight Danish Braids, 36
Overnight Veggie Omelet, 42

P

Pancakes
  Apple Oatmeal Pancakes, 32
  Baked Apple Cranberry Pancake, 31
  Melt-in-Your-Mouth Pancakes, 33
  Pumpkin Pancakes, 32
Parmesan Garlic Popcorn, 27
Parsley Pasta, 123
Parsley
  Herb Rolls, 53
  Parsley Pasta, 123
Parsnips
  Honey-Roasted Parsnips, Sweet Potatoes
    and Apples, 163
  Roasted Harvest Vegetables, 184
Party Beets with Pineapple, 191
Pasta with Beans and Greens, 118
Pasta with Szechwan Peanut Dressing, 126
Pasta, Angel-Hair
  Sesame Noodles, 126
  Summer Pasta, 125
Pasta, Bow-Tie
  Farfalle with Tomatoes, Garlic and Basil, 122
  Five-Ingredient Pasta Toss, 125
Pasta, Fettuccine
  Asparagus Fettuccine, 120
Pasta, Lasagna
  Black Bean Lasagna Rolls, 109
  Easy Black Bean Lasagna, 112
  Slow-Cooker Fresh Veggie Lasagna, 110
  Spinach Lasagna, 111
  Summer Squash Lasagna, 110
Pasta, Linguini
  Linguini Salad, 223

Linguini with Mushroom Sauce, 120
Linguini with Sun-Dried Tomato Pesto, 117
Pasta with Szechwan Peanut Dressing, 126
Vegetable Stir-Fry with Peanut Sauce, 185
Pasta, Macaroni
  Cheesy Slow-Cooker Macaroni, 116
  Crumb-Topped Macaroni and Cheese, 114
  Homey Mac Dinner, 119
  Horseradish Macaroni and Cheese, 116
  Macaroni Coleslaw, 225
  Mushroom Goulash, 119
  Slow-Cooker Macaroni and Cheese, 116
  Veggie Macaroni and Cheese, 115
  Zesty Macaroni and Cheese, 115
Pasta, Manicotti
  Mushroom Manicotti, 107
Pasta, Noodles
  Cabbage with Noodles, 189
  Sauerkraut Casserole, 114
Pasta, Penne
  Baked Pasta E Fagioli, 113
Pasta, Ravioli
  Creamy Spinach Ravioli, 121
Pasta, Rigatoni
  Italian Pasta Pie, 112
  Rigatoni with Grilled Vegetables, 122
  Rigatoni with Roasted Cauliflower and
    Asiago, 124
Pasta, Rotini
  Feta and Vegetable Rotini Salad, 222
Pasta, Shells
  Cheese-Stuffed Shells, 109
  Garbanzo-Stuffed Shells, 108
  Spinach- and Cheese-Stuffed Shells, 108
Pasta, Soba Noodles
  Pasta with Szechwan Peanut Dressing, 126
Pasta, Spaghetti
  Baked Spaghetti Corn, 113
  Garlicky Tomatoes and Olives with
    Spaghetti, 121
  Homemade Spaghetti Sauce, 105
  Large Quantity Pasta Bean Soup, 79
  Spaghetti Pizza, 114
  Summer Pasta, 125
  Vegetarian Spaghetti, 107
Pasta, Spiral
  Bedspring Salad, 223
  Spinach Pasta Salad, 222
Pasta, Tortellini

Tortellini Soup, 89
Pasta, Ziti
  Italian Pasta Pie, 112
  PB&J French Toast, 33
Pea and Rice Soup, 80
Peach Dessert, 242
Peach Sherbet Popsicles, 254
Peaches
  Fruit Mixture Crisps, 249
  Hot Fruit Casserole, 192
  Maple Peach Crumble Pie, 243
  Peach Dessert, 242
  Peach Sherbet Popsicles, 254
  Peachy Carrots, 179
  Texas Peach Cobbler, 247
Peachy Carrots, 179
Peanut Butter Bread, 50
Peanut Butter Chocolate Chip Oatmeal
  Cookies, 256
Peanut Butter Waldorf Salad, 234
Peanut Butter
  African Peanut Soup, 92
  Chocolate Peanut Butter Slow-Cooker
    Cake, 239
  Christmas Popcorn, 27
  Energy Balls, 28
  Flourless Peanut Butter Bars, 259
  Fruit & Nut Chocolate Balls, 257
  High-Energy Trail Bars, 28
  Jimmy Carter Dessert, 253
  Pasta with Szechwan Peanut Dressing,
    126
  PB&J French Toast, 33
  Peanut Butter Bread, 50
  Peanut Butter Chocolate Chip Oatmeal
    Cookies, 256
  Peanut Butter Waldorf Salad, 234
  Vegetable Stir-Fry with Peanut Sauce, 185
Pears
  Fruit Salad with Yogurt and Nuts, 194
  Hot Fruit Casserole, 192
Peas
  Almond Cranberry Rice Pilaf, 143
  Aloo Gobi with Peas, 187
  Cheese Sauce with Rice and Peas, 147
  Chickpea Curry, 135
  Coconut-Curried Spinach Pea Soup, 95
  Couscous Salad, 230
  Curry Pilaf with Garbanzos, 134

Index

Index

Index

About the Author

Phyllis Good is a *New York Times* bestselling author whose books have sold more than 12 million copies.

She authored *Fix-It and Forget-It Cookbook, Revised and Updated*, which appeared on *The New York Times* bestseller list, as well as the bestseller lists of *USA Today*, *Publishers Weekly*, and *Book Sense*.

In addition, she authored *Fix-It and Forget-It Lightly* (which also appeared on *The New York Times* bestseller list); as well as *Fix-it and Forget-It Christmas Cookbook*; *Fix-It and Forget-It 5-Ingredient Favorites*; *Fix-It and Forget-It Vegetarian Cookbook*; *Fix-It and Forget-It Cooking Light, Revised and Updated*; *Fix-It and Forget-It Slow Cooker Diabetic Cookbook, Revised and Updated* (with the American Diabetes Association); *Fix-It and Forget-It*

BIG Cookbook; *Fix-It and Forget-It Kids Cookbook*; *Fix-It and Forget-It Slow Cooker Magic*; *Fix-it and Forget-It New Cookbook*; *Fix-it and Forget-It Slow Cooker Champion Recipes*; and *Fix-It and Forget-It Baking with Your Slow Cooker*.

Her commitment is to make it possible for everyone to cook who would like to, even if they have too little time or too little confidence.

Good, who holds an M.A. in English from New York University, has authored many other cookbooks. Among them are *Fix-It and Enjoy-It Healthy Cookbook* (with nutritional expertise from Mayo Clinic), *The Best of Amish Cooking*, and *The Lancaster Central Market Cookbook*.

Good spends her time writing, editing books, and cooking new recipes.